JANUA LINGUARUM

STUDIA MEMORIAE
NICOLAI VAN WIJK DEDICATA

edenda curat

C. H. VAN SCHOONEVELD

Indiana University

Series Maior, 55

KENNETH L. PIKE

Selected Writings

TO COMMEMORATE
THE 60TH BIRTHDAY
OF KENNETH LEE PIKE

edited by

RUTH M. BREND

1972

MOUTON

THE HAGUE · PARIS

Printed in The Netherlands by Mouton & Co., Printers, The Hague.

2-12-85

TABLE OF CONTENTS

PART II: RELIGIOUS

PART III: POETIC

INTRODUCTION

This volume is designed to fill two major purposes: to provide in one place, for the scholarly world, a large number of the major articles written by Kenneth L. Pike, many of which originally appeared in rather inaccessible publications, and to mark Professor Pike's sixtieth birthday. It is felt that this volume is indeed a fitting commemoration of that event, more so, perhaps, than a traditional festschrift.

General guidelines followed in deciding which selections to include herein included a desire to indicate the scope and depth of Pike's scholarship and interests (which accounts for the inclusion of a few religious essays and poems), to show the chronological development of his research and study, and to show the wide divergence of problems which he has tackled. Although several publications were excluded because of their availability, others which have had wide circulation (e.g., "Grammatical Prerequisites to Phonemic Analysis") have been included because they are central to the development of Pike's linguistic theory. (The editor has simultaneously been compiling two volumes of readings in tagmemics and of studies in tone and intonation by members of the Summer Institute of Linguistics, in which several of Pike's articles are included. Duplication in the three volumes has been avoided wherever possible).

Pike's sister, Eunice, wrote the biographical sketch, drawing on personal knowledge of various periods of his life. The bibliography is as all-inclusive as possible, although some items, especially notations regarding the reprinting of some included items, may have been inadvertently omitted.

This collection is far from exhaustive, and is not even really representative of Pike's wide interests. Apart from the omission of important published works, Pike's ongoing productivity is not included. At this time approximately six items are in the hands of editors, and Pike is currently in Nepal, directing a workshop from which undoubtedly will come various published studies. A sequel to this volume, it is hoped, will appear at a not-too-distant date.

PART ONE

LINGUISTIC

TAXEMES AND IMMEDIATE CONSTITUENTS*

[Critical examination of the grammatical chapters in Bloomfield's *Language*, with suggestions toward a procedure for grammatical analysis.]

1. TAXEMES AND TAGMEMES

1.1. Many students of Leonard Bloomfield's *Language*[1] have been inspired, by the extraordinary insight into grammatical phenomena there shown, to attempt descriptive analysis from that basis. Frequently, however, their hopes of success are dulled somewhat by the singular fact that the material proves more elusive in application than it did in appreciation.

In an attempt a couple of years ago to use Bloomfield's principles to analyze the complicated syntax of Mixteco, an Indian language of Mexico,[2] I came to the conclusion that a slightly different statement of the actual procedure of analysis would facilitate syntactic description; this involved a number of criteria which could be applied consecutively in order to arrive at the ranks and labels of construction.

It was only recently, however, that I reached a further conclusion: that part of the difficulty of Bloomfield's material for the beginning student was the lack of clarity in his statements of the relationship between taxemes and tagmemes, and the actual operation with these principles.

This paper,[3] then, has two goals: first to point out this confusion, and second to outline a procedure which a student can apply to the easier stages of syntactic analysis. The illustrative English material, the phonetic transcriptions, and the definitions are deliberately taken from Bloomfield, and constant references are given to his material, to enable the student to correlate this brief study with his more complete descriptive presentation.

* *Language* 19:2 (1943), 65-82. Reprinted by permission.
[1] Leonard Bloomfield, *Language* (New York, 1933).
[2] The research in Mixteco was carried on under the auspices of the Summer Institute of Linguistics, Oklahoma.
[3] The preparation of this paper was made possible by a Faculty Research grant from the University of Michigan, 1942-1943, in connection with my work for the English Language Institute.

1.2. Bloomfield parallels TAXEME with PHONEME in that both are said to be meaningless: "Like a phoneme, a taxeme, taken by itself, in the abstract, is meaningless" (166); also, the PHENEME includes phoneme and taxeme (264).

Obviously, a phoneme means nothing by itself. It is only occasionally that a single phoneme is a morpheme (as in -s plural, etc.); the occurrences are, in a sense, mere coincidences.

Taxemes are quite the opposite. A large percentage of taxemes have meanings; where there seems to be no meaning, there frequently is one present, even if it be simply connotative and too ephemeral for ready description. Let us consider meanings of various types of taxemes. There are only four types (163–168): ORDER (word order or morpheme order); MODULATION (secondary phonemes of stress and pitch); PHONETIC MODIFICATION ([djuwk] to [doč] in *duchess*); and SELECTION (i.e. choice of verb, adjective, etc.).

(1) As for selection, EVERY taxeme of selection has a meaning — the meaning of the selected form class. These are perhaps the most important of all taxemes. Bloomfield says of them (190), "Taxemes of selection play a large part in the syntax of most languages; syntax consists largely in defining them — in stating, for instance, under what circumstances (with what accompanying forms or, if the accompanying forms are the same, with what differences of meaning [NB!]) various form-classes (as, say, indicative and subjunctive verbs, or dative and accusative nouns, and so on) appear in syntactic constructions." This confuses one who has previously read (167) that "none of these taxemes [in an illustration showing a sample of taxemes of selection, order, modulation, and modification], taken by itself, has any meaning …." The choice of a member of a form class involves a taxeme of selection — which must also include the choice of the class meaning (146, 247, 266-267) of the form class.

(2) Taxemes of order are closely related to the position and function in which words may occur. Thus the difference between *you* in *he hit you* and in *you hit him* may be stated on the one hand in terms of position or function, as actor or goal, and on the other hand in terms of the order of items which concomitantly controls this position or function. Bloomfield describes many of these meanings — always, of course, with the reservation that "class-meanings, like all other meanings, elude the linguist's power of definition", "class-meanings are … only vague situational features" (267-268). Among various samples given on 267, this is typical: "English substantive expressions occur, for instance, in the position of actor in the actor-action construction (*John ran*), with the positional meaning 'performer of an action'." Elsewhere (163) he says that "Sometimes differences of order have connotative values; thus, *Away ran John* is livelier than *John ran away*".

(3) The taxemes of modulation — "the use of secondary phonemes" (163) — also usually have meanings. This is especially true of pitch features. Thus Bloomfield defines the meaning of "exclamatory final pitch" as "strong stimulus" (166) and states that in *Run!* it is both a taxeme and a tagmeme. Stress acts somewhat differ-

ently from pitch; it would seem preferable to treat it as of two types. Sentence stress (or "loudest stress"? [91]) might be defined as "calling attention to the stressed item", e.g. *I ''will go. ''I will go. I will ''go.* Lexical stress may possibly have no meaning of itself, but may rather contribute, like segmental phonemes, to the basic features of the word, as in *con'vict* versus *'convict* (but see modulation by stress, 220-221).

(4) The taxeme of phonetic modification plays a far less prominent part, and the meanings are even more vague. Bloomfield says, however, that *don't* and *do not* have "a difference in connotation" (164).

If taxemes have meaning, it is obvious that they overlap with tagmemes, which are defined by Bloomfield (166, 264) as "the smallest meaningful units of grammatical form".

1.3. A second and related basic confusion arises from this definition of tagmemes as the smallest meaningful units of grammatical form (166) when we find situations in which the tagmemes are composed of several taxemes, said to be meaningless, of which some, at least, seem to have meanings fully as concrete as those mentioned above and attributed to tagmemes. In other words, tagmemes are not always minimal units of grammatical form and meaning.

For example, the definitions of tagmeme and taxeme are immediately followed (166-167) by three illustrations to show the contrast between them.

The first of these illustrations (*Run!*) is said to have two taxemes and two tagmemes, which must be here equated ("exclamatory final-pitch, and the selective feature which consists in the use of an infinitive verb"); in this illustration, no clear borderline can be seen between taxeme and tagmeme.

In the second illustration (*John ran; poor John ran away; the boys are here; I know*) there is said to be just one tagmeme, composed of several taxemes. The tagmeme (made up of the taxemes "taken all together") means "that the one constituent (the nominative expression) 'performs' the other constituent (the finite verb expression)", while none of the taxemes "has any meaning". But at least some of these taxemes do actually have meanings as specific as items given elsewhere in the book: for example the taxeme of phonetic modification of *John's here* parallels the *don't* of 164 which has a "difference in connotation" from *do not*; the taxeme of selection of one constituent, the "nominative expression", parallels what is elsewhere called (267) "the positional meaning 'performer of an action'". The other constituent, "finite verb expressions", parallels (267) "the class-meaning of the larger form-class of verbs as 'action'"; the meanings of the taxemes of order overlap the functional positions which they help establish, as can be inferred from the words (267), "this statement defines for us the meanings of the two positions; the meaning of the actor-position is 'performer of B', and that of the action position is 'performed by A'". The modulatory taxeme in *I know* [aj 'now] might be defined as meaning "attention concentrated upon the knowledge".

In the third illustration (*John ran!*), the first tagmeme, exclamatory pitch, is also a meaningful taxeme, "strong stimulus" (cf. 166); the second, "(object) performs (action)", is similar to the preceding illustration; the third, "complete and novel utterance", selection of an actor-action phrase as a sentence, is elsewhere (171-172) called a taxeme of selection.

If meaningful tagmemes are at times composed of several meaningful taxemes, then tagmemes are not minimal in the sense that taxemes or phonemes or morphemes are minimal. One may conclude, furthermore, that the criteria of size (smallest unit ...) and meaningfulness have not yet provided an easily applied methodology for separating taxemes and tagmemes; and that there is no clear methodology whereby one knows the number of tagmemes or taxemes he may expect to find in an utterance.

1.4. Presumably, Bloomfield meant to use the term tagmeme to label a composite unit of a type not yet dealt with here; perhaps he meant the most embracing or basic of all features of a given construction. This might be indicated by the parentheses around 'object' and 'action' in the tagmeme '(object) performs (action)'; here a layer of tagmemes may be indicated, in which the top layer is the full actor-action sequence and a lower layer is the features of object and action. The absence of a statement of his methodology for labelling such levels of analysis must be considered a third major source of difficulty to the beginner.[4]

1.5. A fourth difficulty is that the term taxeme, defined as minimal, sometimes is used in situations where several smaller taxemes are actually involved. Only on the basis of differences of rank for taxemes and constructions, where different layers of form are postulated for the analysis, might this be warranted; but no adequate differentiation between them is made. Several different layers may be observed in Bloomfield's analysis of the form *duchess*, 167-168.

Under "selection", several features are mentioned: (1) *duke* "belongs to a special class of English forms which combine with the form *-ess*"; it is (2) male, (3) personal, and (4) a noun. He might also have added that it is (5) singular, (6) bounded (205), (7) common (205), (8) substantive (249). In addition, (9) *-ess* constitutes a form class of its own. Now since he says (265) that "the functions of lexical forms are created by taxemes of selection", and "Lexical forms which have any function in common, belong to a common *form-class*", it would seem that EACH of the form-class divisions just enumerated would constitute a separate grammatical feature which equals (166) a taxeme: these may be compared with the 'subsidiary taxemes of selection' described on 192, 190-194.

Specifically, for example, Bloomfield says (202) that "the noun is a word-class; like all form-classes, it is to be defined in terms of grammatical features", so that the classes of 'noun', 'male', 'singular', etc. would each involve a separate taxeme.

[4] A misprint in the third line of 264, corrected in later printings of the book, defines tagmemes as features of arrangement. The term should be taxemes; cf. 166.

Yet he states that "all these facts [numbered and referred to in the preceding paragraph], taken together, may be viewed as a single taxeme of selection" (168). If a 'fact', then, can be equated with a 'feature', and a taxeme has been defined as a feature, it is clear that in the present instance several smaller taxemes are viewed for structural convenience as constituting just one, new, composite taxeme.

Under "order", similarly, he implies that there is but one taxeme — that "-*ess* is spoken after the accompanying form". Yet the reciprocal — that *duke* precedes -*ess* — is equally a separate taxeme, from the point of view of *duke*. Under "modulation", Bloomfield actually divides the description into two such parts: -*ess* is "unstressed", but *duke* "has a high stress", presumably because here the relationship is not quite reciprocal (i.e. both might have been unstressed).

All of these features are compressed on this level into four units — of selection, order, modulation, and phonetic modification; and "these four grammatical features" are said to describe fully "the complex form *duchess*" (168). It is evident that this layer of analysis combines several features into single features still described as minimal.

1.6. In the sentences immediately following this statement, however, a higher layer begins to appear, in which these four are ignored as such and the entire word is treated in the actual utterance *Duchess!* as a single lexical form accompanied by two taxemes: one of selection ("substantive expression") and one of modulation. The full statement (168) may well be quoted: "Any actual utterance can be fully described in terms of the lexical form and the accompanying grammatical features. Thus, the utterance *Duchess!* consists of the lexical form *duchess* and the two taxemes of exclamatory final-pitch and selection of a substantive expression".

In other words, Bloomfield no sooner describes *duchess* as having four taxemes, than he immediately describes it as having one. Obviously his point of view has shifted, and a different layer of analysis is under attention. The student, however, is confused by this shift, and by the fact that four 'smallest' units of form (each composed of several 'facts') may by a shift of attention become one.

In the paragraph following the two just referred to, Bloomfield shuffles the items again, but this time in terms of (three) tagmemes rather than taxemes — the first tagmeme includes the arrangement of *duke* and -*ess* (the first four composite taxemes described); the second, modulation by exclamatory final pitch; and the third, the selection of a substantive expression (viewing the term *duchess* as a single grammatical entity).

1.7. The difficulties which seem to be present in Bloomfield's material may be summarized as follows: the taxeme, defined as meaningless, very frequently appears to have meaning; both taxeme and tagmeme, defined as minimal units, appear at times to be composite; the relationship appears clear-cut in definition but vague in operation; different layers of analysis which are the basis for certain operations are not presented with sufficient clarity for the student to recognize them.

2. DEFINITIONS OF TAXEMES AND TAGMEMES

2.1. Somewhat diffidently I suggest the following classifications and relabellings as perhaps being a bit easier to handle than Bloomfield's.

FEATURE (of arrangement; grammatical feature): a single fact of grammatical arrangement; a SIMPLE taxeme. E.g. the fact that [doč] precedes -*ess*.

TAXEME: a complex, composite, or simple feature of meaningful or meaningless grammatical arrangement, of the basic type of selection, order, modulation, or phonetic modification. E.g. the facts of selection of the male personal noun *duke*.

TAGMEME: a composite view of the basic composite taxemes of a linguistic form, at any one specific layer of structure. E.g. the total arrangement features of the form *duchess* considered as a single entity.

LAYER OF STRUCTURE: an isolated utterance (a sentence type); or the immediate constituents of a construction. E.g. *Poor John* as one layer; *Poor* and *John* as the next layer.

LAYERS OF TAGMEMES AND TAXEMES: A linguistic form can have no more than one tagmeme to a sentence type or to an immediate constituent of a construction. One tagmeme may be composed of no more than four complex (or simple) taxemes — one of selection (i.e. TYPE of item), one of order (i.e. POSITION of item), one of modulation (i.e. the use of secondary phonemes), and one of phonetic modification. The top layer, or tagmeme of a sentence type, may be called a MACROTAGMEME, and is the composite picture of the basic taxemes of an isolated utterance. The second layer cuts the form into its two (or rarely more) immediate constituents; each of the immediate constituents, in turn, may likewise have one tagmeme composed of no more than its four possible complex (or simple) taxemes. The analysis of the syntax ends when one has arrived, by successive layers of immediate constituents, to the tagmeme and the taxemes of each individual word; for a total grammatical analysis one continues with the morphology and ends with the tagmeme and the taxemes of each morpheme.

ULTIMATE TAGMEMES and ULTIMATE TAXEMES: the tagmemes and taxemes of the ultimate constituents.

2.2. Under this organization of features of arrangement, we see that simple taxemes or features may combine into single complex taxemes of selection, order, modulation, or modification respectively, on a single layer of structure. The composite of these four complex taxemes is a tagmeme; tagmemes, then, appear as a kind of super-taxeme on the same structural layer. The layers themselves PYRAMID, until at the top one finds the largest, most inclusive tagmeme — the macrotagmeme.

Frequently a tagmeme will have only two of its taxemes — order (including position before and after zero) and selection. The modulation taxemes usually apply to phrases or words, and hence rarely appear as ultimate taxemes. Phonetic modification is less frequent than order and selection. This differs but slightly from Bloomfield's statements and implications at the top of 169.

2.3. These definitions pave the way for a presentation of a methodology, in the illustrative analysis of a sentence. Where it seems possible, illustrations and definitions of form and meaning have been taken or adapted from Bloomfield; page references indicate the specific sources.

3. SAMPLE ANALYSIS OF A SENTENCE

3. In Table I, Roman numerals indicate successive layers of structure; lines show the division into immediate constituents; Arabic numerals indicate the order in which forms will be discussed. M marks a constituent in a morphological construction.

TABLE 1

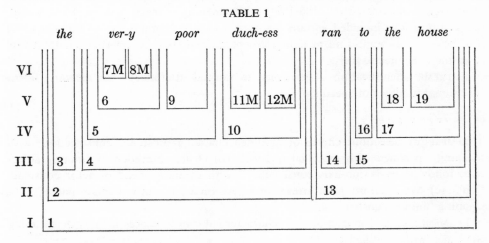

(1) *The very poor duchess ran to the house*

TAXEMES: (a) Selection: choice of an actor-action favorite sentence type (172); with meaning '(subject) performs (action)' (cf. 165). (b) Order: preceded and followed by zero; with meaning 'isolated utterance'. (c) Modulation: falling final pitch; with meaning 'end of sentence' (170). In cases of several modulations in a single sentence, the subdivisions should be treated as having separate taxemes of pitch.

TAGMEME (or MACROTAGMEME): isolated actor-action narrative sentence type; with meaning 'complete and novel utterance' (cf. 172).

(2) *The very poor duchess*

TAXEMES: (a) Selection: choice of determination-substance construction as a substantive expression (see 202, 165); with meaning 'specifically limited object' (cf. 202, 165). Additional features — singular, feminine — will be given under *duchess*. (b)

Order: followed by action-axis construction; with meaning 'performer'. Order and selection will often overlap in meaning, since taxemes of order usually "occur along with taxemes of selection" (197) or "supplement taxemes of selection" (198). The fact that it follows zero has already been covered, because the present form is included in position (1b) above. (c) Modulation: a rhythmic unit; with meaning 'grammatical unit'.

TAGMEME: determination-substance nominative expression; with meaning 'specific performer'.

(3) *The*

TAXEMES: (a) Selection: choice of a limiting adjective (202) of the subclass definite determiner (203); with meaning 'identification' of specimen (203). (b) Order: precedes the head, partially closing the construction (196-197); with meaning 'identificational modifier of specimen'; for item which it follows, see (1b). (c) Modulation: atonic, unstressed (cf. 186-189); with meaning 'normal lack of prominence'. (d) Modification: included variant (183), of a special compulsory sandhi type (187) [ðo] before consonants; no meaning, except normal style as differing connotatively from the over-precise [ðij].

TAGMEME: identification of specimen in normal utterance; with meaning 'identificational modifier of specimen'.

(4) *very poor duchess*

TAXEMES: (a) Selection: choice of modified character-substance construction; with meaning 'specimen with modified quality'. (b) Order: preceded by limiting adjective; followed by action-axis construction; with meaning 'head of actor construction'. (c) Modulation: level stress, or stress on each word without pause; with meaning 'unified construction'.

TAGMEME: unified but modified character-substance expression; with meaning 'specimen with modified quality'.

(5) *very poor*

TAXEMES: (a) Selection: choice of modified adjective construction; with meaning 'modified quality'. (b) Order: precedes the head; with meaning 'attribute of specimen'; for item which it follows see (4b). (c) Modulation: see (4c).

TAGMEME: modified adjective expression; with meaning 'modified quality of specimen'.

(6) *very*

TAXEMES: (a) Selection: choice of an adverb; with meaning 'modification of a qualitative expression'. (b) Order: precedes the adjective; with meaning 'modification of a quality'; for item which it follows, see (4b). (c) Modulation: lexical pattern, first syllable stressed, second unstressed; normal stress on roots.

TAGMEME: adverbial modifying expression; with meaning 'modification of a characteristic of a specimen'.

(7M) *ver-*

TAXEMES: (a) Selection: choice of a bound root, as one form of a derived complex primary word (cf. 209, 240-244); with meaning 'unique lexical constituent'. (b) Order: the root precedes the primary affix; with meaning 'unique root'. For the item which it follows, see (4b). (c) Modulation: see (6c).

TAGMEME: Selection of bound root; with meaning 'unique lexical constituent'.

(8M) *-y*

TAXEMES: (a) Selection: choice of a bound primary affix determinative (209, 240-244); with meaning of lexical extension of root. (b) Order: affix follows root; with meaning 'obligatory accompaniment of the root' (cf. 240). (c) Modulation: see (6c).

TAGMEME: primary affix; with meaning 'obligatory lexical extension of root'.

(9) *poor*

TAXEMES: (a) Selection: choice of descriptive adjective (202); with meaning 'qualitative character of a specimen' (202). (b) Order: follows the adverb modifier as head of the modified adjective expression; with meaning 'qualitative attribute of specimen'. (c) Modulation: see (4c).

TAGMEME: descriptive adjective; with meaning 'qualitative character of a specimen'.

(10) *duchess*

TAXEMES: (a) Selection: choice of singular female bounded personal substantive expression (168, 205); with meaning 'one female object' (cf. 250-251) or 'species occurring in individual indivisible specimens' (cf. 249, 205). (b) Order: follows the adjective expression, as its head; with meaning 'object'; for the item which follows it, see (2b). (c) Modulation: see (4c).

TAGMEME: singular female substantive; with meaning 'one female object'.

(11M) *duke*

TAXEMES: (a) Selection: choice of singular male substantive expression, of sub-class which can occur with *-ess*; with meaning 'one male object'. (b) Order: the underlying form of the derived secondary word precedes the bound form (209-210). (c) Modulation: the underlying form is stressed (210, 168), as is usual in English morphology (210). (d) Modification: [k] replaced by [č] and [uw] by [o].

TAGMEME: singular male substantive, of sub-class combining with *-ess*; with meaning 'one male object'.

(12M) *-ess*

TAXEMES: (a) Selection: choice of an affix of secondary derivation: a unique form class, because it alone may combine with a certain small list of permitted underlying words, e.g. *prince, actor* (167); with meaning 'classification of the accompanying form as female rather than male'. (b) Order: the bound form follows the underlying form (168); no meaning; for the item which follows the bound form, see (2b). (c) Modulation: the bound form is unstressed, as usual (210, 168).

TAGMEME: a bound suffix in secondary derivation of a singular female substantive; limited to a small list of underlying forms; with meaning 'classification as female'.

(13) *ran to the house*

TAXEMES: (a) Selection: a finite verb expression (165, 267); with meaning 'performed by an actor' (267). (b) Order: follows substantive expression; with meaning 'performed by an actor'; for the item which follows it, see (1b). (c) Modulation: contains the final pitch mentioned in (1c); with meaning 'end of the sentence' (170).

TAGMEME: finite verb expression; with meaning 'performed by an actor'.

(14) *ran*

TAXEMES: (a) Selection: finite verb; with meaning 'action' (267); and in its alternate form as 'past action'. (b) Order: precedes adverbial relation-axis expression, as its head; with meaning 'action'; for the item which it follows, see (13b). (c) Modification: [o] replaced by [ε] (164) in the underlying form, as a substitution alternate with (the now zero alternant) *-ed* (cf. 216); with meaning 'past time' (but see 272, 274, tense and aspect).

TAGMEME: finite verb in past time; with meaning 'action in the past'.

(15) *to the house*

TAXEMES: (a) Selection: choice of a relation-axis exocentric construction (194) as a modifier of the verb (194); with meaning 'directional qualification of the action'. (b) Order: follows its verb head; with meaning 'modifier'; for the item which follows the construction, see (1b).

TAGMEME: an exocentric relation-axis verb modifier; with meaning 'directional qualification of the action'.

(16) *to*

TAXEMES: (a) Selection: choice of a preposition as one of two exocentric heads of a phrase (194, 268); with meaning 'relation' (271). (b) Order: precedes the other constituent of the construction; with meaning 'relation'. (c) Modulation: atonic, unstressed; with meaning 'normal lack of prominence'.

TAGMEME: preposition as one exocentric head of the phrase; with meaning 'relation'.

(17) *the house*

TAXEMES: (a) Selection: choice of a determination-substance substantive expression

(202, 165); with meaning 'specifically limited object'. (b) Order: as a second exo-centric head it follows the first head, *to*; with meaning 'center from which a relation holds good' (267).

TAGMEME: determination-substance expression as second head in a relation-axis construction; with meaning 'center from which a relation holds good'.

(18) *the*

TAXEMES: (a) Selection: same as (3a). (b) Order: same as (3b), except that it is preceded by the preposition. (c) Modulation: same as (3c). (d) Modification: same as (3d).

TAGMEME: same as (3).

(19) *house*

TAXEMES: (a) Selection: choice of singular bounded substantive (205); with mean-ing 'species of object which may occur in more than one specimen, such that the specimens cannot be subdivided or merged' (cf. 205). (b) Order: follows the deter-miner as head of the substantive expression; with meaning 'object' (267); for the item which it precedes, see (1b). (c) Modulation: the significant part of the final pitch mentioned in (1c) is principally applied to this substantive.

TAGMEME: singular bounded substantive; with meaning 'indivisible object'.

4. IMMEDIATE CONSTITUENTS

4.0. One may observe that the preceding analysis is utterly void, if the initial separa-tion of constructions into immediate constituents is not based upon a valid assump-tion or procedure. Constituent items form the basis for analysis by layers, so that if the layers are incorrectly separated, the analysis fails.

Bloomfield again and again insists upon the essential fact that the analysis must proceed upon the assumption of the principle of immediate constituents (161, 209). It is to be regretted, however, that he failed to provide us with a separate chapter on the criteria for such division, since I for one have frequently been quite per-plexed as to the application of the principle.

For example, one may meet with difficulty in attempting to divide into their imme-diate constituents and to label as endocentric or exocentric the phrases *Away ran John; Away John ran; John ran away; Did he go; John, they say, ran away; Hit him; If he comes, I will sing.* This difficulty has troubled me in the analysis of my own language as well as in the analysis of Mixteco.

In the following paragraphs I shall attempt to gather together some of the prin-ciples implied or mentioned by Bloomfield, and augment them with further illustra-tions, principles, and observations of my own. They are still incomplete and do not operate with perfect ease in difficult situations.

4.1. *Exocentric Division*

Determine if the construction is exocentric or endocentric; these terms Bloomfield clearly explains and illustrates on 194-196. If the construction is exocentric, then two (or sometimes more) forms combine into a phrase, but the form class of neither form is "on the whole" the same as that of the total combination. Thus, "*John ran* is neither a nominative expression (like *John*) nor a finite verb expression (like *ran*)". In an exocentric construction, one should separate the immediate constituents by cutting the phrase at the juncture of the two (or occasionally more) basic contributing forms: *John | ran; Poor John | ran away; the very poor duchess | ran to the house; beside | me; in | the house; by | running away; bigger | than John; if | I can go; that | I can do it; come, | please; John | he ran away; John | broke the lock.*

4.2. *Head-Modifier Division (Endocentric Subordinative)*

If the construction is endocentric subordinative, the total construction will belong to the form class of one of the constituents, the head: "thus *poor John* belongs to the same form-class as *John*, which we accordingly call the head" (195). The other member is the ATTRIBUTE and qualifies or modifies the head, just as *poor* shows one attribute of *John*.

In an endocentric subordinative construction, one should separate the immediate constituents by cutting the phrase at the juncture of the modifier and the thing modified, i.e. between attribute and head: *very fresh | milk* (not: *very | fresh milk*, since *very* qualifies *fresh*, not *milk*); *very | fresh; the | very poor duchess; door knob | wiper* (not: *door | knob wiper*).

In a head-modifier construction, the attribute modifies the whole of the head expression, not just its center. Thus, in *the | great big man, the* modifies *great big man*, not merely *man*; in *buy eggs | tomorrow, tomorrow* modifies *buy eggs*, not merely *buy*. The same principle holds true for *big | black bear; paint the barn | red; elect the man | president; elect him president | if you can.*

A clause may be subordinated to (modify) a main clause: *When he comes, | I will go home; When he goes to the store in the morning | he will find the door closed.*

The labelling of a phrase as exocentric or endocentric cannot always be done by 'rule of thumb', since none of the criteria can be pressed too far because of over-lapping form classes. If we insisted that the head belong to the precise form class and sub-class as the total construction, we should arrive at far fewer endocentric constructions than is expedient. In practice, we are usually concerned with the larger form classes, and with finding whether or not the head belongs "on the whole" (194) to the same one as the phrase, rather than with minute details of permitted position. For example, *the house* is an endocentric construction, since the phrase acts more or less like *house*, in being the actor in actor-action constructions, the goal in action-goal constructions, etc.; but on the other hand, it differs in details inasmuch as the determiner cannot be repeated to form *the the house*, since the construction is closed (196).

The factor of judgment in view of the total situation must therefore be reckoned with. Investigators might differ on some of these decisions. For example, one might say that *hit him* is exocentric because the expression acts neither like the form class 'pronoun' nor like the form class 'transitive verb'; a different investigator might choose to describe the phrase as endocentric because, on the whole, it acts like a finite verb expression and especially like an intransitive verb.

The phrases *Hit him again; Sing again; Hit him if you can; Sing if you can; Sing again if you can* can be satisfactorily described beginning from either starting point even though one or the other might prove to be more convenient (cf. §4.19) for a complete description of English. If the investigator has first decided that in *scolding the boys (would be foolish)*, *the boys* modifies the gerund *scolding*, and that a similar situation exists in *to scold the boys (would be foolish)*, then probably the endocentric expressions would cause him to describe *Hit him* as likewise endocentric (cf. 269, 268; for farther and nearer goals, see 197 and 198; for verb modifiers of manner, 269; for prepositional phrases, 194; for marked infinitive, 268; for anaphoric phrases, 194).

In order to make these criteria for the division of immediate constituents more explicit and to bring to attention the factors which influence one's judgments, a number of further criteria will be given.

4.3. *Division by Ranks of Modifier*

In repeated application of principle (2), one may find layers of rank of modifiers (195, 202-206), taking care that the qualification is from attribute to head: *the / very poor duchess* (not: *the very / poor duchess*); *very poor / duchess* (not: *very / poor duchess*, since *very* qualifies *poor*, as the next layer indicates); *very / poor*. The layers of attribution must be taken off one at a time. See, also, layers or ranks of closure, 223.

4.4. *Separation of Minimal Free Forms; Syntax versus Morphology*

In the initial stages of analysis one need not be too sharply aware of borders between morphology and syntax, but may work down through all layers both of morphology and syntax on the basis of the general principles of ranks of endocentric head-attribute constructions (or underlying versus bound forms): *the / large singers; large / singers; singer / s; sing / er*.

Minimal free forms (smallest items which are spoken by themselves, in isolation) are conveniently called words (178); arrangements of words are customarily handled with one terminology and arrangements within words with another. The boundary line is somewhat vague, with phrase words (180, 207, 239), compounds (227-237), and a few special features (232) all preventing a perfectly clear separation.

Frequently, in an analysis of a language foreign to him, an investigator may hesitate for a long time before determining boundaries. This does not prevent him, however, from proceeding with an analysis of immediate constituents and a partial classification of the grammar.

4.5. *Division by Structural Order*

Rank, in syntax, is paralleled by structural order in morphology (210). Layers here, too, must be taken off in proper sequence: *old maidish | woman* (not: *old | maidish woman*); *old maid | ish* (not: *old | maidish*); *old | maid*.

4.6. *Underlying and Bound Forms*

Instead of calling these head and attribute, the terms in syntax, we speak in morphology of UNDERLYING FORM and BOUND FORM, and cut immediate constituents at their juncture (210): *gentleman | ly*.

4.7. *Separation of Underlying Free Forms*

In cutting morphological items, one tries to leave at least one constituent as normal as possible. Frequently, in English, this means cutting so as to leave one constituent a permitted free form, since complex forms are so often built up by adding a bound form to a free form: *un | gentlemanly* (not: *ungentleman | ly*); *manifest | ly* (not: *mani | festly*); *battl | ing* (not: *batt | ling*); *un | fasten* (not: *unfast | en*).

This will apply to secondary derivation (209), but in primary derivation no underlying free form is present (209): *per | ceive; fath | er*.

4.8. *Division by Theoretical Underlying Form (Stem) and Bound Form*

The setting up of theoretical underlying forms (stems) allows one to divide certain items as if they were secondary derivatives composed of underlying free form plus bound form (237): *scissor | s; oat | s*.

Underlying theoretical free forms plus underlying actual free forms give a slightly different list (237): *cran | berry; oat | meal; scissor | bill*.

4.9. *Division by Inflectional-Derivational Layers*

If an inflectional layer has been shown to be different from a derivational layer (222) on the basis of the other principles, then the division into immediate constituents first cuts off the inflectional bound form: *actress | es*.

4.10. *Division by Primary Affixes*

In derived primary words, which contain more than one bound form (209), the division comes between the primary affix and the root (240-242): *hamm/er; spid/er; ver/y; bott/le; furr/ow; hamm/ock; con/tain; re/ceive.*

4.11. *Division by Morphemes*

Since morphemes are the smallest lexical units of grammatical form and meaning (cf. 161, 264), they are never divided in this procedure: *cat* (not: *ca/t*); *a boy* (not: *a b/oy*); *complex* (not: *co/mplex*).

A few residues provide marginal exceptions. Of these one may mention the root-forming morphemes (244-245) which may cause morphemes otherwise normal to be broken into two constituents: *sl/ime; sl/ush; sl/ump; th/ump; b/ump; th/is; th/ese; th/e; th/us; th/en.*

4.12. *Division Involving Noncontiguous Members of a Constituent*

Sometimes one immediate constituent of a construction lies within the non-contiguous parts of the other constituent.

Infixes are of this type, in morphology. Tagalog (222) ['pi:lit] 'effort' takes the infix [-um-], giving [pu'mi:lit] 'one who is compelled'. Parentheses (186) frequently act similarly, in syntax: *John, so they say, ran away = John ran away + so they say; I saw the boy — I mean Smith's boy — running across the street = I saw the boy running across the street + I mean Smith's boy; Won't you please come? = Won't you come + please.*

Note also the noncontiguous members of one constituent in *Give them up = Give ... up + them; Give the man those books = Give ... those books + the man; Elect us a good man president = Elect ... a good man president + us.* Cf. (*a building*) *which you must pay to enter*, possibly *which ... to enter + you must pay*, but preferably *which / you must pay to enter* (see §4.13, and cf. [*the man*] *whom / I saw*).

4.13. *Division by Positional Structural Weakness*

There are many forms which at first sight one might regard as containing noncontiguous members of a constituent, on the analogy of the same lexical items with normal narrative actor-action word order. Thus, *When he comes, I will go home* might be analyzed as composed of the constituent *I* and the constituent *When he comes, will go home* (partially analogous to *I / will go home when he comes*; but this rather *I will go home / when he comes*); similarly *Who did he send?* might be divided into *he + who did send* (partially analogous to *John / ran away*).

In spite of these partial analogies, however, it seems preferable to me to handle them thus: *When he comes, | I will go home* (endocentric, cf. §4.2); *Who | did he send?* (exocentric); *Away | John ran* (endocentric), and *Away | ran John* (endocentric) — analogous to: *Really, | I must; "Why", | I asked; Why | did he go?; If | he went; If | he go.*

Here, the position just preceding the actor-action heads has so many analogies with forms exocentric to the actor-action unit (e.g. *When he comes; If he comes; why he comes; and he comes*, etc.), and with forms separated by pause (*of course, if you can't go ...; Never, I said; Look, he's coming; Hurray, he's here*) that the position may be said to carry the meaning 'loosely united to the actor-action construction', and the structural break tends to come there regardless of analogies which entail changed word order. Some of these forms are endocentric, modifying the following clause; some are exocentric to the clause, and form with it a new construction type.

This positional pressure would likewise raise the hypothesis for the cutting of certain other phrases in a similar way: *Did | he go?; Has | he gone?; Will | he choose it?* This would necessitate a rather complicated description of constituents such as *he gone*, and hence on the basis of convenience (§4.19) one would probably prefer to treat *has ... gone* as noncontiguous members of a single constituent. If so, the immediate constituents of the sentences just cited would be: *he + did ... go; he + has ... gone; he + will ... choose it.*

4.14. *Division by Coordinate Head and Coordinate Attribute, Contiguous and Noncontiguous*

Endocentric constructions may be coordinate, involving two or more heads. In the sentence *Books, papers, pens, all were lying ...*, the prior constituent consists of the three coordinate heads *books + paper + pens*. Each one may have its own attributes, resulting in a complex endocentric phrase with head and attribute alike consisting of noncontiguous members: *The large books, the important papers, the new pens ... = the large ... the important ... the new + books ... papers ... pens.*

The attribute may alone be coordinate and noncontiguous: *twelve good men and true = twelve good ... and true + men; Bloomfield's Chapter Three = Bloomfield's ... Three + Chapter.*

4.15. *Ambiguous Phrases*

Some phrases are completely ambiguous (if no pauses are present in the phrase). Thus [ðo 'sonz ˌrejz 'mijt] may be either *the sons raise meat* or *the sun's rays meat*. A pause after [sonz] would force the former interpretation; a pause after [rejz] would force the latter. Apart from such a pause, the decision as to the immediate constituents would have to be made on the basis of the semantic context. This need not disturb us any more than the homonymy of [sij] 'sea' and 'see', or [bijt] 'beat' and 'beet'.

Another such phrase is [ðo ˈkiŋ ov ˈiŋglondz ˈajl], *the king | of England's isle* or *the King of England's | isle.*

In the two illustrations above, the problem is to determine the size of the modifier; when that has been done, the head is apparent. In some cases, however, the presence of a modifier is evident enough, but one is not certain which of two items may be its head, because one does not know the structural layer in which it must be broken off. Thus, in (*The man*) *paid for a bench in the park*, two analyses are possible: *paid for a bench | in the park* (i.e. *paid in the park*), or *paid for | a bench in the park* (i.e. *a park bench*). In the former case, *in the park* breaks off in the first layer as a modifier of the entire verb expression; in the other case, as attribute of *a bench* only, it breaks off in the second layer. In this particular choice, the stronger pressure seems to be towards choosing for the final phrase the potential head which is as close to it and as small as possible. If the context forbids this (e.g. if the listener knows of a certainty that the bench has never been in the park but that the man frequently does incidental business there) then one makes the second choice. If the speaker expects that the second choice will be made, but the listener is unaware of the context, the speaker will be 'misunderstood'. When no context is present, the analysis follows the stronger pressure, i.e. towards the selection of that phrase as head which is closest to the attribute and smaller than any other potential head expression.

Rarely, there may be two additions on a structural level so close to one another that the division is made arbitrarily until a decisive formal difference can be found. Compare, for example, *un/gentlemanliness* and *ungentlemanli/ness* — both *un-* and *-ness* coming from the inner derivational layer, and both, when removed, leaving acceptable free forms, or both removed together to leave *gentlemanly.*

4.16. *Division to Preserve Component Meanings*

In separating immediate constituents, one attempts to disturb as little as possible the relationship between the meaning of the parts of the combination and the meaning of the combination as a whole; or to cut in such a fashion that the resultant meaning can be seen to have proceeded readily from the combination of the meanings of the separate parts plus the added grammatical meanings: *gentleman | ly* (not: *gentle/manly*); *door knob | wiper* (not: *door | knob wiper*); *paper | ticker tape* (not: *paper ticker | tape*); *telephone bell | cord* (not: *telephone | bell cord*). On the syntactic level, this principle has already helped provide some of the clues for the operation of principle (2), the finding of head and modifier.

In some types of items, however, the resultant meaning cannot be found as a combination of constituent meanings: *Jack | in-the-pulpit; jail | bird; the | big cheese.* This also includes various types of jesting, etc. (cf. 142).

4.17. *Testing for a Division by Optional Use of Pause and Intonation*

Pauses are frequently introduced between important constituents of expressions. Such pauses are used to indicate separation (and its corollary, grouping) of phrase units. Pauses of this nature are not permitted if they destroy the meaning of the phrase. In a doubtful situation, one who investigates his own speech may therefore attempt to insert pauses, in order to study their effect upon the total meaning of the phrase. Compare §4.13, where pauses help to indicate structural weakness. On the syntactic (but not upon the morphological) level, a permissible pause may usually be inserted between immediate constituents, especially if one also adds the intonation appropriate to such a situation: *Poor John, ran away*; but not *Poor, John ran away*.

This criterion must be used with caution. With determiners, for example, it might not work. Thus in *the / very fresh milk*, one would be more likely to pause after *fresh* (to separate *very fresh* from *milk*) than after *the*. The pause quite frequently may occur at the first layer break with another at a second layer break: *Tom, is here, but not John*. Compare also *He is foolish, who says so*.

In the ambiguous phrases cited in §4.15, this test is helpful (but only when the context is known), since the context will force interpretation of the lexical items, and the grammatical interpretation will follow and carry the pauses with it.

4.18. *Testing for a Division by Parallels*

Choose the division which shows permitted analogous and parallel constructions. Thus (222):

actor	plus	-*ess*	=	*actress*
count	plus	-*ess*	=	*countess*
and *lass*	plus	[-ez]	=	*lasses*
hence *actress*	plus	[-ez]	=	*actresses*
but not *actor*	plus	-*esses*	=	*actresses*

"because there is no parallel for a division" of the last type — i.e. there is no *lass* plus -*esses* = *lassesses*.

In syntax also one looks for parallel instances of form which, by eliminating some of the superfluous and confusing factors of any one particular form, leave the pattern more clearly in view (see illustration in §4.13).

The chief dangers of such parallelism are, first, that one may try to parallel constructions by equating meanings (or by 'logic') instead of by their construction type, and second, that one may falsely assume that the same lexical items with the same general meaning have the same immediate constituents even if the order of the components is shifted. This does not follow, as we saw in §4.13. The parallelism, to be valid, must be within the same positional format or frame (see §5.1), since positional changes bring changes in taxemes of selection (of construction type) and taxemes of order (of constituents).

"A grammatical pattern (sentence-type, construction, or substitution) is often called an *analogy*" (275). A speaker utters forms "*on the analogy* of similar forms which he has heard" (275). "The regular analogies of a language are habits of substitution" (276). Analogies (or patterns) are used to build up new utterances, as in the sample (276)

$$\left.\begin{array}{l} dog : dogs \\ pickle : pickles \end{array}\right\} radio : radios$$

or in analogic change (405-410; samples there also). When an investigator experiments with permitted parallels, he is exploring the range of the habits of substitution by analogy, to get clues to the basic pattern features — in the present case, a clue to their immediate constituents. In a specific position where a form occurs, one may substitute various other permitted forms to gain a broader view of the function of that position.

4.19. *Testing for a Division by Convenience of Description and by Classification of Residues*

Where a construction can be described or cut into its immediate constituents in two or more alternative ways (cf. §4.15; see also §4.13), all the alternatives should be tested, and that one chosen which will "in the long run" give the "simplest possible set of statements" (cf. 212) in view of parallel and related data. This criterion is one of convenience of description (cf. §4.2). It goes without saying that 'convenience' should not be allowed to suppress data.

Regardless of the alternative chosen, there is certain to be a residue of items which do not readily fit the basic classificatory system chosen for the language as a whole. The alternative description to be preferred is the one that leaves the smallest or least troublesome types of residues, which in turn may be either subclassified or described as unique features.

4.20. *The Test of Intuition and Common Sense*

A person will understand and react to his own language if he is spoken to. The naïve English speaker knows by intuition that *pin, bin, sin, fin, shin, thin*, are 'different' in some way. On the other hand he cannot readily (if at all) analyze the difference in terms of phonemes. This inability does not invalidate his differential reaction.

In a somewhat similar way, but perhaps not as strongly, a native speaker reacts to grammatical patterns or 'feels the pressure of word order'. When an investigator of his own language is serving as his own informant, his 'hunches' of structural breaks are very important clues. His hunch may be an unanalyzed reaction to some analogy.

Likewise, any well-organized description of syntactic structure should appeal, at most of its basic points at least, to the common sense of the naïve speakers of the language. The chief difficulty with this conclusion is that native (structurally formed) intuition may become partially obscured when an individual tries to rationalize his language, and thereupon his sophisticated common sense may become erroneous.

Bloomfield implies a unity between speakers of a dialect, in this respect, when he says (161) that "Any English-speaking person who concerns himself with this matter is sure to tell us that the *immediate constituents* of *Poor John ran away* are the two forms *Poor John* and *ran away*" etc.

5. FORM CLASSES, POSITIONS, AND MEANINGS

5.1. A technical principle of equal or approximately equal importance with that of immediate constituents is the identification and classification of form classes. Bloomfield has excellent discussions of this feature (see 264-280, and other references in index). Members of a form class often can be determined by utilizing a test phrase, one element of which can be replaced successively by other items; this testing device is a FRAME and can be used best when the investigator is his own informant.

The phrase *John ran away* might be used for a frame, for example, if one removes *John* and substitutes for it the following replacement items, which constitute a form class of nominative substantive expressions: *he, the horse, the poor boys, everyone who could, the dogs in the kennel*, etc.

If we change the frame, we begin to discover sub-classes. (*John*) *runs away* limits the items which can substitute for *John* to the form class of singulars; *This* ( ) *ran away* eliminates all of the items mentioned here except (*the*) *horse*.

The test for parallels (cf. §4.18) is largely based on a type of exploration in terms of frames or analogous phrases so as to determine the form class of constituents.

When one is working with a limited volume of written materials, rather than using oneself for informant, one may be forced to collect expressions which occur in similar rather than identical grammatical contexts; but the results are the same if one is careful to control possible interfering subclassification.

5.2. The meaning of a form class, the class meaning, is the least common denominator of the members of a class in all the positions in which they may occur (cf. 146, 266-267); such meanings are at times extremely vague and difficult or impossible to state (cf. 'singular' vs. 'plural': *wheat grows* vs. *oats grow*, 190; see also 280).

The meaning of a syntactic position is similarly determined (269).

Where a list of forms is limited to a single position, the class meaning and the positional meaning coincide or overlap. If the list may occur in several positions the class meaning will be somewhat broader than the positional meaning. Thus the positional meaning of the actor position may be 'performer', whereas the class meanning of the performers themselves may be 'object', since the class can also appear as goal, axis, etc. (cf. 267).

In any case, one first determines the list of items which may occur in a syntactic or morphological construction, and then secondly labels the list (class) by its form and meaning; one should never first start with a meaning and then try to arrange a form class according to items which have that meaning (cf. 201, philosophy versus form). Even with a category expressed by several different means, one first obtains the forms (in this case, subgroups) and then connects them into a single category by further formal criteria (cf. gender, 270).

6. GRAMMATICAL DESCRIPTION

Assuming that the grammar of a language has been analyzed by these and other principles, one must next write a description of the data which he has found. The outline for description will differ considerably from that for analysis. Bloomfield's material follows the latter type more than the former (and herein lies a difficulty for students who wish to abstract his analytical principles), but in terms of language in general rather than of one specific language.

One can first describe the largest formal units, the sentence types (171-183); and proceed then to a detailed study of endocentric syntactic constructions (e.g. 202-206), of exocentric syntactic constructions (e.g. 199-200), of morphological constructions outlined according to their types of immediate constituents (209-246), and of substitutions, not discussed in this paper (247-263); and end with a categorical analysis (270-273). Probably no outline can prevent considerable overlapping.

GRAMMATICAL PREREQUISITES TO PHONEMIC ANALYSIS*

0. INTRODUCTION

In recent years various phonemicists seem to have set as an ideal of phonological description and analysis the elimination of all reference to or reliance upon facts about the grammatical structure of the language being investigated. Possibly the most specific rejection of grammar in phonemics is made by Charles F. Hockett: "No grammatical fact of any kind is used in making phonological analysis." Also: "There must be no circularity; phonological analysis is assumed for grammatical analysis, and so must not assume any part of the latter. The line of demarcation between the two must be sharp."[1]

The present article holds that it is impossible for such claims to be realized completely, and that even were it possible, it would at times prove undesirable. It assumes that the best description of any set of data is that statement about them (1) which accounts fully and accurately for all the facts and (2) which at the same time is the most concise and simple and convenient. Since the convenience of a description varies somewhat with the purposes to which it may be placed, the goal of phonemic description for the present discussion is taken to be the purely scientific presentation of the phonology of languages as part of their structural delineation. To eliminate the facts of grammatical relationship and structure from the analysis and presentation of phonological structure is frequently undesirable because many of the phonological facts are inextricably interwoven with grammatical facts and structural relationships; avoiding the portrayal of this relationship means omitting, completely or at least temporarily, an important part of the total structure of the language. When phonological and grammatical facts are mutually dependent, the treatment of phonology without reference to grammar is a concealment of part of a most important set of structural facts pertinent to phonology. The apparent gain in compartmentation or systematization of data at the expense of an early indication of such structural phenomena within the total phonological arrangement is too high a price to pay for neatness of statement.

Furthermore, it may prove unnecessarily complex to establish in every instance

* *Word* 3:3 (1947), 155-172. Reprinted by permission.
[1] Charles F. Hockett, "A System of Descriptive Phonology", *Language* 18 (1942), 20-21.

a distinct terminology to differentiate the phonological structure and grammatical structure, if the same set of facts and relationships may apply to each. If, for example, a grammatical entity is discovered which is clearly a minimum unit of free expression, and which may be conveniently labelled a 'word', and if phonological distributions can only conveniently be described in reference to these same sections of utterances, one has lost something of convenience, simplicity, and clarity of presentation of the language as a whole, if in the grammatical discussion these units are called 'words', but in the phonological discussion they are called, let us say, 'intrajunctures'. Distinct terminology for distinct 'levels of analysis' is valuable only when the facts and relationships are likewise distinct. An artificial distinction based upon different approaches to a single set of data may result in a sharp artificial dichotomy which has no reality.

Such an unfortunate exaggerated distinction already exists within grammatical analysis in the traditional terminological cleavage between syntax and morphology in those characteristics of grammatical analysis which may be similar for both phases of the analysis. This terminology proves especially inconvenient, and is most likely to lead to error, in those languages in which no such basic structural dichotomy can readily be demonstrated.[2]

Although Hockett held that he used "no grammatical fact of any kind" in his analysis, it appears to me that one must inevitably utilize — however unintentionally — facts which are linked so closely to grammatical phenomena that an attempt to separate completely a phonological analysis from a grammatical one proves impossible.

1. FIELD PROCEDURE

The first fact to be noted, which indicates an essential relation between phonological and grammatical analysis, is that the field procedure of linguists in general is to conduct some grammatical research simultaneously with phonemic analysis. Hockett himself admits doing so: "Analytical procedure is a trial-and-error process, in which the analyst makes successive approximations. He gathers phonological and grammatical material at the same time, though he may emphasize now one, now the other. He makes errors of omission and commission, and later corrects them."

This dual research, I maintain, is essential, not accidental; phonemes cannot be analyzed without some knowledge — though it may be very slight — of grammatical

---

[2] On overlapping morphology-syntax nomenclature see K. L. Pike, "Taxemes and Immediate Constituents", *Language* 19 (1943), 76; for a language without pronounced cleavage between morphology and syntax, see K. L. Pike, "Analysis of a Mixteco Text", *IJAL* 10 (1944), 113-138, esp. 113, 125-128, 131-132; for problems in English, see *ibid.*, 128, fn. 8, and K. L. Pike, *The Intonation of American English* (= *University of Michigan Publications in Linguistics* 1) (Ann Arbor, 1945), 81. Also note M. Swadesh, "Nootka Internal Syntax", *IJAL* 9 (1939), 77ff, esp. 78: "... the combination of morphemes into a single word in a synthetic language has the same function as the juxtaposition of independent words in an analytic language."

facts. Furthermore, it appears to me that one must assume that any elements of unavoidable procedure must in turn reflect something of the structure being analyzed. Generally used field procedures imply that phonemes can be analyzed only in reference to grammatical facts.

B. Bloch and G. L. Trager[3] take a different view in saying: "The procedure by which we analyze the grammar of a language is in principle the same as that used in phonemics. Here again we examine a collection of utterances, list the recurrent fractions, and establish classes by grouping together parts of different utterances which are alike in form and function. Phonemic analysis must come first (cf. §3.2); for the utterance fractions listed and compared in grammatical analysis are not sounds but meaningful forms phonemically recorded."

Their assertion that phonemic analysis must come first is, indeed, partially true: a succinct, adequate, complete statement of the grammar can only be given when the forms are presented phonemically; otherwise, many postulated minor 'rules of grammar' might prove to be nothing more than statements regarding subvarieties of phonemes (allophones) where occurrences are determined by the phonetic environments as they change with substituted or added grammatical elements.[4]

If, however, one interprets their statement to mean that NO grammatical analysis can precede phonemic analysis, or to mean that a COMPLETE phonemic analysis either CAN or MUST precede even a partial grammatical one (and these are implications of their statement as given), then serious errors are involved. Many of the most significant grammatical facts of a language can be deduced from a crude and inaccurate phonetic transcription: morphemes can often be identified even by rough similarity in form and meaning; indeed, even accurate phonemic transcriptions sometimes show the morphemes in variant forms. Once the morphemes are identified, they can be grouped into major and minor form classes: into stems, affixes, and the like; into tenses, aspects, etc.; into words, compounds, or phrases; into structural layers of immediate constituents. Boundaries between morphemes, words, clauses, utterances and so on, may then usually be established. That is to say, many of the most important structural facts which differentiate two languages can be discovered from crude phonetic data, subject to some omissions if pertinent sounds are overlooked, or unnecessary complexity of form at those points where allophones, instead of phonemes, are transcribed.

These facts seem sufficiently pertinent, at least, to counterbalance somewhat the hyperbole of Bloch and Trager (*Outline*, 39): "In short, a purely phonetic description makes it impossible to distinguish the really significant features of the vocabulary and the grammar from the accidental and personal features which inevitably form part of every utterance; as a scientific procedure it is about as fruitful as it would

---

[3] *Outline of Linguistic Analysis* (Baltimore, 1942), 53.
[4] It is to these difficulties which Bloch and Trager call attention in §3.2, referred to in the previous quotation. These facts are not sufficient, however, to justify their sweeping instructions to the beginner that ALL phonemic analysis be completed before ANY grammatical research be undertaken.

be for a biologist to assign two cats to different species because one had more hairs in its tail than the other." Hockett, however (*Language* 18, 20), admits that "Grammatical work is carried on, of course, in cases where phonological information is incomplete, either slightly deficient as it is for Old English, or sadly inadequate as it is for ancient Egyptian."

2. IDENTIFICATION OF MORPHEMES

The phonemic analysis cannot be completed until some initial grammatical steps are taken. Perhaps the most important of these is the identification of at least a limited number of morphemes. Thus Hockett,[5] and Bloch and Trager[6] utilize pairs of utterances which (1) have different meanings, and (2) are minimally different in their pronunciation.

Recognizing that the utterances are different in meaning is a grammatical process,[7] not a phonemic one. It is thus absolutely essential that a minimal grammatical identification be achieved before phonemic analysis can be carried on: the irreducible minimum prerequisite is that the investigator know enough about two items to be certain that they are 'different'. One might at first conclude that morpheme identification is a lexical problem instead of a grammatical one. This objection, in my opinion, is overruled by at least three facts. (1) Many morphemes, to be identified at all, must be studied in larger utterances, since they do not occur in isolation. In longer sequences the processes of grammatical comparison, and structural classification become very evident; the abstraction of these morphemes is not a mere listing of lexical items. (2) Even in situations commonly called isolation, morphemes must be abstracted, by processes of grammatical comparison of occurrences in the same or different practical situations, from a host of speech characteristics such as intonational modifications, variable voice qualities and the like. (3) Meanings can be determined only in context. The pertinent contexts may be practical (gestures and so on) or linguistic. Especially in matters of linguistic context, grammatical analysis must be used in finding the meanings.

The phonemic analyst must have some knowledge of when he is hearing repeated pronunciations of the same morpheme or sequence of morphemes. If this were not true, he might sometimes think he heard variation in the pronunciation of what he assumed was a single 'word', whereas he had actually heard two different words with

---

[5] *Language* 18, 7.
[6] *Outline*, 38, 40.
[7] Hockett himself (*Language* 18, 20) acknowledges this fact, without noting that it contradicts a statement in his succeeding paragraph to the effect that "no grammatical fact of any kind is used in making phonological analysis". He says: "The criteria for grammatical classification are (1) recognition of morpheme, word, and construction, and of borders between them, (2) the phonemic shape of morphemes, words, and constructions, and (3) bisocial function, or meaning; the third is used in determining the first."

two different sound sequences. M. Swadesh evidently recognizes the need for knowing what constitutes repetitions of the same word in such a methodological statement
as:[8] "Except for word variants... different occurrences of the same word have the
same phonemic make-up. If differences are observed in different pronunciations
of the same word, these are to be taken as showing the range of deviation of the
component phonemes." The identification of repetitions of a morpheme involves
the grammatical segmentation of the utterances containing it.

Based upon this field procedure, is another highly important one, even though subject
to abuse: the gathering of clues as to positional variation of a phoneme by noting
the changes of a morpheme in different grammatical contexts. If, for example, a
certain suffix ends in voiceless *l* when that morpheme comes at the end of an utterance, but ends in a voiced *l* when a further suffix is added to it,[9] the investigator
assumes that *l* and *l* are submembers (or allophones) of a single phoneme unless or
until he finds these two sounds in direct contrast elsewhere, in phonetically and
grammatically analogous positions. There must be something wrong with present-
day phonemic theory if workers agree on the practical value and validity of a procedure (and of evidence) in the field which they then rule out in theoretical discussion
and in presentation.

Certain types of phonemic description require considerable grammatical knowledge — more than a mere differential knowledge of morphemes. An example is
L. Bloomfield's "Stressed Vowels of American English",[10] whose introductory summary describes it as a "Description of the stressed vowel phonemes of Central Western
Standard-English as spoken in Chicago. The article possesses a more general interest
as an example of the technique of analyzing phonemically the structure of a dialect."
In giving a description "of the combinations in which the phonemes occur", the
author states, for example: "*Type 1.* As the basis of our description we take morphologically simple one-syllable words ... *Type 1a.* Such combinations are made
with suffixes and enclitics of the form [s, z, t, d], added without phonetic modification ...". One should also note that Bloch and Trager (*Outline*, 54) treat identification of free forms in their morphological analysis, not their phonemic one.

3. CONTRASTS IN UTTERANCE-INITIAL

A field which receives wide usage,[11] although not as much attention as word pairs, is the
study of sounds in contrast at the beginning of utterances. At the outset in the pho-

---

[8] "The Phonemic Principle", *Language* 10 (1934), 123.
[9] A situation existing in some of the Mayan languages, including Cakchiquel of Guatemala (data
from W. C. Townsend). For a problem in which this type of evidence proves important, see N.
Weathers, "Tsotsil Phonemes with Special Reference to Allophones of *b*", *IJAL* 13 (1947), 108-111.
[10] *Language* 11 (1935), 97-116.
[11] Note, for example, references in Bloch and Trager, *Outline*, 40-41; also M. Swadesh, "A Method
for Phonetic Accuracy and Speed", *Am. Anthropologist* 39 (1937), 728-732, esp. 730, step 2.

netic study of a language it is no arbitrary whim which dictates the observation of the sounds occurring at the beginning of utterances. Rather, at that place the analyst can be certain that he is at the beginning of a phoneme, of a syllable, of a stress or rhythm group, of an intonation contour, of a phonological sequence of some type. These facts eliminate some of the variables and uncertainties which he would inevitably face in the middle of an utterance. At no other place, except at the end of utterances, can he be certain, before he has studied the structure of the language, that he will find such dependable conditions.

By studying sounds at the beginning of utterances the analyst also knows that they are simultaneously at the beginning of a word, and at the beginning of a construction.[12] These positions are grammatical. By the mere focusing of his attention on the phonological characteristics at the beginning of utterances, the analyst does not thereby eliminate the grammatical characteristics at that same point. The value of utterance-initial position in phonological analysis is in part due to the potential influence of these grammatical units on the sounds, not just to the potential phonological conditioning factors. The assumption that one can treat utterance-initial sounds without being affected by grammatical relations seems therefore to be incorrect.

4. JUNCTURES

Now, what are so-called junctures? Are they phonemes in their own right, or are they special kinds of joints between phonological units, or are they joints between grammatical units with occasional phonological characteristics?

I cannot recall having seen a careful discussion of the problem.[13] I am under the impression, however, that some workers in the field are tending toward the conclusion that junctures are phonemes of some sort. Thus junctures appear in lists of phonemes in the writings of Z. S. Harris,[14] C. T. Hodge,[15] and others.

If one wishes to treat junctures as phonemes, one must be ready to answer the following questions: Are junctures phonemes similar to segmental and prosodic ones? If not, how do they differ? If a juncture is a phoneme, can one describe its variant forms or indications as allophones? And how will one treat allophones of a juncture phoneme if they have nothing physically in common with each other, or if close 'juncture' is phonetically zero?[16] Most important of all, what must be

---

[12] See K.L. Pike, *Phonemics: A Technique for Reducing Languages to Writing* (Glendale, 1946), 63-65. In that edition, as well as the editions of 1943 and 1945, I have presented phonemic techniques with reference to grammar.

[13] Hockett, however, states (*Language* 18, 15) that "Junctural phones are not matters of grammatical segmentation, although a junctural situation may define phonological segments which are of grammatical significance."

[14] "The Phonemes of Moroccan Arabic", *JAOS* 62 (1942), 318.

[15] "Serbo-Croatian Phonemes", *Language* 22 (1946), 112.

[16] Note, for example, Bloch and Trager, *Outline*, 47 — varieties of phenomena preceding and following open juncture.

done when the analyst is convinced that a space should be written because of morphological parallels at a place where no known phonological justification exists for placing a 'juncture phoneme'?

The last question is a serious one. At the moment, those investigators treating junctures as phonemes seem to be writing spaces at such points and calling them junctures, but postulating the existence of phonological data which they have as yet been unable to hear but assume — on grammatical grounds — that it must be there. Bloch, for example, says of Japanese:[17] "Pauses do not occur within a word: every pause marks a word boundary. On the other hand, many word boundaries are never marked by pauses. In our transcription we separate words by spaces, but these have no phonetic value." Since Bloch has claimed that phonemic analysis must precede a grammatical one, where does he obtain this morphological transcription? Since he states that only a phonemic transcription is constructive for grammatical description, why does he include nonphonemic — even nonphonetic — elements in his transcription?

Several other quotations of a similar nature can be given: Trager says of Taos,[18] "Word-division has here been determined by morphological criteria when the available phonemic description does not suffice."

W. E. Welmers says of Fanti,[19] "However, for practical purposes, since such junctures will always parallel morpheme boundaries, it may be pointed out that, in learning Fanti and most other languages, the recognition of morphemes proceeds more rapidly than the recognition of the minute phonetic details that may possibly be present to establish junctures in such cases ... for the time being then, such junctures are written arbitrarily but without apology." This statement occurs in the paragraph immediately following one which begins thus: "It must also be pointed out that the establishment of phonemic junctures is independent of any considerations as to morpheme boundaries."

Harris, for Moroccan Arabic,[20] states that "The segments of various lengths (word, etc.) are not defined by the morphological terms used in this section, but by the points in which the junctures are placed, and the place of the junctures is in turn determined by the sound types in whose environment junctures are included." Contrast this quotation with others taken from the page immediately preceding it in the same article: "The junctures are not in themselves heard as sounds ... We have to count as phonemic those junctures which are necessarily mentioned as environments of sound types which we consider automatic or include as positional variants of phonemes ... it is only because we recognize a morpheme juncture after *l* 'the' that the *u* in [l-ųŭžh] 'the face' does not contrast with the *u* in [kursi] 'chair'... The ad-

---

[17] "Studies in Colloquial Japanese II: Syntax", *Language* 22 (1946), 202.
[18] "An Outline of Taos Grammar", *Linguistic Structures of Native America* (= *Viking Fund Publications in Anthropology* 6) (New York, 1946), 189.
[19] *A Descriptive Grammar of Fanti* 21 (= *Language Dissertation* 39) (Baltimore, 1946).
[20] *JAOS* 62, 318.

vantage of these junctures is that in addition to helping set up successive (linear) and simultaneous (contour) phonemes, they also divide the flow of speech into morphologically distinct segments: morphemes, words, and the like."

For Kingwana-Swahili, Harris and F. Lukoff[21] likewise utilize some grammatical junctures, with attempted or implied phonemic justification for them: "In order to establish the tone-stress sequences, we have had to recognize word juncture /#/. We may now recognize junctures which mark the boundary of utterance intonations ... No other junctures have had to be recognized on phonemic grounds."

We must now ask ourselves the following questions: If phonemic analysis, including junctural phonemics, must be completed before grammatical analysis is begun, as Bloch and Trager imply, how does it happen that Bloch and Trager in analytical publications utilize junctures established by grammatical procedures instead of by phonetic data? If junctures are phonemes, and if the allophones of such a phoneme have some underlying phonetic characteristic, why is it that Trager and Welmers failed to find such characteristics and were forced to use grammatical ones? If, as Bloch implies, a phonemic analysis is the only convenient one for grammatical description, why do Harris, Lukoff, and Bloch himself write spaces bolstered by grammatical analysis?

If phonemic analysis is the most practical one as a background for grammatical description, there must be something amiss with any statement of phonemic theory (1) which must be abandoned in difficult spots, or (2) contradicted by actual field procedure, or (3) executed with dependence upon extremely obscure phonetic data which elude even expert observers and which are called upon to support junctures set up by other (grammatical) procedures rather than for serving those practical advantages claimed for phonemic transcription.

I am inclined to believe that, when research workers such as Bloch, Trager, and Harris fail to find phonetic data at these points, then (1) either no such data exist, or (2) the data are so obscure, and so minute, as to be below the threshold of useful signals for communication, or transcription by the analyst.[22]

What constitutes the mysterious element which forces investigators to write junctures in contradiction to their theories? In my opinion it is grammatical structure. Hockett asserts that, for phonological analysis and grammatical analysis, "The line of demarcation between the two must be sharp." Why? If it can be demonstrated that a grammatical approach to phonemics gives a simpler, easier, accounting for

---

[21]   "The Phonemes of Kingwana-Swahili", *JAOS* 62 (1942), 337.

[22]   This does not completely eliminate the possibility of groupings of a physiological type, which at present elude us but which may ultimately be isolated in such a way that we can train ourselves to record them. R. H. Stetson (*Bases of Phonology* [Oberlin, 1945], 57) says: "The foot includes one or more chest pulses, syllables, grouped by abdominal-diaphragmatic contraction of expiration. This is the movement which binds the syllables together and gives junctures and the main stress." Can this involve something in addition to what we respond to in writing stress, pause, intonation, and the like?

ALL of the FACTS, why should we follow an *a priori* separation of the two?[23] If language actually works as a unit, with grammatical configurations affecting phonetic configurations, why should we not describe the language and analyze it in that way? If forced to do so, why pretend we are avoiding it?

I conclude that in many languages certain grammatical units — say 'words' — have as one of their characteristics the induction of subphonemic modification of some of the sounds. When modifiable sounds happen to occur at the borders of such units, the juncture becomes phonologically recognizable. If no modifiable sounds happen to occur at a grammatical boundary, the boundary is not phonetically perceptible but is nontheless present and just as important in the total structure of the language. The phonemics of a language, in other words, cannot be presented completely until something is known of the grammar, just as the grammar cannot be presented completely until something is known of the phonemics.

5. OPTIONAL OR POTENTIAL PHENOMENA

As a corollary of these statements I conclude that grammatical units such as words, or grammatical borders, may carry various potentials which are not actualized as phonetic data at every occurrence of these words or borders, but which are important to practical orthographical symbolization of a language and to its phonemic analysis.[24]

Perhaps the most important of such potentials — long recognized and utilized by other workers, but not under the arguments presented in this paper — is the ability of certain grammatical items to occur as free forms. Such items are usually called words, and are frequently set off by spaces in the orthography.[25] The point I wish to emphasize here is that the potentiality of free occurrence remains in force even when the words are included in longer utterances, and that the grammatical unit is capable of affecting phonemic structure even although it may not in every instance be phonologically definable or observable in terms of stress, characteristic clusters of sounds, or other objective phenomena. Presumably it is this potential which, in part, led Trager, Bloch, Welmers, and Harris to set up certain word junctures without phonological evidence, and to symbolize them with 'phonemic' spaces in their orthographies.

In many languages it seems to be these word units which control the types of

---

[23] Hockett (*Language* 18, 9) sets up simplicity, under economy, as a criterion. In the following quotation from his writing (*Language* 18, 15-16), simplicity seems to be on the side of grammatical, not phonological, definition (I have no description by Hockett, available to me at the time of writing, of a modern language as a whole): "Our phonetic information for Latin is defective, but it seems quite possible that the stress in early classical Latin was not an accent but part of a junctural phone. It can be located mechanically if certain borders are assumed. Grammatically these borders are clear, but without adequate material it is impossible to tell whether they were also phonological or not."
[24] See my *Phonemics*, 66-67.
[25] E.g. Bloch and Trager, *Outline*, 54.

permitted sequences of phonemes or of the specific allophones which occur in various positions within the words. Thus M. Swadesh says,[26] "Each language has a characteristic word and syllable structure. Some of the limitations of occurrence of phonemes are best accounted for as connected with principles of word structure ... The limits of the word are often marked in special ways ... Such elements (e.g. aspiration, glottal stop, accent) are not phonemes, but mechanical signs of the limits of word units."

A second type of potential which is highly important for English,[27] and possibly for some other languages, is that the end of an intonation contour may occur at the end of any word. The end of every word is potentially the end of such a contour whether the word is found in isolation or included in a longer phrase. Note the following set of sentences; the numbers indicate pitch from 1 as highest to 4 the lowest; the degree sign indicates the beginning of a primary contour, and the syllable carrying it is stressed; hyphens link the elements of a single total intonation contour; the accent mark indicates innate lexical stress, which is reduced or eliminated unless a degree sign occurs with the same syllable — but syllables with accent marks and no degree sign are potentially stressed, so that the actual stress may reappear normally on that syllable at any time that the intonation is modified:

(1)   'Thomas   is   'coming, (but ...)
          o2 -4-3   3-   o2 -4

(2)   'Thomas   is   'coming, (but ...)
          o2-   -4 -3

(3)   'Thomas   is   'coming, (but ...)
          o2 -4   o2-4   o2 -4

In the first sentence an intonation contour ends with the word *coming*; in the second, with the word *Thomas* as well; in the third, another contour is completed on the word *is*. The potential for a contour end existed on the words *Thomas* and *is*, in the first two sentences as well as the third. This potential helps to establish grammatical junctures (word junctures in this instance) which are phonologically pertinent, even though perhaps not phonetically marked, between the words in the first sentence in rapid speech.

Another type of pertinent potential may be illustrated with these same sentences. Pauses may optionally occur between words; usually, but not essentially, an intonation contour ends at every pause — but many contours end where no pause occurs. The intonation break is often accompanied by a change of speed. In the third sentence, repeated here, note the pauses, symbolized by a virgule:

(3)   'Thomas   is   'coming, (but ...)
          o2 -4/   o2-4/   o2 -4/

26   *Language* 10, 122.
27   See Pike, *Intonation*, esp. 78-88 and 29-39.

These English potentials of permitted placement of pause and end of intonation contour normally occur at word ends. The potentials are lost in compound words.[28] This formulation eliminates the necessity of postulating a 'compounding stress', which appears difficult to maintain in the light of occasional homophonous phrases and compounds.

A further kind of potential occurs in the illustration above, but does not seem to affect English junctures so directly: Lexical stress may be reduced considerably in intensity or, with sufficient speed of utterance, — reduced below the threshold of contrast perceptually discernable. Note, for example, loss of stress on the word *coming*, in the first sentence, if the word *Thomas* is heavily stressed. Nevertheless, if an intonation of the type seen in sentence (2) is then given to the utterance, the stress returns to the word *coming*, and — let it be noted — reappears on the same syllable as before. This potential (for reappearance of stress on a specific syllable of a specific word) can be predicted only if the word is known from other contexts, or if the stress is not completely eliminated in the other pronunciations.

In a somewhat different analysis one may note that so-called 'secondary stress' on words like *vaccination* may be (1) very weak or (2) nondetectable by auditory analysis, or (3) moderately weak, or (4) as strong as the primary stress. Even in the weak pronunciations, however, the potential remains for the recurrence of stress in other contexts.

So also various nonphonemic modifications of sounds, such as 'drawling' of voiced consonants or vowels at word ends, are potentially but not essentially present. Likewise the phrase *an aim* may be phonetically distinct from the phrase *a name*, but optionally, or with rapid pronunciation, the phrases may be homophonous. If the grammatical juncture is symbolized with a space (and the options or potentials at such borders defined in a phonemic statement), the total admissable series of pronunciations is symbolized. If, however, one insists on writing a space only where phonetic criteria can be heard, the problem of the writing of the space would be complicated by the necessity to decide at what point the phonetic characteristics of the one juncture had faded into the other, or disappeared altogether. The failure to treat optional but normal pronunciations of various kinds is a deficiency in Bloch and Trager's discussion[29] of 'internal open juncture'.

6. PROBLEMS OF TRANSCRIPTION

It appears necessary to solve two problems before grammatical junctures can be utilized as such in phonemic analysis and presentation:

(1) How could a beginner, given a phonemic alphabet and a statement of allophones by an early worker in the field, take dictation in the language and write all

---

[28]   See Pike, *Intonation*, 79-88.
[29]   "Syllabic Phonemes of English", *Language* 17, 228.

the sounds and junctures, if the junctures are grammatical and at times reflect no positive phonetic characteristic?

The answer is: He could not. The beginner would have to be able to recognize some of the morphemes, and know something of the grammatical structure, before he could correctly leave spaces in places where phonetic clues were not present. But can he do any better with a phonologically defined set of juncture symbols if, as in the cases presented by Welmers and Trager, certain spaces are written morphologically in spite of the definition? The answer is again: No. If, however, phonetic phenomena characterize the presence of a certain juncture, the beginner has as good a chance to record it whether it is defined in terms of a 'phonemic phrase'[30] with phonetic markers, or of a grammatical 'word' with the same markers.

(2) If one uses grammatical units or their borders for the description and analysis of phonemes, which kinds of units must one use and symbolize? Morphemes? Words? Short constructions? Long constructions? Noun constructions? Verb constructions? Suffixes? Or what? And how can he know when he has symbolized enough kinds of grammatical units?

A partial answer: the analyst studies grammar and phonology simultaneously, allowing phonemic hypotheses to give him clues for finding grammatical facts, and grammatical hypotheses to give him clues for finding phonemic facts; grammatical analysis can be begun with phonetic data, and phonemic analysis can be begun with a small amount of grammatical data plus the phonetic data. He assumes that any specific phone is a phoneme in its own right unless he finds two similar sounds occurring in mutually exclusive phonetic environments, from which he concludes that they are allophones of a single phoneme and writes the two with a single phonemic symbol. Similarly, if two similar sounds are restricted to mutually exclusive grammatical environments, he concludes that they are members of a single phoneme; he then uses a single symbol, but he must also symbolize in some way the grammatical environment causing the modification.

Three rules, related to the preceding statements, may help the beginning analyst:

(a) Phonemes must be defined, in so far as grammatically conditioned varieties are concerned, only in terms of those grammatical borders which are symbolized in some way — such as by space, or by hyphen.

(b) Symbols for grammatical borders should be utilized only for those types of junctures by which the analyst wishes to define subphonemic variation or for highly important nonphonetic potentials such as ability to occur in isolation.

(c) Once a certain kind of juncture is symbolized at one point in the language, the investigator must write that same symbol at every occurrence of the same kind of border, even though no phonetic modification is there observed.

Experience seems to show that a fourth rule should be added:

(d) The investigator should avoid utilizing small or (even large) specific grammatical categories for these purposes. Although one may conceive, for example, of a

<hr>

[30] Term used by Bloch and Trager, *Language* 17, 226.

situation in which the symbolization of every noun in a way different from every verb would reduce the number of phonemes postulated,[31] this type of transcription should be avoided. I shall not attempt to state here the reasons which give rise to this practical conclusion. In any event, the previous rules hold: a noun-verb distinction must not be used for defining the environments of allophones unless the analyst is prepared to symbolize this distinction at every occurrence of a noun or a verb; such a symbol should not be set up unless needed for phonological reference; once used at all, the symbols must be used consistently throughout the language. It is because of the uncertainty with regard to rule (d), that I have called this discussion a partial answer, only, to the last question proposed. When, however, the analyst (1) has accounted for all his phonetic data, (a) by symbols for the phonemes themselves, or (b) by symbols for those grammatical junctures which modify the phonemes and produce subphonemic phonetic phenomena, and (2) has symbolized all highly important and widespread potentials such as possibility of occurrence in isolation, he needs no further analysis of the grammar for phonemic purposes.

7. PHONOLOGICAL CHARACTERISTICS OF MIXTECO MORPHEMES

In previous sections of this paper I have affirmed that morphological units could affect phonemic units. I now wish to indicate several ways in which the Mixteco morpheme unit (a) is sometimes marked and (b) controls sequences of vowel phonemes.[32]

7.1. Every Mixteco morpheme in its full form consists of one of the following bisyllabic sequences (C represents a consonant, V a vowel, n nasalization of final vowel): CVCV, CVɁCV, CVV, CVɁV; CVCVn, CVVn, CVɁVn. Any medial consonant may be optionally but nonphonemically (noncontrastively) lengthened. If the listener hears a long consonant, he knows that he is at the middle of a morpheme, since such consonants do not occur elsewhere. If the consonant is extra long it signals general intensity or emphasis. In this form one might choose to analyze a prosodic phoneme superimposed on the phrase. However, it is probably best treated as a type of socially significant gradation[33] rather than as a contrastive phoneme, since there seems to be no line of demarkation between the normal and the emphatic lengthening.

The first syllable of any morpheme may optionally be marked by stress. The

---

[31] Harris and Welmers considered and rejected such a possibility in "The Phonemes of Fanti" (*JAOS* 62, 325): "If we could indicate by their form which words are verbs, we would not have to mark tones on them. However, it is not quite possible to make a phonemic distinction between verbs and nouns, for there are a few possible cases where the same form could be either ...."

[32] I am discussing in these paragraphs morphemes of native origin only. Loan words introduce new sequences.

[33] See Pike, *Intonation*, 98-99.

second syllable is never stressed. If the listener hears a stressed syllable he knows that he is at the beginning of a morpheme. The first syllable, nevertheless, is not necessarily stressed; frequently I can detect no extra intensity on it whatever.

It is the morpheme unit which controls these two optional phenomena. When neither special length nor stress is present, the potential must still be symbolized by an indication of morpheme beginnings, since the reader without such symbolization would tend to make some syllables more intense than others but would frequently stress the wrong ones. This type of mispronunciation by foreigners frequently leads to misunderstanding by the natives.

The indication of potential initial stress and potential medial lengthening is complicated by the phenomenon of morpheme reduction, by which the basic two-syllable form is reduced to a monosyllabic proclitic or enclitic that attaches to another full morpheme. To set all morphemes apart equally by space would not show whether a reduced element goes with the preceding or following full morpheme, with consequent confusion of meaning. To place a stress mark at the beginning of every morpheme would misrepresent the facts by insisting on a feature that is frequently absent. My solution has been to use spaces and hyphens.[34]

7.2. Once the morpheme unit has been recognized in Mixteco, one finds that there are systematic restrictions in the sequences of vowels that may occur within it. The vowel sequences are correlated with the syllabic pattern of the morpheme, CVCV, for example, being less restricted than CVʔVn. Contiguous sequences (as in CVV) are much more heavily limited than noncontiguous ones (as in CVCV), and the types found with final nasalization (CVCVn, CVVn, CVʔVn) are more limited than corresponding types without nasal. There are also restrictions in consonant sets, but these have not yet been fully worked out. Also toneme sequences and sandhi changes of tone are not treated here.[35]

The six vowels, *i a u ə e o*, fall into two groups according to the freedom with which they occur in sequences within stems. The first three, forming the outer points in the vowel triangle, are relatively unrestricted. The second three, occupying inner points in the vowel triangle, are very considerably restricted. Examples illustrating all the sequences that occur in the different stem patterns are given below:

[34] See texts published in *IJAL* 10, 113-138; 11, 129-139, 219-224; 12, 22-24. In *cuendu ñānga* [Funny Stories] (Oaxaca, Mexico, San Miguel el Grande, 1946), designed for native readers, I use hyphens to set off postclitics but spaces after proclitics; this cuts down the number of hyphens without creating ambiguity.
[35] For Mixteco tone, see Pike, *Tone Languages* (Glendale, 1945). The treatment of morpheme make-up as attempted here would be 'morphophonemics' in Hockett's definition (*Language* 18, 20): "the branch of grammar which deals with the phonemic shape of morphemes, words, and constructions, without regard to their meaning". However, Bloch and Trager (*Outline*, 57) define morphophonemics as "the study of the alternation between phonemes in morphemes related to each other by internal change". The data given here were presented at Ann Arbor to a summer meeting of the Linguistic Society of America about eight years ago. I have been able to add several specific vowel sequences which have since been discovered by my colleague, Donald Stark.

CVCV with unrestricted vowels: *ʔini* 'to become late', *ʔísá* 'day after tomorrow', *lítú* 'a kid'; *čáká* 'a fish', *kačì* 'cotton', *ʔañú* 'heart'; *žúžú* 'dew', *ⁿduči* 'bean', *žùča* 'river'. None lacking.

CVCV with one or two restricted vowels: *meke* 'brain', *žeha* 'craw', *lelu* 'lamb'; *səkə̀* 'back', *tə̀ka* 'grasshopper', *təñí* 'mouse', *ñìtə́* 'sand', *katə* 'shade', *kutə* 'short'; *sókó* 'a spring'. *ʔoⁿdè* 'up to', *víló* 'lizard', *kʷažo* 'rubbish'. Some speakers add: *təku* 'for sewing'. Lacking sequences: *a-e, i-e, ə-e, u-e, e-i, o-i, e-ə, o-i, e-ə, o-ə, e-o, ə-o, u-o, o-u.*

CVʔCV with unrestricted vowels: *kʷiʔñì* 'a crack', *kʷiʔnà* 'the devil', *čiʔⁿdù* 'an oak ball', *saʔma* 'cloth', *kaʔni* 'sweat' (from illness), *ñaʔmù* 'tuber', *suʔnù* 'shirt', *kuʔni* 'to wring', *suʔmà* 'tail'.

CVʔCV with restricted vowels: *téⁿdé* 'torn', *ⁿdə̀ʔži* 'a sore', *sə́ʔbə́* 'a name', *kóʔⁿdó* 'frog'. Some speakers: *liʔlò* 'rabbit'.

CVV with unrestricted vowels: *níí* 'you' (polite), *kʷià* 'year', *bìu* 'green sprout'; *náá* 'I' (polite), *kai* (short form of *kahi*) 'eat', *žau* 'century plant'; *ⁿdúú* 'both', *ⁿdua* 'arrow'. *Cui* is lacking.

CVV with restricted vowels: *bèe* 'heavy'; *nə́ə́* 'whole', *hiò* 'griddle', *róó* 'you' (familiar).

CVʔV with unrestricted vowels: *líʔi* 'rooster', *kʷiʔà* 'expensive', *ⁿdiʔù* (or *ⁿdiʔbù*) 'closed', *naʔa* 'thatch pole', *ⁿdaʔì* 'to cry', *báʔù* 'coyote'; *žuʔu* 'mouth', *ⁿduʔa* 'a plain'. *Cuʔi* is lacking.

CVʔV with restricted vowels: *kʷeʔè* 'illness', *sə́ʔə́* 'female', *híʔo* 'spice', *žoʔo* 'root'.

CVCVn with unrestricted vowels: *ⁿdihìn* 'wing', *ⁿdihàn* 'sandal', *tisùn* 'June bug', *kakàn* 'ask', *žahìn* 'gourd', *kasùn* 'to bake'; *čúkún* 'a fly', *a-ⁿduhìn* 'last year', *žuhan* 'dough'.

CVCVn with restricted vowels: *žə́kə́n* 'infantile', *ⁿdoson* 'breast'.

CVʔCVn does not occur at all.

CVVn with unrestricted vowels: *sìin* 'side'; *čaàn* 'forehead', *taìn* [tañì] 'sweat' (from working); *tùun* 'feather'; others lacking.

CVVn with restricted vowels: *ʔəən* 'one'.

CVʔVn with unrestricted vowels: *kiʔin* 'take', *síʔàn* 'eagle'; *saʔàn* 'doctrine', *saʔùn* 'fifteen'; *kuʔun* 'put on' (clothing); others lacking.

CVʔVn with restricted vowels: *səʔə̀n* 'a post': also, as an alternate of *Cuʔun*, *tò ʔon* 'word'.

Examination reveals a considerable amount of patterning in the sequences that occur and fail to occur. Except for the two least frequent of the stem types ending in nasality (CVV*n* and CV*PV*n), there are occurrences for all stem patterns of: (a) all repeat sequences (*i-i, e-e*, etc.) both for outer and inner vowels; (b) all possible sequences of outer vowels (*i-a, i-u, a-i, a-u, u-i, u-a*). Sequences of inner vowels with each other are almost completely lacking: *o-e* in the morpheme *Po*ⁿ*de* 'up to' is the only case that has been found. The most usual combination of inner vowels is the repeat: *ə-ə, e-e, o-o*. No simple general rule for the occurrence of inner with outer vowels can be given. The vowel *e* is the most restricted of all, occurring only in C*e*C*a*. No combinations of *o* with *u* are found; since the same is true of *e* with *i*, one can generalize to the extent of pointing out that (except for repeat sequences) no combinations of palatal with palatal vowel or of labial with labial vowel occur.

The different patterns of stem form can be graded from high to low in terms of the number of vowel sequences they admit. The pattern CVV*n* shows the least number (only *a-i* in addition to repeat sequences, and even two of the latter, C*ee*n and C*oo*n, are lacking). Slightly better is CV*PV*n. Then follow CV*P*V and CVV; then CV*P*CV; and finally CVCV, with the greatest number of sequences. Using arrows to show the combinations that occur (other than repeat sequences) and the order of the vowels, the diagram of Fig. 1 shows the occurrences for the CVCV pattern. Since this is the type that has the maximum possibilities, the diagram at the same time can serve as the total for all patterns except for one item, C*iPo*.

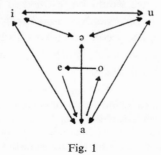

Fig. 1

8. SUMMARY

Grammatical analysis of an initial kind is prerequisite to phonemic analysis.

Field procedures of necessity carry on grammatical and phonemic analysis more or less simultaneously.

Partial identification of morphemes is one of the grammatical prerequisites to phonemics; utilization of contrasts in utterance-initial position, so as to be certain of initial position in various grammatical units, is another.

The fact that the proponents of phonological juncture phonemes are by their own admission forced in their analytical work to symbolize many nonphonetic but grammatical junctures indicates that grammatical juncture should be one of the bases of phonemic analysis. Various optional phonetic phenomena need to be symbolized; these potentials are most readily indicated by symbolizing grammatical junctures. All grammatical junctures which are used as a basis for describing modification of sounds must be symbolized.

Mixteco morphemes show a highly organized phonological structure. The morpheme is marked by optional initial stress and optional length of medial consonant. In its phonemic make-up it is marked by a complicated series of permitted vowel sequences involving restricted and unrestricted vowels.

If a language structure is to be described realistically, the interweaving of grammatical and phonemic facts must not be ignored. A language system represents a structural whole which one cannot compartmentalize mechanically without doing violence to the facts.

A note on zero allophones

Since this paper was submitted for publication, two articles have appeared which suggest or utilize 'zero allophones' of juncture and bear closely on matters discussed in §4 of the present paper.

Thus Rulon S. Wells, in "Immediate Constituents", *Language* 23 (1947), 108, says in fn. 45, "If we could reckon the silence at the beginning and end of an utterance as one allophone of juncture, we would be justified in positing another allophone, a zero-allophone, which occurs for example in *night-rate*." It appears doubtful that such a solution would be completely consistent with his general phonemic approach, concerning which he says (*Language* 23 [1947], 271), while reviewing *The Intonation of American English* (emphasis mine):

Phonemics takes the point of view of the hearer. Now the hearer, in order to interpret correctly an utterance that he hears, must rely on two separate sources of information: (a) the HEARD SOUNDS (supplemented, it may be, by the sounds of previous or following utterances); (b) the extra-linguistic context (including his knowledge of what the utterance may or must mean). For the purpose of sharply distinguishing between what can be learned from one source and what can be learned from the other, phonemics makes a point of recording NOTHING BUT WHAT IS CONVEYED BY (A). All else belongs to grammar (and lexicography). This is why one wishes to avoid intersection (overlapping) in phonemics but not in grammar. And a fortiori, 'potentialities' (as of stress to become totally suppressed, and of an intonation break or a pause to be inserted into a rhythm unit) are not indicated in a purely phonemic transcription. We do not say that phonemics and grammar must be separated, but only that the separation is feasible and serves the above purpose. ... Pike's system of transcription is not purely phonemic. (1) Extra-phonemic information is sometimes required to determine the boundaries of his complexes, particularly the primary contours (§11). (2) Pike proposes (cf. §16, §26) to take morpheme boundaries into account in determining the stress phonemes.

Now Wells does not illustrate in detail how such a proposed zero allophone would work, so it may be that he ultimately would prevent its being written at any place except where phonological clues occurred preceding or following it. On the other hand, he might himself be tempted to write such zero allophones of juncture where the phonetic clues were zero, and thereby utilize the very procedure to which he elsewhere objects (*Language* 23, 107): "The validity of juncture phonemes is open to grave doubts on phonetic grounds. Linguists find themselves tempted to institute 'junctures' simply as notational devices for reducing the number of phonemes." It is difficult to see how a strictly phonetic zero could be considered part of the 'heard sounds' which Wells postulates as the only data pertinent to phonemics.

A more detailed treatment of proposed zero allophones is given in "Juncture in Modern Standard German" (*Language* 23 [1947], 212-226) by William G. Moulton, following out a suggestion from Bernard Bloch (see p. 220, and fn. 13). "This segmental phoneme + has the following allophones: at the beginning or end of an utterance it appears as a pause of indeterminate duration: +'tail+, +ta'blet+; within an utterance it appears either as a pause of brief duration or, in *free variation with this* [emphasis mine, KLP], as zero: +'ʔan+ˌtraːt+, +ʔix, ʔantvorte+te'rase+." A similar statement is given on 223, Section 4.2; however a limitation is indicated later (225): "only the zero allophone occurs at morphological boundaries within words (usually only between the constituents of compound words)." By these statements, one might gather that the phonemic symbol + reflects a POTENTIAL placing of pause, rather than actual phonetic data. Such symbolization of potentials must in turn reflect morphemic structure, since it is the morphemic or grammatical structure which controls such options.

Moulton gives a grammatical statement of the occurrence of the postulated phoneme (224): "The places where + occurs usually coincide with syntactic and morphological boundaries. The only exceptions are a few words (all of foreign origin) in which open juncture and the onset of strong stress precede a voiceless stop or a vowel: +pa+'piːr+ 'paper', ... +ruː+'iːnen+ 'ruins', etc." In a footnote on 225 he asks, "Should we accept syntactic and morphological boundaries as part of our phonemic analysis if, by so doing, we can limit the scope of — or even avoid assuming — open juncture?" His answer is negative, as follows:

First — and this is a purely methodological reason — I believe that the phonemes of a language should be analyzed without reference to syntax or morphology. ... Secondly, we could not do so successfully even if we tried, because of the cases (noted above [i.e. the words of foreign origin]) in which open juncture does not coincide with a syntactic or morphological boundary. Finally, it would seem that the phonetic marking of morphological and syntactic boundaries is more clearly described precisely by the assumption of open juncture.

The present paper implies that the first of Moulton's reasons is arbitrary and conceals, rather than reveals, total linguistic structure. The third line of reasoning is weakened by his occasional use of perplexing phrases such as that on p. 225: "...words which are not separated by a syntactic boundary ..." — but, we ask, are not all words so separated, by definition? The second reason is serious, but one should

hesitate to allow a small residue of words of foreign origin to prevent a general formulation, at least until vigorous attempts have been made to follow the analysis
which otherwise would more easily represent the total grammatical-phonological
structure of the language; possibly a descriptive expedient might be found which
would preserve the easier formulation without doing violence to the facts.

Such an attempt is especially in order here when the difficulties of a residue from
a grammatical approach are offset, in part at least, by difficulties of a residue within
Moulton's nongrammatical approach. His Section 5 discusses the problem of a
certain few items which do not follow the rules for distribution of allophones as he
has set them up, but which might respond with less difficulty to an attempt to describe them in terms of grammatical rather than phonological junctures. In "the
sequence r plus unstressed vowel", the "one phoneme behaves as if it were followed
by a pause, but the following phoneme does not behave as if it were preceded by
a pause ... (In the speech of my informant, r behaves in this way at the end of any
word or constituent of a compound word)."

One other question should be asked of Moulton's material, for which I did not
find an adequate answer within the article (but see his §4.31 for a partial answer):
Does the "brief pause", "in free variation with [zero]" ever occur within the sentence
at points where the preceding or the following sounds do not indicate its phonemic
presence? That is to say, if aspiration, or glottal stop, or a fronted x, or some other
marker is not present, but the zero allophone as a free variant of pause does so occur,
then Moulton's entire structure falls. In any such instance the writing of the $+$ for
representing the zero allophone would be accompanied by no phonological mark
of its presence; the reason for its occurrence would then be (1) the potential occurrence of the pausal allophone, or (2) a grammatical juncture. In either case, grammar would enter, since the potential for pause would be controlled by the morphemic
structure.

An attempt to utilize grammatical junctures for the symbolization in his phonemic
orthography would presumably have necessitated at least the following: (1) the
writing of spaces between words; (2) the writing of hyphens within certain types of
words, such as compounds; (3) the writing of a phoneme of pause at the time it
actually occurred, especially in slow speech (but not when it was an unactualized
potential), — and all spaces might be points of potential pause. If it be objected
that this is more complicated than the writing simply of $+$ to represent pause and
nonpause, one may answer that we are not after simplicity first, but rather a representation of the structure of the language as it functions, whether the result be simple
or complex.

COEXISTENT PHONEMIC SYSTEMS*

with CHARLES C. FRIES

1. SYSTEMS IN CONFLICT

The speech of monolingual natives of some languages is comprised of more than one phonemic system; the simultaneously existing systems operate partly in harmony and partly in conflict. No rigidly descriptive statement of the facts about such a language accounts for all the pertinent structural data without leading to apparent contradictions. These are caused by the conflict of statements about one phonemic system with statements about another system or part of a system present in the speech of the same individual.

This paper attempts to demonstrate the validity of the assumption that two or more phonemic systems may coexist[1] in the speech of a monolingual, and to outline a procedure for determining the nature of these coexistent systems. We[2] believe that an approach to linguistic data by way of this assumption is necessary lest otherwise certain types of problems remain unsolved.

The problems referred to are of several types: (1) the analysis of the conflict between the system of sounds in words of native origin and an interjected set of one

---

* *Language* 25 :1 (1949), 29-50. Reprinted by permission.
[1] The basic assumption of this paper thus differs from the conclusions reached by Bernard Bloch, "A Set of Postulates for Phonemic Analysis", *Language* 24:7 (1948), §1.7: "The totality of the possible utterances of one speaker at one time in using a language to interact with one other speaker is an *idiolect*.... The phrase 'with one other speaker' is intended to exclude the possibility that an idiolect might embrace more than one STYLE of speaking: it is at least unlikely that a given speaker will use two or more different styles in adressing a single person." We suggest, however, that a speaker — even in the middle of a sentence — may suddenly lower his voice to a whisper, or burst into tearful speech, or shift to a caressing quality, or the like. Socially pertinent differences of style cannot safely be ignored; they must be handled in some way in our phonemic assumptions and procedures.

[2] The authors of this article approach phonemic study from widely different types of experience. Fries has concentrated on historical studies, Pike on reducing languages to writing. This article springs from discussions between them. Fries contributed especially to the discussion of historical change and to the principles outlined in Part 1; Pike was largely responsible for implementing these principles with the procedures and assumptions given in later parts of this paper.

An abstract of this paper was presented to the summer meeting of the Linguistic Society of America, July 31, 1948. Upon that occasion we were pleased to hear from Professor J.R. Firth of the School of Oriental and African Studies, University of London, that he had been making abstractions on various levels which might be related to these. See now fn. 30.

or more unassimilated sounds from other contemporaneous dialects or languages; (2) the interpretation of the total phonemic reaction of bilinguals in such a situation — i.e. the investigation of the possible existence for the bilingual of a total phonemic pattern which transcends the specific pattern of either of the languages by itself; (3) the discovery of a conflict in the system of sounds of a single speaker during a transition stage wherein a phonemic contrast is being introduced or lost or replaced by linguistic change of some type over a period of time within a single dialect; (4) the result of treating on a single descriptive level the 'normal' system plus various types of special signals such as interjections, extra schoolroom contrasts, and the like; (5) the avoidance of internally inconsistent and self-contradictory analyses which result if one treats on a single descriptive level (a) those particular differences of sound which occur in one uniform style, and (b) those which are due to a qualitative or stylistic change, in whispering, song, extra-fast utterance, extra-precise pronunciation, or the like, in the speech of one individual.

Most of our attention will be given here to the first of these types, the problem of unassimilated loans. The discussion will be centered around an illustration from Mazateco.[3] In words of native Mazateco origin, all voiceless stops become voiced after nasals. If loans are ignored, one would be forced to conclude that [t] and [d] are sub-members (allophones) of a single phoneme /t/, and could both be written with the single symbol 't'.[4] Yet certain facts make this conclusion dubious: one very frequent word — *siento* 'one hundred', a Spanish loan — and a few other rare loans have [t] after nasals in the speech of some Mazateco monolinguals. For these speakers the loan words prevent or contradict the desired statement that all stops become voiced after nasals. No native word for 'one hundred' is now in use; all speakers of the language use the Spanish loan.

The following question, therefore, arises. Should one or two loan words be considered strong enough to break the occurrences of native /t/ into two phonemes, /t/ and /d/? The analyst might easily reply in the affirmative, were it not for a fact of a nondistributional kind: the monolingual natives referred to, as well as the bilinguals (as reported by Eunice V. Pike), find it easier to learn to read [nd] when it is written 'nt' than when it is written 'nd'. This evidence we interpret as indicating that the monolingual speakers still react[5] to the native [t] and the native [d] as composing a single phonemic unit, just as if the loans with [nt] were not used by them at all. If that is true, then monolingual Mazateco speakers are operating at this point with two conflicting systems of arrangements and contrasts of phonemes and sub-mem-

---

[3]   Taken from Kenneth L. Pike and Eunice V. Pike, "Immediate Constituents of Mazateco Syllables", *IJAL* 13 (1947), 79, with supplementary data from the second-named.

[4]   Brackets enclose phonetic symbols; virgules (slant lines) enclose phonemic symbols; quotation marks enclose letters of a suggested orthography.

[5]   We do NOT imply that a native's uncritical remarks are to be accepted as valid analyses. Rather we claim that a linguist can objectively observe the behavior of the native and draw certain structural implication from his observations.

bers of phonemes. And if this in turn is true, then a procedure is needed which will lead the linguist by descriptive methods to locate, analyze, and describe such situations.

The development of such a procedure is not an easy task, since one wishes to avoid various errors. The analyst must not be guilty of utilizing historical data to prejudice his conclusions, even though the situation being studied is a result of a mixture of language material over a period of time. He must not consider the naïve native speaker capable of analyzing his own language, even though the naïve remarks (occasionally right, but often wrong) are part of the objective data which must be scrutinized for evidence concerning the structural organization of the native sounds. He must be wary about utilizing data other than those provided by the techniques growing out of his phonemic postulates, but must be ready to speculate upon the sources of his accepted postulates and to receive non-distributional, non-phonetic data from the language being studied if those data are of the very kind which in his study of other languages have helped tacitly or explicitly to establish those postulates.

Before presenting the methodology that we suggest for tackling the problem, it will be good to consider a few general principles which bear upon it. In a purely descriptive analysis of the dialect of a monolingual speaker there are no loans discoverable or describable. An element can be proved to be a loan word only when two dialects are compared. The description of a word as a loan is a mixture of approaches: the mixing of purely descriptive analysis with dialect study, comparative work, or historical study. Dialect mixture cannot be studied or legitimately affirmed to exist unless two systems have previously been studied separately. It follows that in a purely descriptive analysis of one particular language as spoken by a bilingual, no loans are discoverable.

Such statements may appear to be truisms, but they by no means go without saying. Linguists often call items loan words in grammars which are purportedly purely descriptive of one dialect. The Mazateco problem was described in the same way in the article referred to in footnote 3. Yet if a descriptive procedure is to be presented which will handle the Mazateco problem, it must be capable of leading the linguist to the discovery of the difficulty, and to an analysis of it in terms of conflicting overlapping systems, without reference to or reliance upon the origin of the disturbing items. This a linguist is more likely to do in instances in which he cannot indicate the source of words which may be loans; presumably it is in cases where the foreign origin is obvious that loans are more often referred to or recognized as such.

Another assumption should also be made. Phonetic facts are not significant in themselves, but only as parts of a speech system. We conclude, therefore, that systems must be compared with systems — not isolated facts with isolated facts. It is for this reason that the investigator should attempt to classify as elements of further systems those small residues which resist analysis as parts of the principle phonemic system of a language. Instead of postulating various types of extra-systematic characteristics,[6] he assumes the existence of a further — though admittedly defective — system or set of systems to accommodate the data.

The Mazateco evidence points to the conclusion, then, that two or more phonemic systems may coexist within a single dialect, even though one or more of these systems may be highly fragmentary. Since Mazateco readers find [nd] easier to learn to read when it is written 'nt' than when it is written 'nd', and since no phonetic [t] occurs after /n/ except in the few special words referred to, we conclude that the principle phonemic system of Mazateco includes a phoneme /t/ which has a voiced sub-member after /n/, but that a coexistent though fragmentary phonemic system in the language of some of the same monolingual individuals includes a phoneme /t/ following /n/ in a few special words. We reach this conclusion in spite of the fact that [d] and [t] would have to be considered separate phonemes (since the [d] and the loan [t] contrast after /n/) if the investigator adhered without exception to the principle that two sounds belong to separate phonemes if they contrast in analogous environments.

It will not do, however, to make such assumptions and leave their application to individual momentary fancy. An intolerable inconsistency might be found in the work of only one analyst, and even more so in a comparison of the statements of several investigators, unless some procedure can be developed which can be utilized independently and somewhat uniformly: by various investigators or by a single investigator at various points of time.[7] We turn now to our suggested methodology, with some of the assumptions needed to develop it.

2. PROCEDURES AND ASSUMPTIONS FOR ANALYZING DIALECT MIXTURE

Two kinds of procedure may be utilized to discover conflicting coexistent phonemic systems. One of them appears at first to be much more objective than the other, but is incapable alone of leading the investigator to satisfactory positive conclusions. The other utilizes data which are much more nebulous (though it is not 'mentalistic') but, when the evidence can be found and safely evaluated, does lead to a definite statement or a basis of sound judgment. In neither of them does the analyst pre-judge the case by describing aberrant items as 'loans'.

In the first of these two procedures the linguist studies his data carefully and attempts to make the simplest description which includes all the facts. If in attempt-

---

[6] This was the method of Pike in *Phonemics: A Technique for Reducing Languages to Writing* (= *University of Michigan Publications: Linguistics* 3) (Ann Arbor, 1947), 142-143. It is precisely the premises given in the first part of the present paper which allow the gathering together of various items presented in the book, and the further procedural advance.

[7] Even the most widely accepted procedures of the current type do not yet result in complete uniformity in the analysis, say, of English. Without considerable discussion it is highly improbable that we can get as much agreement on the new procedures as there is on the old ones. It appears to us, however, that the attempt to set up tentative procedures will be justified if it promotes more intensive investigation of pertinent problems.

ing to do so he finds that almost all the data of some particular type can be covered by a simple statement, but that a few items cannot be accommodated in that statement, he considers two hypotheses: (1) that the excluded data are parts of a co-existent conflicting system; or (2) that a single system is present, even though it appears unsystematic and leaves unexplained some types of native behavior — e.g. difficulties in learning. Thus for the Mazateco material he could soon state tentatively (1) that stops become voiced after nasals, but that in a few items such as *siento* the data do not fit the statement and may be supposed to be parts of a conflicting system; or (2) that voiced and voiceless stops constitute separate phonemes, since they contrast in one position, namely after nasals, but that voiceless stops in that position are very rare.

For the Mazateco data this approach is inadequate, since it does not allow the linguist to determine which of the two hypotheses must be considered correct. Although the first suggests that two systems are in conflict, no evidence is brought forward to establish that hypothesis, except the relatively low frequency of occurrence of voiceless stops after nasals. The second hypothesis is also unsatisfactory since it fails to account for data of a different kind: it does not explain the reason why the native still seems to learn to read and write native [nd] more easily when it is written 'nt' than when it is written 'nd'.

The whole approach is inadequate, furthermore, to handle whispering or other similar characteristics in, say, English; it would force the linguist either (1) to postulate a conflict of systems between whispered utterances and utterances spoken aloud, without methods or assumptions to prove the existence of such a set of systems, or (2) to postulate a single series of vowel phonemes which includes both voiced and whispered types in contrast. The second conclusion would be untenable in that it fails to account adequately for the reaction of English speakers to whispered and spoken utterances as each being 'the same' in some way. Nevertheless, since whispered and vocal conversation carry different social connotations, a rigid phonemic procedure might force one to describe whispered and voiced vowels as different phonemes, e.g. as /ʌ/ and /a/.

It becomes evident, then, that a different kind of procedure is necessary: one which allows the careful introduction of evidence of a non-phonetic kind. It must be one which can handle unassimilated loans before and after they are recognized as such, and can care for qualitative differences (such as whisper and song) which are socially significant, and can give suggestions also about sound types limited to interjections or to special morphemes. We are now ready for the discussion of such a procedure, and for the building up of the axioms necessary to justify it. Again we utilize the problem of Mazateco /nt/ as a starting point in the consideration of dialect mixture. We shall then turn briefly to a study of stylistic differences, special sounds, and the orthographical representation of such data.

The suggested procedure for the analysis of problems of conflicting phonemic systems within the speech of a monolingual includes the following steps. (1) A description of all available data from the language, utilizing premises current in the field for determining contrastive sounds, conditioned variation, non-phonemic free variation, and phonetically complex unit phonemes.[8] This work is to be done under the tentative assumption (later to be modified) that all sounds in the language are parts of a single non-contradictory system of contrasts. (2) A survey of the types of data and methodology which have given rise to the phonemic postulates utilized in Step One, or which prove their validity, with a check of the data from the language in question to see if evidence of this type, also, can be found there. (3) A description of the way in which the two types of conclusions differ, if any conflict arises between the results of Step One and the evidence from Step Two. (4) The setting up of a hypothesis which attempts to reconcile any such conflict by suggesting the simultaneous presence of two or more phonemic systems. (5) A check of this hypothesis against a known earlier stage of the language or any other known languages or dialects which might prove to be sources of the conflict; a further check against general speech styles which may have modified the entire conversation or part of a conversation of some speaker; and a check against special situations of surprise, gesture, disapproval, facetiousness, and the like.

In the Mazateco problem under consideration the linguist would in the first step be forced to separate [t] and [d] into the two phonemes /t/ and /d/, but would then find that /d/ had a limited distribution (after nasals only) and that /t/ and /d/ contrasted only after nasals.

In the second step he would speculate upon the types of evidence which were behind the assumptions of Step One. He might decide that evidence could be obtained (a) by watching the reaction of persons learning to write their own language, or (b) by analyzing their difficulties in studying the phonetic minutiae of their language, or (c) by considering the problems they face in learning a language new to them. In each of these instances he would watch for errors, difficulties, special facilities, and naïve remarks or naïve attempts at analysis. He would not need to make mentalistic statements about the speakers of these languages, but would objectively study their reactions to the underlying phonetic facts of their own phonemic system and to the conflict between two systems. Since the present procedure is dependent upon such types of evidence they must be reviewed here.[9]

An untrained person who is attempting to write his own language with phonetic symbols frequently fails to record differently two sounds which the investigator knows are actually different.[10] A speaker of English, for example, might write *tatter* as 'tætr' even though the letter 't' would then, at least for certain dialects of American English, represent first an aspirated [tʰ] and then some kind of flap. Natives learn

[8] The underlying premises and methods for handling them are to be found in Pike's *Phonemics*.
[9] Some of them have been presented by Pike in his *Phonemics*.
[10] Edward Sapir used this type of evidence in his article, "La réalité psychologique des phonèmes", *Psychologie du langage* (= *Journal de psychologie* 30 [1933]), 247-265, summarized by W. F. Twaddell, *On Defining the Phoneme* (=*Language Monograph* 16) (Baltimore, 1935), 10-14.

to differentiate certain sounds of their language in writing with much less difficulty than other sounds. An assumption is implied here: In his writing the native learns to separate with relative facility those sounds which are in phonemic contrast. Occasionally, however, some evidence weakens the force of this assumption. When, in a certain phonetic position, a sound type appears which is roughly halfway in acoustic quality between the norms of two phonemes, the student may have difficulty in deciding which he should write; thus American students of some dialects often are troubled to know whether they should write 'o' or 'ɔ' before /r/.

Further evidence appears when a student attempts to learn to identify the various sounds of his own language. He may find it difficult to recognize any difference between certain sounds which are objectively different. Thus, American students usually have great difficulty in learning to distinguish between the two vowel qualities heard in *above*, provided the stress differences are eliminated.[11] On the other hand, they have little difficulty in learning to hear the difference between [ɛ] and [æ] — a distinction which causes great difficulty to native speakers of Spanish. An assumption is implied: Speakers have little or no difficulty in learning to hear a difference between any two phonemes of their own language.

Another assumption is related to the last one: Native speakers can learn with some facility to isolate, one after another, the phonemes in any particular sequence which occurs in their language. Thus, in English, a student of phonetics can in a few moments be taught to separate *sip* into [s], [ɪ], [p] (or into the same sounds accompanied by a vowel or other characteristic to make them more easily pronounceable, such as [ɛs], [ɪ], [pʰ], but maintaining the same number of units isolated). One should note that most students easily learn to separate [aᴵ] into [a] and [ɪ] or [i], but tend to have more difficulty with [oᵁ] and [ᵁᵘ]; this difference in the facility of the English speaker implies a difference in the phonemic structure of the diphthongs,[12] since we assume that the phonetic differences involved are not great enough to account for this reaction. Spelling difficulties may interfere temporarily, but are not as hard for the student to overcome; he may, for example, divide *ax* into [æ] and [ks] (instead of into [æ], [k], and [s]), until he is cautioned to listen to the individual sounds of the word.

A further assumption accompanies the one just given: When the speaker tries to abstract a sound from the middle of an utterance, he tends to substitute for it another sub-member of the same phoneme, but one which is appropriate to the pronunciation of that phoneme in isolation (or appropriate to the pronunciation of the name of the phoneme — e.g. as utterance final in /es/, the name of the phoneme /s/). In isolating the sounds of the English word *matter*,[13] speakers who use a flapped

[11] If, however, the student is told to write 'ɔ' whenever he hears the /ə/ unstressed, but to write 'ʌ' whenever he hears it stressed, he learns to apply the rule easily (though without necessarily hearing the quality difference) simply by listening to the stresses.

[12] For an elaboration of this evidence, see Pike, "On the Phonemic status of English Diphthongs", *Language* 23 (1947), 151-159.

[13] In a dialect which distinguishes between *matter* and *madder*.

[t] are unlikely to pronounce the abstracted element in the same way in isolation, but tend to say [tʰ]. They are usually very much surprised if it is pointed out to them that the [t] which they isolated is different from the one which they pronounced in the word. When the analyst observes that a speaker of some language reacts thus to its sounds, he considers it objective evidence (though not conclusive, because of potential sources of error)[14] that the sounds are sub-members of the same phoneme.

The native is likely to encounter some difficulty, however, in isolating sounds (such as English /-ŋ/) which do not occur initially in an utterance. Likewise there may be hesitation in isolating phonemes when two of them coalesce, as /u/ (or /ʊ/) and the first /n/ in the pronunciation [mą̃ᵁʔtn̩] /maᵁntn̩/ *mountain*. Yet even here the naïve English speaker is likely to isolate the sounds in such a way that the first /n/ appears as a separate consonant. He is not likely, however, to analyze the syllabic /n̩/ into two parts [ə] and [n], but will more probably pronounce it as a single syllabic. It may be that this type of reaction is part of the unstated reason why some analysts prefer to assume the presence of phonemic syllabic consonants in English rather than treating [n̩] as /ən/. Stressed syllabic [ɾ] may sometimes be broken into two elements by the same speakers who isolate [n̩] as one. The implication of this fact is not clear.

In attempting to correct the mispronunciations of foreigners, the native may himself use exaggerations or slow speech which involve the substitution of one sub-member of a phoneme for another, without his being aware of the fact. If the foreigner has trouble in saying *matter* with a flapped [t], the native may repeat the word slowly, using an aspirated variety of the phoneme — i.e. [mætʰɾ]. If the foreigner uses a strong [s] at the end of the words *was* and *beds*, the native may repeat them with a completely voiced [z], rather than with [ˢ] or a weak [z] the end of which slurs to [ˢ] (the raised [ˢ] denotes a lenis variety of the voiceless sound). An assumption is needed to cover this situation: The native has not substituted one phoneme for another when he insists that he has not changed his pronunciation. Thus, if he states that the sound is the same in [bɛdz] as in [bɛdˢ], one should conclude that this constitutes objective (though non-conclusive) evidence tending to prove that lenis [ˢ] and voiced [z] are sub-members of the same phoneme.

Various naïve remarks of the native, or his early attempts at phonemic analysis, may give the linguist a clue to the phonemic structure. These remarks may be in response to queries by the linguist. Even though the linguist knows that two pronunciations of a word have varied phonetically, the native may say that they have the same sound. In English such a response tends to be heard if a native is asked about pronunciations of words like *sit* in which the final stop is at one time released with aspiration, and another time unreleased. The assumption: The native usually does not call sounds the same if they are phonemically different. Also: The native is more likely to notice or comment on substitution or loss of phonemes than sub-

---

[14] We assume that traditional spelling cannot be the whole source of the pressure which causes speakers of English to isolate the middle consonant of *matter* as [tʰ].

stitution of sub-members of phonemes. When a word has two alternate pronunciations with different phonemes, the response may be that the 'words are the same', but further query tends to elicit the addition that 'the word is pronounced in two ways'.

The last assumption may become useless if the native has had a modicum of phonetic training; even a few moments of instruction may make him conscious, for instance, of differences in non-phonemic utterance-final aspiration. Occasionally, also, untrained speakers will make interesting phonetic observations concerning non-phonemic detail if their attention is focused on some part of a word. Before knowing anything about phonemic theory, some students are puzzled about word-final /z/, and do not know whether to write it as 's' or as 'z'. These facts lessen the usefulness of the last assumption.

When he learns a foreign language a person finds certain sounds easy to distinguish but others difficult. An assumption based upon this fact: If two sounds are phonemically distinct in the speech of an individual, he will have little difficulty in distinguishing between two similar sounds in a language foreign to him; but he will have considerable difficulty in distinguishing two phonemes of a foreign language if in his own language those sounds are sub-members of a single phoneme. Here the linguist may get objective clues to phonemic structure by watching the native speaker attempt to pronounce words of a language foreign to him. If in his own language the native has aspirated and unaspirated stops, and in a foreign language has no difficulty learning words whose difference lies wholly in the presence or absence of aspiration, the probability is that in the native language also, the aspiration makes a phonemic difference between stops. The converse is also true: English had unaspirated and aspirated stops, but American students have considerable difficulty in learning to hear the difference in Mazateco, which has phonemic aspiration.[15]

Transfers of sequences present related problems. The assumption: If a sequence of segments constitutes a sequence of phonemes, the native should have little difficulty in pronouncing either a part or all of that same sequence in comparable positions in a foreign language. Yet American speakers whose dialects include diphthongized [o^U] and [ʊ^u] have considerable difficulty in pronouncing non-diphthongal [o] and [u] in languages foreign to them; this may constitute evidence that the English glide is not a sequence of phonemes.[16]

One should notice that the assumptions given above are assumptions as to tendencies, rather than assumptions which can be rigidly and universally applied with-

---

[15] For an experiment in the problem of transfer from Spanish to English nasals, see A.H. Marckwardt, "Phonemic Structure and Aural Perception", *American Speech* 21 (1946), 106-111; for a similar experiment with voiceless sibilants and affricates, see Marckwardt, "An Experiment in Aural Perception", *The English Journal* 33 (1944), 212-214. Marckwardt finds that in recording a series of dictated words there is less confusion when a phoneme appears in a strange position than when sub-members of a phoneme of one language appear as separate phonemes in another language.
[16] See the reference in fn. 12.

out exception; a few bits of evidence which seem to run counter to the assumptions were introduced into the discussion to demonstrate that fact. The assumptions, therefore, must be applied with caution and checked against one another. It is for this reason, among others, that our usual phonemic procedures are more easily utilized than are these added ones. The investigator should use these additional assumptions only (1) for demonstrating the validity of the basic premises of the traditional type; (2) for obtaining clues which may lead him to set up hypotheses for further checking by traditional methods; and (3) for determining the existence of simultaneous phonemic systems, since rigorous application of a one-system assumption or one-system procedure based on traditional methods to languages in which there are coexistent systems will lead to contradictions, absurdities, or omission of some kinds of data. In general, then, the TENDENCY to reactions of this type is important even when it is not invariable.

We have now discussed the types of evidence which might be found by using the second step of the outlined procedure. The investigator is now ready for the third step, which looks for conflicts between the results of his initial phonemic analysis and the evidence gained from applying these listed assumptions of step two. This step has already been implied and illustrated in previous paragraphs, and needs no further discussion here. In Mazateco, for example, the rigid one-system phonemic analysis would at first postulate a phonemic contrast between /t/ and /d/, since both are found after /n/; but conflicting with this analysis is the fact that the Mazatecos seem to learn to read and write [nd] as 'nt' more easily than as 'nd', which implies that [nd] is phonemically /nt/.

As a fourth step, if such evidence is found, the investigator now sets up a hypothesis which suggests that two conflicting phonemic systems are in simultaneous use in a language. This possibility, also, has been earlier stated and occurs in the speech of Mazateco monolinguals. In one Mazateco system, [nd] is phonemically /nt/, and [nt] does not occur; in the other system, [nt] does occur, as in [siento], and is also phonemically /nt/.

In the fifth step this hypothesis is checked against any other language(s) known to be in the area, in order to discover the source of the mixture of phonemic systems. Spanish is spoken by many people in the Mazateco region; the word [siento] means 'one hundred' in Spanish as it does in Mazateco; the Spanish word has obviously been borrowed by the Mazatecos. Evidently, however, the loan has not yet been completely assimilated into the Mazateco phonemic structure; the conflicting patterns exist there side by side.

Such a conclusion raises the following question: What are the criteria one uses to determine that a borrowed sound has or has not been completely absorbed into the native phonemic system? In terms of the procedure set up, the answer is now not hard to give. The assumption: When (a) the results gained by Steps One and Two (i.e. by a rigid one-system initial analysis, without reference to loans, and by the observation of the reactions of speakers as they learn to write or analyze their own language or to speak a foreign language) are no longer in conflict, and (b) when the loan is in common use by monolingual speakers of the language, a borrowed sound is to be considered completely assimilated. This is assumed to be true regardless of the manner in which it forces modifications in the description of the phonemic system by addition of new phonemes or by redistribution of phonemes. So long as it is not used by monolinguals, or so long as the results of Steps One and Two lead to different conclusions, a borrowed sound has not been assimilated completely.

In addition to the phonemic conflicts just discussed there are various related problems which might be partially solved by a similar technique. (1) When the large majority of words constitute a systematic set of structural sequences of phonemes, but a small residue of words contain a different pattern, one may suspect that this residue is composed of loan words and search neighboring dialects for evidence supporting that judgment. Note, for example, the sequence /šn/ in some English pronunciations of the name *Schneider*. (2) When the large majority of a certain set of phonemic sequences are similarly related to morpheme boundaries, an exceptional instance not so related can be suspected of being a loan. Compare /ts/ in *bats, cats, hats, sits, resists* (in which a morpheme boundary interrupts the sequence) with *Ritz* and *Fritz* (in which the sequence is not thus interrupted). (3) When various phonetically similar but different segments could be analyzed as complementarily distributed sub-members (allophones) of a single phoneme except that the distribution of a small residue of those segments occurs in another and conflicting distribution, the analyst may suspect that the nonconforming residue occurs in a few unassimilated loans which constitute a coexistent phonemic system. This approach may support the exploitation of grammatical borders in phonemic analysis, and weaken the arguments in favor of the necessity of postulating junctures as phonemes.[17] (4) When evidence of some type points to the existence of two LARGE groups of non-uniform material in the speech of a monolingual, two coexistent systems may be suspected, but two which are more nearly of equal size than those previously mentioned.

The preceding statements lead to the following assumption: A loan sequence of phonemes can be considered completely assimilated when (a) it parallels the se-

[17] In a recent paper, "Juncture in Modern Standard German", *Language* 23 (1947), 212-226, W.G. Moulton writes: "The places where /+/ [open juncture] occurs usually coincide with syntactic and morphological boundaries. The only exceptions are a few words (all of foreign origin) in which open juncture and onset of strong stress precede a voiceless stop or a vowel: /+pa+ piːr+/ 'paper', ... /+ruː+ iːnen+/ 'ruins', etc." (224). Since these loans are the specific data (cf. Moulton's note on 225) which caused his rejection of grammatical borders as criteria in his phonemic analysis, Pike suggested ("Grammatical Prerequisites to Phonemic Analysis", *Word* 3 [1947], 171-172) that "one should hesitate to allow a small residue of words of foreign origin to prevent a general formulation, at least until vigorous attempts have been made to follow the analysis which otherwise would more easily represent the total grammatical-phonological structure of the language; possibly a descriptive expedient might be found which would preserve the easier formulation without doing violence to the facts." We now raise the question whether the postulation of a coexistent system might be such an expedient.

quences occurring in native materials, or is analogous to them; when (b) its occur-rence in relation to grammatical boundaries is the same as sequences in native words; and when (c) the words containing it are in common use by the monolinguals; or a loan sequence may be considered completely assimilated when it serves as a pattern for the development of new sequences in the native materials.

Thus far the analysis has been concerned with the conflicting phonemic systems of monolingual persons whose language has received unassimilated loans from an-other language. We must now inquire whether the analysis must be made in the same or in a different way for the speech of bilinguals who speak both their native language and (with less facility) the language from which the loans are derived.

We conclude that the procedure of analysis must be similar, with similar assump-tions, but that the results obtained in a particular language may differ considerably for its monolingual and bilingual speakers. This, also, may be stated in the form of an assumption: New sounds may be completely assimilated into the native system by the bilingual sooner than they are completely assimilated by his monolingual friends or by the monolingual members of his own household. We further assume that the conflict of coexistent phonemic systems found for the monolingual may be entirely or largely lacking for the bilingual. The implication, then, is that an analysis of the speech of monolinguals and of bilinguals must be made separately if one wishes to determine whether or not a specific loan or phonetic phenomenon has become completely assimilated.

The difference between monolinguals and bilinguals includes the following types. (1) The bilinguals tend to use loan words before the monolinguals do; monolinguals learn them from the bilinguals, unless they learn them by the gestures of demon-strating foreigners. (2) The monolinguals are more likely than the bilinguals to force the loan words to conform to the native phonetic and phonemic pattern. Thus some[18] of the Mazateco monolinguals (but not all of them — and not the group we have been discussing) retain the [t] of [siento] but drop the [n] while nasalizing the preceding vowel. For these Mazatecos the word [siento] becomes /sįe²to⁴/, and leaves no conflict of patterns, since nasalized vowels are frequent in the native mate-rial, and the sub-member [t] of the phoneme /t/ is found following them in words of native origin. (3) It is also theoretically possible that for bilinguals the effect of their second language may be the phonemic breakup of conditioned variants of phonemes in their native language, even when no loans have been adopted which would force such a modification of the native system. If, for example, a native speaker has the phoneme /v/, which unvoices to [f] at the end of words, but the second language has /v/ and /f/ in phonemic contrast, a bilingual speaker may in some instances react to his native language as if there, also, [v] and [f] were separate

---

[18]   When the present article was undertaken, neither Pike nor Eunice V. Pike had observed this fact. The latter now reports it to us. No count is as yet available to show the proportion of monolinguals or bilinguals using each of the two pronunciations. A detailed investigation, with close attention to the assumptions here listed, would probably yield further interesting observations.

phonemes. This may be true even though the two sounds do not appear in contrast anywhere in the native language or in loans in that language.

A situation of this general type may possibly occur in Cakchiquel, a Mayan language of Guatemala. There /v/ non-phonemically unvoices at the ends of words, whereas Spanish initially distinguishes /v/ and /f/. Although loans with [f] seem to be highly restricted (possibly to a few names) in Cakchiquel, the bilinguals have strongly insisted upon using both 'v' and 'f' in preparing written materials.[19]

If such a breakup of the phonemic system of the native language of the bilinguals is caused by their second language, this fact could only be determined by some such procedure as that outlined in the preceding pages; it would not be found by a distributional study of the sounds in the native language alone. In the form of an assumption — and with no assurance that it is correct — we might present this conclusion as follows: In the speech of some bilinguals the sub-members of one phoneme in native material may be broken into separate phonemes by the pressure of the structure of a second language, even without loans from that language. But this situation must be determined by an objective study of the reactions of the bilingual speaker during his attempts to write or analyze his two languages, or in analysis of his naïve statements (whether they be right or wrong) about the two languages.

Such situations may prove to be the technical source of many practical problems of providing an orthography for peoples who are bilingual — especially if they are literate in the second language, and if this training has aided in their ability to notice phonetic differences which are non-phonemic in the speech of monolinguals of the first language. The Cakchiquel evidence reported above may prove to be an instance of this type. Morris Swadesh[20] reports a somewhat similar problem for Tarascan, in which bilinguals literate in Spanish were attempting to indicate in their writing the non-phonemic voicelessness of phrase-final vowels. Some of the bilinguals started to write the voiceless vowels with the reversed apostrophe which was being used to mark Tarascan aspirated stops. Swadesh's explanation: "The phenomenon [of phrase-final voiceless vowels] remained from the Spanish standpoint an unusual feature and was represented by ', a symbol also used to represent what is an unusual feature from the Spanish standpoint. Phrase final unvoicing, while it does not contrast with voiced pronunciation in Tarascan, does contrast with the normal treatment of final syllables in Spanish. From the Spanish standpoint, it had to be specially represented and a logical way to represent it was with the diacritic for aspiration."

For a language situation in which most of the speakers appear to be bilingual, Wonderly[21] has given us by implication the following assumption: When (a) a very

---

[19] Information from W.C.Townsend of the Summer Institute of Linguistics, as reported to Pike.
[20] "Observations of Pattern Impact on the Phonetics of Bilinguals", *Sapir Memorial Volume*: *Language, Culture and Personality* (Menasha, Wis., 1941), 49-65. Many other illustrations of problems discussed in the present paper are to be found in Swadesh's article; but he does not attempt to set up a procedure to handle them.
[21] W.L.Wonderly, "Phonemic Acculturation in Zoque", *IJAL* 12 (1946), 92-95, reprinted in Pike's *Phonemics*, 202-206.

large number of loans have passed from a foreign language to the native language, and when (b) other loans are accepted with great ease, the loans currently in normal use must be considered assimilated. These criteria should, however, be carefully checked against Step Two above. In addition, they must be supplemented in ways which have been suggested if one wishes to study the difference between the speech reaction of monolinguals and of bilinguals in the same area, or if one studies the language of monolinguals whose speech contains only a few loans.

Up to this point in the discussion, the mixed systems which we have described are largely paralleled by independent systems operating in the same general period of time without such mixture. That is to say, the Mazateco with Spanish mixture is paralleled by Spanish without that Mazateco mixture. The mixture has resulted from a GEOGRAPHICAL proximity of speakers of the different systems, whether the systems are closely or distantly related or unrelated. We now turn to problems which must be handled in much the same way, but which have a somewhat different origin. In this case, as before, two systems or parts of systems are found to be overlapping; but the conflict has developed within a single language over a period of TIME. Assumption: In the process of change from one phonemic system to a different phonemic system of the same language, there may be a time during which parts of the two systems exist simultaneously and in conflict within the speech of single individuals. The incoming contrasts or sounds may be already present, but not completely extended throughout all the words of the language, or the old contrasts or sounds may not yet have completely disappeared; in either instance an overlapping of coexistent systems may be the result. This mixing of systems due to linguistic change over a period of time is not completely distinct from change caused by borrowing; the process of borrowing occurs over a period of time also. Furthermore, borrowed sounds once completely assimilated to the native system tend to be modified over a period of time in the same way that words of native origin are modified; new words, in turn, may then be borrowed, leaving unassimilated loans. For convenience, nevertheless, we shall make a few statements concerning change over a period of time which amplify the assumptions and procedures given for the analysis of loans from a separate language.

How can one detect in some one language the existence of simultaneous but conflicting sound systems or parts of systems which are due to historical change? The solution begins with the steps indicated in the previous directions. A rigid analysis is attempted on the assumption that only a single, consistent system of sounds is present in the language; regardless of complexity, the results are tentatively described on this basis; these results are then checked against the investigator's analysis — in accordance with the assumptions given above — of the reaction of the speakers of that language as they try to write or analyze or describe the sounds and the system of sounds of that language, or to learn another language; if the analyst seems to discover any conflicts in the results of the two approaches, he looks at all geographically neighboring dialects or languages with which the people have cultural contact, to see if the presumably small number of words containing the conflicting data appear to have their origin in one of the foreign dialects. If he cannot locate the source of the conflict in the geographically neighboring dialects, he then looks to available evidence concerning the phonemic system of the language itself at a somewhat earlier (but not a remote) period, to see if it is reasonable to suppose that the conflicting items are a residue of an earlier system which has largely disappeared, but has left traces in the form of conflicting elements in the present system. If these conflicting elements were not present in the older layer of the language, he may set up the hypothesis that they constitute an incoming layer. In the latter event he may have to wait for a few years to find evidence of further change which will substantiate or refute his hypothesis.

This last possibility brings us to a further set of assumptions: It is impossible to give a purely synchronic description of a complex mixed system, at one point of time, which shows the pertinent facts of that system; direction of change is a pertinent characteristic of the system and must also be known if one wishes to have a complete description of the language as it is structurally constituted. This can be discovered only by a study of the language over some period of time, whether long or short, or by comparative work among neighboring dialects, or by setting up a plan to record future data, or by studying the speech of informants of different ages.

Two non-linguistic illustrations may help to make the last assumption seem reasonable. If an investigator wishes to give a description of the current fashion in women's hats, it will not be enough merely to go to the corner and sketch, classify, and count the kinds of hats going by. For a culturally complete description he must also determine those few which represent the latest style (and are increasing in frequency), and those few which represent a nearly lost type (and are decreasing in frequency). To a person who is interested in 'pure description' such differences of frequency over a period of time might appear utterly immaterial to the system — but probably the wearers of the hats would disagree with him violently. Similarly, a description of the architecture of a city would need a time perspective; even a short period of time might suffice to determine trends. So, for the study of changing phonemic systems, a time perspective is needed; this, as well as the study of loans as they exist at a particular time, is part of what we subsume under the study of coexistent phonemic systems.

If it be objected that a time perspective is inessential to the functioning and hence to the description of a language system (inasmuch as the speakers of that language do not know its history), the illustration about the hats may again prove helpful in explaining our point of view. The wearer of a young lady's hat may not be aware of the history of decades of change in styles of hats. Yet she may be highly conscious of the fact that certain types are APPROPRIATE TO OLD PEOPLE or commonly worn by them, and she may shun those types accordingly. Similarly, children may recognize, without reflecting on the matter, that certain styles of speaking are common to old people. Parents recognize that children mimic the speech of other children more vigorously than they copy the speech of their elders. This helps to explain the fact that the speech of one age group tends to be more uniform than that of different age groups. In addition it supports the following assumption: It is possible to obtain a time perspective by a descriptive approach to the speech of living speakers even when written documents are not available.

We do not attempt to state how much time would be required for a reliable perspective for any particular type of change. Presumably the time would vary considerably from one problem to another. In some instances ten years might suffice, for others sixty years; for still others, sufficient data might be gathered by observing differences between the speech of informants of different ages.

In centuries past, various changes have occurred which have caused the modification of phonemic and grammatical systems in such a way that the changes can be documented by written materials. For English many individual changes seem to have taken about a hundred years to appear and become established. In a language in which historical data are available over a long period of time, it is possible to compare one approximately consistent system with another system which likewise is approximately consistent but which has become quite different from the first. The scope of this paper does not permit any detailed presentation and analysis of such historical changes, since the assumptions, criteria, and procedures needed to work with written materials differ considerably from those which we have suggested for use with speakers of a language.[22]

In Zapoteco[23] the investigator at first finds pairs of words which in certain positions seem to differ principally by the length of their vowels (e.g. *ya·* 'steam bath', *ya* 'bamboo'), although there may be concomitant minute differences of pitch as well as differences in abruptness or sharpness of 'attack'. If on this evidence the analyst postulates the existence of phonemic length, he then meets various difficulties: except for its occurrence in these few monosyllabic morphemes, length seems to be either freely variable or conditioned by the position of the vowels in the word or in relation to fortis or lenis consonants, etc. It is only after much study that he is likely to discover that the three (level) pitch phonemes also cause conditioning of length; vowels with high tone are shorter than those with mid tone, and after a low tone a high-toned monosyllable in utterance-final position has its pitch lowered until it is approximately of the same height but not of the same length as one with mid tone. Thus, in that position, the pitch contrast is 'actualized' largely as a difference of length, although in other positions the same morphemes occur with easily heard pitch contrasts. A study of Zapoteco over a future period of time might reveal

---

[22]   An attempt to deal with this problem in English will be included in Fries' *History of the Structure of English from 1100 to 1900*.
[23]   Data from Eunice V. Pike, "Problems in Zapotec Tone Analysis", *IJAL* 14 (1948), 161-171; dialect of Villa Alta, Oaxaca, Mexico.

a tendency to develop phonemic length — or comparative studies might prove that phonemic length has been lost in this dialect.[24]

3. SPECIAL SOUNDS AND CONTRASTS

If the investigator finds a conflict between the results of a rigid description in terms of an assumed single consistent system on the one hand and a study of observable native reactions to that system on the other, but cannot explain the conflict by a study of dialects adjacent in time or in space, he must consider other possibilities as the source of the conflict. A number of them may be briefly mentioned here,[25] and may constitute SPECIAL elements inserted into the basic phonemic structure of the language but not a systematic part of it. These elements may themselves constitute minor fragmentary systems coexistent with the full normal system. One type consists of a special contrast between sounds which otherwise do not occur in contrast, but are heard in over-precise or schoolroom speech. In such instances the extra system may distinguish between sounds which in normal situations are sub-members of a single phoneme.

In some areas of the United States, for example, a special variety of /a/ may be used in over-precise speech. In other areas a contrast between voiced and voiceless /w/ may be introduced into the classroom by a teacher who does not observe it in her normal speech, or it may be taught to pupils who do not have it in their own dialect. In parts of Latin America where [b] and [v] are not phonemically distinct, schoolteachers may nevertheless deliberately introduce the distinction, with exaggerated lip movements, while discussing spelling or pronunciation, even though they themselves do not use the contrast in normal speech. In the phonetics classroom, where many varieties of sounds are discussed, many contrasts exist in the directed speech of the instructor and students for varied lengths of time, and obviously constitute an extra-systematic set of sounds which leaves the regular native system more or less intact, though possibly modified in ways yet to be investigated.

A situation similar to that of the classroom, but much less artificial, may arise when a layman attempts to correct a foreigner's mispronunciations. If the layman is unsatisfied with the foreigner's pronunciation of the middle consonant in *matter*, for example, he may repeat the word slowly and — he claims — 'distinctly'. While accomplishing his aim of clarity he may substitute a different sub-member of the phoneme /t/; he may replace the flapped variety with an aspirated one. By this change of style he has unconsciously changed his system of sounds, so that a contrast now exists between the flapped [t] of the one system and the aspirated [t] of the other, with a concomitant change of meaning (i.e. connotation) — something

---

[24] Length is phonemic in the Zapoteco of Juchitan. Data gathered by Pike in collaboration with Velma Pickett and Marjorie MacMillan.
[25] For further discussion of these types see Pike's *Phonemics*, 65-66, 124-125, 142-143.

like 'word pronounced distinctly' as against 'word pronounced normally'. Notice that this difference caused by style is unlike the substitution of allophones caused by isolated pronunciation, and cannot readily be handled by a procedure which is based on the assumption that a language contains one and only one consistent, non-conflicting system of sounds.

With this particular kind of extra-systematic addition the investigator can often observe the following: the naïve comments of the native often indicate that he is largely unaware of the contrasts thus introduced; he talks about the new pronunciation as if he had merely slowed it down without changing the quality of the segments at all. A similar modification may be seen when a 'clear' pronunciation for foreigners is given of words with the final /z/; instead of being largely unvoiced they may in the slower pronunciation be completely voiced. This type of extra-systematic contrast must not be considered as paralleling the contrast of /s/ and /z/ in *seal* and *zeal*.

A few special sounds may belong to specific morphemes only, and may thus constitute special systems in addition to the normal phonemic system, even though they occur as non-phonemic varieties of other sounds in the normal system. Thus the glottal stop seems to be an essential part of English /mʔm/ or /ʔmʔm/ or /həʔə/ (each with dropping pitch) 'no'; elsewhere it may occur as a sub-member of /t/ in words like *Scotland* or *mountain*. An alveolar click may constitute a morpheme indicating commiseration; and so on.

4. MODIFICATIONS OF PHRASES

If the investigator follows the assumption that only one phonemic system is operating in a language, he will probably encounter a curious phenomenon: for many languages all voiced phonemes will be paralleled by contrasting whispered ones; all voiced sounds will also probably occur in two sets, one spoken and the other sung. In most languages some people occasionally whisper and occasionally sing, even though in some languages whispering and singing are very rare.[26] In addition to the whispered and sung varieties of sounds there may be others reflecting various additional styles of vocal utterance — e.g. chanted utterances, or utterances with stress-timed versus syllable-timed rhythm.[27] In a language where people communi-

---

[26] It is difficult, for example, to find whispering among the Mixtecos; Pike, after a considerable period of residence among them, cannot recall a single instance. For privacy, they speak in low voices. Pike found it difficult to teach Mixtecos to whisper when on a few occasions he wished to compare whispered with voiced speech. Similarly, in the dialect of San Miguel el Grande, Pike can recall hearing only three persons sing, without urging, even a single Mixteco song; and what they sang was heavily mixed with Spanish loan words. Yet certain other Mixteco dialects have numerous native songs.

[27] Pike, *The Intonation of American English* (= *University of Michigan Publications*: *Linguistics* 1) (Ann Arbor, 1945), 34-35.

cate extensively by whistling,[28] one can see that whistled pitches are highly important and constitute a system distinct from but related to the vowels.

By what procedure can the analyst discover that the apparently separate phonemes consisting of whispered, sung, and spoken vowels are not all to be handled as equivalent (i.e. contrastive) types in the language system? The analyst makes two observations: (1) that a number of whispered vowels (or sung vowels, etc.) tend to be found in sequence, if the utterance contains more than one vowel; and (2) that any utterance which can be whispered (or sung) can be duplicated (a) with the retention of the same words, morphemes, and general meaning, but (b) with the substitution of voiced vowels for the whispered (or sung) ones. It is the entire utterance, therefore, which is affected in each of its vowels, reflecting as a whole a slight difference in the general social situation in which it is used. No new basic types of qualitative contrasts between vowel and vowel are introduced within any single utterance.

On the basis of this type of evidence the analyst concludes that whispered or sung quality is SUPERIMPOSED upon the basic phonemic system of the language, and constitutes a second type of system operating simultaneously with the first, modifying it though not in conflict with it in specific average utterances. The occasional instances in which a speaker may burst into song in the middle of a sentence or lower his voice to a whisper in the middle of an utterance do not invalidate this general conclusion, but only make more difficult a statement of the circumstances in which such additions occur.[29]

Changes in the speed of utterance may introduce further complications into the original analysis. In rapid speech some sound types may be added or some may disappear, so that the distribution of sounds is affected. The shortening of some sequences of sounds would not upset the analyst's statement concerning the types of sounds encountered, but might cause considerable modification of his description of the phonemic content of specific morpheme types. More serious would be the fusion of a two-sound sequence found in slow speech into a single distinctive sound found only in fast speech. In such a situation he would have to conclude that his analyses of slow and fast speech (identified, say, by counts of the relative number of syllables per second) give evidence for the simultaneous existence of overlapping conflicting phonemic systems in the language.

Differences of speed in the utterance of certain kinds of phrases introduce a problem in the analysis of borders between words and modifications of sounds which occur at those borders. In the utterance *ice cream* [aᶦs. ˈkʰrim] there appears to be a syllable boundary at the morpheme boundary: the [-s] is part of the first syllable; the stress of the second syllable seems to begin with the [k-]; and an aspiration, in

---

[28] See G. M. Cowan, "Mazateco Whistle Speech", *Language* 24 (1948), 280-286.
[29] The investigator must also determine, by further analysis, whether these additional characteristics are in turn subdivided into an intricate system of contrasts (like the intonations of American English). So far, no such contrastive system has been observed for whisper. In song, such a system is obviously constituted by the tones of the musical scale, even though the contrasts are artificial (not 'natural to the universe') and different in different cultures.

the form at least of partial unvoicing of the [r], follows the [k-]. In exceptionally fast speech the same morpheme sequence *ice cream* may become [aⁱ. ˈskrim], homophonous or nearly homophonous with a very rapid pronunciation of *I scream*. The phonetic characteristics which distinguish the two utterances in slow speech have in this case disappeared in fast speech, even though the two utterances are different in their potentials (since they will revert to their earlier phonetic forms if their pronunciations are slowed down, and will again constitute an easily recognized contrast). Extra-slow speech likewise shows special phonetic phenomena and morphemic modifications which do not appear in speech of normal speed. These characteristics of changing speed, as well as those of whisper and song, necessitate an analysis of a language into a series of coexisting but related phonemic systems.

5. SYMBOLIZATION OF CONFLICTING SYSTEMS

Once the analyst decides that in the language which he is studying he has found some of the various types of conflicting phonemic systems discussed here, he may wish to symbolize these characteristics in an orthography. He may be preparing the material for one of two general types of audiences: for a technical audience of native or foreign linguists, or for natives who will use it in a practical vernacular literature. The symbols chosen will sometimes differ considerably according to the audience which will be reading them.

In presenting to a technical audience a set of materials whose conflicting patterns are caused by unassimilated loan words, the linguist may introduce added symbols for any added phonemes; from the description furnished him, the reader will recognize their origin when he sees them. When the native material conflicts with the unassimilated borrowed material in such a way that a single symbol must be interpreted in two different ways, according to the origin of the word in which it appears, the foreign word must be accompanied by some added symbol which indicates that it is unassimilated and that it must be read according to a separate set of orthographic conventions. A small dagger[30] preceding the word might be a satisfactory sign for this purpose: e.g. Mazateco 'nta' for [nda] 'good', but '†siento' for [siento] 'one hundred'.

If, for the same audience, one wishes to write loans which have been adopted into the vernacular, but which carry new sounds with them, the problem is much simpler. The linguist merely adds to the vernacular writing those extra symbols necessary to represent the new sounds. From the description of the sounds and symbols furnished him, the technical reader can both pronounce the sounds and recognize the fact that the words containing them are probably not of native origin — except that, after a considerable period of time, vernacular words may be ana-

---

[30]   In the Mazateco article cited in fn. 3, an asterisk was used for this purpose. A dagger seems better, to avoid confusion with the traditional use of the asterisk to mark unattested forms.

logically created or modified in such a way that the new sounds appear in them.

In a vernacular literature prepared for a non-technical audience, any sounds added by loans can usually be written best with the same symbol which they would have in the second language, provided that no conflicting phonemic systems are caused by the presence of these loan sounds. If, however, a conflict of phonemic systematization of sounds exists because of the presence of unassimilated loans, no completely satisfactory solution is available. The writer may consider symbolizing the loans in some way (by italics, by a dagger, or the like); but if only one or two loans are involved, it is probably best to ignore the conflict and leave the orthography ambiguous at that particular point. Probably this is preferable both in the literature prepared for monolinguals and in that prepared for bilinguals. In Mazateco, Eunice Pike is now testing the use of orthographic 'nt' both for the native material and for the few loans, with no symbolization of the conflict between the 'nt' which symbolizes [nd] and that which symbolizes the few occurrences of [†nt]. So far, no serious difficulty has been reported as a result of this method.

When the phonemic systems of the monolingual and the bilingual speakers of a community differ, the linguist who is preparing a practical orthography must decide first of all whether he wishes to adapt the orthography to the monolingual or to the bilingual phonemic system. His orthography may prove to be quite different according to the way he decides this crucial question. In order to reach such a decision he must study (1) the extent and nature of the phonemic conflicts in the linguistic systems of the monolinguals and the bilinguals; (2) the nature, direction, and speed of phonetic or phonemic changes over a period of time; (3) the nature, source, and strength of social pressures favoring such trends; (4) the potential hindrance to a literacy program for monolinguals if the orthography is adapted to the needs of bilinguals; (5) the potential hindrance to bilinguals if the monolinguals are favored; and (6) the probable strength of opposition which may develop from those bilinguals who consider themselves capable of adequate linguistic judgment (simply because they know how to read and write their second language) and who will oppose any orthography which does not correspond to that of the second language. With these and any other pertinent cultural data in hand (such as the influence of professional linguists in the government or the power of conservatives), the linguist can then reach a decision as to the orthography which will give the best practical results in the field. He must be prepared to modify this decision if tests or experience or both show his judgment to have been wrong.

The most critical differences between bilingual and monolingual systems, and the ones which may cause the most severe problems, are likely to be those in which two sounds are phonemically distinct in the second language but constitute sub-members of a single phoneme in the vernacular speech of monolinguals, and in which the bilinguals speak the vernacular just as the monolinguals do but react to spelling decisions like monolingual speakers of the second language. For the monolingual it is easy to see that one symbol alone is best to represent the two variants of the phoneme — unless the linguist assumes that the monolingual will soon be bilingual, and that the orthography for monolinguals should foreshadow their later bilingualism.

A decision as to the best orthography for the bilingual is more difficult to make. Should the linguist assume that the bilingual's second language actually constitutes part of a super-system which includes both languages, or should he conclude that the languages are to be treated separately? If he decides to treat each language separately, he will use a single symbol for two sounds which are in mutually exclusive distribution in the vernacular; but he may receive vigorous criticism from the bilinguals themselves for doing so. If, on the other hand, he transcribes the two sounds differently, paralleling their known phonemic difference in the second language, he implies that the sounds of the two languages constitute a single system for the bilingual, and has made an orthography which is not well adapted for the use of the monolinguals.

In Latin America, in a number of instances, social pressure from the bilinguals — who tend to carry much more prestige than the monolingual speakers of the vernacular — has forced the decision. In one instance among the Quechuas of the Andean region, Pike found extremely strong insistence from bilingual schoolteachers and bilingual government officials that a five-vowel Quechuan orthography be used, even though all the monolinguals and many of the bilinguals of the region have a three-vowel system. Here the practical problem was severe, since [o] and [u] in the vernacular are sub-members of a single phoneme /u/, but their occurrence is partly conditioned and partly free. Because of this distribution, it proved impossible to set up any rule by which the native could be taught to write 'u' or 'o' in specific words with the assurance that its pronunciation in a particular instance would parallel that of a Spanish vowel written in the same way. Individuals literate in Spanish, furthermore, would sometimes arbitrarily select certain Quechua words to be written with only one of the vowel letters, even though no conditioning environment occurred in the word to determine which variant must occur; they would be highly incensed if someone else suggested spelling the word with the opposite vowel letter. The best practical compromise seemed to be to write 'o' immediately adjacent to back velar consonants, but to write 'u' elsewhere, regardless of the phonetic variety of the sound which happened to occur in a particular utterance of some specific word.

Summary

Some languages contain phonemic arrangements which are not completely in balance; they contain conflicting elements which may be analyzed as coexistent phonemic systems. The points of conflict can be determined by first studying the sounds of a language on the assumption that they compose a single completely systematic unit, and by then looking for elements of the postulated system which contradict evidence separately obtained by analysis of the objectively observable reactions of native speakers to the writing or analysis of their own language or to the speaking of a foreign language. Sounds are pertinent only as they are parts of a system, so systems must be compared with systems. Coexistent systems may include, among other types, a vernacular (1) with sounds borrowed from other languages, or (2) with relics or advance elements of linguistic change, or (3) with special segments of an interjectional type, or (4) with general differences of quality, style, or speed. Monolingual and bilingual speakers may have an identical pronunciation of the vernacular but different reactions to it. Various assumptions and procedures have been suggested here for determining the existence and characteristics of coexistent phonemic systems, but these procedures need further development before linguists can reach agreement on valid methods for their application in specific instances.

The chief assumptions propounded in this paper lead us to the following conclusion. Evidence for the phonemic structure of a language is of two kinds: (1) phonetic and distributional data of the traditional kind; and (2) the observable reactions of native speakers as they attempt to write or analyze their own language or to speak a foreign language. If, as we believe, the second kind of evidence is actually the foundation on which postulates concerning the first kind must be built, then the two kinds should lead to similar or identical results, provided the phonemic system of the language is uniform; but since they sometimes lead rather to conflicting results, we are driven to the conclusion that in some languages two or more phonemic systems coexist.[31]

[31] Since this article was in proof, various related items have come to my attention.

A group of British scholars are making various levels of abstraction which, if pursued further, may overlap with the analysis given here. J.R. Firth and B.B. Rogers, in "The Structure of the Chinese Monosyllable in a Hunanese Dialect (Changsha)", *BSOAS* 8 (1935-1937), 1055-1074, discuss sequences of permitted sounds: an 'alternance' is a list of single sounds or clusters substitutable for each other in contrast in any one 'place' (position) in the syllable. N.C. Scott, in "The Monosyllable in Szechuanese", *BSOAS* 12 (1947), 197-213, carries this analysis further, using boldface type for phonetic sequences and italics for 'systematic' (approximately phonemic) writing, paralleling somewhat the American usage of square brackets and slant introduced by Bloch and Trager. Eugénie J.A. Henderson, in "Notes on the Syllable Structure of Lushai", *BSOAS* 12 (1948), 713-725, emphasizes the structural contrast between the number of 'places' in the 'phonetic analysis' of the syllable and the number of 'places' in the 'syllabic structure'; the 'structural dividing line' (721) in syllable structure parallels the American use of the term 'immediate constituents': see, for example, the article referred to in fn. 3. J. Carnochan, in "A Study in the Phonology of an Igbo Speaker", *BSOAS* 12 (1948), 417-426, suggests that a phonetic characteristic "may be a feature of a whole utterance" if one sound — e.g. aspiration — non-phonetically conditions other non-contiguous sounds; he uses this type of reasoning to reach the conclusion that a syllable is not a sequence of discrete sounds but a unit. J.R. Firth, in "Word-Palatograms and Articulation", *BSOAS* 12 (1948), 857-864, makes a related but experimental abstraction of a phonetic characteristic from a word or syllable by noting the total effect of some one articulator throughout the whole unit; these effects are not Harris' simultaneous components, which affect contiguous sounds, but may be the result of non-contiguous segments.

Somewhat closer to our assumptions are the conclusions reached by two continental scholars. André Martinet, in "Où en est la phonologie?", *Lingua* 1 (1948?), 34-58, emphasizes the necessity of studying historical phonological changes in relation to the total system of which they are a part. Bertil Malmberg, in *Le système consonantique du français moderne: Études de phonétique et de phonologie* (=*Lunds Univ. Årsskr.* 1.38.5) (1942-1943), briefly foreshadows another of our conclusions, without attempting to develop a procedure for handling it. Cf. the review of this publication by Eli Fischer-Jørgensen, *Acta Linguistica* 3 (1942-1943), 140.

A PROBLEM IN MORPHOLOGY-SYNTAX DIVISION*

This paper[1] sets forth data to document the following propositions:

Proposition 1: FOR THE DESCRIPTION OF SOME LANGUAGES IT IS NOT ACCURATE OR HELPFUL TO POSTULATE A SHARP MORPHOLOGY-SYNTAX DICHOTOMY. Illustration: the Mixteco language.

Proposition 2: A GRAMMATICAL DICHOTOMY INTO MORPHOLOGY AND SYNTAX IS NOT AS CRUCIAL OR BASIC TO LINGUISTIC STRUCTURE AS A DIVISION INTO (A) PATTERNS, (B) POINTS IN PATTERNS, AND (C) LISTS OF POTENTIAL REPLACEMENT ELEMENTS AT THOSE PATTERN POINTS; IN SOME INSTANCES MORPHOLOGY-SYNTAX DIVISION SHOULD BE ON A LATER LEVEL OF ANALYSIS THAN THAT OF THE FIRST CLASSIFICATION INTO PATTERNS, PATTERN POINTS, AND PATTERN POINT REPLACEMENT-POTENTIAL. Illustration of terms: *John came* as a subject-predicate pattern with *John* at the subject pattern point, *came* at the predicate pattern point, and *Bill*, *Jim*, *the dog*, *boys*, and many others as potential replacement items for the subject point of the pattern.

Proposition 3: WORD BOUNDARIES BECOME OBSCURED, AND THE ANALYSIS OF A SENTENCE INTO A SEQUENCE OF SEPARATE WORDS BECOMES AWKWARD OR FORCED, WHEN MAJOR PHONOLOGICAL BOUNDARIES DO NOT COINCIDE WITH MAJOR GRAMMATICAL DIVISIONS OR BOUNDARIES; that is, the recognition of a unit of a type traditionally called a 'word' is most easily attained or justified in those instances in which the borders of major phonological and major grammatical units do coincide, without large scale fusion of morphemes. Illustration: In the extra-rapid pronunciation [wãᵻ tʃə ᵎgo] of *why don't you go* there is considerable fusion; the chief intonational phonological break seems to come somewhere after [wãᵻ], but the major grammatical break would come after *why* — excluding the nasal element of [wãᵻ]; here word boundaries are not easily found.

For Indo-European languages we find it relatively simple to demonstrate that there is a difference between whole words, parts of words, and groups of words. In English, for example, *boy* is a single complete word; *boys* is also a single word,

* *Acta Linguistica* 5:3 (1949), 125-138. Reprinted by permission.
[1] Presented to the Michigan Academy of Science, Arts, and Letters, Apr. 2, 1948, Ann Arbor, Michigan.

For earlier discussion of these principles, see Kenneth L. Pike, "Analysis of a Mixteco Text", *International Journal of American Linguistics* X (1944), 113-138; the second proposition is more fully discussed in an unpublished paper, *Idem*, "Grammatical Structure".

made of the two parts *boy* and *-s*; *boys sing* is a group of two words comprised of the word *boys* and the word *sing*. The criteria which serve as the most adequate rule-of-thumb to determine the classification of a specific item in one of these three groups are the following: (1) Any item which is found in normal native speech pronounced by itself, as a complete utterance, is either a single complete word or a group of words. Thus *boys*, *sing*, and *boys sing*, may all be heard by themselves. (2) If that item cannot be divided into two or more smaller items (with no parts left over), such that each of them may also sometimes be found pronounced as separate utterances, then it constitutes a single word. Thus *boys* can be divided into *boy* and *-s*, but the *-s* is not heard by itself as a normal utterance; *boys* therefore constitutes a single word. (3) Any meaningful pieces of a word, which are smaller than the total word of which they are a part, are obviously parts of words rather than whole words. Thus the *-s* of *boys* is a part of a word, meaning 'plural', whereas *boy* is part of the word *boys* even though it may elsewhere constitute a complete word by itself. Such smallest meaningful units are called MORPHEMES.

Occasionally other criteria must be used to supplement those just given. Notice, for example, that the word *the* is seldom if ever found by itself unless we are talking about the word in a linguistic discussion. In its places of occurrence in the sentence it parallels, however, words like *this*, and *that*; and the demonstratives quoted do occur by themselves and easily meet the requirements for being considered complete words. Thus, (4), an item may be considered a word if it parallels in its usage other items which are undoubtedly words.

The study or system of parts of words we call MORPHOLOGY; that of groups of words, SYNTAX. Indo-European languages tend to have a sharp cleavage between their morphological and syntactic arrangements.

Such a classification does not readily accommodate some of the data of English and other Indo-European languages, however. How many words are to be found, for example, in the rapid pronunciation ['wɛr di go] *where did he go?* The form [di] includes *did* and *he*; must one consider, then, that the [d] is one word, and that the [i] is another?

Notice also ['wətʃɾ nem] *what is your name?* (with intonation °2-4-3). Presumably the [ɾ] represents the last part of *your*, with the first part included in [tʃ]; the [t] of *what*, the [ɪz] of *is* and the [j] of *your* seem all to be fused into the one affricate. In such an instance it is impossible to cut this 'phrase' into separate words with separate boundaries in the rapid form. Notice also ['dəbl̩ju 'dəbl̩ju 'dʒe 'brɪŋʒu ...] *WWJ brings you ...* in which the *-s* of *brings* and the *y-* of *you* coalesce; likewise: [k'mir] for *come here!* Compare, finally, the item [wãˀtʃə du'ðæt] *why don't you do that?* In this last illustration the first [d] disappears, the [n] is heard as nasalization of the preceding vowels, and the [t] and [j] coalesce to [tʃ]. How many words are involved in such an utterance?

In general, for English we analyze these in terms of the slower, fuller pronunciations, and the phonetically broken down words which do not appear by themselves in such reduced forms we may call CLITICS. If, however, no slow forms were available for comparison, but in many utterances the coalesced pronunciations were always given, the investigator would have a much more difficult time in describing the system. If, for English, one were forced to call [wã^{I}tʃə ˈgo] *why don't you go?*, a single word, the complexities of English morphology would be enormous, because the 'paradigm' would include forms like [wã^{I}nti ˈgo] *why doesn't he go* and so on. The description would prove difficult to handle because of the diversity of forms which would enter a paradigm, and because of the grammatical looseness of the parts of words; thus *you* and *why* are not as closely related, in the previous utterances, as were *boy* and *-s* in *boys*.

In Mixteco, an Indian language of Mexico, related problems constitute some of the most severe difficulties of analysis. Certain of its morphemes at first appear to English speakers as if they were suffixes, but are best treated as postclitics; others appear to be prefixes, or fusion of tones and consonants to stems, but prove to be preclitics. Both the preclitics and postclitics must be subdivided into types which appear very loosely joined to the words with which they are pronounced, and into various types which are more closely joined, even though not as closely related as are traditional prefixes and suffixes. Further items appear to be compounds, but are best analyzed as phrases. Samples of each type will now be given.

(1) Postclitics which are likely to be erroneously analyzed as suffixes. Every Mixteco item (whether a phrase or a single morpheme) when it is pronounced by itself, as a complete utterance, must contain two diverse or identical vowels. No word in isolation contains merely one vowel. Whenever, therefore, a morpheme contains only one vowel, it is phonologically incomplete, and must be pronounced with the morpheme preceding or following it.

The morpheme $^{n}du\check{c}a$ means 'water', and this pronunciation of the word is frequent and normal. As unmodified subject or object, however, the morpheme often loses its first syllable. 'The water came up (from the ground)' would be *nì-$^{n}do^{n}da-\check{c}à$*; in this pronunciation the second syllable of the morpheme is retained, but its tone is lowered (grave accent represents low tone, acute represents high, zero accent represents mid); *$^{n}donda$* means 'to come up', *nì-* is a preclitic meaning 'finished'. If, however, the subject is modified by an adjective, the full form of the subject must appear: *nì-$^{n}do^{n}da$ $^{n}du\check{c}a$ bá?a* 'good water came up (from the ground)'. The form *-čà* is a postclitic, loosely joined to the verb preceding it, rather than a suffix which would be tightly bound; a suffix would not be expected to resume a full, independent form at the addition of an adjectival modifier.

A few other morphemes are as loosely bound to the noun or verb phrase which they modify or of which they are a part, as is *-čà*. The most frequent of these is *žúkan* 'that thing', or 'that one', which abbreviates to *-ún* when it becomes a postclitic. Note *čàa-ún* (or *čà-ún*) 'that man'. This item cannot be considered a suffix, since many other free words may be inserted between it and the word it modifies, e.g., *čàa ñáʔnu-ún* 'that old man'; in such instances the *-ún* is postcliticized to the last of the series of words.

A different set of morphemes looks even more like suffixes than do the two just mentioned. Certain nouns may have abbreviated forms, and serve as substitutes for subjects or objects — i.e., they act like 'pronouns'. Yet they cannot be conveniently analyzed as suffixes since (a) they are cognate with free nouns, (b) they are limited in occurrence to specific types of grammatical contexts, but replaced by the two-vowel forms in other contexts, and (c) their treatment as possessive suffixes to nouns or as subjective suffixes to verbs would force into single words various sequences of morphemes which grammatically are quite independent, phonologically pronounceable in isolation, and not homogeneous in structure.

One of these morphemes is *-i* 'child'; it is cognate with *sùčí* 'child', which is a normal noun, occurring as subject, object, possessed item, and so on. Where *sùčí* is the subject of a verb, but at the time it is unmodified by an adjective, or by a qualifying noun, or by a possessor, or by a numerative noun, the full two-vowel form is usually replaced by the one-vowel form, and the one-vowel form is postcliticized to the verb or to the last verb modifier which precedes it. Thus one finds *žáʔa ká-ⁿǰaà-i* '(the) child is seated here', with the abbreviated *-i*, and *žáʔa ká-ⁿǰaà tuku-i* 'here the child is seated again'; but *žáʔa ká-ⁿǰaà əən sùčí* 'one child is seated here'. Note also the forms in which 'child' serves as modifying possessor of a preceding noun: *žáʔa kúu beʔe-i* 'this is (the) house (of the) child', but *žáʔa kúu beʔe sùčí lúlí* 'this is (the) house (of the) little child' and *žáʔa kúu beʔe sùčí-ná* 'this is my child's house'. (These illustrations were taken from the author's "Analysis of a Mixteco Text", *International Journal of American Linguistics*, X [1944], 132.)

If in the preceding illustrations the morpheme *-i* were considered a suffix, then *káⁿǰaàtukui* (and some of the other items) would have to be considered as a single word. This is undesirable since, in addition to implying a strange irregular suppletive relationship between the free word *sùčí* and the suffix *-i*, it would force the parallel analysis of long items such as the following: **tenìkáⁿǰaàžačìşaàntúkumáái* 'and sat down quickly exceedingly again that child' in which one finds the free morphemes *žačì* 'quick', *şaàn* 'fierce' (i.e. 'exceedingly' in this context), *tuku* 'different' (i.e. 'again' in this context); yet the *-i* would have been replaced by *sùčí* had one merely added *-ún* 'that one', so that the same investigator would then presumably analyze the item as consisting of the words *te-nì-ká-ⁿǰaà žačì şaàn túku máá súcí!* That is to say, the analysis of *-i* as a suffix would force the further analysis of various morpheme sequences as comprised of complex verbs or complex nouns entailing large numbers of incorporated (but actually independent) verbs, nouns, and adjectives. Such an analysis would prove much more unwieldy, and less parallel to the observed independence of the incorporated items, than does an analysis of the abbreviated forms as postclitics. Approximately a dozen morphemes act in this way: full and abbreviated forms of 'I' (or 'my', and so on), both polite and familiar: *náá* and *-ná*, *ruù* and *rì*; of inclusive first person, 'we': *žóó* and *-žò*; of 'you', polite and familiar:

níí and *-ní*, *róó* and *-rò*; of 'woman' (abbreviated form usually best translated 'she'):
ñaʔa and *-ña*; of 'man' (abbreviated form usually best translated 'he', and with
phonetic relationship to the full form now obscured by historical sound change):
čàa and *-de*; of 'animal': *kətə* and *-tə̀*; of 'sacred personage': *ʔiʔžà* and *-žà*.

Similar conclusions must be reached when one studies these same elements used
as possessors. In *beʔe-i* one might suspect that *-i* is a suffix, but the probability is
greatly reduced if one knows that there seems to be no theoretical limit to the number of adjectives or other modifiers which can come between the noun and its possessor; note the following, which would be theoretically possible: *beʔe žuù káʔnu
luu kʷíi bàʔa-i* 'the house (which is made of) rock (and is) big, beautiful, green, good,
(of the) child'; it would not do to analyze this as a single word: **beʔežuùkáʔnu-
luukʷíibàʔai*.

(2) Preclitics which may erroneously be analyzed as prefixes: Similar problems
confront the analyst when he studies morphemes which are abbreviated, also, but
which are phonologically dependent for their pronunciation upon the items which
follow them. The crux of the difficulty consists of conflicting grammatical and
phonological relationships: a morpheme may phonologically be tightly joined to
the morpheme which follows it, while grammatically it is loosely joined to that
morpheme; on the other hand a morpheme may phonologically be loosely joined
to the following morpheme, but grammatically be tightly joined to it. Thus in *kətə
káʔnu* 'big animal', the *káʔnu* 'big' is loosely bound phonologically to *kətə* 'animal'
in that both morphemes contain two vowels and are therefore pronounceable by
themselves. On the contrary, the *te-* 'then' (or 'and') is tightly joined phonologically
to the succeeding morpheme to which it is precliticized, and with which it is pronounced, since it has only one vowel in normal speech; in slow speech it is sometimes heard as *tee*, an isolatable word. Yet *te-* is grammatically only loosely bound
to the word immediately following it since it qualifies an entire succeeding phrase
of several words rather than a single word; note *te-nì-kenda tiʔinà* 'and a dog came
out'.

In the following formula parentheses enclose items which are closely related
phonologically; brackets enclose certain items which are closely related grammatically:

> ([te]-[nì-kaʔàn) (čàa-ún])
> ([and] [finished say) (man that]) i.e. 'and that man said'.

Following the *te-* directly (or with full free independent words between) there may
come one of several morphemes which are best considered auxiliary verbs. Of this
set the *nì-* 'to be completed' is a frequent example. Usually it has but one vowel,
and is pronounced with the morpheme following it. Occasionally, however, it may
be pronounced by itself, in slow or hesitation forms, as *niì*; sometimes, also, it forms
a pronounceable unit with the preceding *te-*, so that *te-nì* becomes the initial utterance, preceding a hesitation while the speaker decides what word he will say next.

At first *nì-* might appear to be a prefix, but since in hesitation it occurs by itself, and since a few other full or abbreviated morphemes like (*nì-*) *haʔàn* 'went' which appear to be free may come between it and the main verb, and because of the general tendency of the language to be constituted of sequences of grammatically independent words in various phonological and structural layers, it seems best to consider *nì-* to be a preclitic rather than a prefix. Other similar morphemes are *ná-* 'let it be', *nì-* 'would that it were'; these, like *nì-*, seem to qualify a verb head (and its immediate post-modifiers, if the verbal phrase is comprised of several independent morphemes in a close-knit verbal construction). Note *nì-hani ʔinì-i* 'completed-hit innards-child' i.e. 'the youngster thought'. Here the *nì-* modifies *ʔinì*, as well as *hani*.

When an investigator first studies Mixteco he is likely to conclude that there is a distinct morphological structure very different from the syntactic arrangements of the language. He will find, for example, morphemes with 'potential aspect' in which an incomplete action is signified and then he will discover these same morphemes modified by tone or by tone and palatalization of the first (or more) sounds to indicate 'continuative aspect' or a continuous action. Note *kusù* 'will sleep' and *kišì* 'sleeping'; *kunu* 'will run' and *hínu* 'running'; *kunu* 'will weave' and *kúnu* 'weaving'; *kùči* 'will ripen' and *híči* 'ripening'. Soon the investigator would make various additional observations: the kinds of tone substitutions seen in this instance are paralleled very frequently and mechanically in sandhi elsewhere; the tones of one set of words (in part determined by their innate form, and in part by an arbitrary listing) affect the tones of words which follow them in accordance with a definite pattern. Thus if a word of two mid tones is preceded by a word which causes tone substitutions, the first mid tone will be replaced by a high tone, and so on. The details of these substitutions may be found in my *Tone Languages* (= *University of Michigan Publications: Linguistics*, IV) (Ann Arbor, 1948). These substitutions in sandhi are not dependent upon the basic form class of the word being modified or causing the modification; they apply equally to nouns, verbs, and adjectives — a fact which hints that the tonal change in the verbal 'aspects' is not a characteristic deeply imbedded in the structure of verb stems as such, but a residue of an earlier change. The palatalizing effect of the 'continuative aspect' is also to be found elsewhere: the preclitics *nì-* and *ní-* both cause these changes in certain of the verb stems which they precede. Finally, the investigator will notice that just as the preclitic *nì-* may occur either preceding the main verb stem, or preceding various auxiliary verbs which likewise precede the main verb, so the palatalizing effect of the 'continuative aspect' will also be shifted to the identical auxiliary which would have been affected by the preclitic *nì-* 'completed'. Similarly the tone substitutions of the 'continuative' will be shifted to the same auxiliary, as they would be if the preclitic *ná-* were to precede the verb complex.

The implication of these various facts is that the 'continuative aspect' is not constituted in essence of a stem plus a process of stem change, but rather of a sequence of two morphemes, the second representing the basic verb, and the first comprised of an auxiliary verb morpheme meaning 'to be in process'; this auxiliary parallels in its usage the morphemes *nì-*, *ní-*, and *ná-* already mentioned; it parallels *nì-* in causing palatalization and *ná-* in causing tone substitution of certain items which follow them. Since the preclitics *nì-* and *ná-* (by parallel with the postclitics *-i*, *-ña*, and so on) must be treated as abbreviated dependent words rather than as prefixes, the stem change in 'continuative aspect' must likewise be considered a remnant of a dependent word, with the statement that the remnant consists of sandhi and palatalizing influences only.

The complexity of the analysis of the auxiliary verb preclitics is one of the chief problems in attempting to determine whether there exists in Mixteco a sharp boundary between morphology and syntax. If one concludes, as we have just done, that the remnants of fused items are still best treated as sequences of dependent words, rather than as prefixes or morphological stem changes, then Mixteco does not present any structural arrangement which entails a basic dichotomy between morphology and syntax in the traditional sense. Overlapping layers of grammatical relationship find their points of cleavage (or 'immediate constituents') at different places in the continuum of speech than do the layers of phonological dependence, and make it necessary to describe Mixteco without postulating such a sharp morphology-syntax division as is customarily expected in a language. Succeeding paragraphs of this paper indicate further types of items in the language which illustrate the same point, and cover the remaining principal sources of difficulty in substantiating that decision.

Stem changes involving some type of nasalization of the first consonant of the stem, and meaning 'to be in a state of' constitute a problem similar to that for the fused continuative morpheme. Note *kasù* 'will close' and *ⁿdasú* 'to be in state of closure'; *kuu* 'will be' and *ⁿduu* 'will turn into'; *kuʔnì* 'will tie' and *nuʔnì* 'to be tied up'; *kàbə* 'will enter' and *ⁿdàbə* 'will repeatedly enter' or 'will enter to remain'. The fused nasalizing morpheme which has caused these changes has not been located in its full form elsewhere, and affects an arbitrary list of morphemes beginning with velar or affricate sounds. It appears to be an auxiliary verb type, however, and in the sequence of permitted occurrences of auxiliary verbs before the stem it seems to come between the causative preclitic *s-* and the main verb stem. When *kàbə* receives both the continuative morpheme and the stative morpheme fused directly to it, the resultant form is *ⁿdábə* in which the high tone comes from the continuative morpheme and the nasalization of the first consonant from the stative morpheme; semantic result: 'to be in the process of repeatedly entering (or remaining)'.

An intransitivizing morpheme, likewise applied to an arbitrary list of (transitive verbal) words, seems to result in the substitution of a lower tone than one of the tones of the basic stem. Note *nì-saka-ná* 'I planted (something)' and *nì-sakà* '(it) was planted'; *təən* 'will grasp' and *tə̀ən* 'will take root'. This morpheme, also, comes close to the stem of the main verb, following most other verbal auxiliaries; it is not clear whether it should be analyzed as preceding or following the stative one.

Other changes of stem consonants appear in nouns, when the two nouns appear

in sequence, the second modifying the first, but the first is abbreviated or lost, as in
čòʔó 'flea'. Compare, *kətə búrru* 'animal burro, a donkey' with *tə-saà* 'animal bird,
bird' (in which the first word is *kətə* precliticized in abbreviated form) and with *kətə*
žòʔó 'flea', usually heard as *ti-žòʔó* but occasionally further coalesced to *čòʔó*. For
nouns which now have only the coalesced form the analyst may merely list the present stem form without comment — and in fact may not know of its origin. Similar
items occasionally are found among the verbs: *či-žàʔú* or *čàʔú* 'to pay'. Where the
first morpheme preserves at least one vowel, that morpheme is best considered a
preclitic, a phonologically dependent word, rather than a prefix or a part of a compound.

(3) Phrases which may erroneously be analyzed as compounds: A further problem remains in the analysis of an item like *tə-saà* 'bird': Should it be considered a
compound comprised of *kətə* 'animal' and *saà* 'bird', or a phrase in which the first
element is abbreviated and precliticized, or a single word in which *tə-* is prefixed?

The answer is not an easy one. In the first place, the item has a unified meaning.
Both *tə-saà* and *saà* occur, in normal speech, with the simple meaning 'bird'; *tə-saà*
seems to occur in much the same positions which *saà* can occupy — either form
may be the subject or object of a verb, the possessor or an item, possessed by an
item, and so on. On the other hand near-parallel data make the longer item appear
like a phrase. In Mixteco one finds a great many sequences of noun modified by
noun; the construction is extremely frequent. The relationship between such nouns
is not completely uniform. In general, however, one sees that the pattern is very
productive and almost any noun can modify any other noun if the result 'makes
sense'. Abbreviation of the first item of these sequences usually takes place only
when the first noun has the phonological form CV_1V_1 or $CV_1\text{?}V_1$ (with or without
nasalized vowels); in such instances the final vowel and consonant (and all nasalization) tend to be lost. Often the full form may reappear in slower speech, however;
note *žuʔu ⁿdúča* (slow) or *žu-ⁿdúča* (fast) 'margin of the river (or lake, etc.)' from
'mouth-water'. With patterns CV_1V_2 (in which the vowels are diverse, the one from
the other) and CVCV (with or without nasalization of the second vowel), abbreviation occurs only rarely. Usually the full form of both nouns is retained, and no
loss or substitution of consonants, vowels, tones, or stress, signals the combination.
The sequence of noun-noun appears to be a simple phrase, usually without semantic
specialization, but occasionally with it: note the phrase *žaù kaba* 'hole cliff', i.e.
'cave'. Only rarely does the pattern CVCV abbreviate, and at those times it is likely
to lose the first syllable: note *tə-saà* already mentioned. The freedom with which
noun-noun phrases can be constructed, and the obvious parallels to those which
have abbreviation of the first member of the sequence, plus the fact that the early
abbreviation appears to be nearly mechanical and in general limited to certain types
of phonological patterns, makes items like *tə-saà* appear to be phrases, with the
first word precliticized, rather than compounds.

Certain additional facts support this conclusion: Similar abbreviation occurs freely between words juxtaposed in widely divergent grammatical structures, provided that the phonological situation is similar; the sequence of noun plus adjective (a very frequent and normal pattern of modification): *čàa* 'man' plus *ñáʔnu* 'old' in rapid speech gives *čà-ñáʔnu*; a verb plus its subject: *káa* 'numbers of to be in a position' plus *žuù* 'rock(s)' give in rapid pronunciation *ká-žuù* 'many rocks are (in the road)'; *nìʔi* 'strong', *kée* 'is blowing', *tačì* 'wind', gives *nìʔi ké-tačì* 'the wind is blowing hard'. Like the nouns, the verbs can be modified by other verbs or by nouns or adjectives, and form close-knit units which function more or less like single verbs in the positions of the sentence which they occupy. These, also, are many in number, are very free in the types which can be constructed, and entail abbreviation of the first member of the sequence: *kee* 'going out' plus *kožo* 'to pour out' give *ke-kožo* 'to be rushing out in a group' (but contrast *bài* 'to come' in *bài kožo* 'to come in a group', which does not abbreviate because of the diverse vowels in the first word); *sáʔa* 'makes' plus *ⁿdaà* 'straight' usually is pronounced *sá-ⁿdaà* 'fix up, agree'. It appears, then, that phrases of various types occur, with abbreviated first member, and that noun and verb compounds as such are not found.

Two more types of evidence must be examined, however, before allowing this conclusion to stand: Specialization of meaning may possibly occur in a few instances of abbreviation, and loss of meaning may appear in some abbreviated or unabbreviated sequences. The word for 'jail' is *be-kàa* from *beʔe* 'house' and *kàa* 'metal'. While travelling with a Mixteco Indian in a different section of Mexico we saw a house with a galvanized iron roof; this he described, in a newly constructed phrase (since such roofing is not used in his neighborhood), *beʔe kàa* without the abbreviation; a contrast could easily develop here, though frequent usage might bring the two to be homophones. A more probable distinction exists between *sá-bàʔa* 'to prepare' (or even 'to skin') from *sáʔa* 'to make' and *bàʔa* 'good', and *sáʔa bàʔa* 'to follow a good course of action'; here, also, the unabbreviated phrase is rare, and seems forced when it is elicited.

In some abbreviated sequences we have not yet found the meaning of one of the members. Thus *lì-suʔmá* 'skorpion' includes *suʔmà* 'tail' and an unanalyzed element *lì-*. Similar problems exist with unabbreviated sequences. Note *koʔò kúù* 'an incense burner' from *koʔò* 'bowl' and unanalyzed *kúù*; natives use the term *kúù* only in this context, and cannot explain what it means; *koʔò* is an extremely frequent word, since bowls are used by the people daily. Many kinds of free phrases with *koʔò* are in constant use, and others seem to be freely constructed whenever occasion demands it: thus one may hear *koʔò ⁿdéžu* 'bowl for food', and a new kind of bowl brought into the village by the analyst will be given some appropriate name. It appears that the morpheme *kúù* is paralleled by many other morphemes which are free, full forms. Presumably it must also be analyzed as a free full form, even though it occurs only in this one expression, since no formal characteristic differentiates it from part of a normal phrase. Compare English expressions in which one word occurs only in a specific phrase: e.g. *shrift* in *to make short shrift of*. Similarly, the *lì-* of *lì-suˀmà*, referred to above, parallels abbreviated forms of independent morphemes, even though no meaning has been found for it, and it has not been discovered in other phrases.

Does Mixteco, then, have compound words? We face a dilemma in answering the question. If we reply in the negative, then the English reader may feel that the loss of meaning of some of the morphemes, the abbreviation of certain of them, and the specialization of meaning of others invalidates the conclusion. If, however, we reply affirmatively, then criteria must be established to recognize the compounds. If abbreviation is utilized for the criterion, fantastic results would be achieved; abbreviation occurs between items which grammatically are so loosely bound together and occurs with such an arbitrary set of grammatical sequences — or with all of them, since abbreviation is conditioned at least in part by phonological structure rather than by grammatical type — that the language would be represented as an unpatterned miscellaneous set of unrelated compounds. If semantic specialization is chosen for the criterion, then many of the most flagrant samples of fusion would not be compounds, while many sequences otherwise indistinguishable from normal phrases would be analyzed as compounds; the result would be to disguise parallel structures rather than to illuminate them. A combination of these criteria would not solve the problem, since striking inconsistencies would continue to be seen. No criterion, or series of criteria, has been found which gives a basis for consistent identification of a compound. It seems best to avoid the term in describing Mixteco.

How, then, must one describe Mixteco if one postulates no sharp division between morphology and syntax, or any items which are structurally like forms traditionally called affixes or compounds? Presumably the investigator must list the constructions which do occur, and present in detail the various layers of structure; some items are grammatically more closely related than others, and this degree of closeness constitutes the source of a pyramiding layering in the constructions. Basic morpheme classes — noun, verb, adjective — each have their various types of modifiers, and each in turn modifies the other, in different relationships and groupings.

Assuming for English a clear morphology-syntax division for much of the data, how can fusion of words be symbolized? (1) Complete open space (with or without intonation marks) can be given where the division between words is paralleled by phonetic phenomena such as lengthened sounds or by pitch change: [ˈyɛstṛdi aⁱ ˈkem] (with °2-4-3 intonation on the first word, followed by 3-°2-4 on the next two; note the space after *yesterday*). (2) Space, with ligature, may come between full or abbreviated words which are part of a single rhythm or intonation group marked phonetically by a single abdominal pulse, but at a point where the break between words occurs between two phonemes: [ˈwɛr‿d i go] *where did he go?* (Unpublished data by Paul Garvin on Ponapean have in part suggested this phase of the writing). (3) A ligature may come below any phoneme which is simultaneously part of two words; where necessary, two or more ligatures may occur under a single phoneme, if slow forms and related phrases indicate by additional evidence that it is two or more

words which are thus fused: [ˈbrɪŋʒu] *brings you;* [wãˈtʃə ˈgo] *why do not you go?;*
[ɛd ɛˈˈd ɛdɛdɛd ɪt] *Ed had edited it;* [j̃ ɪnˈjoˈɪt] *Did you enjoy it?* Here, then, space
symbolizes word borders at the time they coincide with the borders (and concomitant phonetic phenomena) of intonational and rhythmic phonological units. Ligature symbolizes the same word borders at the time they do NOT coincide with these
borders of large phonological units; the ligature consequently symbolizes the PO-
TENTIAL for phonological border phenomena at those points, even though slower
forms would be essential before the fused words in some of the instances would become less overlapped and so permit the occurrence of these phenomena.

OPERATIONAL PHONEMICS IN REFERENCE TO LINGUISTIC RELATIVITY*

The phonemes of a language are neither absolutes nor bundles of absolute characteristics, but rather are fluctuating bundles of features identified (1) relative to each other in sequences, (2) relative to a system of fluctuating bundles of characteristics, and (3) relative to structural position in a sequence of such relative elements. Detection techniques, if paralleling phonemic analysis, would need to be able to work with fluctuating relative elements rather than with absolute physical characteristics only.

1. ABSOLUTE AND RELATIVE IN BEHAVIOR

Let us suppose three incidents. In Incident A, a man driving a jeep comes up to a bridge where a second man is leaning against a rail. The driver grabs a revolver, shoots through the open window, and kills the man on the bridge.

In Incident B, some six months later at a different place, a man driving a jeep comes up to a bridge where a second man is leaning against a rail. The driver grabs a revolver, shoots through the open window, and kills the man on the bridge.

In Incident C, sometime later at a different place, a man driving a jeep comes up to a bridge where a man is leaning against a rail. The driver grabs a revolver, shoots through the open window, and kills the man on the bridge.

A movie camera and a tape recorder set up to record these events would have found them approximately 'same'.

Let us suppose, however, that from other evidence we know that in Incident A the driver had a long-standing hatred for the man on the bridge. The driver had taken great pains to determine the habits of the other man and had so timed his movements as to find him at the bridge and deliberately kill him. In the second incident the driver had just escaped from a hospital for the insane and, stealing a jeep, had come to the bridge where he suddenly was filled with a fear that the man standing there was trying to prevent his escape; so the insane man shot him. In Incident C a war was under way and intelligence services had reported that at such a time and place on the bridge an extremely important spy would be standing wait-

* *The Journal of the Acoustical Society of America* 24:6 (1952), 618-625. Reprinted by permission. Presented at the Conference on Speech Analysis, Massachusetts Institute of Technology, June 17,1952.

ing to cause irreparable harm to the home country; he would be protected by extremely strong hidden forces such that any man trying to get at the spy would suffer certain death. Nevertheless, a volunteer rides on to the bridge, kills the spy, and in the next minute after the camera and tape recorder stop turning, he himself is riddled with bullets.

The three instances which the camera and tape recorder portrayed as 'same' are now seen to be extremely different, relative to the cultural situation in which they occurred. The driver of Incident A was a murderer. The driver of Incident B was to be pitied. The driver of Incident C was a hero.

The significance of sounds as culturally 'same' or 'different' we will call a type of cultural relativity in which the particular incident by itself can be seen as an absolute, but its functional significance can be determined only in relation to incidents immediately preceding and following it and in relation to a whole system of behavior of which it is a part.

It is by analogy with this set of incidents that we hope to show that there is a linguistic relativity and that there are sounds which a spectrograph can show are approximately 'same' in physical terms but which in terms of their relation to their context and to the system of which they are part are sharply 'different'. Further, we hope to demonstrate that all sounds or features of sounds must be considered, not as physical absolutes, but rather as shifting points relative to a system of subsystems of types of sounds, whenever we wish to consider their significance in language.

2. SEGMENTS AS QUASI ABSOLUTES

As with the Incidents A, B, and C, segments must be isolated, in order for the analyst to study them in relation to the system and setting of which they are a part. An early task of the linguist in studying speech, then, is to find and record those sound segments which appear to him as 'same' — (as if he were a rather inaccurate physical instrument). He must cut these segments out of a continuum.

One approach is to identify and describe segments in terms of the movements of the vocal organs which have produced them, an approach which I have helped to develop[1] for teaching people to analyze languages which never before have had an alphabet.

Let us suppose, for example, that a person is saying [a...i...a...i]. As we see the tongue and jaw rising and then lowering, we can observe (or 'hear') that there is a point at which the mouth is closest to complete closure during [i] and farthest from

---

[1] (a) *Phonetics: A Critical Analysis of Phonetic Theory and a Technic for the Practical Description of Sounds* (Ann Arbor, University of Michigan Press, 1943), 42-55, 107-120; (b) *Phonemics: A Technique for Reducing Languages to Writing* (Ann Arbor, University of Michigan Press, 1947), 9-11, 29, 30, 68-70, 73-77.

closure during [a]. At each of these points, we can identify (or posit) the center of a segment. It is not possible for us, however, to identify accurately the borders[2] between these segments since the movements slur from one to the other; nor is it necessary for us to do so for linguistic purposes. Rather we choose a symbol, one for each trough or crest of such movement, and tentatively define such a phonetic symbol by the characteristics of the sound, as if it were stationery at the crest or trough of movement, plus— where it seems especially important to communication — its on-glide and off-glide. In the event that two or more parts of the vocal apparatus are moving simultaneously, only one segment is postulated when they reach crest and/or trough simultaneously.

Now, in thus segmenting speech there is a margin of error such that an observer in a new language might fail to detect slight but semantically important differences of quality between two varieties, let us say of [i], yet this margin of error is not sufficiently great to prevent starting the analysis from these data, whereas our analytical procedures are designed to eliminate the errors at a later stage. Needing emphasis here is rather the fact that by this technique we get our absolutes — or because of the margin of error, I shall call them quasi absolutes — to be studied in relation to their significance in the culture just as the action of the jeep driver in the initial illustration is an 'absolute' to be so studied.

3. RELATION OF QUASI-ABSOLUTE SEGMENTS TO STRUCTURAL POSITION IN A SEQUENCE

We turn now to an illustration of a quasi-absolute sound for which it may prove wise to use two cultural interpretations. Take, for example, the segment [u], during which the air stream is coming from the lungs, past the vibrating vocal cords, into the mouth, without friction there, over the top part of the tongue (raised high and fairly back in the mouth), and out between pursed lips. Note, for example, that the [u] of *boot* or *who* might be called 'same' as the first sound in *wick* since all the conditions are fulfilled which were referred to — namely, the air is coming out from the lungs, past the vibrating vocal cords, into the mouth without friction there, over the top part of the raised tongue, and out between pursed lips. Nevertheless, in terms of the procedures by which I for one operate, the [u] of *boot* and the [u] of *wick* are handled as phonemically distinct, not because of their phonetic or absolute differences but because of their structural relationships.

Now if a person speaks only languages in which *w* so occurs, he may be tempted to inquire, "Why is there any problem here? Why isn't the first sound of *wick* simply '*w*'?" But if one has worked with languages such as, for example, Mazatec[3] of Southern Mexico, the answer is that culturally it will simply not do to assume that

---

[2] For a somewhat different view, see B. Bloch, *Language* 24 (1948), 12-13.

[3] K.L. Pike and E.V. Pike, *Internatl. J. Am. Ling.* 13 (1947), 84-87.

presyllabic [u] is a *w*, since ears accustomed to English will there hear as a *w* the kind of a sound which actually is functioning in that language as a vowel (in that it carries the significant tone as other vowels do, and oftentimes in other parts of the grammar where a vocalic suffix does not follow it, even English speakers would hear it as a vowel). The question must be raised therefore, as to how we can decide for a language hitherto unknown, whether such a sound is to be considered a consonantal *w* or a vocalic *u*.

The answer in terms of linguistic relativity is that one must study the relationship of these sounds to the structural positions in which they occur in the particular language, just as the jeep driver had to be studied in terms of his motives and the cultural setting. Just as driver C was in the class of heroes who storm pillboxes and charge trenches, whereas driver A is in a class with robbers and forgers, so in English the [u] of *boot* is in the class with (that is, occurring in the same pattern as) the [æ] of *bat*, and the [i] of *beet*; whereas the [u] of *wick* is in the class with (occurring in the same pattern as) the [s] of *sick*, the [k] of *kick*, the [n] of *nick*, and the [l] of *lick*. It is this parallelism of cultural function (distributional grouping), and not the quasi-absolute nature of the sound itself, which may lead us to treat the [u] of *wick* and the [u] of *boot* as structurally different.

The structural element which is to be noticed here is perhaps the fact that the [u] of *boot* constitutes the center of a syllable, whereas the [u] of *wick* constitutes the margin of a syllable. The identification of syllables is still highly complex and must differ greatly from language to language; no 'absolute' definition of a syllable is adequate, since even here linguistic relativity enters, in that a syllable must be defined afresh[4] for each language in terms of the relationships of the internal elements of that particular language. Persons who do not adopt this point of view might try to treat segments like [u] and [i] as absolutes, and hence *wick* might in their phonemic system be written as /u'iik/, while *yo-yo* might be written as /'iouiou/, or *woo* as /u'uu/, *rotary* as /ə'outəəii/, *aurora borealis* as /əə'əəə bəəii'ælis/, *stirrer* as /st'əəəə/, etc.[5]

(Intertwined with this problem is another: the possible necessity for a phoneme of syllabicity.[6] Instead of using separate consonant and vowel symbols for /y/ and /i/, for example, the same symbol *i* could be used for both, with a syllabic marker under it every time it is the peak of a syllable — not occasionally only, and not replaced by a stress mark on stressed syllables only.[7]

A second complication is the resultant desirability of a set of quasi-absolute phonetic terms definable without reference to sequence and without reference to a particular language system, as distinct from the relative terms defined operationally, or defined afresh in relation to the sequences and system of the particular language

---

[4] K.L. Pike, *Phonemics*, 60*b*, 65, 90*b*, 128-130, 144-149, 181.
[5] Cf. (a) C.F. Hockett, *Language* 18 (1942), 11; (b) Jakobson, Fant, and Halle, *Preliminaries to Speech Analysis: The Distinctive Features and Their Correlates* (=*Tech. Rept.* 13) (Massachusetts Institute of Technology, 1952), 20, 22, 44.
[6] (a) L. Bloomfield, *Language* (New York, Henry Holt, 1933), 92, 121-122; (b) reference 4, p. 141a.
[7] See reference 5(b), pp. 20, 22, 44.

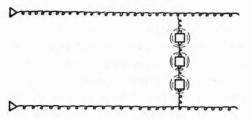

Fig. 1(a). Three weights, not quite at a state of rest, suspended between springs, illustrate three level tones in a tone language.

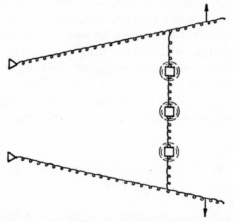

Fig. 1(b). When the supporting springs are spread apart, the weights are spread. Similarly, when a person speaks emphatically the tones may be farther apart.

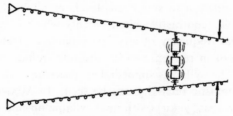

Fig. 1(c). A quiet speaking mood may bring the tones closer together.

being studied. For a pair of such quasi-absolute terms I use vocoid and contoid;[8] for the relative terms, I use vowel and consonant operationally defined.[9] It seems to me that such an approach would help Jakobson, Fant, and Halle in handling 'vowels' sometimes as essentially voiced[10] but at other times voiceless — as in whis-

[8] K.L. Pike, *Phonetics* (especially the 1944 lithoprinted edition), 78-79, 140-147; reference 4, pp. 5-8, 13-24.
[9] Reference 4, pp. 136 (footnote), 128-130.
[10] Reference 5(b) (see, now, Fig. 12 in the second printing, May, 1952, for Comanche voiceless vowels).

pered or unvoiced vowels, whether phonemic or nonphonemic, which would by their principle definition not come into a vowel classification at all. Other less apparent consequences follow from the same general approach).

A similar problem of structure forces us to treat the [h] of *heap* as a phonemic unit by itself, whereas the puff of breath following the [k] of *keep*, although quite similar (in absolute terms) to the [h] of *heap*, must be treated as just a part of the [k]. In fact, English speakers are likely to be completely unaware of the existence of that puff of breath in *keep* which is so similar to the [h] of *heap*.

In languages other than English the 'same' segment sequence [k] plus [h] could be culturally as different from [k] by itself as murder is from heroism. Thus, for example, in Mazatec — to which I have referred earlier — [ki] (plus tones 4-3) means 'he went', but [khi] (plus tones 4-3) means 'he writes'. The reason for the difference between the cultural interpretations of the same sequence in English and Mazatec is again linguistic relativity; in the one language, English [k] plus a puff of breath functions as a single unit, just like [s] in *seep*, or [l] in *leap*, etc., whereas in the Mazatec, the sequence [k] plus [h] functions like sequences such as [hk], [sk], [nk], [k], and so on and hence as two independently variable structural units in sequence.

4. RELATION OF QUASI-ABSOLUTE SEGMENTS TO NEIGHBORING ITEMS IN A SEQUENCE

Linguistic relativity for the interpretation of segments is relevant not only in reference to structural, functional positions in the sequence but also in relation to the specific individual sounds which precede and follow. The clearest situation in which this can be seen is in relation to significant levels of pitch. Let us suppose that a certain language signifies contrastive pitch heights which carry different meanings with them; the physical frequency of any one syllable is irrelevant since a syllable is linguistically high, not in reference to its absolute frequency, but in reference to the relative height of the syllables immediately preceding and following it. Here, most clearly of all, linguistic relativity can be seen. In Mixtec, for example, there are three such levels so that [yuku] (with final syllable on mid pitch) means "mountain" but [yukú] (with final syllable on high pitch) means 'ox-yoke', whereas [yukù] (with final syllable low) means 'brush'. If the speaker happens to be speaking in a high tone of voice, his pitches which are phonemically low may, absolutely, be higher than those pitches which are phonemically high when speaking in a low tone of voice. Note, for example, Fig. 1(a), in which we can assume that three weights tied together with springs are in turn suspended between springs; the weights are not quite at rest, so there is some slight variation in their position. In addition to this slight variation, however, there may be much wider variation in accordance with various stresses; the weights may be pulled farther apart (Fig. 1(b)), or they may come closer together (Fig. 1(c)), or they may be raised (Fig. 1(d)), or by a sudden stress at one point the relative intervals may be affected (Fig. 1(e)). The important factor is that the three are still separated, the one from the other, by relative height. With tones, this separation is determined by the relation of the pitch of one syllable to the pitch of neighboring syllables, so that if two syllables succeed one another and the second is the higher of the two, then (other things being equal, in a two-tone language with unconditioned level tones) the second will be phonemically high and the first phonemically low.

In English we have a pitch system (which is not very well known outside linguistic circles), in which by four levels[11] of relative contrastive pitch we can describe a large percentage of the significant elements of the pitch of the voice. Note, for example, beginning with the lowest of these four: *yes* (4-3), *well* (4-2), and *who?* (4-1). We can transpose these four to a high key, or to a low key, and preserve the same relationships; thus, for example, a poem such as "Mary Had a Little Lamb" can be whistled in two keys, in the one with wide intervals and in the other with narrow intervals.

(It may prove important to engineers who use such materials that they should note that the four pitches referred to are relevant only on certain syllables, i.e. on key points, or contour points.[12] Otherwise they may try to analyze the pitch of a text with equal importance given to the pitch of each syllable. The result is likely to be highly unconvincing. Bolinger, for example, by spectrographic analysis of a few phrases shows[13] that a sequence of several syllables may rise through a series of small steps on many levels, in such a way that four phonemic levels appear to him completely inadequate for representing the structural facts of intonation; it seems to me that no other result is possible from a starting assumption which tends to give equal weight to all syllables.)

Relativity applies ultimately to consonants and vowels as well as to pitches. Thus, for example, a sound [h] will be interpreted as a consonant in an ordinary utterance of *The hat is on the table*, but it will be interpreted as a vowel when all the surrounding sounds are whispered, as in the whispered word "Pat" in the whispered sentence, *I saw Pat yesterday*. A sound must be interpreted relative to the general style, as indicated by a sequence of sounds before it or before and after it.

A definition of vowels by phonetic absolutes would lead to difficulty if, as one of its identifying characteristics, the vowel is assumed to include vibration of the vocal cords; in whispered vowels, there is no such vibration. On the other hand, a phonetic semi-absolute definition of vowels without reference to vibration of the

---

[11]   K. L. Pike, *The Intonation of American English* (Ann Arbor, University of Michigan Press, 1945); for these materials applied pedagogically for foreign speakers see publications of the English Language Institute, 1942, 1943, or later.

[12]   Reference 11, especially pp. 26-30; the contour points are symbolized in that volume by the numerals which are placed directly under the pertinent syllables; the solid line symbolism is easier to read, and hence useful for certain pedagogical purposes (pp. 41-42), but brings in a distortion (p. 43) which implies, incorrectly, an equal structural importance for the pitch of each syllable.

[13]   D. L. Bolinger, *Word* 7 (1951), 201-203, 208.

vocal cords might lead to considerable embarrassment since then [h] (of *hat*) in English would presumably turn out to be a vowel. The way out of this dilemma is to treat vowels not as phonetic semi-absolutes but as members of a system in which the system as a whole can be modified as in 'whisper'; thus in speech aloud the criterion of voicing separates [h] from vowels — and in addition the criterion of structural position in the syllable makes [h] a consonant, even without reference to voicing. Then when speech is whispered, the second criterion of structural function

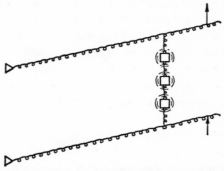

Fig. 1(d). Excitement may raise all the tones, but the system as a system remains the same in spite of absolute changes. The ABSOLUTE position is irrelevant. A vowel system may have similar displacements and detection criteria must in such instances be relative rather than absolute.

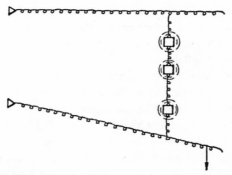

Fig. 1(e). Sudden force at one point may displace one weight more than the others. Tones, too, may be unevenly affected by interfering factors.

still separates a consonantal [h] from a whispered vowel even though as a semi-absolute the whispered vowel is phonetically similar to the [h].

(In reference to the use of the phonetic term vocoid versus the structural term vowel, as suggested previously, an [h] and a so-called 'whispered vowel' might be the same vocoid, whereas the 'voiced vowel' would be a different vocoid; on the other hand, a certain 'voiceless vowel' and a comparable 'voiced vowel' in a particular language might — in different styles or in different positions — be structurally the same vowel.)

Nor is whisper the only style change which can affect a segmental system as a

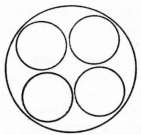

Fig. 2(a).   Four small balloons inside a large balloon illustrate the way in which four level tones in a tone language may constitute a tone system which more or less fills the available 'space' or total range of pitch of the voice at a particular time and in a particular style.

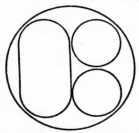

Fig. 2(b).   If, in a particular phonetic environment, two of the tones fuse into one, the resultant entity is still distinct from the second pair and fills the place of the first pair. Such a possibility is difficult to demonstrate for tone, but in vowels it is called a kind of neutralization.

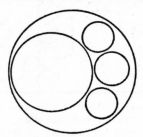

Fig. 2(c).   Under different special surroundings one tone may take over more of the available range [cf. Fig. 1(e)].

Fig. 2(d).   Under further special conditions (like a block between the balloons) the nature of the tone may be affected by extra factors; for example, a glottal stop (the sharp closure of the vocal cords) following a tone often affects its height or gliding direction or speed.

whole. Note, for example, those quasi-absolutes which culturally are vowels in the spoken sentence, '*Johnny came home yesterday*' and the different quasi-absolutes when the same sentence is sung.

Similarly, the quasi-absolutes differ markedly; but the system as such remains the same, in relativistic structural terms, when a relatively high general tongue position gives a clear or child-like quality to all the vowels, or when a relatively low tongue position gives a 'hollow' tone to the vowels, or when a relatively back tongue position gives a 'choked up' quality to the vowels, or when a relatively front general tongue position gives a "lisping" or foreign character to the vowels, or when special faucalized arytenoidal (?) trillization gives a quality of distant ventriloquism.

It should be emphasized that such differences are not differences between separate speakers only[14], but are differences used by the same speaker at different times.[15] For example, in talking to children, the relatively high tongue position may be used; in protest, a relatively back tongue position may be used; in singing, a fronter position may be deliberately assumed; in some kinds of solemn public address, a lowered tongue position or an open throat quality may be assumed. For all of these style changes the phoneme variants become numerous and difficult to analyze in isolation, but rather must be handled in terms of their relation to surrounding segments in the large sub-system or style of which they are a part.

Even within any one style, the articulatory movements producing two sounds

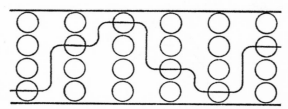

Fig. 3.   This figure represents a sequence of syllables, proceeding from left to right. Each vertical column of circles symbolizes a single syllable, with each circle representing one of the four potential tones of the particular language's tone system, any tone of which might have been chosen for pronunciation during that particular syllable. The actual pitch-path selected for one particular sentence is symbolized by the solid line.

[14]   (a) M. Joos first pointed out to me the differences between separate speakers (see, now, *Acoustic Phonetics* [Baltimore, Linguistic Soc. Am., 1948], pp. 59-65). It has seemed necessary to me, however, to go much further, and to make *all* quality relative, (1) to account for the types of data given here, and (2) to allow a single formula to cover qualitative analysis as well as the pitch analysis which I, with many others, had already been handling as relative. (b) For relative quality see reference 4, pp. 66, 105; (c) for relative pitch, see K.L. Pike, *Tone Languages* (University of Michigan Press, Ann Arbor, 1948), pp. 4, 20. (d) For further differences between speakers, see Potter, Kopp, and Green, *Visible Speech* (D. Van Nostrand Company, Inc., New York, 1947), 45, 272-280; and (e) G.E. Peterson, *Language* 27 (1951), 544, 552.

[15]   A small degree of individual variation is charted by G.E. Peterson and H.L. Barney, in *J. Acoust. Soc. Am.* 24 (1952), 177-178. It would be very helpful if similar systematic chartings were made of a much wider set of deliberate style changes. For spectrograms during whisper, see reference 14(d), pp. 314, 321, 322; also, for speech defects, pp. 329-342.

in sequence tend to slur into one another or tend to anticipate one another. For this reason, certain sounds at first appear to the investigator to be 'different' (as quasi-absolutes) but must be treated as phonemically 'same' since, relative to the system, they have the same functional value, whereas the absolute differences are merely accidental ones of environment and not significant ones of signalling value. For example, the [a] preceding [i] in [ai] ends differently from that which precedes [a] in [au]. These conditioned differences (called allophonic differences, and the segments themselves called allophones of the phoneme) must, because of their relationship to the system, be treated as phonemic 'sames'. Nevertheless, in listening to speech and in detecting the formal signals of meaning, the segments which the listener actually hears are the allophones of the phonemes — not some platonic abstraction; it is these quasi-absolutes which the beginning phonetician must record, and recognize, and interpret as members of significant units of sound.

(Just as in Fig. 1 the weights were not quite at rest, but varied around a statistical norm, so each allophone represents a scattering of slightly different variants consisting of different pronunciations each time the sentence containing it is repeated. The absolute sound, the single event, is frequently ignored by the practical phonetician when the differences seem to him trivial; as a result, his allophonic record may not be absolute, but may be rather quasi-absolute, with a range of tolerance within which deviation is tentatively left unsymbolized — subject to careful checking by later phonemic procedures.)

5. RELATION OF QUASI-ABSOLUTE SEGMENTS TO A RELATIVISTIC SYSTEM OF RELATIVISTIC SUB-SYSTEMS OF UNITS

Just as observers interpreted the killing of the man on the bridge (in our initial illustration) in reference to events preceding and following, and also interpreted it in reference to the whole cultural system of kinds of things which can be done at certain places in the culture, so a quasi-absolute segment is interpreted culturally, that is phonemically, in reference not only to sounds preceding and following it but also in reference to the whole potential set of phonetically related sounds (i.e., having one or more articulatory component in common) which might have been pronounced in that position, and in reference to other sets of phonetically different quasi-absolute segments which might also come in that or different positions.

(One of the problems which has bothered linguists for a long time, for example, is that the [h] of *hat* and the *ng* of *sing* are, in terms of their structural position, mutually exclusive in their distribution, with [h] syllable-initial, but *ng* syllable-final; elsewhere, sounds which are mutually exclusive in their structural occurrence are, if phonetically similar, likely to be considered members of a single phonemic unit since it is assumed that the distributional differences are to be correlated with a 'causal' relationship of slurring into their environment. Here, however, the phys-

Fig. 4.   A phonological system may include many sub-systems (of stops, nasals, vowels, tones, etc.). These combine in a hierarchy of systems within systems. The dotted lines suggest that there is some interpretation or overlapping of sub-systems of sounds or of phonological with grammatical sub-systems.

iological characteristics of [h] and *ng* are so different that it seems improbable that a mere environmental slurring would cause [h] to become *ng* or *ng* to become [h], or for the one to be a member of a phonemic unit of which the other was a member. The solution to this problem, too, seems to rest with linguistic relativity in that [h], is a member of a set of phonemes which have in common the continuous escape of an air stream through the mouth and the lack of vocal cord vibration during their production, whereas *ng* is a member of a set of quasi-absolute segments identified by the escape of air through the nose — but not the mouth — while the vocal cords are vibrating [in speech aloud]. Now other members of these two sets can be shown to constitute distinct phonemes inasmuch as it can be easily demonstrated that culturally the one is a signal independent of the other and that they are not dependent upon environment for differences, since each can be shown to be separately a signaller of meaning; note, for example, that *cuff* ending with [f] contrasts with [m] in the 'same' phonetic environment in *come*; also [s] versus [n] in *case* versus *cane*. Since the labial and alveolar fricatives [f] and [s] are in contrast with the labial and alveolar nasals [m] and [n], we may assume that the fricative and nasal analogous set [h] and *ng* should similarly be considered to be in contrast, even though the evidence is indirect — i.e., an analogous place in contrastive sub-systems of sounds.)

We return now to the problem of tone which illustrates more easily than anything else the nature of linguistic relativity. We have previously discussed the fact that tones are relative one to another in the sequence since high or low has significance

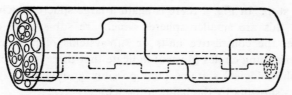

Fig. 5. At each moment a segment of speech represents a complex choice from many sub-systems. The two paths through the cylinder suggest that numerous types of choices within each sub-system are made simultaneously — e.g., tonal and consonantal or vocalic. This figure combines Fig. 3 with Fig. 4.

only in relation to the immediate context; but there is, as we have stated in discussing segments, another element to be considered, namely, the relation of one tone to the total number and type of tones which might occur in a particular place in a particular context. This potential is determined by the system and relates the one tone to that system.

Let us try another model (see Fig. 2(a)). We assume that within a sphere there are four balloons filled with gas. In such a model the balloons may — if the pressures are adequate — more or less fill the space within the sphere, but not overlap. Just so the potential range of variation of any tone in absolute terms is conditioned by its relationship to the total number of tones in the system, and each tone must be kept structurally apart, subject to the penalty of confusing the signals.

Occasionally special problems arise in that in certain environments two segmental phonemes fuse into one (in so-called neutralization, or in what I call a fusiphoneme). The diagram would then have to be modified (Fig. 2(b)) such that the new fused balloon fills the space approximately occupied by the first two but nevertheless remains distinct from the remaining two. Under a different set of conditions, the pressure in one of the balloons can increase so that it encroaches on the area occupied by the other three (Fig. 2(c)); this perhaps illustrates a situation which may occur when, within the system, the immediate environment affects one member of the system.

A related distortion of the pattern may be caused by interference of elements from different sub-systems of sounds in the same sequence. If, for example, at the beginning or end of a syllable containing tone, the vocal cords are sharply closed together (in a so-called glottal stop), they may force the modification of the pitch contours; note Fig. 2(d), where the square box represents a glottal stop intruding from one sub-system into the pitch system.

I now wish to illustrate by a model how the sequence of absolute pitches is a reflection of a choice from the potential of the system as a whole. In Fig. 3, the potential for the four tones is shown vertically, and the sequence of syllables is shown horizontally. Each syllable may carry one of these tones so that the path of the quasi-absolute pitch in terms relative to the system may be diagrammed as a line connecting the tones chosen from the potential of the system.

We now show a model such as the one of the balloons, but involving more than tone and glottal stop. In Fig. 4 there is again a large sphere which is the total system, but within this are smaller spheres which are sub-systems containing again within themselves the contrastive units or sub-systems of pitch or consonants or vowels. The overlapping circles (dotted) indicate that there is some interpenetration between these phonological systems (and possibly grammatical systems) which is not susceptible to showing by the balloon model.

If now we conceive of speech as a long cylinder (Fig. 5) which simultaneously contains the potentials of the consonant, vowel, and pitch sub-systems, and so on, we can then by dotted lines suggest dimly the way in which the actual speech is a composite of several simultaneous paths selected from the various sets of contrastive sub-system potentials always present. Thus, Fig. 5 combines Fig. 3 with Fig. 4.

6. PROCEDURE

By reference to the preceding models (especially with reference to a modification of Fig. 3), it is possible to demonstrate one of the important analytical techniques. In attempting to determine the number of culturally significant relative pitches in a language, for example, I have set up a 'frame technique'[16] in which a person chooses a sentence such as *I saw X yesterday* and at point *X* he has the speaker successively replace one word with another (e.g., *I saw John yesterday, I saw Bill yesterday, I saw Sam yesterday*). In terms of the model, one is looking for the total potential of distinctive pitch ranges at any one point.

Let us suppose, for example, that the starting sentence has a certain general pitch sequence superimposed upon its syllables (see Fig. 6). Then let us suppose that at point *X* certain substituted monosyllabic words show three deviations from the original pattern, i.e., three additional alternate pitch-paths, each of them lower than the original path at that point, and each of the three persistently (phonemically, or contrastively, or semantically) different from one another. We have by this technique, subject to certain restrictions which eliminate other contextual factors,[17] determined the existence of four phonemic pitch levels in the system.

Thus, phonemic procedure at all stages is designed to help the analyst find the total system potential so that he can see how quasi-absolute elements fit into a total system of potential occurrences of relatively distinct quasi-absolutes (and by related techniques he eliminates the possibility that differences between them are due to irrelevant contextual conditioning).

A theory of linguistic relativity more or less as presented here must also be ap-

---

[16] Published first in K.L. Pike, "Phonemic Work Sheet" (Summer Institute of Linguistics, Siloam Springs, Arkansas [now Glendale, California], 1938); since then, reference 4, pp. 105-115, and reference 14(c) (mimeograph editions, 1943, 1945. See now Ann Arbor, University of Michigan, 1948, especially pp. 48-67).
[17] See reference 14(c), especially pp. 28-31, 49, 52-54, 55-57, 61.

plied to all other phases of linguistics — to the study of morphemes, sentences, meanings, and so on. Evidence for this conclusion I hope to give elsewhere.

In conclusion I would raise certain questions which I am not competent to answer.

(1) Are the segmentation devices used by the engineers comparable in theory to the segmentation procedures of phoneticians?

(2) How far does the equipment produced by the engineer take account of the structural 'positions' of sounds rather than merely sequences of sounds?

(3) How far are the present machines equipped to handle purely relative elements, such as units of pitch sequence?

(4) Does this equipment take account of the total system of a particular language such that each language is treated one at a time, in terms of internal relative contrasts, rather than all languages being treated at once?

(5) How do the machines take account of the drastic relative shift of a whole vowel system — as in whisper, song, baby talk, or hoarse throat?

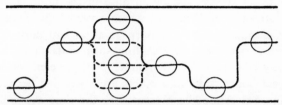

Fig. 6. The linguist studying an unknown language must 'crack its code' — he must find, for example, how many tones (if any) it has. In one technique (or set of operations) for doing so, the linguist selects arbitrarily some sentence, and notes roughly the path of the pitch throughout the sentence. He then has the informant replace a word at one point in the sentence with other words at the SAME PLACE. The number of alternate pitch-paths so discovered permits him to find the potential of the system (Fig. 3). By supporting techniques he discovers any conditioned or irrelevant variation about the norm — i.e., the tolerance within the system itself (see Fig. 1(a)).

(6) How are machines built so as to recognize as 'same' the allophones of a phoneme differing according to the environment in which they occur?

(7) As for psychology, how far can present studies explain the way in which the brain handles these same problems?

MEANING AND HYPOSTASIS*

For the past seven years I have been working on the development of a behavioremic theory in order to explore relationships between the structure of speech and the structure of nonverbal activity. As the material developed, it became increasingly evident that the theory would have many implications for the understanding of problems of meaning in speech and of purpose in the nonlinguistic behavior. At every point in the structure of behavior, whether verbal or nonverbal, components of value, meaning, significance, and/or purpose arise, and must be included within the conceptual framework used for handling such units of activity as are under consideration at any one moment. A number of these elements have already appeared in the project under way,[1] and others are scheduled for inclusion in a later chapter on meaning but cannot be presented in the time available for this paper. One particular crucial problem which has appeared in the first published findings, however, may be summarized for discussion at this Round Table.

What is the relationship between the meaning of a word as deduced by the lexicographer, and the meaning of the word which might be reported by a native speaker of that language? Is there any structural relationship between this problem and that of determining the relationship between the purpose of a nonverbal act as defined by the techniques of observation of the cultural anthropologist and the purpose of the same act as stated by anthropologically-untrained native participants of that culture?

We start by suggesting that the stated purpose of an act — stated by native participants — is by no means irrelevant to the culture; on the contrary, the verbalized purposes of a community are assumed here to be highly relevant to the activity of that community, whether or not these purposes are the same as those deduced by anthropologically-trained observers. Similarly, we suggest that the meanings verbalized by native speakers are relevant to their verbal and nonverbal behavior at SOME point in the system of behavior, whether or not these naïve analyses are 'cor-

* Monograph 8 (Georgetown University, The Institute of Languages and Linguistics, 1955), 134-141. Reprinted by permission.
[1] Kenneth L. Pike, Language in Relation to a Unified Theory of the Structure of Human Behavior, Preliminary Edition, Part 1 (Glendale, Summer Institute of Linguistics, 1954), e.g., 17b-18, 23a, 24a, 39b, 78b-82, 88, 94-98, 100b-101, 104b-105a, 116-117a, 121, 126b, 132-133, 135b-136a, 150a-151.

rect' from the point of view of the trained linguist. Verbalized purposes or meanings can affect behavior even if the verbalizations are not in a form approved by the technicians. Since such verbalizations both CONSTITUTE part of the activity of the members of a culture, and AFFECT the activity of those persons, the verbalizations must be considered part of the data which should itself be analyzed by the technicians, and the possibility of noncongruence, complete congruence, or partial congruence of the technical and naïve statements of meaning should be allowed for in any theory of meaning or of human behavior as a whole.

For some technical analysts, the meaning of an utterance may be considered as the elicitation by a particular utterance of a particular kind of response, or the meaning may be considered as constituted of a response[2] to such an elicitation of response, provided that he does not assume that the response elicited is always performed by the hearer even though the latter understands the eliciting character of the utterance (i.e., the hearer may deliberately refuse to 'shut the door' in spite of a request that he do so). Elicitation of the response and the response itself has a probability aspect rather than a complete certainty.

The discovery by the analyst of the meaning of such an utterance involves the investigation of its occurrence — or the occurrence of repeated fractions thereof — in various contexts, in order to find in the various contexts the kind of responses which it can be seen to regularly elicit, and which can be predicted for it elsewhere. A competent technician, furthermore, is likely to RETAIN AS PART OF HIS ESSENTIAL DATA certain of these contexts as illustrative of and as productive of the meaning deduced. In addition, he is keenly aware of the fact that any one linguistic item may occur in a variety of contexts, and hence have a variety of variant meanings (variant elicitations-of-response) in these contexts.

For the naïve native speaker of a language, however, 'meaning' almost seems to 'reside in' the words, as a mystic entity apart from their phonemic form, apart from the particular contexts in which they happen to occur at the moment, and apart from the regularity of response which he tacitly reacts to while often unaware of the response-elicitation character of meaning. Words seem to 'mean something' to the native speaker apart from what the words 'are' and it is in part this mystic character which he seeks when he wishes to 'define terms' during an argument, or when he wishes to follow an exposition with understanding.

The discovery of meaning by the native speaker in the large majority of instances — i.e., when he is not 'looking them up' in a dictionary or being taught meanings of certain terms in a class in science, etc. — is done in a manner which leaves him, as an adult, unaware of the process involved by which he reached his conclusions about those meanings. Hence he can be quite convinced of the independent existence of mystic meaning units in a particular language even when he has in fact obtained those meanings by a procedure similar to that of the technician, but with

[2] See, for example, Charles C. Fries, *The Structure of English* (New York, Harcourt Brace, 1952), 65.

mental compilations of contexts rather than written ones. In addition, having made his response-elicitation abstractions from these defining contexts he may have forgotten the contexts in most instances (except, for example, in the rare instances for which he can remember the time when he 'first heard' a particular word), and when pressed he may be able to verbalize, instead, only the generalized abstraction itself which somehow is available to his memory, or for which a crude verbalization can be manufactured on the spot without reference to the particular contexts in his personal history which are behind this capacity. Such a tendency to forget the specific contexts which underlie such a capacity carries with it, however, the tendency, also, to fail to call to mind at such a moment many contexts which would lead the technician to set up multiple meanings for his definition of a term; the naïve product is nonsystematic, and has gaps; it may emphasize one kind of response-elicitation at the expense of another, or lead to the definition of central meanings while ignoring metaphorical meanings, etc., which are also relevant to the usage of a term.

Some linguists have attempted the setting up of a theory of meaning which has in common with that of the naïve speaker the postulating of a 'meaning' which is structurally distinct from, but concomitant with, the forms. Other linguists have taken a sharply different view, attempting to describe forms as units, without including their meanings as essential parts of the definition of these units. In the theory which I am developing, however, I am attempting to keep form and meaning more rigidly joined, as a form-meaning composite, such that no structural unit of meaning as such is postulated apart from or within the lexical form which it accompanies, and no lexical structural unit of form as such is postulated apart from the meaning which constitutes one component of the form-meaning composite. This endeavor is part of a more inclusive view of behavior for which I postulate, exclusively, UNITS WHICH HAVE A MANIFESTATION MODE COMPRISED OF A STRUCTURED PHYSICAL COMPONENT. Every structural unit (emic unit, in my technical terms) postulated for language, in this system, has a physical component as its base; no exceptions are knowingly tolerated. It is this more basic starting point which rules out an eme of meaning as such; a morpheme, or a sentence, is a form-meaning composite, NOT an eme of form plus an eme of meaning (nor an eme of form accompanied by a meaning).[3]

This approach seems to be useful for ordinary speech, but now a special problem arises: What are the emic units of activity of the native speaker by which he does discuss meanings as if they were isolatable, as if he thought they had no physical component? The first part of our solution in such an instance is to assume that a physical component DOES appear in these instances, as well as in those of ordinary speech which have their manifesting contexts, but that here the physical component of the 'meaning' which the native speaker proposes is the combination of his neurological activity as he thinks about or utters the words labelling these meanings, plus

[3]   Cf. Pike, *Language in Relation to a Unified Theory*, 24, 74b, 83a, 96b, 98b, 150b.

the physical activity of uttering the words aloud. The verbal activity constitutes the physical manifestation of these activity units just as verbalization constitutes the physical component of ordinary speech in context, so that no non-embodied emes of meaning need here to be postulated.

The second part of our solution is to point out a further generalized dichotomy in kinds of human activity. One kind of activity is the normal occurrence of an event as part of a sequence of events which it helps comprise; ordinary activity occurs in an appropriate context, as the verbal activity comprised of pronouncing the word *Bill* occurs in context as the subject of the sentence activity *Bill ran home*. A quite different kind of activity is the excising of a part of a sequence of activity from its regular context, and viewing it as an isolated unit; a 'viewing context' or 'viewing frame' may be set up as a special 'holder' of the 'specimen' to be examined; note, for example, that in the preceding sentence the phrase *the word* (*Bill*) served as such a viewing context for the word *Bill*, since in that sentence we specifically wished to accomplish the kind of activity which we were at that moment describing — the taking of an activity (the pronunciation of the word *Bill*) out of its normal stream of activity (its pronunciation in such a sequence as *Bill ran home*) so as to view it as if it were an isolatable item (i.e., in this present context, to talk about the activity of pronouncing *Bill* as if it were 'a thing' which existed in its own right, instead of as one component of a system of speech activity).

Any abstraction of an activity from a normal participant sequence for purposes of viewing it, studying it, mentioning it, analyzing it, listing it, cataloging it, or discussing it as such, we shall call HYPOSTASIS[4] of that activity. The mention of a word is an activity of hypostasis. The formation of a dictionary listing is accomplished by the hypostasis of these forms. The practicing of the passing of a football is the hypostasis, and repetition in hypostasis, of the football-passing activity of a normal game, etc.

The native speaker, in quoting a word out of normal context, is performing an act of hypostasis. If he mentions the MEANING of that word, however, he is doing something further: he is making an abstraction from various contexts of some common phase of the elicitation-response characteristics of those contexts, and is giving to his abstraction a name, or 'label'. The physical manifestation of the label is a component of the abstracting activity and, for that activity, fulfills the kind of function which for the non-abstracting activity of normal speech is played by the physical component of that normal speech. Activity units in which a substitute verbalization for hypostasis defining purposes replaces the verbal activity utilized in normal non-abstracting sequences, we may call 'conceptualized hypostasis' to differentiate it from hypostasis which merely repeats, out of context, an item to study it apart from that context.

The technical analyst in making a listing of terms does so by hypostasic activity;

---

[4] Compare Leonard Bloomfield, "... *hypostasis*, the mention of a phonetically normal speech form", in *Language*, (New York, Henry Holt, 1933), 148.

when he defines these terms, the definition is similarly a conceptualized hypostasis of the elicitation-response data. If, however, he were merely to cite the contexts in which the responses could be observed, without attempting to make up a 'definition' from the data within these contexts, his activity in respect to the abstraction of the elicitation-response contexts would be hypostasis, but not a conceptualized hypostasis.

What, then, is the difference between the activity of the lexicographer and that of the native speaker who mentions meanings? Both of them use conceptualized hypostasis in setting out the statement or definition of meanings, but the native speaker is less likely to understand the significance of defining contexts in general or to preserve an awareness of the particular defining contexts relevant to a particular word — and, to the extent that he does operate theoretically in the same hypostasic or conceptualized-hypostasic manner, does so less systematically.

Applied to nonverbal behavior, this same general outlook helps to clarify the relation of the purpose of a unit of nonverbal activity as deduced by the cultural anthropologist to the purpose of that unit of nonverbal activity as reported by a regular participant in that activity. The description, or 'definition', of a purpose by technician or participant is an activity of conceptualized hypostasis. The technician needs to make his own analysis, his own conceptualized hypostasis of the purpose of a particular unit of activity in a culture. In addition, the technician needs to make an analysis of the purpose of that activity as alleged by the regular participants in that activity. This latter activity by the technician is the act of making a technical conceptualized hypostasis of the naïve conceptualized hypostasis of the regular participant, just as the linguist's description of the meaning-abstracting activity of a naïve speaker is a technical conceptualized hypostasis of the naïve conceptualized hypostasis of the native speaker.

Our generalized analytical and conceptual framework has proved fruitful, in this way, by allowing us to bring into a single theory various items which have troubled both linguists and anthropologists.

SEYMOUR CHATMAN (Wayne University): Professor Pike, I would like to raise a question which I think is also pertinent to the previous talk, and I would welcome Professor Read's comment on the subject. It is my understanding that you consider the terms Bloomfield coined, namely 'sememe' representing lexical-meaning and 'episememe' indicating structural meaning, to be useless.

KENNETH L. PIKE (University of Michigan): You are right. I do not work with the sememe in the Bloomfieldian sense for reasons I have given. I think that Bloomfield is inconsistent at this point. His basic assumption of all linguistics is that in every speech-community there are some forms which are alike or practically alike in form and meaning. However, when he later sets up a sememe as distinct from a morpheme, I think that HE ABANDONS HIS BASIC ASSUMPTION. But I would not say that the term 'sememe' is therefore useless. It is useful in order to discuss the kind of analysis which Bloomfield proposes. However, I would not like to confuse the usefulness of a term with what I think is Bloomfield's inconsistency.

ALLEN WALKER READ (Columbia University): Bloomfield's use of the word sememe has troubled me. It involves dangers which he certainly avoided in his practice. He did not reify his sememe in analytical procedures, and therefore I do not consider the term necessary in his formulations.

TOWARDS A THEORY OF THE STRUCTURE OF HUMAN BEHAVIOR*

For many years my esteemed friend Dr. Manuel Gamio has been attempting to study man through the simultaneous application of the techniques of numerous disciplines. This approach to the study of man within the context of the entire range of activities in which he participates is an emphasis which is essential if one wishes to understand man in order to be of service to him, as Dr. Gamio has devoted many years of his life in the service of the indigenous races of Mexico. It is with great pleasure, therefore, that I write this brief contribution to a volume honoring Dr. Gamio.

The thesis which for the past seven years I have been exploring is the following: that every purposeful activity of man is structured, and that certain basic characteristics are common to every such activity, so that it should be possible to develop a theory and a technique which would pass without a jar from the study of the structure of one kind of activity of man to that of any other kind. Ideally, this would result in one basic theory of structure, one basic set of terms, and one basic methodology which could be applied to the analysis of language, the analysis of ritual behavior, the analysis of sports, the analysis of occupational activity, or even to the processes of thought itself. In 1954 I published the first part of a detailed development of this thesis in a work entitled *Language in Relation to a Unified Theory of the Structure of Human Behavior*.[1] In this present article I shall highlight a few of the general principles underlying the detailed presentation given in that volume.

WAVES VERSUS PARTICLES

In order to apply to the analysis of all human behavior, a theory must on the one hand take account of the apparent irreconcilability between the fact that a behavior event is often a physical continuum with no gaps in which the movement is stopped, but on the other hand must take account of the fact that human beings react to their own behavior and to that of other individuals as if it were segmented into discrete chunks.

* *Estudios Antropológicos Publicados en Homenaje al Doctor Manuel Gamio* (México, 1956), 659-671. Reprinted by permission.
[1] Part I, Preliminary Edition; published by the Summer Institute of Linguistics, Box 870, Glendale 5, California.

In order to treat this contrast in the present theory, we may first state that for every purposive unit of human behavior there is an underlying physical base which constitutes this continuum — as in the phrase *I know John* there is no pause between any of the sounds, or as the motions of a conductor's baton may constitute for some time a continuous motion without pause.

Next, we note that this continuum is not a steady non-fluctuating one, but that there are in it some 'waves' of activity. These activity waves are waves of physical motion; there is a flow and ebb of activity, ups and downs of movement, steady states and change states of motion. Within these waves of motion one can detect nuclei (the steady state or the peak of a motion), and troughs of movement (which are the 'change points' or transition areas where one activity is changed to another, or the relatively relaxed points within the continuum of activity). Thus, as the conductor moves his baton, the beat movement constitutes the peak of such a wave, and the trough is constituted of the transition movement between beats. Similarly, a syllable is the peak of a movement, and the break between syllables is a trough between two such waves of movement.

There may be small waves superimposed upon larger waves of movement, furthermore, as ripples may be superimposed upon a large wave of water; a consonant or a vowel is a small wave of movement superimposed upon the larger wave of the syllable, or movements of the eyes may be ripples upon the larger wave of the movement of the head as it adjusts to see some object, and so on.

In addition to this basic point of view, however, the theory indicates that when people react to human behavior in their own culture they react to it as if it were a sequence of separate particles of activity; the actor in such activity and the native perceiver of this activity both tend to ignore or to be unaware of the transition states between the waves of activity. For this reason, a purely physical analysis of human behavior may analyse it as comprised of waves, but a cultural analysis of human behavior must treat it as comprised of particles — discrete behavioral entities. Our theory combines these two by retaining a physical base as postulated for every human event, and, in addition, a discrete structuring of that event in terms of smaller unitary events. The label which we shall apply to any such particle of activity is 'eme' or 'emic unit'.[2] Emes occur not only in speech but in nonverbal activity of all kinds, so that as one basic assumption of our theory, designed to be applicable to all kinds of human behavior, we accept the principle of the simultaneous presence of movement waves and of experiential particles in the physical and cultural data.

STRUCTURE IN RELATION TO NATIVE REACTION TO IT

In the discussion of particles of activity as experienced by the participants in that activity, we were acting upon a further assumption which we now wish to make

[2]   Deriving the terms from the latter part of the world 'phoneme' or the phrase 'phonemic unit'.

more explicit: the emic analysis of the emic units of human behavior must analyse that behavior in reference to the manner in which native participants in that behavior react to their own behavior and to the behavior of their colleagues. This principle implies that no adequate analysis of the structuring of human behavior can be made upon a physical basis only, since the physical basis can deal only with continua of various kinds without reference to the fact that natives (in many instances at least) react to that behavior as if it were comprised of discrete particles.

In addition, this point of view — that structure must be analysed in relation to native reaction to behavior — must be extended until purpose is included within the matrix of the data which is used to arrive at conclusions as to the nature of that structure, and must be included as one of the relevant structural components in many of the definitions of the basic units of the structure. Purpose, within this theory, may be rephrased as implying 'elicitation of response' and response may be rephrased as implying 'reactions to elicitation of response'. In reference to language, for example, Professor Charles C. Fries has insisted "the question itself is part of the frame in which the answer as an utterance operates".[3]

In other words, the analysis of the response to a question cannot usefully be treated without reference to the fact that it is correlated with the prior occurrence of the question which elicits that response, whether the response be verbal or nonverbal. Similarly, in a football game, the feinting of a player, as a device to deceive the opposite side, is an elicitation of a response which will put his opponents in a disadvantageous position; the feint elicits a deliberate reaction.

The studying of response is important, furthermore, because only within a framework of the elicitation of response and of the response itself can one determine the points in the physical continuum at which there are emic breaks. That is, only within such a framework can one determine what are the discrete particles from the point of view of the participants themselves. The technique used is one of substitution frames, in which, within a large sequence of activity, one item can be withdrawn and another put in its place, in such a fashion that the response elicited differs for the two instances. Thus, the sentence *Shut the door* and the sentence *Shut the drawer* elicit different responses, and at the same time indicate that there is a break in the sequence before the words *door* and *drawer* which can be assumed to be an emic transition between emic units.

In order to cover all of behavior, it is convenient — at the early stages of analysis, at least — to equate purpose and meaning. Within the analysis of verbal material one will usually speak of the meaning of an emic unit, whereas in the analysis of nonverbal activity one will usually speak of the purpose of that event. Purpose and meaning are here treated alike to the extent that both of them have reference to the elicitation by a participant of a reaction from another participant, or the predictable reaction of the second participant to his interpretation of the purposes of the first participant.

[3]   *The Structure of English* (New York, 1952), 165-169.

PREDICTABILITY OF DIFFICULTIES IN ACCULTURATION

Every person is emically structured. He has grown up in an environment where the responses elicited from him by his colleagues have developed in him a set of responses to certain continua as if those continua were divided in a certain discrete way, and as if those discrete responses were related to a total system of such responses. This is an essential part of the structure of human behavior. If this were not a part of the structure of human behavior, no person would be able to elicit a reaction from another person, since the second person would be unable to understand the signals of the first; the first would not be able to elicit responses, and the second would not be able to give adequate responses.

As a result of this structuring, a community has developed useful and appropriate cultural norms of reaction of many different types, when within the limits of appropriate alternatives. When an individual in one community attempts to respond to an individual of a different community, however, a great deal of confusion may result: the activity which in the first community would elicit one response might in the second community elicit a very different response. This is most easily seen in such situations as that which I have encountered, for example, when waving good-bye in an American fashion to a Spanish-speaking friend — the friend has thought I was calling him over for an interview, since the calling gesture of the Spanish speaker from Latin America, and the gesture for waving good-bye in my own culture are sufficiently alike in their physical characteristics to be interpreted by a member of the other culture as constituting the quite different unit from his own culture.

The detailed clashing of two emic systems, however, may be much more subtle. In English, for example, the vowels of the word *mate* and *met* may occur in the same context (between the sounds *m* and *t*), such that the words which they in part constitute are distinct from the point of view (i.e. the response) of the English hearer, and for this reason the two vowels likewise come to constitute in English two discrete emic entities. Two Spanish vowels which are somewhat like the two English vowels of *mate* and *met* may be found in the Spanish words *pelo* ('hair') and *perro* ('dog'). In Spanish, however, the response elicitation of the two vowels is quite different from the response elicited by the somewhat similar English vowels, since the two vowels of Spanish are not contrastive but constitute just one emic unit in that language (i.e. just one Spanish phoneme).

In such a situation, one can predict with a very high degree of probability that the person coming from a system containing a pair of emically undifferentiated vowels to a language containing a physically similar pair of emically differentiated vowels will have a great deal of difficulty in responding to this emic contrast, precisely because he has trained himself by millions of practice sessions[4] to ignore the distinction. The Spanish speaker could be expected to have difficulty, therefore, in

[4] That is, by conversations over a long period of time, each of which constitutes a practice session in responding to the elicitation.

learning to discriminate the words *mate* and *met*. Some years ago, in one country in Latin America, for example, I was lecturing on English pronunciation to over one hundred teachers of high-school English and it was difficult to find a single one of them who did not have great difficulty in discriminating these sounds (and, along with these, *mit* and *mat*), even though some of these teachers spoke English fluently.

It is only through an emic analysis of the sounds or of the activities of a community that one can predict the difficulties which members of that community will have in passing to another community to learn its response patterns. But it is on the basis of such considerations that the best techniques for the teaching of foreign languages have recently been developed, especially under the leadership of Professor Fries of Michigan. He insists that textbooks must be prepared separately for every uni-directional language situation — that is, not only for every pair of languages, but for every pair of languages in reference to the direction in which the learning is to take place, so that a textbook for teaching English to Spanish speakers might be quite inadequate if it were translated and used as a textbook to teach Spanish to English speakers, since the emic problems met may not be reciprocal. Certain elements may rather require much greater practice in the one direction than in the other, just as a Spanish speaker must be provided a great deal of practice material to learn to differentiate *mate* and *met*, whereas the English speaker does not need practice to keep from making erroneous responses of a severe nature in pronouncing the corresponding vowels of *pelo* and *perro*.

It is hoped that in the future similar predictions of emic clash and consequent problems of acculturation can be made not only in respect to language learning but also in respect to acculturation in the field of etiquette, or of ritual, or of law, commerce, and so on. A great deal of such prediction may already have been made by anthropologists, but if this theory could be developed in sufficient detail, such prediction might be established in a more systematic fashion and with a higher degree of reliability.

SPOT AND CLASS

One of the basic principles which was developed for our theory, and which has made it possible to go much further than has previously been considered possible by some persons, is the setting up of the correlation between 'spot' and 'class' as an integrated unit. By 'spot' we mean the place at which substitution can occur, just as above we used the phrases *Shut the door* and *Shut the drawer* to show the substitution of the one word for the other. By this theory, all behavior is considered to contain significant spots at which behavior occurrences may be found. At each spot a series of alternatives is possible, so that if no such series of alternatives is to be found in any particular place within a continuum of behavior, it is assumed that no emic spot is covered by that particular area.

The spot may be one in which large emic units occur, or one in which small emic units occur. Smaller spots may in turn occur in sequence in a larger spot, in a hierarchical progression similar to the manner in which ripples can occur on waves within one of the physical continua. In a football game, for example, there are spots for the occurrence of plays, and at the spot for any one play there are a variety of possibilities, such as passing, kicking or running; where alternatives for such plays exist, an emic spot is present. A certain sequence of spots makes up, as a whole, the larger spot for a series of 'downs'; several such series of downs, under certain conditions, fill a larger spot, during which one side has control of the ball, etc.

The particular list of items which are appropriate to a spot constitutes, by virtue of its occurrence in that spot, an emic class of items which is pertinent to the language and not a mere arbitrary aggregation of the analyst. It is this appropriateness for occurrence in such a spot which constitutes one of the criteria for an emic class of items — although the actual delineation of such a class has to take account of numerous other criteria which are not relevant to the discussion here.

The spot-class combination, moreover, constitutes a correlation which, as such, may be considered an emic unit of a type related to but different from a particular emic event by itself. It is the development of this concept which constitutes one of the most useful parts of the theory and one of the greatest departures from traditional analysis. I am acquainted with no other major attempt to show how verbal and nonverbal culture could be integrated into a single theory. Probably the reason for this lack is the fact that persons who have wished to accomplish this goal have in general started from the point of view of attempting to find the cultural correlates of the phoneme and morpheme, which form a very difficult starting point for such integration. Beginning with the spot-class unit, however, this transfer of technique begins in a much more simple fashion, and in a way which can be appreciated with much less difficulty by persons outside of the linguistic field.

The very great advantage of the spot-class start is that, with it, one is able to by-pass the necessity for a *minimum* unit in the early stages of the analysis. At any point within behavior, whether the behavior event under consideration be large or small, the analyst can start looking for substitutable items which elicit, in conjunction with the matrix in which they are imbedded, differential responses from members of the community. Whenever such a situation is found, the investigator can begin his analysis with spot-class units — with a charting of the spots as they occur in sequence, and with a searching for the limits to the membership of the classes which occur in their respective spots. When he has done this with his starting matrix, or with a number of such matrices, he can choose either to advance up the hierarchy to larger units, or to turn his attention to smaller spot-class units within the unit which he has already discussed. He is, therefore, by this technique not stymied with the necessity for beginning at some kind of an assumed minimum such as the cultural equivalent of the phoneme or morpheme.

Another reason why the spot-class approach is helpful is that whereas in linguistics the threshold is quite stable (so that the minimum segmental units of sounds — the phonemes — are the minimum segments within almost any consideration of linguistics), the minimum of nonverbal culture which is useful to treat emically (as the natives react to it) changes with the purpose or attention of the actor. If the actor is an ordinary participant in a football game, for example, we may assume that his attention is usually focused on the plays or on the principal segments of the individual plays, and rarely would be consciously focused on units much smaller than that. When a football coach is teaching the players the rudiments of the game, however, this awareness threshold may be very sharply lowered, to such items as foot placement, and minor body movements in the processes of blocking, tackling or passing. Within the current theory, this difference of participant type is seen to be an essential part of the formula of any activity, and an ignoring of this difference leads to chaos in the analysis. Since, however, this change of participant activity changes the threshold of attention of the participants, the minimum emic units of that activity may themselves change. In spite of these changes, however, the spot-class technique proceeds without jar either upwards or downwards in the hierarchy until it comes to some threshold which seems to be relevant to that particular kind of activity with reference to the particular kind of participant attention being given to it.

HIERARCHICAL STRUCTURE, FOCUS AND THRESHOLD

We now make more specific reference to a number of items treated indirectly in the preceding sections: language and all kinds of behavior are constituted of a hierarchical structure. Small units may make up large units, and large units make up still larger units. Small spots of an emic type occur within larger emic spots, and these larger ones occur in still larger ones. Units occur within units in the hierarchical structure. In addition, a theory which is to take account of behavior other than speech must certainly include within it a difference of participant focus, the changing attention given by a participant to his own activity or to the activity of other participants. This change of focus is relevant to the person's activity, since his responses vary enormously in reference to his change of focus. In the football game, for example, the attention of the fans in the stands may be directed to things widely different from those to which attention is directed by the coach. It would be folly to assume, therefore, that the emic structuring of the activity of a novice watching the game from the stands is structurally the same as the activity of the football coach as he watches the game analytically. The activity of the two must be treated differently, as their focus is different. One's attention, furthermore, may be focused to include larger units or smaller units of the hierarchy, and the threshold of attention, as we indicated previously, can change. Some kind of threshold enters the description of any emic event, and ultimately provides the limits such that minimum emic units of a hierarchy of a system may be postulated.

THE BEHAVIOREME AS A HIGH-LAYERED UNIT

It is convenient to have a label for a unit of behavior upon which the participants are at the moment putting conscious attention, or which they are performing with deliberate conscious awareness of some real or assumed purpose. Such a unit we shall call a 'behavioreme'.[5] A list of some typical manifested behavioremes might include a football game, the reciting of a poem, or — with a lower threshold — a response to a question.

INTEGRATION THROUGH JOINT VERBAL AND NONVERBAL CLASSES

Behavioremes may be constituted either of nonverbal events, or of verbal events, or of composite nonverbal-verbal events. It is this last type which should now be seen to have considerable significance. An event comprised of both verbal and nonverbal activities could not be analysed by the linguist alone — since his techniques do not allow him to analyse the nonverbal activity. Likewise, it could not be analysed by the non-linguistic anthropologist alone, since his techniques do not include the analysis of the details of a sentence. We insist, moreover, that it could not be analysed by the combination of a linguist and a non-linguistic anthropologist, since the current techniques of neither of them is integrated with the techniques of the other, and any joint analysis by the two of them would merely be an aggregate of conclusions, rather than an integrated synthesis of the materials within a single description in which the synthesis would proceed on the basis of a single theory, with a single set of terms, and a single kind of approach.

Consider, for example, a party game in which people sing the stanza of a song; on the repetition of that same stanza, one word is deleted and a gesture is put in its place. For example, from the phrase *Under the spreading chestnut tree* the word *spreading* may be deleted, and a gesture — the arms outspread — may be substituted for it. During the third singing of that stanza, a further word is replaced by another gesture: for the word *tree* a gesture with the arms upright may be substituted. This kind of replacement can continue, until practically all the words in the stanza are replaced by gestures.

What do we deduce from this incident? First, that it is certainly a single emic unit of activity — it is so considered by the participants, who call it a single game, not a composite of several games. They also identify it as a single unit by such state-

[5] Another possible term for this unit is 'behavior cycle', a phrase used by F.S. Nadel, in *The Foundations of Social Anthropology* (London, 1951).

ments as *Well, that was a good game, but we want another one now*, and so on, in which the phrase *another one* indicates their treatment of the party game as a single unit. The integration of the verbal and nonverbal activity is here so complex how- ever, that an attempt to describe it by the mere summation of an atomistic linguistic approach and an atomistic non-linguistic anthropological approach would utterly fail to reveal the structure of that unit. There is no escape, in describing this unit, from setting up spot-classes in which the emic classes are comprised of both verbal and nonverbal materials. It is precisely this substitutability of nonverbal materials for verbal materials — in the same class with them, occurring in the same spot, as structurally integrated in the identical fashion — which allows this party game to proceed as a functioning unit. Only a unified theory of the structure of human be- havior, such as we have been attempting to develop, can possibly describe such a unitary instance as this and do it justice. Yet such a party game, though striking in this regard, is not necessarily different from a wedding in which the verbal "I will" may be integrated to other official parts of the service, such as the signing of his name by the officiating clergyman or other person. A unified theory of the structure of human behavior must allow for the integration — not just the summation — of verbal and nonverbal events.

SIMULTANEOUS MODAL STRUCTURING OF AN EVENT

The previous elements of the theory have lent themselves to discussion one at a time, with only a certain amount of overlap from one to another. We now come to a phase which is much more difficult to handle, inasmuch as it deals with that part of the theory which asserts that any emic event is simultaneously structured in three ways, i.e. in three 'modes'.[6] The attempt to describe the manner in which each of these distinct components can be demonstrated in terms of differential na- tive reaction is a very elaborate procedure which we cannot indicate in detail here. We will, however, hint at the direction in which it goes, and refer the reader to the larger volume for illustrative detail.

The manifestation mode is the hierarchical, segmental structuring of the physical material which is present in every human behavioral event. In language, this im- plies structure in terms of phonemes, which in turn enter a hierarchy with syllables, stress groups, and still higher units. A phoneme such as the consonant *t* is utterly different from a word such as *boy*; the structuring of the hierarchy in which the phoneme occurs is a hierarchy of physical units. It specifically is NOT a hierarchy comprised of the progression from phoneme, to word, to phrase (and hence it breaks here very strongly with much of the current linguistic theory), but is the structuring

---

[6] (i.e., in 'three dimensions'). The use of the term 'dimension' is suggestive of the general idea. It is misleading, however, in that it seems to ignore the physical component which is present in every mode.

of a physical unit within a larger physical unit and so on as we have just indicated.

The feature mode of an emic unit of activity is, in general, comprised of the simultaneous identificational-contrastive components of that unit, with its internal segmentation (and one component of the whole unit) analysed with special reference to purpose or lexical meaning wherever these are detectable. It is in reference to this mode, therefore, that any over-all meaning of a sentence is treated, and the intonational and segmental components of the sentence as well. In addition, the internal segmentation of the feature mode of the sentence leads to the morpheme units as the minimum internal segmental components of its feature mode.

The third mode is the distribution mode, and here reference is made to the breaking up of the sentence into its pertinent major and minor spot-classes. Specifically, the distribution mode is not distribution abstracted as such, but the correlation of spots plus the classes filling those spots. This last statement is extremely important to the theory since, by it, a physical base is preserved not only for the manifestation mode itself, but for the distribution mode and for the feature mode. Within this theory, there is never an emic unit postulated without a physical base; the manifestation mode of the sentence is the physical base of that sentence, but the distribution mode of the sentence also has its own manifestation mode so that the distribution mode likewise has its physical base.

This results in modes within modes, so that every emic unit within every mode of a larger unit has in turn its components which likewise are comprised of a feature mode, a manifestation mode, and a distribution mode. In other words, there is a hierarchical structuring of components of modes within components of modes. The details of this modal hierarchical structuring constitute a kind of chain reaction which becomes extraordinarily complex, and beyond the possibility of illustration in a brief summary such as this.

The presentation of the modal characteristics of an emic unit can also be indicated by a formula — the formula basic to the theory as a whole, and the one which is applicable equally to verbal and to nonverbal behavior. With "U" for emic unit, "F" for feature mode, "M" for manifestation mode, and "D" for distribution mode, this central formula becomes

$$U = \begin{matrix} F \\ M \\ D \end{matrix}$$

CONCEPTUALIZED HYPOSTASIS

It is useful to point out one implication of the theory where it can be easily misrepresented. The theory insists that every emic unit has a physical base, a physical component. Yet the theory suggests that a thought can be such an emic unit. What is the physical base, then, to a thought? The answer which this theory gives, is that

the neural activity within the brain constitutes the manifestation mode of a particular thought — and the theory does not leave room for thoughts 'floating through
the air' without being constituted of the specific neural activity of some specific
individual at some specific time and place.

A further problem must be treated, however: what is the 'meaning' of a word,
when the meaning, for analytical purposes, is abstracted from the form, as indicated
by such a sentence as "The word *boy* is comprised of two parts, one of which is the
sequence of phonemes and the other is the meaning"? Our answer here is that the
abstraction of the meaning, as such, is similar to the 'thoughts' referred to above
— the manifestation mode of the ACTIVITY of abstracting the meaning is comprised
of the neural activity of the person doing the abstracting, and of his verbalization
of that activity (such as 'defining the meaning' of a word). Within the normal activity of participants as they operate, without a deliberate abstraction of the meaning
no abstracted unit of meaning, as such, is postulated by the theory. Similarly, no
form is postulated as emically locatable, without reference to the total purposive
content of some behavioreme — and system of components of behavioremes —
of which it is a part. 'Meanings', therefore, as such, are exclusively a 'conceptualized
hypostasis' — the abstracting activity of the analyst[7] or the product of that activity —
the neural activity of thinking of an abstraction of the responses of individuals.

Here, again, we find it vital to be certain of the kind of participant whose activity
we are analysing. If we are analysing the activity of a non-reflective speaker, his
emic units are treated as wholes without the abstraction of form and meaning, in
the large majority of instances. On the other hand, if we are analysing the activity
of the analyst, then we are certain to find many conceptualized hypostases of a very
convenient type, which constitute the constructs of science. These, too, are tri-
modally structured, within the formula

$$U = \begin{matrix} F \\ M \\ D \end{matrix}$$

[7]   Or of a participant acting as an analyst — as the analyst himself is a participant, as a scientist, in the larger community.

LANGUAGE AND LIFE: A TRAINING DEVICE FOR
TRANSLATION THEORY AND PRACTICE*

In our first lecture we emphasized the fact that a language was a grid, an emic system by means of which and through which communication takes place. In the second, we indicated that such a system had, basic to it, classes of morphemes (or words, or morphemes and words, or words and phrases) with functional slots into which the classes fitted in sentence structures. In this, the third lecture, we are not so much interested in adding new linguistic concepts as we are in exploiting the ones already set forth. In order to do this we shall introduce an artificial system which will serve as the total target language into which passages are to be translated (a technique which I worked out in 1950 and 1952 for the Australian branch of the Summer Institute of Linguistics, but published here for the first time). The system is fashioned in such a manner as to keep it small enough to be manageable within the space of a lecture of this kind, but complete enough to make concrete the manner in which slots and classes enter into the translation process. Even though the example is built to order, artificially, the person studying it carefully and experimenting with it will see in clear perspective some of the most important elements of translation theory and practice. It is the most effective method we have so far been able to develop to demonstrate these principles.

FORMULAS FOR AN ARTIFICIAL TRAINING LANGUAGE

Only one sentence type occurs in this artificial language — a language which I shall hereafter call Kalaba-X. This sentence type has three slots which must always be filled, and filled in a particular order: each sentence has a predicate slot, followed by an object slot, which in turn is followed by a subject slot. If we symbolize the obligatory occurrence by a plus sign (+), the formula in so far as it is implied up to this point would be:

+ Pred.　　　　+ Obj.　　　　+ Subj.

The fillers of these slots must also be specified, however, before the formula is usable.

* *Biblioteca Sacra* 114 (1957), 347-362. Reprinted by permission.

That is, both slot and filler of the three gramemes involved must be known before actual sentences can be constructed in Kalaba-X.

For the fillers we would save a number of difficulties if we invented each word and morpheme — and we do this often for certain training purposes. The unfamiliar morphemes take much longer to recognize, however, slowing down our present demonstration, and are likely to change the focus of the reader away from the point we want to illustrate. In addition, at this stage in training there is very great gain in the shock received from seeing familiar words used in strange slots, according to new patterns. It helps the reader assimilate the implications of the fact, mentioned in the last lecture, that parts of speech are formal elements, formally resultant from the distribution of morphemes and words in functional slots, rather than categorical classes which are universal to all languages. (There is also the possibility that for many languages the concept of a restricted number of parts of speech may best be abandoned, to be replaced by a much more flexible approach to a larger number of criss-crossing groupings.) This in turn leads to a flexibility of conceptualization in a new framework which may prevent an inexperienced translator from stalling in his task when he fails to find the kind of translation equivalents which he expected. With his imagination trained, he is better able to look for a correct and adequate but unexpected path out of his dilemma.

To fill the predicate slot we use any English verb. Since only one kind of predicate grameme is set up, there are no distinctions between transitive and intransitive verbs. All English verbs, despite their restrictions in standard English formulas, may occur in this slot. Each of them, it should be noticed, must be followed by an object. A further convention is adopted for this stage in the training formula: A verb may be borrowed from English in any of its inflected forms, according to convenience; the internal analytical problems raised by these differences are ignored at this point, left to be covered later by other phases of the training process.

Both the object slot and the subject slot of Kalaba-X are filled by English nouns. Here, too, delicate problems arise as to the forms to be permitted, even though it is specified in advance that any inflected form of the noun may be used. The formula, then, now looks like this:

$$+ \text{Pred.}^{\text{Verb}} \qquad + \text{Obj.}^{\text{Noun}} \qquad + \text{Subj.}^{\text{Noun}}$$

One further amplification of the formula is introduced to give more flexibility to Kalaba-X and to provide an artificial language that is very simple but which nevertheless allows for the translation into it of English materials. A modification grameme is added. This grameme, unlike the others so far described, can come in more than one place. It may occur — but is not required to be present — after the predicate grameme, which it then modifies. It may also follow, and modify the object grameme, or the subject grameme. Although a particular sentence may, therefore, contain three instances of the modification grameme (one after each of the basic gramemes), no two modification gramemes come in sequence, since each of the basic gramemes is restricted to one, and only one, modifier.

The filler of the modification slot in Kalaba-X may be any English adjective. Here, as with the other gramemes, some problems arise, since we are assuming that the list of English adjectives will be clearly known to the reader, whereas in fact differences of opinion as to the inclusiveness of the list occur. (In any such particular instance, the student makes his own arbitrary decision if it does not contradict the basic rules laid down, and provided that he remains consistent throughout his work.)

The problem is made much more instructive, however, by a further extension of the list of fillers appropriate to the modification slot. Any noun, or any verb, may constitute an acceptable filler of the modifier slots just as an adjective can do.

Note, then, the revised formula, with the added symbols of slant line (/) meaning 'or', and parentheses to show the basic gramemes expanded by a modifier:

$$+(+P^V \pm M^{N/V/A}) + (+O^N \pm M^{N/V/A}) + (+S^N \pm M^{N/V/A})$$

Note, further, that this formula in part defines a noun for the Kalaba-X structure: it is a member of that list of words which can fill object, subject, or modifier slots. A verb is a word which can fill predicate or modifier slots. An adjective is a word which can fill only a modifier slot.

FROM A COMPLEX TO A SIMPLE STRUCTURE

We now present a paragraph which is to be translated into Kalaba-X. Sentences are numbered for convenience of reference:

(1) ON A BICYCLE DOWN THE MALL — (2) I was doing my best to make my way home from work on my old bicycle and thread my way down St. James' to take a short cut through the Park. (3) But I was forced to dismount. (4) Picked up by the crowd, I was put down again intact at Marlborough Gate. (5) I was going well again when I reached the Mall, and then it dawned on me — the Queen and the Duke of Edinburgh were expected. (6) There was a traffic diversion. (7) Being a very small fish, I had got through the net. (8) The Mall stretched in front of me clear and inviting, with police on each side keeping the crowd back. (9) "This may never happen again," I said to myself, and without a second thought, kept straight on. (10) The good-natured crowd cheered. (11) Even the police had to laugh. — (12) E. T. Sutherland, Torrens Rd., Brixton. — *The Evening News*, London, July 4, 1953.

Now we suggest a translation into Kalaba-X. Many different — and presumably better — translations are possible within the limiting structure. This is not THE correct translation. Differences of judgment as to word equivalences, artistic effects, literalness, and the like, would prevent any two translators from obtaining identical results — a principle easily demonstrable in a classroom by this method. Sentences are numbered to key into the source paragraph, with a running commentary on some points which the student should not overlook. One special caution: the model allows a considerable degree of ambiguity, since in a sequence of nouns a particular noun might be either subject or object or might be object or verb modifier, etc. These ambiguities can only be resolved, if at all, by a study of the context.

(1) "Rides Mall Bicycle Man." The title had to be rephrased into a full sentence, to fit the structure. The predicate *rides* was deduced from later context, and the noun *Mall* used as a modifier of it, i.e., *to Mall ride*, as if we were to say *to Boston go*. The prepositions *on* and *down* disappear; the meaning of *on a bicycle* is carried by the predicate-object phrase, *ride bicycle*. The articles *a* and *the* drop — no such word class appears in Kalaba-X; the distinction of the English definiteness or indefiniteness would be made explicit in Kalaba-X only if it were important to the context. Categories obligatory to a source language must often be dropped in this fashion, lest a translation made to preserve them become exceedingly long and cumbersome.

(2a) "Owned bicycle old speaker present." Since no pronouns occur in Kalaba-X (one of the bits where it is least like a natural language, where *I* would presumably be found), a substitute technique must be used to signal the reader that this is a firsthand account. Note here the subject *speaker present*; and compare sentence 12, which makes the signal less ambiguous. Similarly, *my* drops, and the possession requires statement in new form — here, in a verb with its object.

(2b) "Left work speaker." We were unable to begin with *doing my best* since it has no nominal object, and since the whole concept of the first source sentence was too complicated for a single sentence in Kalaba-X. In order to simplify it, we pulled out the phrases *my old bicycle* and *from work* and made separate sentences of each, to get the setting ready for the main action.

(2c) "Attempted difficulty trip homeward speaker." Now the idiom *was doing my best* is reworked into a predicate *attempted* plus a noun *difficulty* modifying it, i.e., *attempted with difficulty*.

(2d) "Traversed street St.-James' speaker." The change from a complex structure to a simple one often involves repetition of some parts. Here the subject has been repeated, since no pronoun is available, nor can *and* be used to connect the predicates of (2c) and (2d). The compound street name *St.-James'* is treated as a unit — under the assumption that speakers of Kalaba-X mimic the total pronunciation without recognition of its grammatical structure. The lexical change from *threaded* to *traversed* deletes a figure of speech which, to be intelligible, might have needed an expansion which hardly seemed warranted — the progress of the story was not tied in to this figure of speech of needle and thread (but see the *fish* figure in 7).

(2e) "Comprised shortcut Park intention speaker." The source purpose seen in *to* is transferred to a subject noun *intention*, with the old subject *I* buried in *speaker* which functions in (2c) as modifier. The prepositional phrase *through the Park* is handled by *Park* as modifier of the object.

(3) "Forced descent bicycle circumstances." A pseudo-actor, *circumstances*, is added; perhaps *crowd* would have been better. The passive complex verb is replaced by the active one, and *to dismount* becomes the object *descent* (from the bicycle). Perhaps "Dismounted speaker crowd" would have been a better translation.

(4a) "Lifted speaker crowd." The two-word phrase *picked up* is replaced by a single word for the Kalaba-X format.

(4b) "Released Marlborough-Gate speaker intact crowd." As an alternate: "Constituted site release Marlborough-Gate," if *intact* is handled otherwise.

(5a) "Continued succeeded point Mall journey resume." The verbs *succeeded* and *resume* are modifiers of predicate and object, i.e., "The resumed journey successfully continued to the Mall spot." The verb *resume* covers the source word *again*.

(5b) "Clarified suddenness understanding speaker situation surprise." Three noun modifiers — *suddenness, surprise,* and *speaker* — fill modifier spots.

(5c) "Wait appearance Queen crowd expect." The object is *appearance*, with *Queen* as modifier.

(5d) "Wait Duke Edinburgh crowd." Repetitiveness is avoided in (5c-d) by using *appearance* as explicit object only in (5c), with *Duke* as object in (5d).

(6) "Rerouted previous traffic officials." English pseudo-subject *there* must be replaced, and *officials* (or *police*) obtained from context. *Previous* modifies *rerouted*, not *traffic*.

(7a) "Constituted analogy fish small speaker."

(7b) "Penetrated fish net traffic speaker unimpeded." The *fish* analogy is preserved, at a cost of spelling it out in detail. In 7b, *fish* modifies *penetrated*, i.e., *to penetrate like a fish*. It could have been dropped, to yield (replacing (7a-7b) something like "Penetrated restraints traffic speaker unimportant", or "Penetrated restraints traffic vehicle small."

(8a) "Appears front space open Mall extends." The word *extends* is merely a verb modifying *Mall*, i.e., "the extended Mall ..."; it is not a predicate in a new formula.

(8b) "Invites ride Mall."

(8c) "Restrain sides crowd lines police." The noun *sides* modifies *restrain*, deduced from context.

(9a) "Tells speaker speaker." Alternate: "Soliloquized words following speaker," which perhaps more clearly states that a quotation is to follow.

(9b) "Represents probability negative opportunity repeat."

(9c) "Gives negative consideration more rider storyteller."

(9d) "Proceeds direction straight rider."

(10) "Cheered rider crowd pleasant."

(11) "Restrain failure laughter own police."

(12) "Tells story own E.-T.-Sutherland."
(13) "Inhabits Torrens-Rd. Brixton storyteller."
(14) "Published London story The-Evening-News."
(15) "Happened Four July story 1953."

This last set (13-15) is awkward. *Brixton* is assumed to modify the name of the street. *London* modifies *published*. *1953* is treated as a unit modifying *story*, and *July* as modifying *four*.

In summary, various changes may occur when one translates from a complex to a simple structure. Among those illustrated in the above problem are addition of fillers to slots obligatory to the target language but not to the source language; partial loss of some categorical distinctions obligatory to the source language; loss of parts of speech or of morpheme classes present in the source language but absent in the target language; loss of constructions based on these classes; transference of load from lost components to target components, such as when a lexical item — say a particular noun — in the target language carries the functional meaning of a special particle in the source language; change of order of words or slots; shortening of complex sentences into multiple short target sentences; dropping figures of speech or else making them more explicit; replacing idioms with lexical or structural substitutes; drawing on context for interpretive data to fill blanks required by formal structure; the mere sequence of the sentences may be forced to carry implications of time, sequence, or cause, or dependence, or relatedness, etc., which were in the complex structure signalled by particles of some type.

ARTISTIC USE OF SIMPLE STRUCTURES

A person unacquainted with language forms might conclude that a language with a simple structure would lead to a dreary style. This is far from true. Every structure, in the hands of an artist, lends itself to beautiful effects. A simple structure may lead to balanced lines and artistic repetition. An occasional Chinese verse might seem to the uninitiated layman to be built on a model scarcely more complex than the sentence type we have been studying (see the Chinese verse in my *Tone Languages*, 35, footnote 3).

Perhaps the reader would enjoy seeing verse in the format given. The following verse utilizes that pattern, with a few changes; one further sentence type, limited to a single exclamatory word, is added, and some hyphenated two-morpheme items are treated as single slot-filling units:

> Enters bird big, man bewildered.
> Maketh sound loud, bird silvered.
> > Whoosh!
> Aimeth sky top, bird up-flying

Falleth ground face, earth low-lying.
       Wow!
Hideth earth low, clouds heavy.
       Rocketh gentle man, bird steady.
       Nice!
Cover eyes blue, eyelids drooping.
Covers sky blue, darkness stooping.
       Sleep!
Open eyes tired, man wondering.
Breaketh air night, storm thundering.
       Boom!
Rocketh bird poor, storm no-cease.
Reacheth land firm, bird one-piece.
       Whew!

              Dorothy Barnhouse

For verse with no changes other than a comma to make unambiguous by a pause the end of the object, note the following:

Owns lamb little, Mary.
    Loves lamb, Mary little.
    Loves Mary pretty, lamb.
Owns lamb, Mary pretty.

Seems snow, fleece white.
    Equals snow white, fleece.
    Equals snow, fleece soft.
Seems fleece soft, snow.

FIRST-STAGE TRANSLATION INTO A COMPLEX STRUCTURE

Translation from a simple structure to a complex one may entail all of the problems faced in translating English to Kalaba-X, but in reverse. Instead of fewer parts of speech, or distribution classes, there may be more; several simple sentences may need to be combined into a large complex one; the number and function of obligatory slots may be different; and so on. In our next illustration we shall translate from Kalaba-X into English. Instead of emphasizing these same problems, however, we shall use the illustration to demonstrate two other points: (1) A sentence-by-sentence translation can be made, meeting all, or almost all, of the requirements already discussed for adequate translation from structure to structure, but still be awkward, unpleasant, and completely unsatisfactory even though accurate. (2) Satisfactory translation must take account of units larger than the sentence; it must consider the story, or quotation, or paragraph, or document as a whole; it must approximate a choice of vocabulary, choice of sentence type, and choice of general style of exposition which will be appropriate to the age, sex, training, experience, cultural setting, and purpose of comparable speakers or writers in the target culture; it must, in sum, have the flavor of an original document in the target culture.

In order to show these points we will first present a short incident recorded in our artificial language Kalaba-X. Interlined with it we will give a first-stage translation, one sentence at a time, into the target language, which is normal English. Later we will give a second-stage translation of the incident as a whole, modified for better style.

(1) "Made resolutions New-Year writer."
   (Trans.: "The writer made some New Year's resolutions.")
(2) "Constitutes writer speaker."
   (Trans.: "The speaker is the writer.")
(3) "Contained resolution following list."
   (Trans.: "The list contained the following resolution.")
(4) "Necessitate patience increase reactions writer."
   (Trans.: "The writer's reactions need increased patience.")
(5) "Apply need direction daughter patience require."
   (Trans.: "The required patience must be applied in the daughter's direction.")
(6) "Constitutes daughter Janet."
   (Trans.: "Janet is the daughter.")
(7) "Belongs writer daughter."
   (Trans.: "The daughter belongs to the writer.")
(8) "Disregard obligation irritation degreeless writer."
   (Trans.: "The writer has an obligation to disregard irritation of any degree.")
(9) "Necessitates remembrance facts reaction writer."
   (Trans.: "The writer's reaction makes necessary the recollection of certain facts.")
(10) "Attained exclusive years fifteen Janet."
   (Trans.: "Janet is just fifteen years old.")
(11) "Constitutes currently adolescent Janet."
   (Trans.: "Janet is now an adolescent.")
(12) "Exasperates adults adolescence."
   (Trans.: "Adolescence exasperates adults.")
(13) "Discovered accident resolutions different writer."
   (Trans.: "The writer accidentally discovered some different resolutions.")
(14) "Requests imagination reader writer."
   (Trans.: "The writer requests imagination to be used by the reader.")
(15) "Affected feelings writer discovery."
   (Trans.: "The discovery affected the writer's feelings.")
(16) "Belong Janet resolution New Year's."
   (Trans.: "The New Year's resolutions belonged to Janet.")
(17) "Saw resolution first writer."
   (Trans.: "The writer saw the first resolution.")
(18) "Stated words following resolution."

(Trans.: "The resolution read as follows.")
(19) "Requires effort increased situation."
(Trans.: "The situation requires increased effort.")
(20) "Obligated patience mother daughter."
(Trans.: "A daughter is obligated to have patience toward her mother.")
If now we read rapidly the interlinear translation, it becomes clear that it does not yet remotely reach our ultimate goal of an accurate translation which sounds like a document originally written in English.

SECOND-STAGE TRANSLATION INTO A COMPLEX STRUCTURE

A second-stage translation is needed in which the style should be made more normal. Before attempting this we should note the over-all setting, and deduce something of the character of the writers so as to get a clue to the kinds of styles people of a comparable type would use in English. The author is a woman sophisticated enough to keep a diary, old enough — and young enough — to have a fifteen-year-old daughter, alert, resilient, able to recognize and appreciate a subtle joke on herself, and sufficiently articulate to write up the incident to share the pleasure with others. The daughter is adolescent, but sophisticated in sensing that responsibilities must be shared.

Since Kalaba-X and English differ so greatly, there is a corresponding great difference in possible translations from the one to the other. The following attempt is only one of many possible translations:

(1-3) "I made some New Year's resolutions, with this one among them." Note that the sentences are combined, the incident told in the first person, the more informal *this one* replacing *the following*.

(4-7) "I must be more patient with my daughter Janet." The phrase *my daughter Janet* covers (6-7), while (5) is made more idiomatic and informal.

(8-12) "Regardless of the degree to which she becomes irritating, my reaction to her must keep in mind the fact that she is just fifteen, a mere adolescent, and that this age is always exasperating to other people."

(13-18) "But just imagine how I felt when by accident I ran across Janet's New Year's resolutions and saw that the first one read:

(19-20) "A daughter should be patient with her mother; I must try harder with mine."

Many problems can be demonstrated by these techniques, which time does not allow in this lecture. Once the student has learned to adapt his final draft to a desired style it may be necessary to give some illustrations of instances in which the translator has taken too great liberty with the text, in adding speculative material not justified by the context, or by changing content as such rather than the formal matters of the structural grid.

One of the best exercises to teach balance in this regard is to have one group of students translate from English into Kalaba-X, and a second group of students translate back into English without having seen the original. When the two English versions diverge sharply on nonformal matters, or in emotional over-tones, or in style, the two translations should be checked to see if one or the other was inadequate, or whether the cultural setting was too obscure to give the style clues needed.

In line with this suggestion, we now give the original from which the Kalaba-X story about Janet was taken. The reader may wish to modify one of the translations in accordance with these principles:

On my list of New Year's resolutions was: "Be more patient with my daughter Janet. No matter how irritating she is, remember that, after all, she is only 15, and is going through the exasperating period of adolescence."

Imagine then my feeling when, quite by accident, I came across Janet's New Year's resolutions and saw at the head of her list: "Try and be more patient with Mother."

Contributed by Mrs. C.R. Knowles, *The Reader's Digest*, Jan. 1952, p. 79.

ON CULTURAL TRANSLATION

If we turn from the discussion of language to problems of Christian faith and life, how can those translation experiences serve to illuminate them?

The problem of bringing Christianity into a culture alien to the culture within which Christianity was developed can be viewed, in part, as one of translation. Each culture has its own emic structure of customs, its own grid, its own behavior pattern, as we indicated in the earlier lectures. Christianity may be viewed as a message to be translated into the new pattern.

Just as a word-for-word translation following the word order of the source language leads to an incomprehensible utterance, so an attempt to lead tribal groups of the Amazon headwaters, for example, to follow each detail of life of Christians within the United States would be impossible because of technological differences. We obtain our fish from a supermarket cooler, while they obtain theirs from the rivers by bow and arrow.

These mechanical limitations, however, are quite superficial. Much more subtle, and often existing without the 'westerner' being aware of it, are delicate rules of etiquette, intricate SOCIAL OBLIGATIONS, deep-seated MORAL CODES. Christianity insists on kindness as a character trait which must be translated into a culture at points where it may be lacking. But kindness working through the golden rule must be interpreted not as a bookkeeping transaction by which every bit of activity which I myself value as kindly within my culture is transferred to the tribal folks under the assumption that it will be equally evaluated as an act of kindness within their culture. Rather the principle of doing to others as one wishes done to oneself must be interpreted relative to this translation process — kindnesses should be performed with their cultural grid in view, not just our own.

At this point the effective missionary can only be one who is sensitive to the cultural view — the emic grid — of others. The trainee who wishes to be kind within a foreign culture can well afford to learn many things from the anthropologists — whether or not they grant our Christian assumptions. They can tell us something of the nature of such cultures, knowledge which should serve as background to understand the cultural structures into which Christian kindness must be translated.

There is danger of error in understanding any problem if an analogy is carried too far. In this, the translation model for Christianity is no exception. In the language translation, for example, we carefully refrain from modifying the target grid; only the vocabulary is expanded, without the grammar structure being tampered with. When Christianity effectively enters a tribe, however, many customs will be modified, added, or lost — analogous to vocabulary change, perhaps — but, in addition, the basic structural framework is modified as the value system underlying it is necessarily affected. Thus some acts which would appear to the tribe as acts of kindness may nevertheless have to be omitted because they are in conflict with some moral principle — or with needs of self-preservation. Christianity CANNOT countenance infant killing even when the tribal beliefs would indicate that it is necessary to preserve the tribe from some calamity, nor can the physician apply a harmful poultice even though prescribed by local custom. Even in such circumstances, however, the translator of Christian and of hygienic values should be sympathetic in understanding the structure he is attempting to modify, and try to lead the tribe to make the modifications itself, through its own mechanisms of cultural change.

For this kind of result the written Scriptures in the vernacular are important. The tribesmen, in reading them, see principles working out in one culture, as if they were reading a message in a foreign language. Stimulated by this message, they themselves may succeed in translating it freely, i.e., in applying the principle. The foreigner often finds it more difficult to do, since without the Scriptures available in the tribal tongue he must select from the Scriptures the particular bits and emphases which seem relevant to him. To the extent that he fails to understand the tribal culture, however, he may overlook materials in the Scripture which would be appropriate. The tribesman, going to the documents directly, is likely to gain direct benefits for specific problems where the foreigner fails to see the relevance of the selection and sees the problem itself distorted through his own cultural grid. The flower knows what vitamins it needs to draw from the soil better than the farmer does. The Scriptures are the fertile soil rather than an artificial fertilizer which may lack essential trace elements.

One further caution is necessary. The evangelical does not view the Christianizing task as merely a cultural translation. He sees it in part as a cultural task plus an infusion of supernatural power in the individual life. A variety of Christianity which attempts the cultural phases of the task without reliance upon the power emanating from the crucifixion and resurrection of Christ as trustworthy historical events would impress the evangelical as failing to provide the tribe's people with the source of supernatural power which not only leads to present cultural values, such as kindness, but also gives eternal life.

LANGUAGE AS PARTICLE, WAVE, AND FIELD*

What is the nature of language? What are its parts? How is the structure of language related to structural problems in other areas of investigation?

Language, in my view, can be viewed profitably from three distinct standpoints. One of these is traditional, and views language as made up of PARTICLES — 'things', pieces, or parts, with sharp borders. The second view is not at all thought of in lay circles perhaps, and is largely neglected on the technical front. This second view treats language as made up, not of parts which are separated one from the other and added like bricks on a row, but rather as being made up of WAVES following one another. This second view is one which I have recently been developing, and leads to some very stimulating insights as to the nature of language structure. A third view consists in viewing structure as a total FIELD. Technicians have studied semantic fields as part of language, but the handling of the concept systematically in terms of the more ordinary structuring of sentences has not even been attempted. Some components which could enter such a possible view, however, have been developed for other purposes, and I have found the concept fruitful in certain practical situations of applied linguistics.

These three views of language can be summarized in different terms. Language, seen as made up of particles, may be viewed as if it were STATIC — permanent bricks juxtaposed in a permanent structure, or as separate 'frames' in a moving-picture film. The view of language made up of waves sees language as DYNAMIC — waves of behavioral movement merging one into another in intricate, overlapping, complex systems. The view of language as made up of field sees language as FUNCTIONAL, as a system with parts and classes of parts so interrelated that no parts occur apart from their function in the total whole, which in turn occurs only as the product of these parts in functional relation to a meaningful social environment.

It is extraordinary that in the twentieth century we should still be viewing language almost entirely from a static, particle-like view rather than in a dynamic fashion. Only recently have approaches of a dynamic type begun to appear. In my own work the insistence on a wavelike hierarchical blending and fusion of units is designed in part to fill this gap. In the so-called 'prosodic' approach in London, developed by Firth and his colleagues, there are also dynamic elements.

*   *The Texas Quarterly* 2:2 (1959), 37-54. Reprinted by permission.

In spite of the importance of the wave and field concepts of language we shall first, however, discuss the structure of language as made up of particles, since it is easiest for us to grasp psychologically, closest to the lay view of language, and most fully developed in technical exposition. (Later, we will affirm that each of the three views must be retained, supplementing one another, if we wish to preserve an empirically and theoretically adequate view of language.) This particle view reflects a common-sense attitude: Language is made up of words, with sharp boundaries between them. A language, for some people, would appear to be ideally comprised of a dictionary. Once one has the dictionary of a language one seems to have under control the heart of the language, if one thinks in this way. This view appears to be very common in some areas of our culture.

A more sophisticated particle view aims at an analysis of great simplicity. It attempts to reduce high-level language structures to combinations of a few small units in more and more restricted groupings. The unit chosen is the sound — the PHONEME — or a component of a phoneme. If one has a list of the sounds and the possible restrictions on the combination of these sounds, one is assumed to know the structure of the language. This view — though I have oversimplified it — has had high prestige in the United States in the past few years.

Harris has attempted, for example, to study the combinatorial structure of language without reference to meaning and has attempted to go as far as possible in finding the lexical units — the MORPHEMES — by purely distributional techniques. That is, by studying the fashion in which one sound may follow another, he has tried to arrive at successive groupings of sounds in structurally significant combinations on higher and higher levels of organization until the words and sentences are analyzed without reference to the meaning or identification of the morphemes or words or sentences as such. For example, after a sequence of sounds such as represented by the English letters *I th-o-u-g-h-t th-*, there are only a few specific letters which could follow, such as *a* of the word *that*. (The scholars referred to, however, would be very careful to handle such a problem in reference to the pronounced sounds, not in reference to spelling by letters.) Here, then, is a 'thing-centered' view of language, but with the particular parts made up of small sound units rather than of word units. It tends towards a philosophical reductionism, with sounds or sound components as the ultimate and only primitive units and with all other units as merely combinations of these in a distributional relationship.

This view has been very fruitful in stimulating linguistic discussion and development. Some of us feel, however, that characteristics inherent in language structure will prevent its complete fulfillment. (The pendulum has in the last year or two begun to swing for these authors, however, away from complete rejection of meaning to a basic reliance upon it in specified areas of study. Harris, for example, now treats of some grammatical problems in which a basic constant necessary to identify the relations between, for example, *John hit Bill* and *Bill was hit by John* is a retention of certain lexical meanings. He appears to avoid destroying his earlier work — that based on an attempted rejection of meaning-relevance in grammar — by a semantic device. He calls the one type 'combinatorial' or 'descriptive' grammar, and the kind based on meaning relations 'transform' grammar. In my view, a synthesis of these extremes into a single hierarchical approach would seem to reflect the data more effectively.) Most linguists have not in practice attempted as formally 'rigorous' an analysis of language into meaningless discrete parts as this latter view seems to imply (with 'rigor' used in a mathematical sense as 'nonintuitive' — rather than as 'coherent, consistent presentation of the data'). Nevertheless, the development of the analysis both of the phoneme and of the morpheme is very intricate, very extensive, and represents one of the greatest achievements of twentieth-century linguistic science.

A phoneme may include within its various pronunciations a large number of different varieties of pronunciation. The *t* at the beginning of the word *time*, for example, is much different from the single consonant sound in the middle of an American pronunciation of *Betty* (which in turn is very different from the pronunciation of the *t* in *bought*). (The first has a puff of breath following it, the second is made by a quick flip of the tongue, and the last may be heard sometimes as cut off rather sharply at the end of an utterance.) Some scholars, however, prefer to work more extensively with a unit smaller than the phoneme as the basic unit, namely one or more of the components which make up the phoneme, as atoms can make up a molecule. The sound *d*, for example, has a component of voicing — produced by the vibrating vocal chords — as well as a component of mouth closure by tongue tip, plus a component of nasal passage closure by the soft palate, and so on.

The second unit, the morpheme, would include such lexical items as *boy*, *dog*, *house*, and, in addition, meaningful lexical units such as the suffix *-s* of *cups* or the prefix *un-* of *unpleasant*. Morphemes, like phonemes, have been studied heavily in reference to their varieties. The plural suffix *-s* of *cups*, for example, occurs in a special form *-es*, in *houses*, and in further forms in *feet*, *children*, and *data*. The development of techniques to discover, describe, and systematize the phonemic and morphemic variants has required a great deal of research by some of the most competent linguistic scholars of our generation and is by no means finished.

While still keeping within the view of language as made up of parts, pieces, or units, a third small unit, it appears to me, must be postulated. This is a unit of grammar, comparable to the units of phonology and lexicon just discussed. Some of my recent research has been the introduction of a TAGMEME unit into linguistic theory, on a par with the phoneme and the morpheme. (The term itself is given to us by Bloomfield, although his particular attempt to define, describe, or isolate such a unit has not been fruitful and has not entered into current linguistic theory or practice.) The new concept (of the same name) has already proved helpful in analyzing languages in field situations. The layman would recognize some such units or unit classes if he were told, for example, that there may be in an English sentence several kinds of subject, each of which is a separate tagmeme. Thus a subject-as-actor unit in the sentence *John came home* would be one tagmeme, whereas subject-as-person-affected would be a distinct tagmeme in the sentence *John was hit by Bill.*

In my current researches I am applying to such units the same kind of linguistic development which has been so successfully applied to the phoneme and morpheme. Variants of tagmemes occur just as one finds variants of phonemes and morphemes. A subject variant, for example, might be a simple one such as *John* in the sentence just quoted, or a complex subject in a sentence such as *My big Johnny came home yesterday.* Both the simple subject and complex subject here are variants of the English subject-as-actor tagmeme. The tagmeme concept, it should be noted, resists the reductionism of language structure to meaningless sounds. It points in the direction both of preserving a meaningful lexical unit and of introducing a meaningful grammar unit as primitive terms in linguistic theory.

The structure of a complex word in the Candoshi language of northern Peru may serve to illustrate the way morpheme, phoneme, and tagmeme pieces function together. (The data utilized are chosen from those published by Doris Cox in the *International Journal of American Linguistics* and by Lorrie Anderson and me in *Lingua Posnaniensis.*) In the word *kopáako* 'She washes' the consonants and vowels are quite audible and easily analyzed with an 'ordinary' (from the English viewpoint) stress on the first part of the second syllable. A few 'special' sounds, however, occur in the language. The phrase 'She cooks', for example, differs from the one quoted only by the fact that the first vowel is whispered rather than spoken aloud. We may write that vowel with a capital letter thus: *kOpáako.* Only once elsewhere in the history of the world, in the information which has reached me, has careful documentation been published of this phenomenon; this other instance concerns the Comanche

±	±	±	+(∓	±	±	±)	±	+	±
-ka locative	*-ya* recent	*-ran* past	*-k* indicative	*-ma* durative	*-ch* incomplete	*-sha* 2nd order	*-t* individualizer	*-i* 1st person sg.	*-ya* emphatic
-mpa intensive	*-ta* punctiliar		*-r* current	*-shin* movement	*-nch* complete	*-masi* 1st order		*-ish* 2nd person sg.	*-pa* potential
				-tar habitual				*-o* 3rd person sg.	*-shi* negative
				-ts possible				*-ini* 1st person pl.	*-a* interrogative
								-is 2nd person pl.	
								-ana 3rd person pl.	
								-ich impersonal	

Fig. 1. Chart of independent indicative suffixes.

of Oklahoma, as found in the researches of Canonge. (Such differences are highly important to Bible translators, such as Cox and Anderson, in pairs of words such as these, in passages like Revelation 1:5 "[Christ] washed us from our sins in His own blood". In a head-shrinking or cannibal culture these must not be confused!)

The consonants and vowels make up the parts which, going together, produce words. Compare the word *táyanchshatana* which means 'I have stayed there then'. It is made up of the parts *tá* (the stem, 'to be'); *ya* 'recently'; *nch* 'completely'; *sha* 'next'; *t* 'individually'; *a* 'I'; *na* 'emphatically'; —that is, 'Emphatically-I-individually-next-completely-and-recently-was-there'.

In turn these morphemes, made up of phonemes, are members of classes of morphemes which are replaceable in particular slots in a potential structure. The combination of such a functional slot, along with the class of morphemes which can fill that slot, makes up one of the tagmemes interior to the verb. Note the chart of independent indicative suffixes (Fig. 1), which suggests how (with certain unimportant exceptions) words — among them the word quoted — can be made on this particular 'mapping' pattern. The ± on the chart means that a particular class is optional in the verb. The ∓ followed by ± within the parentheses indicates that some one or more of these classes must be represented. A + indicates obligatory occurrence of some member of the class in every word of that type. In the particular form quoted, furthermore, certain special sub-varieties of these morphemes occur. In our illustration above, for example, the first person instead of being represented by the vowel *-i* is represented by *-a* (which is found always replacing *-i* after the *t*), while the normal variety *-ya* 'emphatic', is replaced following *i* by a variety spelled *-na*, which is especially restricted to its occurrence there.

With some special restrictions, any morpheme can be chosen from its respective column to go toward making up a word.

Other quite different mapping must be made for independent desiderative suffixes, independent imperative suffixes, independent optative suffixes, dependent conditional suffixes, and nonpersonal dependent suffixes.

The tagmemes in the chart are represented (1) by the column (which indicates the functional positions of the suffixes), correlated (2) with the particular class of morphemes listed in that column. For the learning of the language, such a chart provides the morphemes and tagmemes upon which practical substitution drills can be based for the assimilation of the language structure.

The minimal particles — phoneme, morpheme, tagmeme — are not the only 'particles', however, which some of us treat as basic. Each of the three is rather, in a hierarchical view of language, merely the smallest unit of several units in an increasing complexity of organization leading to larger and larger units. The phonological minimal unit of sound (the phoneme) is part of a larger phonological unit which may be called the SYLLABLE.

In much of the technical linguistics in America during the past two decades, however, due to a phonological reductionism and nonhierarchical treatment, the syllable has either been denied theoretical status or ignored in theoretical treatments. It is only within the last few years that this unit, so well known to the layman, has begun to be handled in our country by more structural theoreticians. The reason for this has been a kind of reductionism which has wished to eliminate all higher level units of complexity as primitive terms (although occasionally they replace these units, in description, with units of the same name which were defined merely as aggregations of sequences of lower level units; that is to say, that the term SYLLABLE while appearing in such writings would be treated not as a new KIND of unit, but merely as the resultant of specific distributions of sounds which gave the characteristic effect we call syllables). A scholar by the name of Stetson for many years objected to this, but only recently has his work had the impact necessary to force a few structuralists to begin to work the syllable into their theories as both a physiological and distributional element.

Above and beyond the syllable in size and complexity within the phonological hierarchy lie other units. These include the stress group (or rhythm unit), the pause group, and other units with phonological characteristics such as the rhetorical period.

In a hierarchical approach we assume that the morpheme is at the base of a lexical hierarchy, distinct from the phonological hierarchy in structure. Groups of morphemes make up specific words on a higher level of that hierarchy. Thus *boy* plus *-s* makes up the word *boys*.

For the layman, some of the most easily seen units on the next levels of the lexical hierarchy are idioms. *To step on the gas* is a high-level unit of the lexical hierarchy. It differs from a different kind of high unit, *putting one's foot on top of the gasoline*. Still higher in this same hierarchy are items like sonnets, limericks, and other integrated specific verbal pieces.

The grammatical hierarchy, on the other hand, may be illustrated as proceeding from a particular kind of subject (but with the particular subject unspecified — whether it be *John, Bill, Joe*) to a higher unit such as a subject-predicate complex which makes up a clause. Clauses in turn make up complex sentences, and so on. The problem of distinguishing between the lexical and grammatical hierarchies is a very technical one which is crucial to this point of view — but which at the moment seems to be more in doubt from the point of view of the technician than from that of the layman. I shall not set forth here the intricate arguments which I have been developing to attempt to make the essentiality of this distinction clear to my colleagues.

Thus far it has been difficult to show how modern linguistics and current literary criticism have much in common, although some scholars such as Hill and Jakobson have attempted to exploit this area. It seems to me clear, however, that once linguistics turns its attention more fully to higher hierarchical levels, it will begin to look at many of the problems which have taken part of the attention of literary scholars. In some of their formal aspects, linguistics study and literary study of such high-level units might mutually complement one another in a way more fruitful than can be seen at present.

In my own hierarchical emphasis, for example, I am attempting to develop techniques by which the separate lexical, phonological, and grammatical hierarchies can maintain their identity in the analysis, and yet at the same time, the intricate overlappings between each of the three, at various levels of the three, can be pointed out. It seems to me that one would achieve only a 'flat' picture of communication — especially of literary communication — if one were to attempt to treat literary structure exclusively with low-level units such as phoneme, morpheme, and tagmeme. Even when these three are supplemented by studies of pause, intonation, and stress — as is currently being done — the result comes far from reaching the subtlety of actual literary communication. It would seem to me that the subtlety with which the poet operates can begin to be analyzed or approximated by the linguist only when he is able to study the crisscrossing of effects of one hierarchy upon another at various levels. The level of sound-sequence structure must be seen to affect the choice of words, as in alliteration. The level of word choice affects the structure of syllable-type sequences, for meter. The level of grammatical functional units provides key turning points for forced interpretation of homophonous words or for simultaneous dual meanings of passages. The simultaneous double function of one physical unit in two separate hierarchies, or on two levels of one hierarchy, allows for some of the extraordinary richness of interplay of subtle innuendo which must be accounted for if one is to analyze literary composition. These and other items not adequately explored by the linguist must be developed further in a hierarchical multiphase conceptual framework before the linguist can hope to have full converse with his literary colleagues.

Nevertheless, once these views are developed more fully, it is clear that a particle view of language will allow for an understanding of an enormous amount of complexity built from a few elegantly simple items such as morpheme, phoneme, and tagmeme in intricate crisscrossing hierarchical arrangements.

Once one has sensed the thrill of understanding language organization as such an interweaving of sound and sound complexes, lexical units and lexical complexes, grammatical units and grammatical complexes, it comes as a shock to find that despite this insight it is possible to deny the relevance of almost every statement made thus far by beginning from a different point of view. Language, one can affirm, is not made up of particles at all! Language contains no phonemes, no morphemes, no tagmemes! One must not go around looking for bits and pieces, whether small or large, whether on a low hierarchical level like phonemes and morphemes, or on a higher hierarchical level like syllables, pieces of sentences.

In this second view there are no sounds as such, no syllables as such, no words as such, no isolatable sentences as such. Rather what one meets is a constant flux of total physiological or acoustic movement in a total physiological or acoustic field. Here, language is seen as a sequence of waves of activity; the train of waves is one continuous behavioral event. That which was labelled earlier as a sequence of 'separate' sounds would in this view be nothing but a series of waves of movement or of sound with the peak of a particular wave identifying the place in a sequence where a particular 'segment' was supposed to have occurred.

One's natural view of a language sequence, after one has been taught to read by letters of an alphabet, is that there are little 'gaps' between each pair of sounds in a sequence. Sounds would appear to hang together by some kind of mysterious, invisible cement. But in the view which we must now consider, the wave view, no such thing occurs. Investigation by acoustic instruments shows that the sound sequence may be a continuous unbroken chain. In a sentence such as *Bob did go there?* no single gap appears in the acoustic record. One sound flows into another with no point at which the voice completely ceases. Where, then, are the 'separate' sounds? They have disappeared.

This conclusion is strengthened by articulatory studies through motion-picture X rays in which one sees that the articulations of the mouth form continuous sweeping movements. There are no points of rest in a rapid sentence to allow for gaps between sounds.

What then shall we do to salvage in some fashion the idea of 'sounds'? And units of sound? The answer, in part, is that we must treat sounds not as separate bits or pieces but as waves in a wave train. At the peak of each movement — at the peak of a 'wave of articulation' — we recognize the fact that a sound has been uttered even though the borders between the sounds are not sharp-cut. That is, we replace the concept of a bead-like separation with that of a wave fusion, but retain the general idea of sounds as sounds in a fused sequence. This leads tentatively to a 'wave segmentation', with no sharp division of sounds at their borders, but with the general principle of units in sequence undisturbed.

Even this comfort, however, is soon torn from us. Joos tells us that if one pronounces syllables such as *pop* versus *tot* and records them on tape, and if one then, with a pair of scissors, cuts off the consonants from the tape at the point where segmentation would seem to occur by either a particle view or a wave view of the type just mentioned, and if one then plays back on the recorder the vowel sound only, the two syllables are still distinguishable as *pop* and *tot*! This extraordinary and unexpected result forces us to investigations which show clearly that not only is there fusion at the points where sounds bump into one another in the sequence, but that sounds which are 'due to appear' late in the sequence may actually be in part anticipated early in a sequence. The anticipation affects the early sounds. And sounds which appear early in the sequence, from the point of view of normal, ordinary segmentation, actually decay so slowly in articulation and resultant effect that their influence is felt late in the sequence.

Practical phoneticians recognize, furthermore, that these anticipatory or decay characteristics of a sound are oftentimes extremely important for the recognition of the sound. If, for example, one wishes to listen to certain kinds of *r* sounds or pharyngeal consonants, it is frequently much easier for the beginner to 'recognize' the presence of the consonants by listening to the neighboring vowels which are modified by these consonants than it is to try to listen directly to the consonants themselves. More recent acoustic experiments on the nature of perception would seem to indicate that this is true not only for the phonetics beginner, but that to some extent it reflects the normal experience of the native speaker.

Where does this lead us? Certainly to the view that sounds cannot be considered as segmentable in the sense that one can cut up with a pair of scissors a sequence on tape and have left in segment form all the relevant components of one sound after another. It leads to the view that the totality of any one sound is not necessarily found in any one segmentable section of the sequence. Rather, part of the sound's relevant characteristics may be at the wave peak in the sequence, but various other parts may be extended forwards and backwards over several segments. Since this is true in experiment and practice, where then does a 'sound' lie? AND HOW CAN ONE SPEAK OF A 'PARTICLE' ANY MORE? The particle view is seen to be inadequate at this point.

Does the wave view, however, do any better? Yes. To begin with we spoke of a wave view as if it dealt with a train of waves as in Fig. 2.

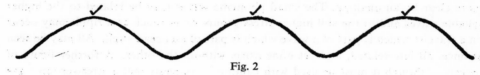

Fig. 2

This diagram would imply that one sound 'follows' another; that at each peak (identified by a little check above it) a sound is heard, but that the borders fuse into each other in the troughs of the waves. Our later comments implied that this diagram must be revised, however, in order to allow for the overlapping characteristics which we discussed. Note the diagram of Fig. 3.

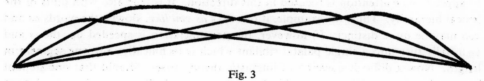

Fig. 3

In this diagram each wave begins and ends at the same two spots respectively. The difference in the waves is in the place where they come to a peak, and in the relative concentration of their characteristics at any one spot in the total sequence. The linguistic interpretation of such a sequence includes the fact that there are a number of sounds, phonemes, each sound identified by its respective peak, but with its borders completely indeterminable. Borders within the continuum cannot be found by any practical experiment, on the one hand, and from the theoretical point of view it is hopeless to expect to develop future experiments to do so inasmuch as their characteristics are smeared throughout. Here, then, seems to be the death of a simple particle view. It would appear that a wave view must replace it. (Later, however,

we shall affirm that BOTH the particle AND the wave view must be retained simultaneously.)

What has been said for sounds applies also to syllables, on a higher level of the
phonological hierarchy. Syllables may occasionally be sharply separated — just as
on occasion sounds may be sharply separated — but on other occasions they may
fuse in such ways that the borders between them are not clear. Thus in *bad dog* a
boundary may be clear in slow speech, but in *biting*, the *t* phoneme comes at the syllable juncture and makes indeterminate the point at which the first syllable begins
or ends. This is similar to the fact that phonemes fuse into one another at their
border points. Syllables may also be partially anticipatory of each other, within
higher units of the phonological hierarchy, so that their phonetic characteristics must
in part be picked out as waves just as phoneme characteristics must. Syllables, too,
disappear as 'particles' — as sharp-cut segments — and can only be identified by
peaks in a complex wave train. Similarly, on a still higher level of the phonological
hierarchy, stress groups fuse into one another within pause groups, and so on.

The general relation of a low-level unit to its including high-level unit may be made
more clear by an analogy: The small phoneme waves may be related to the higher
syllable waves and to the still higher stress group waves much as a ripple may occur
on a wavelet which is part of a wave which is part of an ocean swell. All may be seen
at once, all interrelated, and yet none exists without the other. A further figure of
speech — though it must be used with caution — suggests that a stress-group wave
is like a low harmonic, a syllable wave a higher harmonic, and a phoneme a still
higher harmonic. These articulatory movements all fuse into a total articulatory
complex which in turn produces a single complex sound wave which reflects components of these differing articulatory wave sources.

It is not only in the phonological sphere that particles seem to disappear and waves
to appear, once attention is focused in this direction. It is true also with units of the
lexical hierarchy. Thus, for example, if one says *as you like*, slowly, the words *as* and
you may be quite distinct. If, however, the pronunciation is speeded up, the -*s* and
y- usually fuse into a single palatal sibilant which is technically only one segment in
length. Now a difficult question of linguistic theory arises: Should that one sibilant
be considered part of the first word but not of the second? Or part of the second word
but not of the first? Or should it be somehow divided into components so that the
sibilant component belongs to the first word but the palatal component belongs to
the second? Current particle linguistic theory has no answer to this question except
the arbitrary one which leaves alternate solutions equally valid (although a particular
linguist may find one of the solutions preferable or more economic for certain purposes). Our wave view of language, however, would insist that all three of these
answers are artificial and that the empirical facts require that one flatly refuse to
segment at such points. One must rather insist that the two words *as* and *you* have
an indeterminate border which is fused in a wave-like fashion. In spite of this fusion
the PRESENCE of the two words is fully clear, in that the vocalic peak of each of the

words serves as the peak of the syllables by which the two words are respectively pronounced. The wave view insists, furthermore, that this indeterminacy is an essential part of a language — the wave-like fusion of forms in sequence — and that, rather than force an artificial segmentation upon language, one should adopt a wave theory of language which does not require this artificial treatment.

Going still further, one can look for illustrations on the lexical level which are somewhat parallel to the phonological ones wherein there was anticipation and decay of sounds which affected more than adjacent sounds. For example, in such a pronunciation of *Why did not you go?* as *Wainchago* the total pronunciation of *did* may disappear; *not* also may disappear as such (including the segment *n* written here), except for a residue of nasalization throughout the first syllable or two. The abstraction of these words from the total sequence cannot then be easily handled by a particle theory, whereas wave theory has not yet remotely come to the place where it can systematically handle such things smoothly. Nevertheless, the wave theory toward which I am pointing indicates clearly that some such approach must be developed if we are to handle language as it actually functions.

In grammar, also, such fusions exist in grammatical situations where one word functions doubly in two constructions. Note, for example, the following sentence (from Fries) in which the second *have* serves simultaneously in reference to the infinitive relation and in reference to the verb *pay*: *They have to have the students pay*.

The language of a wave view may include words such as PROCESS, DYNAMICS, CHANGE, FUSION, and the like. The language of particles includes phrases such as IS FOUND IN SUCH AND SUCH DISTRIBUTION, OCCURS UNDER THESE CONDITIONS, IS ENCOUNTERED IN VARIOUS ALTERNATE FORMS, etc. Currently the latter set of terms is in favor in the United States because of the heavy emphasis upon a particle view. The earlier set of terms was found in earlier American literature of a generation ago, but has been largely abandoned in current presentations. In a wave view of language, these former terms must be re-utilized, with more careful definition. A wave view implies process, development, change, and fusion.

It would seem probable, also, that no variety of a static, particle view of language can provide the most useful conceptual framework for the description of dynamic historical change. Within a wave view of language, change over a period of time or over a geographical area could presumably be described more easily through intermediate, transitional, fusion stages than is provided by a particle view. To allow for this approach, however, one must assume that fusion can take place not only between particular segments in a sequence, but between systems in time, and that these systems in some sense act as waves with identifiable components.

It is here that the wave view is seen to be a dynamic one. The dynamics of change in time are the dynamics of waves of movement of one system to another system with indeterminate areas between. In a historical change one system does not cease and another one begin with a gap between them. Rather there are transition states. And yet all is not transition in a single 'flat' sense. Rather there are periods and peaks when certain items or certain phases of systems are prominent. The dynamics of a wave view of language and of historical change would allow this to be treated in a sense that cannot easily be handled by the particle, static view of human behavior which by extension treats a system 'synchronically' (i.e., in terms of a fiction, extremely convenient for certain purposes, that a system can be studied at a point of time as if change were irrelevant to it at that time).

Reference to system, however, forces us to turn to the discussion of a field view of language. As with the wave view of speech, so within this view separate particles as such disappear and melt into one another. There is one major difference, however. Instead of looking at language as a sequence of waves in a single flat wave train, language is viewed somehow in 'depth'. A word is seen not as part of a sequence alone, but as part of a whole class of words which are not being uttered at that particular time but are parts of the total potential behavioral field. A word is viewed against this larger background; it is viewed in reference to its contrastive relationships with words which are not being uttered at that particular moment. A word is seen as part of a total language system. It exists only as part of that system. Its meanings develop only in contrast to other words in the system. Its function is explicable only against the backdrop of the total language behavioral events of that system.

In this view, therefore, CLASSES of words or language events come more into prominence, and patterns of language behavior occur and are analyzable and describable only as part of and in reference to the over-all total behavioral potential of the community. This total behavioral potential, this reservoir of possible activities within a behavioral system, comes into focus, and any one particular sequence of events drops in significance as over against the whole dynamic potential or structure of the system.

This field view is a necessary antidote to an over-segmentation which treats as the only object of study the particular bits and pieces in a particular sequential relation or event. The necessity for this correction derives from the nature of language behavior itself. Language is a vehicle for communication. Yet communication cannot be done with abstract sequences by themselves. Communication requires understanding, and understanding requires a MEMORY reservoir, or pool of common experience, or field, against which particular speech events at a particular moment stand out as figure on ground, and provide the structure which provides the potential for patterned events. Without the total ground, the figure has no meaning, and no perceptual impact.

The concept of field is also useful in terms of fused forms, but on a much more restricted plane. Instead of viewing words as bits which are pasted together in a line (in a particle view), or instead of viewing them merely as fused at their borders, or overlapping (in a wave view), in a field view one is more ready to deal as wholes with elements which resist analysis by the earlier two approaches. Here one is able to deal with a total complex and state that in the complex two or more elements are PRESENT, but that it is impossible to abstract or identify phonologically these two elements without doing violence to the data. It emphasizes the 'wholistic' nature of phenomena. It emphasizes that in communication it is not the bits and pieces which communicate, but the total speech event which carries communication impact only against a behavioral background of structured experience, structured memory, and structured potential.

Specifically, from this field view, we get clues to the reason why, when fusions go far enough, it is no longer useful on a practical level — and in the field view it is seen to be no longer useful on a theoretical level — to try to separate and indicate exactly the formative parts as they currently are present in the fused whole. In a rapid pronunciation of *Did you enjoy it?*, in which the first syllable rhymes with *gin* for *ginjoyit*, a field view would imply that the total overlapping of *did* with *you* and with the first part of *enjoy* is such that it is no longer useful to try to segment the separate elements. If one rejects a field view at this point, one is faced with the alternative of an elaborate particle or wave analysis of a type. Notice, for example, the following conjugation which might result in rapid speech of a certain type:

Die enjoy it?	'Did I enjoy it?'
Dee enjoy it?	'Did he enjoy it?'
D'they enjoy it?	'Did they enjoy it?'
D'we enjoy it?	'Did we enjoy it?'
Jew enjoy it?	'Did you enjoy it?'

So far no one has seriously attempted the analysis of any extensive body of English of this general type. It seems to me that before it can be done neatly a field theory must be more fully developed.

Turning now to look at the problem as a whole, in the light of these three views of language — particle, wave, and field — what attitudes should we now adopt? Should we consider, for example, that the particle view is invalid since a wave view is useful for describing physical continua? And must the wave view then be discarded because a field view provides better for functional relationships? By no means. As I see language structure, we need the three views, all preserved in our total descriptive statement, to approximate more closely the manner in which language operates as a behavioral structure in an active community.

The phoneme concept, specifically, must not be discarded, but supplemented. It reflects more truly than any other approach some of the structuring of data which is called to one's attention as one watches people struggle to learn languages other than their native one, as they attempt to understand the articulatory characteristics of their own speech sounds, and as they begin first to read and write. No wave view, nor field view, as adequately accounts for such psycholinguistic phenomena.

Moreover, in an attempt to avoid the particle implications of the phoneme we must not rely upon a retreat to the syllable, or to other pieces of the sentence, as basic units. This stratagem merely leads to a delay in facing the basic issue. Syllables, words, stress groups, or other units are also types of particles — a part of a segmenting approach — and are ultimately subject to the same attacks which can be leveled against the phoneme. To retreat from phoneme to syllable is to remain within the same phonological hierarchy, of the same basic particle view. If the syllable can be preserved, so can the phoneme. If the phoneme disappears, so inevitably will the syllable and — from another particle hierarchy — the particular morpheme, and word, and sentence!

The solution to our problem does not lie in this direction. Rather, a view of the multiple structuring of data, in three particle hierarchies of phonology, lexicon, and grammar, must be retained. But this hierarchical-particle approach must be supplemented by wave and field outlooks for providing dynamic and functional components within the analysis.

It is worth pointing out another major conclusion — by no means accepted by many linguists — that seems evident to this writer, at least. This is the conviction that LANGUAGE IS A VARIETY OF BEHAVIOR (not merely a code, or set of symbolic forms, or a mathematical logical pattern). This I firmly hold. It comes as no surprise, therefore, that problems of figure and ground which are relevant to perception and to other behavioral forms are relevant to language. The problem of relevant segmentation of non-language behavior, furthermore, requires a concept of purpose which is analogous to meaning in language study, and is essential for the detecting of those parts of events which are significant to the participants in those events. The conflict between studying ordinary behavior from the point of view of significant events, with indeterminate borders between events, as over against studying them as physical continua in which no gaps or borders as such can be found, is also common to language and other behavioral forms. In language, however, the particle view of behavior has been very heavily developed. If we can add to it wave and field views of behavior and develop them as extensively, we should then be ready to apply some of these concepts to other forms of behavior in a way that will help us to focus on some structural characteristics of events whose relevance has previously evaded us.

Language study is the first discipline to exploit in mathematical detail certain structural relationships which may also be found in other forms of behavior. It is, from this point of view, a historical accident that behavior structure, studied in quasi-mathematical terms and in terms of particle and wave, is developing in linguistics before developing in the same sense in other behavioral sciences. As a matter of fact, my interest in the extension of such language structural concepts to non-language areas was an accident. In 1949 when I was developing the theoretical material which I have referred to in this article, I was trying to get an over-all definition for any and all language units. Part of the definition required a component of distribution of the unit in a larger matrix of some type. When, however, I tried to define language itself within this same framework, the distribution requirement forced me to state that language was distributed in culture. Once culture entered the formulas at this point, it was only a matter of time until culture itself, in order to help meet this requirement adequately, had to be viewed within a framework sufficiently comparable to allow it to enter into unified statements with language. The transition therefore was gradual and forced upon me empirically rather than being set up *a priori*.

Now, following this experience, I am convinced that all forms of human behavior can be studied in terms of a hierarchy of particles, a sequence of waves of events, and a background field within which there are manifested concentrations of energy which we call events.

NUCLEATION*

The purpose of this article is to illuminate initial problems of language learning by analogy with problems in the formation and growth of crystals.

Two problems interest us: (1) The first few words of a new language may be more difficult to learn than the same number of words later on in the course of study. (2) A person may memorize a large number of vocabulary items and of grammatical rules and paradigms and yet find himself unable to talk with any feeling of ease or facility.

Persons may study a written language for a long time and yet be unable to speak it. Some scholars who have studied dead languages for twenty years have told me, for example, that a feeling of uneasiness has remained with them all this time: whenever a piece of unfamiliar Greek is put before them, they may be a bit disturbed as though they might not be able to read it. One of these scholars told me that after two decades of working on Greek, he for the first time was able to look at a page and have the proper psychological expectation of understanding it — and reacting to it as 'a language' — after he had studied modern Greek orally for a while.

Each of these difficulties can be explained by a single technical statement: None of the scholars concerned in each of the difficulties mentioned above had achieved language nucleation.

NUCLEATION IN PHYSICS

When a droplet is condensed out of a gas, or when a crystalline solid is precipitated out of a liquid, NUCLEATION[1] has occurred. Nucleation is involved in the first small clustering of atoms or molecules — say the first two or three dozen — into a structural pattern which will then be extensively duplicated in a repetitive fashion to form a crystal. It is difficult to get these first molecules to clump together. It is for this reason that liquids may be substantially undercooled, below the saturation point, before

* *The Modern Language Journal* XLIV:7 (1960), 291-295. Reprinted by permission.
[1] For my first interest in physical nucleation I am indebted to Professor Ernst Katz, of the University of Michigan, who presented the concept in an interdisciplinary seminar on the theory of growth at the University of Michigan in 1953.

nucleation in fact occurs. Yet once nucleation has begun, growth may proceed with great rapidity, so that "In fluid droplets the time of crystallization after nucleation is generally negligible compared with the nucleation period."[2]

In gases, in fact, the growth following delayed nucleation may be so fast — inasmuch as "matter is transported rapidly in gases at low pressures" — that the available material in supersaturation decays onto the growing nuclei quickly, "often within a second".[3] "Thus, it appears that the energy barrier opposing nucleation is much greater than that opposing growth."[4] The initial formation of starting nuclei is very difficult. The growth of these nuclei into larger units is very rapid and relatively easy and simple.

In contrast to the fact that substantial supercooling is necessary for initial nucleation to occur in a pure liquid or gas, only a very tiny degree of supersaturation is needed if within the gas are suspended dust particles around which nucleation can occur.[5] Some two hundred years ago Fahrenheit pointed out, similarly, that "the freezing of ordinary bulk liquids generally begins on suspended foreign particles and/or on the walls of the containing vessel".[6]

If, on the other hand, no impurities are present — as may be the case with small droplets — a liquid may be undercooled "an extraordinary amount relative to bulk liquids"[7] before nucleation occurs. In a larger bulk of liquid there are certain to be a few stray particles which are preferred nucleation sites for the formation of crystals, and this nucleation then spreads by growth very rapidly throughout all the liquid even where no impurities might happen to have been. (Other sites at which nucleation occurs, in addition to suspended particles in the liquid or gas, are the walls of the containing vessel itself.)

This phenomenon is hard to understand until one adds to it two other factors: (1) A PERFECT crystal, once formed, does not easily serve as a nucleus for further growth. (2) A crystal in which there are surface imperfections, however, serves for growth. Even more strongly, growth proceeds with great rapidity when a crystal is so distorted that half way through one of the sides a depression has lowered one or more rows of molecules to leave a kind of 'step' or terrace halfway through the crystal. Such a dislocation serves as a growing edge or terrace halfway across the crystal to which new molecules stick; the step front advances like a row of soldiers, pivoting around the center point where the step begins.[8]

[2] David Turnbull, "Phase Changes", *Solid State Physics* III (1956), 225-306, esp. p. 282.
[3] Turnbull, 263.
[4] Turnbull, 256.
[5] Turnbull, 263.
[6] Turnbull, 281.
[7] Turnbull, 282.
[8] This results in various kinds of spiral growth going round and round on top of the crystal. Extensive discussion of these spiral growths is found in Ajit Ram Verma, *Crystal Growth and Dislocations* (New York, 1953). A simple summary of this material, easily read by nonphysicists and amply illustrated, is seen in an article by Robert L. Fullmann, "The Growth of Chrystals", *Scientific American* 192 (1955), 74-80.

We now suggest that there are certain useful analogies between the nucleation of crystals and language learning.

NUCLEATION IN SPEECH

(1) As it is difficult for the first few molecules to cluster together in physical nucleation, so it is difficult for a person learning a foreign language to learn his first few words. The first words may be more difficult to memorize than later ones.

(2) Some persons have memorized long lists of vocabulary items, and even extensive rules of grammar, without being able to speak the language. One might say that their learning is in a supersaturated condition, without nucleation. That is, though they have many of the elements necessary for a conversation, they cannot in fact handle these. Specifically, they lack the STRUCTURE, the 'crystallization', which gives a characteristic patterning to sentences and conversations.

(3) In lacking a basic structural 'seed' — the basic initial conversational ability — it follows by analogy that we would expect them to find it difficult to learn new materials. Once the basic nucleation has begun, conversations utilized in ordinary contexts, further materials would be learned more easily.

(4) Some persons who do not know grammar extensively, nor have extensive vocabulary, nevertheless are able to use the language in speaking more readily than persons more 'learned' — they have in fact achieved a nucleation even though it be around an 'impurity'. From this situation it seems evident that one can get a deeper understanding of the reason why certain current teaching practices are useful, as well as the implication for certain emphases in practical pedagogy: The custom of having early words memorized in a social context — in a 'social crystal' — becomes clear. LANGUAGE NUCLEATION OCCURS WITHIN THE SOCIAL CONTEXT. Language is more than organized verbal sound. It is a structural part of a larger whole — part of life's total behavioral action and structure, intimately linked to social interaction. Greeting forms in a classroom situation, simulated marked scenes, and the like, provide the larger structural niches within which added bits of learning fit — whether lexical, grammatical, or social.

The student should be encouraged to USE the language in such social situations, even though he cannot do it with complete correctness. Nucleation will occur much faster around an inaccurate though functioning dialogue than it will about a completely abstract though correct set of words. (Drill in pattern practice can be used to eliminate such early errors, while leaving the student with the advantages of nucleated behavior.)

(5) Psychological nucleation in reference to language would seem to be accompanied by a feeling of 'naturalness' of language use. An individual with psychological language nucleation does not have to be instructed to 'think' in the language — he is already thinking in the language the moment he has necleation. Nucleation here

is not at all dependent upon the EXTENT of the vocabulary which he has mastered, nor accuracy, but upon the capacity to use a small set of forms in a natural way automatically in a natural context.

(6) The fact that we emphasize nucleation should not, however, be interpreted to mean that the learning of grammar or the memorization of vocabulary has suddenly become irrelevant. On the contrary, it continues to be important. It is these items, learned, which provide the supersaturated solution out of which the language crystallization can take place. There is a danger, furthermore, that a person getting nucleation without systematic instruction will never grow 'pure crystals' — errors will remain in his speech. Thus, the average person who 'picks up' a language without formal instruction may never learn the language well. Nucleation, as such, neither guarantees accuracy nor replaces hard work.

(7) On the other hand, the understanding of nucleation emphasizes the need for an oral approach to accompany (or precede) the reading approach. It seems very difficult — perhaps impossible — to get psychological nucleation exclusively from the study of written material. I interpret this to be the explanation of the Greek professor who after twenty years felt uncomfortable with classical Greek, and responded to it as in some psychological sense 'real language' only after he had spoken a bit of modern Greek. The modern Greek contributed to him linguistic and psychological nucleation which extensive reading was unable to do. It should be noted, furthermore, that recent attempts[9] to use more extensive oral components in structural contrastive approaches in the teaching of Latin are presumably successful precisely because these newer techniques are in fact capitalizing to some degree upon psychological nucleation. The difference here is that the achieved nucleation in learning a dead language by oral techniques is an artificial one to the extent that the language is not normally used as a national language — but the artificiality, nevertheless, serves the psychological purpose.

(8) We shall suggest that the 'step' in a dislocated crystal is analogous — for certain purposes — to a 'slot' in a grammatical structure. In each instance the step provides the 'growing edge'. By a slot, in grammar, we mean a position in the structure at which substitution of one element for another may take place, and a point at which new words may easily be introduced to the system. Thus in the sentence *The big boy came home* there is a slot where *boy* may be replaced by *girl, man*, etc. New vocabulary is learned most easily not through rote memory alone, but through the hearing or speaking of new words in such grammatical positions. The 'substitution tables' of British scholars or the 'pattern practice' of the English Language Institute, University of Michigan, etc., take advantage of this fact. Here the successfulness of such drills is not exclusively the result of sheer repetition, but to a very significant degree to the psychological ties between the substituted words and their contexts. Such a linkage is analogous to the sum of 'energy' units which are greater

[9]   Note Waldo E. Sweet, *Latin: A Structural Approach* (Ann Arbor, 1957).

and more effective when a molecule can attach itself to a step (with binding energies in two or three directions instead of just one), then when it can attach itself only to the surface of a crystal. The extra linkage points between a word and its linguistic environment within the slot of a structure seem to yield much firmer psychological 'energy bonds' than when one attempts to attach this word merely to the background system of words memorized in isolation.

(9) Every language has its characteristic grammatical structures — its characteristic 'crystal formations'. In our view these are best described as a series of grammatical units (tagmemes),[10] each of which is composed of a slot plus a characteristic set of lexical units which are appropriate to it. Thus a 'subject-as-actor' tagmeme occurs early in an English declarative sentence, and has as lexical units appropriate to it various kinds of substantive phrases.

(10) A sequence of units comprised of slot-plus-class enter into higher level structures — constructions. Constructions may be of word type, various kinds of phrases, clauses, sentences, or even high-level units such as sonnets or limericks. Initial nucleation, to be effective, must give to the speaker control of enough tagmemes and constructions on various levels to allow him to operate within some one social situation. He must have, that is to say, control of tagmemes which begin and end some discourses, of paragraph-opening sentence types, and of sentence types for continuing a description. In addition, he must control enough structures within the sentence to be able to control the substitution of relevant items within the sentence types. Drills designed to help in the mastering of these structures are part of the design of adequate pattern-practice materials.

(11) The structuring is 'hierarchical'. Language units are not all of the same size, nor all on the same level of relevance. The tagmemes are units within higher structures — the constructions — which in turn serve as units to fill slots on still higher levels of structure, up through the discourse level itself. (This hierarchical arrangement constitutes one of the sharp differences between the language of men and the communication units of — say — dogs or birds.) Here, as for the elements mentioned above, we may draw analogies between language structure and crystal structure. Crystal structure begins with a small initial clump of molecules organized in a 'cell'. These increase in size or in groupings of larger and larger accretions of cells. The hierarchical structuring of language, however, is much more elaborate than that of a simple crystal, since the high-level units of the language hierarchy are more than repetitions of low-level units. The analog here is more like that of the structure of a single complex organic molecule, in which there are radicals comprised of a number of atoms, which in turn may enter into various kinds of amino acid intermediate groups, and join to make the full organic molecule.

Nucleation in language learning requires drills which involve various levels of the

---

[10] For this viewpoint worked out in detail, see my *Language in Relation to a Unified Theory of the Structure of Human Behavior*, I, II, III (Glendale, 1954, 1955, 1960). See also Robert Longacre, "String Constituent Analysis", *Language* 36 (1960), 63-88.

hierarchy. Early drills may teach simple structures; later drills teach expansion of these by optional parts. Effective language lessons, therefore, may seek for initial nucleation by dealing with the obligatory components of the simplest entire discourse, followed by progressive expansion of this learned structure with optional elements at various levels of their hierarchy.

A TRI-HIERARCHICAL VIEW OF LANGUAGE STRUCTURE

Some of the complexity of language learning is due to the fact that the units of the language are not exhausted after one has studied the hierarchical components of grammar. In addition to the hierarchical grammatical constructions already referred to, there is present in language a hierarchical structure of phonology as well. Sounds combine into syllables. Syllables combine into rhythm groups related to some kind of accentual system. Rhythm units combine into higher pause groups or breath groups. Such units may in turn combine into rhetorical periods. Language learning, insofar as it is dealing with pronunciation, cannot adequately stop with the teaching of the isolated sounds — nor with words as made up purely of sounds in sequence.

Rhythm units[11] may differ in type from language to language. The adequate mimicry of them is extremely important to adequate pronunciation. Some languages, for certain purposes, have an accentual crescendo early in a word; in other languages a crescendo may occur late in a word. Decrescendo from a stressed syllable, furthermore, may be rapid, or slow. The number of syllables in any one such accentual group, or the placement of them in relation to stress, makes enormous differences in the ultimate result. Differences such as these occur from style to style within a single language as well as across language boundaries.

The lexicon, also, is structured in a hierarchical manner. Separate morphemes (in general comprising meaningful minimal parts of words) combine to join into words — as *boy* plus *-s* make up *boys*. Words combine into specific phrases or into idioms such as *to step on the gas*, etc. On a still higher level of the lexical hierarchy an entire jingle may carry a single meaning, as a kind of high-level lexical unit. A counting rhyme used by children may have no useful meaning derived from the particular words of the rhyme itself, for example, even though the total impact (i.e., meaning) is that of specifying the person selected to play the leading role in the game.

With hierarchies of grammar, phonology, and lexicon in view, one has a tri-hierarchical[12] approach to language analysis. These hierarchies crisscross and affect one another in various ways. A syllable may comprise an entire morpheme — as in *boy*,

---

[11] For a technical description of some of these materials note my "Abdominal Pulse Types in Some Peruvian Indian Languages", *Language* 33 (1957), 30-35. See also my *Intonation of American English* (Ann Arbor, 1945), 34-36, for differences between syllable-timed and stressed-timed rhythm patterns.
[12] For further details see my "Language as Particle, Wave, and Field", *The Texas Quarterly* II (1959), 37-54.

or parts of a morpheme — as in *ticket*, or a cluster of morphemes — as in *boys*. Such crisscrossing between the hierarchies is a crucial datum which forces theoretical separation of these hierarchies.

At least these three hierarchies are in language, according to our analysis. Others may later have to be postulated. Crawford,[13] for example, splits the phonological hierarchy into a 'phonotagmemic' hierarchy, embracing the arrangement of sound elements into phonological slot-plus-class units, comprising the specific units, on various levels, filling the phonotagmemic slots.

Nucleation, to be effective, must lead us to use efficiently, rapidly, automatically, and easily, certain selected units on the various levels of each of these hierarchies. The intricacies of their interrelations are too great for a speaker to handle them by conscious direction on the basis of consciously applied rules. He must, rather, learn to control them automatically on the basis of experience. In nucleation the speaker first integrates all of these kinds of components into at least a small, coherent whole, functioning automatically. This frees the mind to get on with the business of communicating meanings, making choices, and building social rapport.

---

[13] See John C. Crawford, "Pike's Tagmemic Model Applied to Totontepec Mixe Phonology", unpublished dissertation (Michigan, 1960).

STIMULATING AND RESISTING CHANGE*

The purpose of this article is to classify some of the conditions under which change is likely to be successfully stimulated (or successfully resisted) and to imply some kinds of steps which may be fruitfully taken if one wishes to stimulate the occurrence of change. The technique of discussion is to set up a 'model' which is a systematic way of viewing the problem. The prescribed model implies that certain consequences may follow if the conditions can be met. The discussion is therefore a theoretical one, and some of the argument is based on linguistic change. Some readers will find it easier to read first the sections entitled "Stimulating Change" and "Resisting Change", in order to see the practical implications of the model before going back to read the whole article.

This model is an attempt at the SCIENTIFIC statement of components of change. It is, therefore, attempting to suggest components relevant to ALL change and not to set forth conditions leading to any one particular desired change. EVERY educator is involved in changing his students — for what he believes to be the better, and according to his own code of values and morals. Yet my personal biases are not, so far as I know, relevant to the model proposed. The model itself is neutral. Once developed, its use will be determined by other than scientific considerations — that is, by one's own value system.

Thus the model is relevant if one wishes to educate, modernize, Christianize, or, for that matter, to disrupt, destroy, or degrade a culture. The price of progress includes the building of bridges over which people may pass backwards. The model sets forth CONDITIONS for change, without predicting the DIRECTION of change. Change may pass over it in either direction.

THE MODEL ITSELF

The principles suggested here were first developed in reference to linguistic change. They are being published in an article entitled "Toward a Theory of Change and Bilingualism".[1] Persons wishing a fuller statement of the linguistic model should consult that article.

* *Practical Anthropology* 8:6 (1961), 267-274. Reprinted by permission.
¹ To appear in *Studies in Linguistics*.

A crucial concept in the model is that of SHARED COMPONENT. The assumption is that, IF CHANGE IS TO OCCUR, SOME RELEVANT COMPONENT OF THE UNITS TO BE AF-FECTED, OR OF THE MATRIX WITHIN WHICH THE UNITS ARE TO BE AFFECTED, MUST BE SHARED. In this sense the model allows no 'action at a distance'. Units may affect one another only if they share a component between them, or if they share a matrix of behavior or of environment.

A component shared is RELEVANT to a particular desired change when it may either assist or retard the particular change one has in mind. It is especially relevant when the shared component is an essential condition which must be met before change can take place. A component is relevant also, if the item cannot, in the view of its participants, be shared without destroying or injuring one of the systems in-volved.

The shared component may be at the MARGIN of, or incidental to, the units involved, in which case one is dealing with ACCULTURATION. On the other hand, the shared component may be the CORE of the total system of units involved, with the change occurring incidentally to the system, and introduced from within the system, in which case one is dealing with INNOVATION.

A further concept built into the model is a difference between SEQUENTIAL change versus SYSTEMIC change. In some instances behavioral events occurring in sequence affect one another. In other instances the impact of a system of behavioral events upon another system causes change.

These various items of the model can be combined to show certain of the relation-ships implied. We gave a few illustrations of linguistic items filling the respective 'pigeon holes' in the model. The numbers in the succeeding paragraphs correlate with the numbers on the accompanying chart (Table 1), which is based upon one given in the linguistic article cited, with some modifications.

(1) SHARED MARGINS OF SEQUENCES. Non-violent, gradual change in the margins of units is most fruitfully illustrated by the manner in which a phoneme of one syllable can gradually pass over to a second syllable. If one tries to say rapidly and repeatedly the syllable [op] (following an experiment of Stetson), gradually, as he speeds up, he changes to the syllable [po]. At some point before [op] has changed to [po] there is a point in which the sound [p] belongs neither to the first nor to the second syllable alone, but simultaneously to both. The consonants, as margins of the syllables, have been affected in their placement in the syllables themselves. The post-syllabic con-sonant of the first syllable has become a pre-syllabic consonant of the second. The change has occurred over the BRIDGE of the placement of the consonant at the time it was shared by the two syllables.

The bridging across the two syllables is made possible, furthermore, by the WAVE CHARACTERISTICS of the syllable. An articulatory wave, with vowel at peak and con-sonant at trough, is such that the phonemes constitute small articulatory waves or ripples on the larger syllable wave itself. The position of the ripple can change in phase with reference to its place on the wave.

TABLE 1

Model of conditions for change

Relevant Shared Component Changed Component	Components Viewed as Items in Sequence or as Parts of a Complex	Components Viewed as Parts of Systems in a Hypersystem
Margin — and Acculturation	(1) Consonant passing over syllable boundary; op.op o.pop — Dress, work, play, visits, values, history, legends, events	(4) Systems merging at loans — Joint endeavors, or syncretism
Core — and Innovation	(2) Dissimilation of sounds in a word — Internal growth (or decay) of art, philosophy, economics	(5) Styles, interlocking — Community outlook types or specialties
Matrix — as Favorable Climate	(3) Sentence accepting a loan — Climate of social, political, religious, and intellectual opinions or actions, with functional substitutes and additions	(6) Cultural matrix with replaced language — Replacement of linguistic, political, economic, or religious systems

(2) SHARED CORES OF SEQUENCES. When change is developed by forces within a unit, rather than from impact with the neighboring unit in sequence with it, innovation occurs in that unit. In language this may happen when the sounds of a word interchange in some way.

This may be the situation, for example, in dissimilation: Our word *pilgrim* has an [l] and an [r] both of which seem to go back to the Latin *peregrinus*; the change of the first [r] to [l] is an internal matter. A sequence of sounds is involved, but the relevant component shared is the total word — the core of the word, we might say, rather than merely margins of adjacent words.

(3) SHARED MATRIX FOR SEQUENCES. Change occurs when, in a particular matrix of a sequence of units, there is an intrusion of a word from an outside system into some slot of that matrix. Suppose, for example, that in the English 'frame' *I like to eat strawberries*, a bilingual Spanish speaker replaces the word *strawberries* with the loan word *tortillas* 'corn cakes'. The accommodation of the loan into English is made possible by the structure of the sentence — which, say, leaves a subject 'slot' in its matrix, for nouns — into which the borrowed word is inserted.

(4) SHARED MARGINS OF SYSTEMS. As these first loans become assimilated to the system, the system of the receiving language itself becomes changed in terms of the new components added to its inventory and in reference to differences in the pattern of distribution of sounds which the loans may introduce.

Two languages, as systems, have overlapped, at their periphery, when loan words have passed from one of them to the other. From this point of view we choose to assume the presence of a HYPERSYSTEM which includes the two languages as a whole. The two systems form a single larger system, in some vague sense, by virtue of the fact that a reciprocal acculturation is possible between them. A hypersystem appears to occur in the personality structure of the bilingual speaker, who HIMSELF may be viewed as a shared component of the interacting behavioral systems.

(5) SHARED CORES OF SYSTEMS. When dealing with two systems which are in some sense 'the same' but in other senses different, one may have styles of speech, or dialects, of a language. Here the OVER-ALL PATTERN, the central core, may remain the same, with the differences treated as innovation rather than as the acculturation of (4). Informal versus formal address would contain differences of style treated in this way. So, also, would the English of Boston versus that of Texas. Most of the points in the dialect or style concerned would find a corresponding point or component in the other styles or dialects of that language.

(6) SHARED MATRIX OF SYSTEMS. Where violent change affects a total system, some matrix must have been shared. Thus, a geographical matrix must be shared if one language is to replace the other. This may happen, for example, after an invasion.

Systems, like phonemes and syllables, can be treated as waves, with the loan words treated as ripples on the waves, spreading across from one language wave to the other. Changes of dialects in geographical location can be treated in this way, as can changes in time.

STIMULATING CHANGE

We now look at the various pigeon holes in the model to see if they can lead to questions which one may ask, or principles which the 'agent of change' may follow, when change is desired, or when one wishes to explain change which has occurred.

(1) SHARED MARGINS OF ITEMS IN SMALL SEQUENCES OR COMPLEXES. One who wishes to stimulate change may profitably ask: What do the two activity complexes share? Of these elements, which ones are relevant to the desired change, so that they could serve as a bridge over which the desired change could pass?

If no relevant component seems to be shared, one asks: What component could be DEVELOPED as shared, so that it could then be used as a bridge to introduce further change?

The innovator needs to study the folklore, legends, general philosophical background, and values to see what social and moral elements are shared. EVERY society has moral and value components which overlap at some major points. In every society there is SOME value attached to certain assignments of roles to varying individuals, to communication techniques, goals, regulation of affective expression or of disruptive behavior, etc.[2] For the person interested in Christianization, some of these become especially relevant, since it is precisely at this point that all peoples share some desires for internal controls, and it is here that the Christian view attaches moral responsibility to a social structure. The moral imperative here is the basis of responsibility with which Christianity in part deals.

On an activity level, shared components which the innovator may need to develop are opportunities to work together, visit together, exchange stories, and so on. Negatively, note that destructive influences also operate here with the same shared components that the constructive innovator must use.

One of the most crucial of the shared components effective in eliciting change is the language itself. When one speaks of 'communication', one is speaking, in this model, of a crucial shared component. This component is UNDERSTANDING. Understanding comes best through the vernacular. Language is a 'clearing house' for cataloguing and teaching almost all cultural habits. If, therefore, one knows thoroughly the language and literature of a people, he is likely to have at least a nonanalytical knowledge of the habits of that people, and recognize more readily the relevance of shared components.

(2) SHARED CORES OF ITEMS, IN A SEQUENCE OR IN A COMPLEX. How can one encourage initiative? How can one preserve the core of a culture and its forms, as a formal entity, while stimulating it to modify itself usefully? And, as a part of Christianization, how can Christian morality elicit acts of kindness or of altruism in areas of the culture where they would be helpful, and encourage elimination of harmful practices (such as infanticide and feuding)? And how can this be done without losing those habits of courtesy or kindness already engrained in that particular social structure? How can Christianity, for example, be a yeast to permeate cultural forms with unselfish values rather that a hammer to destroy them?

Negatively, note that the incoming of certain kinds of trade values — relative, say, to opium or firewater — could infuse a culture with some kinds of degrading motives hitherto foreign to it.

(3) SHARED MATRIX FOR ITEMS. What kind of climate of opinion is favorable to change? How can such a climate be promoted? Beyond the particular items which the innovator wishes to see changed, how much other material in the climate must be changed in order for the desired changes to be accepted or to survive? Note that this implies that more than the initiation of a particular habit is necessary for effective change of that habit. Rather, one must attempt to affect sources of general public opinion which will make such a habit acceptable, or even desirable, within the value system of the changees or of their colleagues. If it cannot be made acceptable, it must be made tolerable, on the part of others, or it may be wiped out after it is set up.

---

[2] See David F. Aberle, and others, "The Functional Prerequisites of Society", *Ethics* 60 (1950), 110-111. See also a summary of this material (and numerous other bibliographical references) in Kenneth L. Pike, *Language in Relation to a Unified Theory of the Structure of Human Behavior* 3 (Glendale, Calif., Summer Institute of Linguistics, 1960), 119-121.

Where does the new custom fit into the former structure? Can the desired item be treated so that it merely is added to a class of other items in the culture and can be assimilated by the old structure without major revamping of that old structure? Or is the change desired that of eliminating an old item — and, if so, is it most effective to provide a substitute for it in the same slot of the structure?

Specifically, also, how can any such new items be introduced gradually enough that the impact is held within the tolerance limits of the culture? Will the change contemplated be accompanied by so many readjustments that the impact will be violent?

(4) SHARED MARGINS OF SYSTEMS. Are the borrowings forcing a redefinition of the pattern? Does a new pattern force into attention in their system philosophical subtleties or inconsistencies which previously did not trouble them? Has the reworking of the receiving system been useful in terms of its own value pattern, or damaging?

How has the ecology of the total system been affected? That is, has a chain reaction been started by a relative simple borrowing which affects the whole pattern? J. Lauriston Sharp[3] has shown, for example, that the introduction of steel axes set going a far-reaching set of changes in the culture of the Yir Yoront aboriginals of Australia. Studies in ecology[4] show, on a naturalistic front, the upsets which may occur when a small environmental change is made.

To what extent do the two systems in contact together form a total system, interlocking at the borders? Do people feel that they are in a transition stage moving from the changing culture to the innovating culture? If so, how does this affect group loyalties? Emotional drives? Ambitions?

(5) SHARED CORES OF SYSTEMS. How can one encourage a variety of sub-systems of a culture in order to fill up available niches in the environment, to promote helpful specializations and diversity? How can one encourage specific groups to attempt to adapt themselves to the particular set of conditions in which they are living? Here the innovator may wish one kind of fundamental education provided for jungle peoples and a quite different set for the same ethnic group of people after they have moved to a large industrial area.

(6) SHARED MATRIX OF SYSTEMS. As for a cultural matrix within which one system completely replaces another, we note that this may lead to violent replacement if, for example, a total language system is replaced by military pressures. One asks, however, whether such replacement can sometimes be for the good. The reply seems to be that the good values of total replacement can be obtained only if the people themselves desire the change. Thus, if peoples of a minority group themselves wish to adopt wholly the language of the dominant group in order for their children to achieve

---

[3] "Steel Axes for Stone-Age Australians", *Human Organization* 11:2 (1952), reprinted in *Practical Anthropology* 7:2 (1960), 62-73.

[4] See Samuel A. Graham, *Forest Entymology*, 3rd ed. (New York, 1952). See also Stanley A. Cain, "Some Principles of General Ecology and Human Society", *American Biology Teacher* 22:3 (1960).

the privileges which go with that language, then many of these people will, in fact, achieve such total replacement. In the change-over period, however, the innovator helping the people to reach this goal must realize that if the transition is attempted with too great rapidity, serious damage can result. Some of the children may end up with no vernacular and with the dominant language only partially learned, with which they can express only the crudest of the materials needed for full social and intellectual development. In effect, such people may be partly detribalized.

RESISTING CHANGE

In general, theory and practice for resisting cultural change are the reciprocal of those for eliciting change.

Resistance to cultural change can be either good or bad from the point of view of the particular culture involved, or from the point of view of modernization, or education, or Christianization. That which the innovator may wish to elicit as modernization, the culture may choose to resist in terms of conserving old values. That which the innovator may wish to introduce to enhance the values in a society, the society itself may resist in terms of conviction that its own values are preferable. That which the innovator may wish to introduce in order to disrupt a system to his own economic advantage may be resisted by the culture in order to preserve the society.

If we start with the assumption that a certain change is good, and that a desired state resulting from the change is good, and if both the innovator and the changee are agreed at this point, nevertheless both must now resist certain kinds of further change, or the desired state, when attained, will itself collapse. This is most easily illustrated by ecological examples: If one wishes to raise potatoes, and therefore to get a concentration of potato plants in a particular area, this makes a prime feeding target for predatory insects. A disastrous infestation of such insects may develop. This heavy infestation would not have occurred before the cultivated situation was developed, and now threatens to eliminate the desired growing crop — a change which must be arrested by insecticides.[5] In cultural terms, the development of an educated citizenry in an area where previously formal education was unobtainable may open the way to a kind of undesirable academic competition, intellectual pride and excessive nationalism.

Similarly, there are reported to have been some instances in which the introduction of Christianity and kindnesses to a cultural group has in fact led temporarily to the lowering of morals (e.g., through misuses of concepts of forgiveness)[6], or the increase

[5]   See Graham, *Forest Entymology* 94.
[6]   Note, for example, John C. Messenger Jr., "Reinterpretations of Christian and Indigenous Beliefs in a Nigerian Nativist Church", *American Anthropologist* 62 (1960), 268-278. See also, by the same author, "The Christian Concept of Forgiveness and Anang Morality", *Practical Anthropology* 6:3 (1959), 97-103.

of witchcraft. The task of the innovator, therefore, is to elicit change where he wishes it, and then to develop the ecological climate in such a fashion that the change will not be overdone or destroyed by correlative developing forces which destroy the effect of the innovation.

(1) SHARED MARGINS OF ITEMS OR ACTIVITIES. As one utilizes a shared component as a bridge over which changes may pass, so resistance to culture may try to fend off change which threatens to reach it through shared activities. DIFFERENCES can be emphasized which tend to negate or resist the change at that point. If shared components are not easily present, and the innovators are attempting to introduce them, the resisters would attempt to shield themselves and their colleagues from all attempts at building such components. Joint activities of all types might be avoided, on social, economic, or religious fronts. Isolationism would be encouraged by physical and ideological means.

(2) SHARED CORES OF ACTIVITIES. The stimulus to develop initiative and independence may move faster and farther than the innovator feels wise. Or changes may occur faster, though encouraged by the people themselves, than they desire. Here the desideratum seems to be to preserve effective cultural continuity between the new and the old. If the change occurs too fast, then it scarcely represents controlled, peripheral innovation but rather TOTAL replacement of the core. The change becomes qualitative rather than merely quantitative. On the other hand, conservative forces of various kinds may choose to dampen creativity, in order to preserve the status quo.

(3) SHARED MATRIX FOR SEQUENCE. When change needs to be resisted the effective way of doing so is by a cultural dampening of the climate. A mobilization of social forces to frown on change helps to preserve the status quo. By lowering the 'violence' threshold to where small changes are met with violent rejection, major changes are in turn resisted, since the shared-component bridges are kept to a minimum. Similarly, the slots where cultural substitution might take place with functional replacement of the parts are vigorously policed so that no substitutes are allowed for the old acceptable alternatives.

(4) SHARED MARGINS OF SYSTEMS. By refusing to allow small substitutions of detail, such a culture refuses to allow a fusion of two systems as such. If initial small loans from the innovating system cannot enter the resisting system, then no relevant, single, overall hypersystem can develop with its extensive bridges of shared components over which large systemic change can pass.

Change can be undesirable in terms of the overdevelopment of the hypersystem. If the two contacting systems share a great deal of material, the resultant syncretism may in fact weaken the distinctive characteristics of both of the systems. A Christian innovator who brings into a culture certain Christian ceremonies over a bridge of older ceremonies attached to names, places, environments, and other characteristics of the receiving culture may end up with a so-called Christian system which in fact is a hypersystem largely characterized by older values.[7]

(5) SHARED CORES OF SYSTEMS. Innovators may wish to discourage the development of sub-varieties of changes. Or the culture itself may adopt measures to preserve uniformity of opinion and action, unaffected by different local conditions. Development of such local styles of behavior is resisted either by movement of personnel from one area to another to prevent development of local outlook, or by discouragement of initiative at the local point, or by a positive attempt to teach and enforce conformity regardless of local conditions.

(6) SHARED MATRIX FOR SYSTEMS. In reference to resisting total replacement of one structure by another, a resisting group may attempt to enforce isolation by trying peaceably or forcibly to keep out foreign innovators so that people who would constitute a bridge between the two systems do not get a chance to work. The isolation may be accomplished on a smaller front by cultural institutions — as by training in parochial schools.

The innovator must accept the responsibility for the implications of his own value system, including as a value the respect for other values. When, in this circumstance, he feels justified in seeking education for or change in other people, he may assess some of the problems involved by studying the situation in the light of this model.

---

[7]   For a discussion of early Jesuit policy which adopted an approach leading to syncretism, note Peter Duigan, "Early Jesuit Missionaries: A Suggestion for Further Study", *American Anthropologist* 60 (1958), 725-732, and commentary on this by Eugene A. Nida, "The Role of Cultural Anthropology in Christian Missions", *Practical Anthropology* 6:3 (1959), 110-116.

DIMENSIONS OF GRAMMATICAL CONSTRUCTIONS*

This paper[1] begins with a question. It gives empirical data in order to show that the question appears answerable in principle. It discusses some problems that require an elaboration of the preliminary solution. Finally, it summarizes a few of the implications of the study.

1. THE QUESTION

Can grammatical dimensions be charted like phonetic ones? Is it possible to develop a format for presentation of the construction types of a variety of languages in such a way that it will be as useful for grammar as has been the charting of phonemes according to contrastive features? Is it possible to develop a chart of the constructions? Specifically, for grammar, what would be the analogy of

$$
\begin{array}{ccc}
p & t & k \\
b & d & g \\
m & n & \eta
\end{array}
$$

with one set of contrastive features in rows, another in columns, and with phones in the cells of the matrix? Would this approach allow for presentation — simply, comparably — of the construction types of a large number of languages as a basis for a universal etics of grammar? Our answer to these questions is affirmative.

Several difficulties in early tagmemic descriptions would be lessened by such a presentation. Redundancy — most annoying, perhaps, of the characteristics of current tagmemic presentation — would be sharply cut. Where sentence (or clause, or phrase, or word) features have been repeated in order to allow for multiplied sentence types, single presentation of the intersection of two features could be made, with later cross reference to this total complex.

Where a basic kind of sentence is modifiable in various ways for emphasis, or to

* *Language* 38:3, Part 1 (1962), 221-244. Reprinted by permission.
[1] Presidential Address delivered at the meeting of the Linguistic Society of America in Chicago, December 28, 1961.

make interrogative sentences, various devices have been used to avoid a listing of each basic type repeatedly, plus the modifications. Helen L. Hart[2] sets up for Amuzgo a single emphatic sentence type to cover relevant emphatic variants of all basic sentences. Similarly, one query sentence type, one response type, and one quotative type are set up to handle varieties of all the basic sentence types.

Velma Pickett for Zapotec[3] points in the direction of dimensions by charts of constructions in reference to contrastive classes of clause[4] and phrase constructions. This charting serves elegantly as a basis for checking the internal contrastive features of constructions, but has the tagmemes themselves in the cells of the chart — whereas for our goal we must have contrastive features at the side and top of the chart, with separate total constructions in the cells as the unit analogous to phones of a phonetic chart. Pickett's chart, however, will serve us later (42) when we wish to show contrast between differing construction types.

2. DATA ILLUSTRATING GRAMMATICAL DIMENSIONS

During a field seminar which I directed in Peru in 1960-1961, several members of the Summer Institute of Linguistics attempted to apply this theoretical suggestion. First to succeed was Mildred Larson, for Aguaruna.[5] She gives separate dimensional matrices for the various structural levels of verb root, affix, base, stem, margin, and word, and for the clause. It became clear that dimensional analysis is relevant to any such level of structure, not just to one of them.

The matrix for Aguaruna independent clause classes is reproduced here as our example (1). The transitive-intransitive-nominative dimension intersects with the imperative-stative-active-equative dimension. The nominative type is limited to equative clauses. Active and equative both subdivide into declarative and two varieties of interrogative, and hence imply further dimensions for these sub-systems.

The symbols for clause types are in the cells, as we wish them to be. These labels are chosen componentially — with letters from the name of each dimension and subdimension, as well as from the matrix as a whole (i.e., independent clause), which is in contrast with other matrices both on the same level and on different levels. Although the dimensional labels on the charts of the matrices are drawn from meaning components, the dimensions themselves are based on formal contrasts of structure paralleling these semantic elements. The tagmemic nature of the contrast will be in view below, in Section 5.

---

[2] "Hierarchical Structuring of Amuzgo Grammar", *IJAL* 23 (1957), 143-144.
[3] *Hierarchical Structure of Isthmus Zapotec* (=*Language Dissertation* 56) (Baltimore, 1960).
[4] See the reproduction of a part of the Zapotec clause chart in (42) below. For Pickett's phrase chart, see her p. 35.
[5] Of the Jívaro family. Her paper will appear in 1962 in *Peruvian Studies* I (=*Linguistic Series of the Summer Institute of Linguistics*). Materials cited here are based on that article, where specific illustrative sentences may be found.

(1)   *Aguaruna Independent Clause Classes*

	Transitive	Intransitive	Nominative
Imperative	TImpCl	ItImpCl	
Stative	TStCl	ItStCl	
Active			
Declarative . . .	TDACl	ItDACl	
Inter. of Pred.. .	TInPACl	ItInPACl	
Inter. of Item.. .	TInIACl	ItInIACl	
Subjunctive . . .	TSjACl	ItSjACl	
Equative			
Declarative . . .	TDECl	ItDECl	NoDECl
Inter. of Pred.. .	TInPECl	ItInPECl	NoInECl
Inter. of Item.. .	TInIECl	ItInIECl	

Not until the entire article had been drafted was it seen that the apparently arbitrary arrangement of the Aguaruna clause dimensions was in fact structurally determined. The transitive-intransitive components of the horizontal dimension were carried by the verb root or stem, whereas the modal components of imperative, stative, active, and equative of the vertical dimension were signalled by the verb margin.

Both the root and the margin can be arranged in subdimension matrices, as in (2) and (3). In (2), for faster reading, I have not inserted the abbreviated clause names in the cells, but have merely inserted an x to show the occurrence of each type.

(2)   *Aguaruna Verb-Root Types*

	Singular	Plural	Neutral
Transitive.	x	x	x
Intransitive	x	x	x

(3)   *Aguaruna Verb-Margin Types*

Imperative	ImpVM
Stative	StVM
Active	
Declarative . . .	DAVM
Interrogative 1 .	In_1AVM
Interrogative 2 .	In_2AVM
Subjunctive . . .	SjAVM
Equative	
Declarative . . .	DEVM
Interrogative 1 .	In_1EVM
Interrogative 2 .	In_2EVM

One practical value of the dimensional approach begins to emerge here: it forces decision as to class membership — or lack of such membership — of a construction in particular class types. Similarly, it forces into awareness various gaps in the description.

Since the margin material in (3) is not arranged in intersecting-dimensional form, Larson is not forced to make explicit on her chart whether the imperative and stative are assumed to be active, declarative, or neutral in some way. Structurally, also, the interrogative-declarative dichotomy is treated by Larson as less central to the verb system than the imperative-active one. (See Section 3 for nuclear components of a system.)

A theoretical value of the dimensional approach also emerges: forced into attention is a formal interlocking of structural levels. Classes of related constructions from one level may have dimensions coordinate with the dimensions of the classes of some of their members from lower structural levels. This relationship might be called interlevel concord. It is seen most easily when tagmemes of the same structural meaning occur in each level — dependent subject affix and independent subject word, for example.

A second attempt at setting up a dimensional clause matrix was made by Mary Ruth Wise, for data from Candoshi,[6] a language family geographically near the Jívaro. The contrastive features are somewhat similar to those for Aguaruna. In (4) we see the basic outline. Further contrastive subclasses are found in formulas within the article.

(4)   *Candoshi Clause Types*

	Transitive	Intransitive	Equative
Independent			
Indicative			
Declarative	x	x	x
Interrogative	x	x	x
Subjunctive			
Declarative			
Desiderative . . .	x	x	–
Imperative	x	x	–
Potential.	x	x	–
Interrogative			
Desiderative . . .	x	x	–
Imperative	x	x	–
Potential.	x	x	–
Dependent Conditional	x	x	x

---

[6] In Lorrie Anderson and Mary Ruth Wise, "Contrastive Features of Candoshi Clause Classes", *Peruvian Studies* I.

Although other articles on tagmemics have not explicitly attempted to chart dimensions of constructions, one can nevertheless often deduce from them — and, of course, from articles written without reference to tagmemic theory — dimensional matrices. In Záparo sentence types, for example, Catherine Peeke postulates no transitive-intransitive dichotomy.[7] In this it appears (5) quite different from the analysis of the neighboring Jívaro and Candoshi families. Mode and action dimensions are given greater prominence.

(5)   *Záparo Sentence Types*

	Active	Stative
Indicative	x	x
Interrogative	x	x
Imperative	x	—

Note that when one desires, this Záparo matrix, like any such matrix, can be resymbolized as (6) (like a matrix of *p t k, b d g, m n ŋ*) — with only the cell fillers given.

(6)   AInd   StInd
         AInter   StInter
         AImp   —

In Capanahua,[8] clauses with obligatory absence of object lead to a contrast with clauses having optional object. The contrast is not labelled (7) directly transitive versus intransitive by Loos, since the objectless form with causative occurs with a stem in a form which is elsewhere called transitive.

(7)   *Capanahua Clause Contrasts*

	−O		±O	
	−C	+C	−C	+C
Declarative	x	x	x	x
Narrative	x	x	x	x
Exhortative	x	x	x	x

The causative, here, is not merely an addition to a basic matrix, since in contrast to the straight intransitive clause, for example, there are differences in the included predicate tagmemes and also — if these optional tagmemes happen to be present — in the independent subject, the associative, the relative, and the locative tagmemes. The matrix can be restated as (8):

(8)   (D − C − O, DC − O, D − C ± O, DC ± O, etc.)

[7]   Matrix based on "Structural Summary of Záparo", *Ecuadorian Studies* I (=*Linguistic Series of the Summer Institute of Linguistics*), to appear in 1962.
[8]   Of the Pano language family of Peru. Based on data from Eugene E. Loos, "Capanahua Narration Structure", to appear in *Texas Studies in Literature and Languages*.

In data from Cashibo,[9] related to Capanahua, the transitive-intransitive dichotomy is seen to be important on several levels of structure. Roots occur which are basically transitive or intransitive. In addition one finds intricate classes of derivational suffixes of which some are neutral, others transitive or transitivizing (occurring, that is, both with transitive or intransitive roots), and others intransitive or intransitivizing. A verb may be transitive or intransitive whether in a principal or in a subordinate clause. In the subordinate verb, however, whether itself transitive or intransitive, inflectional suffixes reflect transitive-intransitive concord of subordinate verb with the transitive-intransitive base of the verb of the governing principal clause. This set of relations may be seen by comparing (9) and (10). (In Section 4.1, however, clause types from the same column of the two subordinate rows would turn out to be allosyntagmatic.)

(9)   *Cashibo Verb Bases* (*Core plus Suffix*)

	Derivational Suffixes		
	Neutral	Transitivizing	Intransitivizing
Transitive Core.	x	x	x
Intransitive Core	x	x	x

(10)   *Cashibo Verbs*

	Transitive	Intransitive
Principal		
Personal.	x	x
Imperative.	x	x
Purposive	x	x
Subordinate		
With inflectional concord to transitive principal verb	x	x
With inflectional concord to intransitive principal verb	x	x

Dimensional systems even more elaborate than those for Aguaruna and Cashibo are emerging from current study of various languages.

3. MULTIPLICATION OF A MATRIX BY A CONSTANT

In working the dimensional materials into display form various difficulties arose. When the number of dimensions increased, for example, the charts became unwieldy. This awkwardness was especially unpleasant when one of the dimensions seemed in some sense to be subsidiary to the remaining dimensions, and when it cut across the

[9] See Olive A. Shell, "Cashibo II: Grammemic Analysis of Transitive and Intransitive Verb Patterns", *IJAL* 23 (1957), 179-218.

remainder in such a fashion that it modified all of the constructions on that level.

In order to reduce this complexity, we now (a) set up a basic pattern of dimensional contrasts as a small matrix, (b) add a notation which labels the total matrix with a single letter symbol, (c) label the new simple factor by a symbol, and (d) treat the derivative matrix as a product of the small matrix multiplied by a constant.[10]

If, for example, (11a) is a single-column matrix of transitive and intransitive declarative clauses, and if we call this set the systemic kernel M_k (i.e., the nucleus)[11] of the system, then $M_k \cdot Imper$ (kernel matrix times imperative) gives a derived Imperative matrix M_{da} (11b). If each of these matrices can in turn be modified by the addition of an emphasis tagmeme, then we have M_{d3} (11c) from $e \cdot M_k \cdot Imp$.

(11a)	TD	(11b)	TImp	(11c)	$_eTD$	$_eTImp$
	ID		IImp		$_eID$	$_eIImp$

In materials currently available, probably the features most easily treated in this way are interrogation, emphasis, quotation, and negation. Several of these are candidates for such handling in Amuzgo[12] description. Hart's Amuzgo 'Uttereme V: query' merely modifies the various basic sentence types by the interrogative marker. The emphatic characteristic is achieved by placing at the beginning of the sentence the particular tagmeme which one wishes to emphasize. Here, then, a set e of related units (e_1, e_2, e_3) must be used to modify the kernel matrix. If e_1, e_2, e_3 represent fusions of the emphatic with some other tagmeme (subject, predicate, location, etc.), the kernel matrix can be separately multiplied by each of them — and symbolized thus:

$$(12) \qquad (e_1, e_2, e_3) \cdot M_k = {}_eM$$

In Zapotec[13] a set of derived sentence types is made by using special interrogative forms in any one of several tagmemic slots, with another kind of tagmeme in double function. The form simultaneously represents subject and interrogation, or location and interrogation, and so on. These, also, could be represented as a multiplication of matrices.

---

[10]   I take the use of the term 'multiplication' from John G. Kemeny, J. Laurie Snell, and Gerald L. Thompson, *Introduction to Finite Mathematics* (Englewood Cliffs, N.J., 1957), 198. (A row or column in a matrix may be called a vector; a vector by itself is a special case of a matrix.) When, however, one total matrix is to be multiplied by another, their stipulations as to the relation between the number of rows and columns of their matrices are not at the moment useful to our linguistic dimensional analysis. Their treatment of partitions (77-111) and cross-partitions of sets and subsets is closer to the remainder of our approach here.

[11]   See my *Language in Relation to a Unified Theory of the Structure of Human Behavior* 3 (Glendale [now Santa Ana], Calif., 1960), §11.6. Transformation of construction types, therefore, is developed in tagmemic field theory as a phenomenon of matrix multiplication — appearing first of all as a characteristic of the relationship between subsystems in a field, rather than primarily as a set of rules. Passage from kernel matrix to derived matrices and to productive application of the field notation in speech is mediated by tagmemic (plus lexemic and phonological) formulas.

[12]   Hart, 143-144.

[13]   Pickett, 77-80.

Negation in Chontal of Oaxaca[14] could perhaps be displayed usefully by matrix symbols with appropriate commentary to indicate changes or restrictions of particular occurrence, intonation, tagmeme content, or word order. This minor clarification of sentence relationships might become a major one if intensity and interrogation could be integrated in some such formula as:

(13)　　negative · intensive · query · M_k

Matrix multiplication obviates the need for publishing full patterns, as in (14), a display of an artificial clause system.

(14)

		A			B		
I		a	b	c	a	b	c
	1	x	x	x	x	x	x
	2	x	x	x	x	x	x
	3	x	x	x	x	x	x
II		a	b	c	a	b	c
	1	x	x	x	x	x	x
	2	x	x	x	x	x	x
	3	x	x	x	x	x	x

By a combination of (15) and (16), matrix (14) is restated and simplified. First, the dimension (1, 2, 3) times dimension (a, b, c) forms M_k. Then M_k times the new dimensions (I, II) and (A, B) forms M_z.

(15)　　$(1, 2, 3) \cdot (a, b, c) = M_k$

(16)　　$(I, II) \cdot (A, B) \cdot M_k = M_z$

Note, however, that the components (I, II) with (A, B) do not of themselves form a filled matrix (if we think of them as emphatic and negative elements, for example), since they lack sufficient content to give a complete independent clause in any one cell. The basic material of M_k is needed (with subject and predicate, for example). Therefore we do not set up a matrix M_y formed simply by intersection of (I, II) with (A, B).

Let us suppose, on the other hand, that in a different language no constructions fill the lower right quadrant IIB of (14). We represent this gap in our formula by placing a minus before IIB in (17):

(17)　　$(M_x - IIB) \cdot M_k = M_w$

With this kind of notation, systems of substantial complexity can now be shown, as for Mazatec.[15] We first set up a nuclear set (18), with a kernel matrix made up of a single column.

---

[14]　Viola Waterhouse, *The Grammatical Structure of Oaxaca Chontal* (University of Michigan dissertation, 1958), §1.2, to appear as a supplement of *IJAL*.
[15]　For some illustrative data, see Eunice V. Pike, "Mazatec, Huautla de Jiménez Dialect", to appear in a volume of studies on Middle American Languages, to be edited by Norman McQuown. Her dimensional analysis reached me through correspondence.

(18)   *Mazatec Kernel Clause Types*

	Declarative
Transitive. . .	x
Intransitive . .	x
Impersonal . .	x

This proves much more useful than setting up the matrix (19) in two columns, since the intransitive-impersonal gap persists throughout the larger system as a whole, and since the three-row column as a nuclear set reappears frequently and usefully in other formulas, as we shall see.

(19)

	Personal	Impersonal
Transitive. . .	x	x
Intransitive . .	x	–

Next we add a demonstrative set, and a partial equational set with gaps which also persist throughout the total system. This gives (20), the extended nuclear matrix M_k, with sub-nuclear sets M_{k1}, M_{k2}, M_{k3}.

(20)

	M_{k1}	M_{k2}	M_{k3}
	Declarative	Demonstrative	Equative
Transitive. . .	x	x	–
Intransitive . .	x	x	x
Impersonal . .	x	x	–

Multiplying by either a yes-or-no interrogative Q_y, or by a request for information Q_r, we then obtain all forms implied by (21) and (22).

(21) $Q_y \cdot M_k$ (22) $Q_r \cdot M_k$

Various restrictions affect the use of particular particles of the set $Q_r \cdot M_k$, but these data enter the accompanying tagmatic and allosyntagmatic formulas (§6), not the emic-construction matrices given here.

Next, Mazatec imperative (Imp) and emphatic (E) forms can be displayed. But these occur (23) only on the declarative base.

(23) $Imp \cdot M_{k1}$ and $E \cdot M_{k1}$

In addition, rare forms occur (24) with any two or three of (E, Imp, Q) with M_{k1}.

(24) $(E \cdot Imp, E \cdot Q, Imp \cdot Q, E \cdot Imp \cdot Q) \cdot M_{k1}$

Although we began with an attempt to strengthen grammatical theory by using techniques developed in connection with phonology, it now appears probable that this grammatical approach can in turn feed back to phonological problems. For some time I have attempted to treat voice quality and style factors as leaving the bulk of the phonological system not profoundly affected.[16] Such data can in our matrix

---

[16]   See my *Language* for congruent systems with topological distortion or systemic modification: (1955), 13, 20b-21a, 23a, 48a; (1960), 75-76.

theory be in part simply restated as a kernel phonological matrix multiplied by a style constant. Phonetic detail would be specified by formulas. A kernel set of phonemes may have a quality modification. In the kernel part of the total phonological system, furthermore, inner kernels could be set up to allow a set of vowels qualitatively different to be modified by nasalization — or by tone, stress, length, etc.

4. SEARCHING FOR MATRICES

If matrix theory is to be a useful tool not only for displaying structure, but for finding it, any available heuristic hints and essential principles would be welcome. Section 4 gives a few procedural suggestions, and Sections 5-7 give certain requirements for the usefulness and valid application of the method.

The divisions of an outline may point toward the needed dimensions. When, however, the outline has subdivisions which are not related to each other, the implication may be drawn that the outline includes two different sub-systems of the structure rather than a single one dimensionally oriented. Thus outline (25) can be displayed as matrix (26). But outline (27) cannot be handled this way.

(25)	I		(26)		A	B		(27)	I
	A			I	x	x			A
	B			II	x	x			B
	II								II
	A								X
	B								Y

Occasionally this observation leads to interesting results. In Larson's Aguaruna material, a chart of affix classes (28) shows — in addition to other details — an outline of derivational and inflectional affix types.

(28)   *Aguaruna Verbal Affixes*

Derivational
   Voice
      Causative. . . .   x
      Referent   x
   Aspect   x
Inflectional
   Negative   x
   Imperative   x
Mode
   Declarative . . .   x
   Interrogative . .   x
   Subjunctive . . .   x
  Stative   x

These do not form an intersecting matrix, for the reason just given. But precisely this fact now becomes relevant since, as we have already seen (1, 2, 3), the outer layer has a sharply different function in its relation of affix to verb clause from that of the stem to which the derivational affixes belong. The two layers of affixes enter different submatrices of the same affixal level but serve as distinct dimensions of a larger matrix at the word level.

An outline in the form of a tree diagram is an alternative method of seeking some of the essential relationships. It proves helpful in trying to grasp quickly some of the substructures seen at each structural level of the outline of a grammatical description. We must, however, note carefully that the crucial branching needed here is not the branching of a sentence into smaller and smaller constituents. (Not, that is, from sentence to immediate-constituent clauses, to phrases, to words, to morphemes.) Rather this is a tree representing the logical dimensional structure of the contrastive classes of that system at some one level of the system.

This requirement once more calls attention to the fact that we desire through the matrices to display the structure of the grammatical field itself, not the structure of some one particular construction in that field. For the display of the structure of particular constructions, when these are desired, tagmemic theory uses formulas which are made up of sequences of tagmemes hierarchically ordered. (See §§5-7)

By looking at a tree diagram of the contrasting features of a construction set, one sees that a dimensional array can be made whenever, below a certain node, each member of the branching pair in turn branches into the same respective features. Thus (29) forms a matrix like (26), but (30) — like (27) — does not.

(29)   1   2   (30)   1   2
           a   b   a   b   a   b   x   y

5. TESTING FOR WELL-DEFINED UNITS: CONTRAST

The making of a satisfactory (emic) matrix of this type requires that each unit of the set be well-defined[17], so that it can be placed in some one cell.

Tagmemics early focussed its attention on the nature of well-defined units[18] of all

---

[17]   The term comes from Kemeny *et al.*, 54; see also 79. For us, a linguistically well-defined unit is emically structured.

[18]   Through the formula U = FMD; unit has feature mode, manifestation mode, and distribution mode. This high degree of generality applied to the definition of all linguistic units is characteristic of tagmemic theory, which avoids centering its attention on the well-formedness of any one selected unit of any one hierarchy — say the unit named sentence — or giving it analytical, presentational, and theoretical priority.

kinds, with special reference to slot and class characteristics of tagmemes, and in reference to defining characteristics of contrast, variation, and distribution.

5.1 *The Dual Structural Criterion*

Two constructions, to be in contrast, must differ in form and meaning. Yet this requirement is not sufficient to handle the data. Robert E. Longacre has shown[19] that the formal difference must be dual. It appears to me unfortunate that this crucial theoretical contribution is in part obscured by Longacre's focus (reflected in the title of his paper) on the number of segments within a grammatical string. Much more important is his theoretical breakthrough in pinpointing the necessity for identifying minimal contrast between constructions. How would our field procedures of phonemic analysis and our descriptive statements differ if we had no concept of a 'minimal pair' — a set of items differing by the addition or replacement of a single phoneme? Yet only by the Longacre criterion can the analogues be treated in grammatical constructions. A basic difference between phonemes and constructions is involved, however, in that a pair of phonemes minimally contrastive may differ by only one component; a pair of constructions must differ by two formal components.

For the differing components Longacre requires a difference of two tagmemes, or of one tagmeme plus a transformation potential. Thus, with X, Y, and Z as tagmemes, (31) and (32) form a minimal pair of constructions, but (31) and (33) do not.

(31) $+X+Y$ (32) $+W+Z$ (33) $+X+Z$

Since, for Longacre, an optional tagmeme can be diagnostic, (34) also contrasts with (31).

(34) $+W\pm Z$

In my view a difference in the distribution of two constructions in higher-layered constructions may, like a transform difference, count as one of two required differences provided this distributional difference is paralleled by a substantial difference in structural meaning (such as 'declarative' versus 'interrogative'). If T represents a class of transforms, and D of distribution, then by these criteria (35) contrasts with (36), and (37) with (38).

(35) $+X+Y+T_1$ (36) $+X+Z+T_2$
(37) $+X+Y+D_1$ (38) $+X+Z+D_2$

Without the dual structural requirement, however, every optional tagmeme would add a new construction to the classification; *John came home* and *John came home*

---

[19] "String Constituent Analyses", *Language* 36 (1960), 75. Careful work on contrastive constructions on the sentence level is done by Waterhouse (1958), who for Oaxacan Chontal gives detailed indications of structural contrasts as she passes from the discussion of one type to the next. But it is not until Longacre's work that the relevance of a minimal essential difference comes into view.

yesterday would — unfortunately — turn out to be contrastive constructions. Long-acre wished to leave (39) and (40) as free variants of (31).

(39) $+X+Y\pm Z$ (40) $+X+Y\pm Z\pm W$

5.2 *Display via Unit-Times-Component*

Our matrices, in order to present constructions in the cells, as in previous sections, required for both horizontal and vertical dimensions at least one[20] pair of contrastive components. (Otherwise components, not constructions, end up at the dimensional intersections.) This display we may call one of Component-Times-Component.

Now, however, we are not trying to present the relationships between constructions, but to display the internal characteristics of the constructions in a manner best suited to the application of the dual structural criterion.

When an arrangement is presented with total construction units as the vertical axis but contrastive components of those constructions on the horizontal axis, the cells are filled not by constructions but by $+$, $-$, $\pm$, or zero, representing the relevance[21] of that component to the construction. This provides a matrix of Unit-Times-Component. Relevance or occurrence, not constructions, appears in the cells. The Unit-Times-Component display is very useful in predimensional analysis in order to find out what tagmemes occur[22] with each construction. In (41) this kind of chart is illustrated.

(41)

	Subj.	Obj.	Pred.	Time	Location
Construction 1	$+$	$\pm$	$+$	$\pm$	$\pm$
Construction 2	$\pm$	$-$	$+$	$\pm$	$\pm$
Construction 3	$+$	$-$	$+$	$-$	$-$

Although the information of (41) is useful, it proves too condensed for many situations. 'Predicate', for example, may represent a class of various predicates, each of

---

[20] After the first pair was placed at the top, however, all the others could arbitrarily be assigned as subdivisions of the first vertical pair. Elegance of results and the innate structure of a particular language — not the matrix approach as such — influence judgment as to further arrangement of the dimensions.

[21] Note, therefore, its analogy to displays of contrastive features — a type exploited effectively by Roman Jakobson, Gunnar M. Fant, and Morris Halle, *Preliminaries to Speech Analysis* ($=$*Technical Report* 13, second printing, Acoustic Laboratory, Massachusetts Institute of Technology, 1952). If grammatical dimensions turn out to be few in number, as these authors consider the phonological ones to be few, the implications for grammar will be very great. I personally believe that the similarity of the types we have used for illustration, above, is not only due to their geographical source, or to the English etic bias of the authors, but in part reflects some phases of such a limitation.

[22] Harwood Hess, for Otomí, has in preparation extensive test displays of this kind.

We should also be able to prepare Unit-Times-Unit matrices to parallel Component-Times-Component and Unit-Times-Component matrices. Perhaps this would help us define some types of matrix multiplication in which pairs of distinctive matrices serve as the dimensions, and complicated or compound constructions are placed in the cells.

which — say transitive and intransitive — is relevant to the use of the dual structural criterion. If in these cells one is prepared to place more information than plus or minus, but less than a total construction unit, a Construction-Times-Tagmeme-Class display can be given. Here constructions are in the rows, but classes of tagmemes head the columns. Specific tagmemes from these classes fill the cells. This arrangement leads (42) to the type of display given for Zapotec.[23]

(42)   *Some Zapotec Clause Types*

1 IntrDecl	+ IntrDeclPred	+ DepS	± IndS	—	—
2 TranDecl	+ TranDeclPred	+ DepS	± IndS	+0	—
3 PRefDecl	+ PRefDeclPred	+ DepS	± IndS	+0	± PRef
4 IntrImp	+ IntrImpPred	+ ImpDepS	—	—	—
5 TranImp	+ TranImpPred	+ ImpDepS	—	+0	—
6 PRefImp	+ PRefImpPred	+ ImpDepS	—	+0	± PRef

Note, for example, that the first tagmeme column has a class of six different predicate tagmemes; the second tagmeme column has two dependent subject tagmemes; the third column has only the independent subject tagmeme. Information is also provided for a Unit-Times-Relevance (or Occurrence) type, since in two of the constructions the tagmeme is symbolized as optional but in three of them occurrence is shown to be obligatory.

This type of display serves as an extremely important testing ground for contrast between constructions before componential dimensional matrices are finished.

For a presentation of tagmemic contrasts between constructions, Anderson and Wise have sample material in a form easily accessible to the reader, with dimensional analysis of part of the system.

5.3 *Diagonal Matrices and Dual Structural Contrast*

In a number of our first matrices we found a pattern with only diagonal occurrences. This appeared surprising, since the phonological analogue (p, d, ŋ) did not seem to have structural relevance.

An illuminating sample (43) can be deduced for Ixil.[24] The four clause types intransitive, transitive, semitransitive, and equational fill the diagonal set of cells. Four contrastive predicate types give the horizontal dimension, while combinations of absent or optional object with four varieties of topic (with differing focus on subject, actor — structurally distinct from subject — agent, and entity), provide the vertical dimension.

---

[23] Abbreviated from Pickett, 56.
[24] Based on Ray Elliott, "Ixil (Mayan) Clause Structure", *Mayan Studies* I (=*Linguistic Series of the Summer Institute of Linguistics* 5) (1961), 127-154. This particular arrangement was suggested to me by George Hart.

(43)   *Ixil Clauses*

	P_1	P_2	P_3	P_4
$\pm T_{subj} - O$	Intran.	—	—	—
$\pm T_{actor} \pm O$	—	Tran.	—	—
$+ T_{agent} \pm O$ . . .	—	—	SemTran.	—
$+ T_{entity} - O$ . . .	—	—	—	Equa.

But why the diagonal pattern of cells? We note (44) that the cells of any such display can be rearranged (by transposing any two columns or any two rows) to destroy the diagonal but preserve the contrasts.

(44)

	a	b	c
1	x	–	–
2	–	x	–
3	–	–	x

	a	c	b
1	x	–	–
2	–	–	x
3	–	x	–

	a	b	c
1	x	–	–
3	–	–	x
2	–	x	–

Therefore the one cell per row per column must be relevant, rather than the diagonal as such.

The frequency of the pattern, however, implies a deep source. Our analysis of that source is Longacre's underlying assumption concerning the nature of contrast between constructions. To be in contrast a pair of constructions must differ in two formal respects. If three (or more) constructions share none of their dual contrastive components, then to have the constructions fall into the cells the members of each dual set of components must be arranged one on the horizontal and one on the vertical dimension. This would lead to the diagonal matrices observed.

If, then, we wish to fill all the cells of a matrix, the dimensions must be set up so that contrastive features of the dimensions are shared by two or more constructions. But how, if no one component is so shared? Our solution is to add several components together into a single class. Then several constructions share the class, even though not the same member of the class.

The Ixil data, for example, can be reworked into a totally filled simple matrix (45) if the predicate tagmemes are first grouped into subclasses, and topic tagmemes are ignored. The four predicate types are grouped into a dimension made up of the two classes of active (A) and nonactive ($-A$) units.

(45)

	$-O$	$\pm O$
A.	Intransitive	Transitive
$-A$.	Equational	Semitransitive

Matrix display, therefore, supports the assumption of the relevance of a dual structural difference between contrastive constructions.

5.4 *Graph Display of Contrasts*

A different presentation of the Ixil system emerges if the components of (43) are shown in a geometric figure.[25] With the predicate type left distinct, but the topic tagmemes grouped into a set subdivided only by obligatory versus optional occurrence, one can give a simultaneous presentation of three components of the system in a manner analogous to some of the Prague School displays of phonemic systems. In (46) the pyramid has as the four edges of its base the four predicate types of the respective clauses. The four ascending edges represent obligatory versus optional

(46)

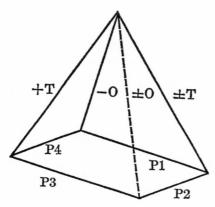

topic tagmemes, and optional versus obligatorily-absent object tagmemes. The faces of the pyramid each represent one clause type. Any two clause types share the components which meet at the edges of their faces; transitive and intransitive share $\pm T$, intransitive and equational share $- O$, and so on. The base of the triangle represents the total set of clauses presented here — in contrast to phrases, sentences, and units of other levels.

6. TESTING FOR WELL-DEFINED UNITS: VARIATION

In Section 5 we showed how the dual structural criterion for testing contrast between constructions is relevant to achieving well-defined units for putting into the cells of Component-Times-Component matrices. Now we leave the test for contrast and turn to tests for variation, with the same goal in mind. Constructions in contrast go into different cells, however, whereas all variants of one construction go into a single cell, symbolized by the notation for the emic construction (the syntagmeme) as a whole.

---

[25] Suggested to me by Ilse Lehiste.

Just as there are construction analogues of phonemic minimal pairs so there are alloconstruction (allosyntagma) analogues of allophones. Unless prior assumptions (and field procedures built on them) allow the analyst to eliminate from his inventory of emic constructions the subunit variants, the overall picture will be cluttered or obscure.

Allo units of any one construction must be tagmatically similar but need not be identical, just as allophones of a phoneme are in some sense phonetically similar but not identical. Problems of indeterminacy and personal judgment remain, however, as in phonemics when one attempts to answer the questions: How much alike must two alloconstructions be to fit the requirement of similarity? By what methodology can two (or more) sequences of tagmas or tagmemes be united into one emic construction?

English illustrations of tabular classification of syntagmeme variants into some thirty types according to environmental source of the modification (lexical, phonological, grammatical, stylistic) and the kind of modification, I have given earlier.[26] Here I wish to add a more formal sample notation for several of these types.

6.1 *Via Concord*

If, for example, we wish to treat the English subject-as-actor and the intransitive-predicate as making up the nucleus of an intransitive clause, then we also wish, as a consequence, to symbolize the judgment that the concord of singular subject with singular verb, and of plural subject with plural verb, leads to etic variants of that emic clause type. If we let S represent the tagmeme subject-as-actor, S_s the singular allotagma, and S_p the plural allotagma of that tagmeme, with P_s, P_p the comparable tagmas of the predicate, and $[R_1]$ the particular relationship of intransitivity between the subject and predicate, then (47) and (48) are alloconstructions of (49).

(47) $S_s[R_1]P_s$ (48) $S_p[R_1]P_p$ (49) $S[R_1]P$

In more general terms, we may say that the alloconstructions of (50) are in local free variation, while $X_1 \sim X_2$ are tagmas in reciprocally-conditioned[27] variation with the tagmas $Y_1 \sim Y_2$ respectively.

(50) $(X_1[R_1]Y_1) \sim (X_2[R_1]Y_2)$

---

[26] In my *Language* (1960), 20-22. Part I §7 gives extensive discussion of contrast, variation, and distribution of tagmemes (under the earlier label 'grameme'); revised, tabulated treatment of tagmeme variants is found in (1960), 18-19.

[27] For etic concord symbolized in Zapotec, see Pickett, 43. For Cashibo concord across clauses, with a dependent clause marked for the expected occurrence of a same or of a different subject in the next clause, see Shell, 203-205. The anticipatory marking in the dependent clause of the coming transitive (or intransitive) independent clause could be similarly handled. See, however, our adding of these allosyntagmatic elements to the Cashibo matrix, in (10) above.

Concord can be more explicitly symbolized, as in (51), as a dual relationship. The construction relation (CR) must be maintained in the two alloconstructions. The tagmatic relation (TR) must also be maintained between the comparable tagmas of the alloconstructions. Conditions of (51) are rephrased in (52). Sequences of (51) are concord alloconstructions if the subscripts a and b are concord symbols.

(51) X_a————$[CR_1]$————Y_a
                | |
           $[TR_1]$ $[TR_1]$
                | |
           X_b————$[CR_1]$————Y_b

(52) $X_a : Y_a = X_b : Y_b$; and $X_a : X_b = Y_a : Y_b$

6.2 Via Zero Allotagmas

A second type of conditioned alloconstructions can be postulated for Chontal of Oaxaca.[28] Here one finds, in a certain construction, either the first or the second person pronominal affix obligatorily present, or — where the meaning implies third person — no personal affix. Although one can, if one chooses, posit a third-person morpheme which is always zero, the tagmemic approach implies a solution which is more elegant: no zero morpheme is set up. (No emic unit of any kind is allowed if all its variants are zero.) Rather, the tagmeme of person is assumed to be always present (the slot is always there) but the tagmeme occurs in two allotagmatic forms, of which the second is zero.

Thus zero, as an allo in both morphemics and tagmemics, is used only as allo of a unit which elsewhere contains overt forms. With Pr representing the pronominal tagmeme, Pr_{-3} the zero third person pronominal allotagma, and $Pr_{1/2}$ the overt pronominal allotagma, we get in Oaxacan Chontal (53) the two alloconstructions of the one emic construction.

(53) $(... Pr_{1/2}) \sim (... Pr_{-3})$ in $\{(X[R_1]Pr_{1/2}) \sim (X[R_1]Pr_{-3})\}$

6.3 Via Order

A further complex of allotagmatic membership, this time in relation to alloconstruction order, occurs in Zapotec.[29] If we let IS_c represent independent subject in concord for number and person with dependent subject DS_c attached to P predicate, and if w/x/y/z represent four third-person morphemes, of which x is the 'identified' depen-

---

[28]   See Waterhouse, §1.1.2. Larson's paper contains a zero allotagma of tense. For discussion of hesitation at setting up a totally-zero morpheme, see Eugene A. Nida, *Morphology*[2] (Ann Arbor, 1949), 46, fn. 44. Note also bibliographical discussion in my *Language* (1960), 64-65.
[29]   Pickett, 58, also 61.

dent subject, then alloconstructions of (54) are seen. The independent subject freely varies in order from before to after predicate, but the position conditions the members of the pronominal tagmeme which may occur.

(54) $(IS_c \ PDS_c w/x/y/z) \sim (PDS_c z \ IS_c)$

6.4 *Via Division Subclass*

A type of freely variant alloconstruction occurs when one tagmeme has allotagmas with differing internal structures. The filler class of one tagmeme slot may contain members of different construction types. If p, q, r, s are four distribution classes of morphemes (or of morpheme sequences), and if R_1, R_2, R_3 are different relations between tagmemes of a construction, then (55) shows two variants of a construction.

(55) $\{X_{(p[R_2]q)}[R_1]Y\} \sim \{X_{(r[R_3]s)}[R_1]Y\}$

English illustrations for $(p[R_2]q)$ and $(r[R_3]s)$ are *Big John* and *The boy*, in *Big John came* and *The boy came*.

Note that caution must be used in assigning them both to the same construction. A dual structural difference exists between the phrases *Big John* and *The boy*. Their head slots differ by personal-noun versus count-noun fillers. The first tagmemes of the two phrases differ by optional versus obligatory occurrence and by morpheme class. These structural differences imply that somewhere in the total string there are contrastive constructions. We have here, therefore, set up the noun phrases as being contrastive constructions filling the same subject-as-actor slot of the clause. Otherwise, their included tagmemes would be assigned to the clause level, and the clauses themselves would have been analyzed as emically different constructions.

This points up the fact that Longacre's criterion of dual structural difference must be applied to specific levels of structure, not to an indiscriminate mixture of them.

Free variation between alloconstructions occurs, furthermore, as the product of tagmemes optionally present in a construction (i.e. without relevant differences of distribution and of relational meaning). This has already been illustrated in (39, 40). It was precisely this type of variant which Longacre wished to treat as noncontrastive, and which led to his dual structural criterion for contrast.

6.5 *Via Morpheme Conditioning*

In Tzotzil[30] we find an elaborate differentiation of alloconstructions which are caused by the particular pronominal affix used in the verb.

In the passive, for example, single pronominals are (in Delgaty's numbers) first

[30]   Data abstracted from Colin C. Delgaty, "Tzotzil Verb Phrase Structure", *Mayan Studies* I (= *Linguistic Series of the Summer Institute of Linguistics* 5) (1960), 82-126.

person 511, second 512, third 513. The third person, if it takes a pluralizer, has plural 411 preceding the pronominal affix; first person and second person are followed by their respective 711 and 712 pluralizing morphemes (or morphs); first person, in addition, may be followed by an element 611 to indicate that it is exclusive ('I and he', not 'I and you'). The pronominal relationships of Delgaty's alloconstruction formulas 3 and 4 may then be seen abbreviated in our (56).

(56)   ... + 511   ± (± 611 + 711)
       ~   ... + 512   ± 712
       ~   ... ± 411 + 513

Even more elaborate variation is seen in the alloconstruction formulas 5, 6, 7, 8, 9, 10 of his Chart IV.

Once it is clear that the Tzotzil system allows substantial differences in alloconstructions due to personal pronouns, the way seems to me to be open, by somewhat parallel analysis, to unite into a single emic construction his substantially different hortatory and imperative clauses. The hortatory (his formula 1) has an explicit first person prefix 2011; the imperative (his formula 2) has second person implicit only. Hortatory has suffixal pluralizer 711 of first person subject; imperative uses the same pluralizer 711 of first person object. Hortatory has either a modal marker 311 before or exclamatory marker 821 after the plural marker of subject, imperative has an obligatory model marker 312, with optional exclamatory marker 821. Hortatory has no personal object; imperative has first person object 511, with pluralizer of object 711 distinct from pluralizer 411 of second person implicit subject. Imperative carries a relative marker 211 obligatory with first person object 711, but apparently optional when the object does not occur. Stems, for both, are transitive.[31]

Note, in (57), our restatement of Delgaty's data. I have treated his formulas 1 and 2 as alloconstructions, with each of them including a second-degree alloconstruction (an alloconstruction of an alloconstruction).

(57)   *Tzotzil Hortatory-Imperative Alloconstructions*

1:	+2011	+StemT		+311			+711	
~	+2011	+StemT					+711	+821
~2:		+StemT	±211	+312	±411			±821
~		+StemT	+211	+312		+511	±[±611 +711]	±821

6.6 *Via Preliminary Matrix*

In field work a preliminary dimensional display of phones serves as a useful testing

---

[31] A few of the irregularities might disappear after checking further with an informant. This possibility does not negate our method. On the contrary, if our approach forces irregularities into attention for checking, it is useful to us in that respect as well.

guide. If an experienced worker wishes to help the beginner check his phonemic analysis, it is very useful to have (a) a preliminary chart of phonemes; (b) a set of phone pairs which are phonetically similar listed with evidence (minimal word pairs, for example) showing their contrast; (c) pairs listed with rule and evidence showing their complementary distribution or range of free variation; (d) patterns of phoneme sequences listed with rule and evidence to show their occurrence in high-level phonological units (and also any observable relation of sequences in reference to tagmeme or morpheme types as to size, distribution, or foreign origin). In this form, gaps in the data are seen more rapidly.

We are just beginning to learn that, similarly, a set of preliminary dimension charts for grammatical constructions helps the consultant to alert the beginner to gaps in his data by allowing him to see more clearly the overall grammatical structural system. Delgaty's material, for example, would have profited if he had had available, before writing, a systematic series of dimensional questions: Can a single dimensional chart (in addition to his morpheme-order charts) be prepared from his data? If so, are there contrasts between units of each column? of each row? What are the suspect pairs of constructions in the cells? Which of these can be shown to be contrastive by Longacre's criterion? Which would be joined as conditioned or free variants of an emic construction? Should the revised larger matrix be broken into smaller ones, with formulas for multiplication of matrices?

In addition to such a Component-Times-Component dimensional matrix (with constructions in the cells), can the extensive formulas of the tagmemic and tagmatic differences between constructions (or alloconstructions) be arranged into a display of Unit-Times-Tagmeme class (the Pickett type) to facilitate testing for contrast and complementation?

Dimensional displays are best prepared by the author, who has available to him data not known to the reader. Nevertheless, the reader who wishes to grasp the pattern of a grammatical article will often do well to make his own chart, as he reads, just as he might for a phonemic article.

With this in mind we suggest arrangement (58) to help the reader sense the dimensional characteristics underlying Delgaty's material. Stem differences provide data for the horizontal dimension. Modal affix elements, in general, give the vertical one. The roman numerals in the cells refer to the numbering of his charts (in which he attempts 'to give structural differences without minor substructural restrictions and variation', 85). Arabic numerals add the reference to his formulas (which attempt to 'give specific allotagmatic detail', although he was aware that he was 'not able to achieve consistency in this regard'). Further study, in the light of the method suggested here, might lead to changes in some of his conclusions and to a dimensional display sharply different from the preliminary one suggested here. This one — or any other — needs careful checking to establish the contrast between each pair of rows, and between each pair of columns, and to justify inclusion of all allo units listed in any one cell.

(58)   *Preliminary Tzotzil Verb-Phrase Matrix*

	TRANSITIVE (object prefix)	(object suffix)	INTRANSITIVE	DESCRIPTIVE
Indicative	VIII.19, 20	IV.5, 6, 7, 8, 9, 10; VII.16, 17, 18	XIII.25	XXI.23
Imperative		I.1; II.2; V.11	IX.21; X.22	XIV.26; XV.27; XVII.30
Stative		III.3, 4; VI.13, 14, 15	XI.23	XVI.28; XIX.31
Subjunctive		V.12	XII.24	XVII.29; XX.32; XXI.34

Our matrix implies, for example, the guess that positional, descriptive, and stative stems are not accompanied by a second structural difference adequate to require emic phrase differentiation; and that imperative, hortatory, and certain subjunctive items may be joined. Other such hunches are implied whenever two roman numerals occur in a single cell.

Delgaty's article comprises a fruitful source of data for studying alloconstructions differing because of pronouns, as we saw in (56), (57). I know of no equal to it for this purpose. But the article becomes extremely difficult to read because of the lack of a consistent underlying dimensional analysis. Reading would have been much easier, furthermore, if the morpheme-order charts were labelled by function as well as by form — by slot as well as by class. Pronominal prefixes 3010 *i*, *a*, and # serve as intransitive subject but transitive object; prefixes 2010 *h ~ k*, *a ~ v*, *s ~ y* serve as transitive subject or noun possessor; suffixes 510 *un*, *ot*, # as transitive (and imperative) object or as stative (including his passive) subject. Final analysis, in addition, would require availability of data on distribution of the verb phrases in clause types, as implied above in (37, 38).

7. TESTING FOR WELL-DEFINED UNITS: DISTRIBUTION

The third characteristic of a well-defined unit is its distribution. Seen through tagmemic theory, however, distribution turns out to be a complicated concept. Specifically, it must be treated in reference to slot, to sequence, and to matrix — and each of these elements has extensive ramifications which we shall barely hint at here.

7.1 *Via Slot, Class, and Segmentation*

Every unit — to be recognizable as an emic unit, to be well-defined — must be in principle replaceable in some emic slot in some larger emic context. Apart from this relationship to its environment, no emic unit emerges as figure against ground.

Here lies the relevance of substitution classes as units replaceable in the same functional (emic) slot. By this occurrence they become members of — or distributed within — the same class. From here, also, comes the possibility and relevance of segmentation and of string- (or immediate-)constituent theory. Only by substitution potential can segmentation breaks occur structurally.

Tagmemic theory has placed prime emphasis on a tagmeme construct relating emic slots to the emic classes of units within those slots. Tagmemic analysis is an accompaniment to matrix theory, since tagmemes make up the constructions which we wish to put well-defined into the matrices.

7.2 *Via Sequence*

The distribution of a tagmeme unit in a slot implies distribution of the tagmemes in sequences leading to and comprising constructions. Apart from the constructions no slots or tagmemes occur. Similarly (like the hen and the egg) without the constructions no tagmemes occur.

Constructions, as emic units, are themselves not relevant to linguistic structure unless (like phrases in clauses, clauses in sentences, sentences in discourse) they fill slots in still larger structures. Well-defined constructions are hierarchically ordered in that within them are sequences of slots (or, more carefully stated, of tagmemes) while they themselves are distributed within higher-level slots of higher-level tagmemes.

This material, like that of the tagmeme, is not the focus of our concern here. It must be mentioned in passing however, as prerequisite to the development of adequate matrices.

7.3 *Via Matrix*

The distribution of constructions is definable not only by occurrence in tagmemic slot and class, and in sequences of larger constructions, but in reference to the whole grammatical system of which they are a part. Matrix theory attempts to display the larger grammatical system. In this sense, constructions are well-defined only when viewed as part of the system — as in a grammatical matrix.

Tagmeme, class, construction, and matrix, then, are mutually relevant to each other's definitions. Together they make a system such that the description of each part is incomplete and tentative until all is finished. Spiral procedure[32] is needed in grammatical analysis or definition — with tentative, etically-defined units used to arrive at the emic system.

8. MATRIX AS FIELD

Matrix theory integrates with tagmemic theory in another direction also. From the

---

[32] As I indicated for phonology in my article "More on Grammatical Prerequisites", *Word* 8 (1952), 120.

latter has come the suggestion that language as a whole, and sub-systems of language, may be viewed as particle, wave, and field.[33]

If grammar is viewed in this way, the tagmeme can be seen as a particle, as a point in the wave. Constructions are waves[34] in which the tagmemes occur. System or matrix is the grammatical field within which the interlocking relationships of the constructions find relevance. In (59) the point relevance of particle substitution is suggested. In (60), the sequence characteristic of the construction wave is indicated. In (61), the spacial display reflects relationships of the matrix.

(59) ↕   (60) ↔   (61) ⌐────────⌐

(In reference to the matrix itself, the concept of particle, wave, and field again finds application, but on a different layer of the analysis. Here, the constructions comprise the particles entering the cells. The sub-system treated as a wave finds the kernel matrix as its nucleus. The dimensions of the total grammatical system serve as the larger field within which the sub-system is distributed.)

An extended paradigm (with, say, a dimension of noun declension classes as over against a dimension of cases) becomes a matrix on the level of word structure. A simple paradigm[35] of one declension would comprise a submatrix of the larger one. Matrix theory, therefore, integrates the traditional usefulness of paradigm displays as growing out of an underlying assumption of a grammatical field.

With this in mind, another theoretical puzzle finds a solution. The former difficulty of relating item-in-paradigm[36] to other approaches lies in the lack of field theory.

If, now, item-and-arrangement is seen as methodology or theory designed to treat particles, with item-and-process as methodology or theory to treat the fusion of waves in sequence, then item-and-dimension (or item-and-matrix, with the special case of item-and-paradigm) is seen as a method of treating an item in relation to field. All three approaches, in our view, have theoretical validity — as well as theoretical limits.[37]

---

[33] *Language* (1960), 30-39; and my article "Language as Particle, Wave, and Field", *Texas Quarterly* 2:2 (1959), 37-54.
[34] Pickett, 91, discusses constructions as waves with nuclei.
[35] Some graphic displays of contrasts — semantic or structural — between inflectional morphemes of paradigms have been given by other authors. See, for example, John Lotz, "The Semantic Analysis of the Nominal Bases in Hungarian", *Travaux du Cercle Linguistique de Copenhague* 5 (1949), 185-197.
[36] See Charles F. Hockett, "Two Models of Grammatical Description", *Word* 10 (1954), 210-231, §1.1. The word-in-paradigm approach is recognized by him as deserving "the same consideration" as item-and-process and item-and-arrangement. But Hockett gives "apologies for not having worked such consideration of WP into the paper". No theoretical basis for a possible treatment is suggested.
The objection to WP referred to by Hockett — that the paradigm approach is not sufficiently general to organize "efficiently the facts of a language like Chinese" — is met in our treatment through matrices and tagmemic formulas to represent dimentional components of constructions on levels higher than the word. A simple paradigm may be merely a one-vector special instance of a matrix of one grammatical level.
[37] For some of the distortion involved in any one separate view, see my *Language* (1960), 59-65.

9. MATRIX AND PRODUCTIVE POWER

Just as one does not know how to pronounce a phoneme in all or any of its specific variants merely by looking at a phonemic transcription or chart of the system, but needs a phonetic commentary to describe the articulatory-acoustic details lying behind the system, so a grammatical matrix is not designed to allow one to speak directly by looking at it.

For productive use, syntagmemic, allosyntagmemic, tagmemic, and allotagmemic formulas must accompany the dimensional matrices. To the degree that the accompanying formulas are complete,[38] the speech produced by the user on this model will be grammatically correct. The combination of matrix and formula gives a tagmemic display of the productive potential — the generative power — of the system.

Those of us who work with the Summer Institute of Linguistics have been interested for a long time in such productivity of formulas. Precisely because our aims include the producing of literature in the languages described, we were forced early to see that analysis of a closed corpus was inadequate for our needs. Perhaps the most explicit statement to this effect comes from William L. Wonderly:[39]

We need, therefore, to balance our formulas representing observed sequences with formulas representing the productive potential of the Zoque language as a functioning, productive system. In order to provide this balance, Chapter IV includes generalized formulae and tables of relative order.

And, in spite of limitations in the approach,

the productive potential is relevant to any study of the language, since a language does not operate as a limited series of frozen sequences of morphemes but rather as a system which includes the free construction of new forms on the analogy of patterns known to the speaker.

A matrix display gives the stranger a quick insight into the structural possibilities of a system as they are available to convey desired meaningful relationships. The tagmemic formulas allow him to implement these relationships with speech.

10. SUMMARY

Dimensional displays of constructions should contribute in various ways (a) toward the display of grammatical structure to help the reader gain insight into the nature of grammatical systems, just as a phonetic chart helps him to grasp quickly the dimensions of a phonemic system; (b) toward cutting descriptive redundancy; (c) toward the typology of constructions, though much further work must be done before a generalized etics of construction[40] types is analogously as useful as current general

---

[38]   Gaps and errors need filling and correcting here, as they do for any approach.
[39]   "Zoque: Phonemics and Morphology", *IJAL* 17 (1951), 2-3.
[40]   Begun in my *Language* §5.53; 3. §11.52.

phonetics; yet dimensional analysis should point the way, and this will prove especially rewarding if the number of dimensions or contrastive features at any one level turns out to be few, as we now suspect; (d) toward testing for validity of grammatical conclusions by preliminary displays of constructions leading to checking for contrast, variation, and distribution; and (e) toward the study of grammatical systems as having properties related not only to particles, but also to waves and to field.

STRESS TRAINS IN AUCA*

I am delighted to have the opportunity, by this article, to pay tribute to the world's elder statesman of phonetics, Professor Daniel Jones. Early in my reading I learned a great deal from his publications, both from his original contributions and, through him, from the line of earlier British and continental phoneticians to whom we all are, often unknowingly, indebted.

Here I would like to share with him some data gathered in the Auca[1] language of Ecuador, as a result of the application of some of my recent theoretical studies in high-level phonological units.[2] The crucial datum concerns a train of alternating stresses, starting from the beginning of a word, which clashes with a different wave train keyed into a mora count beginning from the last suffixual syllable. Junctures and complex vowel nuclei combine with grammatical composition of the word to affect the final result. Yet the merging pattern is predictable if all these elements are known. The data are presented, therefore, in the form of morphophonemic rules for stress placement.

RULE 1A: A wave train starts from the end of words, with final suffixual syllable unstressed, alternating backwards to penultimate stress, antepenultimate nonstress, pro-antepenultimate stress, until the stem or fourth syllable is reached. Thus the

---

* *In Honour of Daniel Jones* (London, Longmans, 1964), 425-431. Reprinted by permission.

[1] Norman McQuown, in "Indigenous Languages of Latin America", *American Anthropologist* LVII (1955), 501-570, lists Auca as equivalent to Sabela (517); unclassified as to language family (512-513); and as extinct (513, 537). One group of fifty — some speakers survive in the Upper Curaray River area – and one known somewhat larger group and a few scattered individuals, a total of two hundred or more, farther east. Gunter Tessman in *Die Indianer Nordost-Perus* lists items closely related to our Auca data under title of Ssabela.

Our informants, Dayuma, Kẽmõ ('Kimo') and his wife Dắwã with Mĩŋkáye ('Minkayi') and his wife Õmpódæ ('Ompora') have recently received world-wide attention. For biographical details see Ethel Wallis, *The Dayuma Story* (New York, 1960).

The phonemic data were largely gathered by Rachel Saint of the Summer Institute of linguistics. She is a sister of the late Nate Saint of the Missionary Aviation Fellowship, who was involved in the recent history of the tribe. The stress data were worked out in collaboration with her. Phonetic sequences written here as mb, mp, nd, etc., may prove to be better analysed as unit phonemes, with the homorganic nasal component as conditioned by the presence of a preceding nasal vowel.

[2] K. Pike, *Language in Relation to a Unified Theory of the Structure of Human Behavior* 2 (1955), Chs. 8 and 9, and 3 (1960), Chs. 13 and 15.

regular patterns are Cá.Ca; Cá.CáCa; Cá.CaCáCa; Cá.CáCaCáCa. In the formulas the symbol *C* represents any consonant or consonant cluster; the letter *a*, any vowel (or vowel sequence joined by ligature). The lowered dot indicates the end of the stem, both in formulas and in illustrations.

Note the following words each of which begins with the single-syllable stem /go/ and is followed by one, two, three, and four syllables, respectively:

/gó.bo/ 'I go' (/go/ 'go', /bo ~ mo/ 'I')
/gó.bópa/ 'I go' (/pa ~ mpa:mba/ 'declarative')
/gó.tabópa/ 'I went' (/ta ~ nta:nda/ 'near-past tense')
/gó.támõnápa/ 'We two went' (/mõ/ 'first person plural', /da ~ na/ 'dual')

RULE 1B: In a chain of five suffix syllables, the stress pattern is Cá.CáCaCaCáCa.

/gó.kǽdõmõnáĩmba/ 'We two would have gone' (/kæ ~ ŋæ/ 'near-future tense', /dõ ~ nõ/ 'contingent-past tense', /ĩ/ 'is')

RULE 1C: Enclitics added to the suffix train do not affect the mora count for stress placement. Compare Cá.CaCáCa and Cá.CaCáCa-Caa. The hyphen symbolizes the beginning of the enclitic.

/pṍ.ŋãndápa/ 'He came' (/põ/ 'come', /kã ~ ŋã/ 'third person singular')
/pṍ.ŋãndápa-dia/ 'He came – what do you think of that!' (/dia ~ nia:ndia/ 'What do you think of that!')

The enclitics themselves may be unstressed, or stressed.

/ǽ.ŋĩmo-to/ 'I will not say!' (/ã/ 'say', /kĩ ~ ŋi/ 'future tense', /-to/ 'disgust')
/gó.bo-táye/ 'I go!' (/táye ~ ntáye/ 'emphasis')

Note in the following illustrations that the noun is followed by that enclitic which was used with a verb in the preceding illustration:

/nḗmõ-táye/ 'Star!' (with the noun used as a personal name, and the enclitic added as emphatic call for attention)

RULE 2: A second wave train starts from the beginning of the word — whether noun, verb, or attributive. When the stem is made up wholly of a single root, or of a sequence of roots without derivative suffixes, this stem train begins stressed and produces an alternating stress-nonstress syllable sequence (with a few special restrictions). Thus the regular patterns are Cá.Ca, CáCaCá.Ca, etc.

/wǽ.ŋa/ 'He dies' (/wæ/ 'die')
/kíwẽ ṍ.ŋa/ 'where he lives' (/kíwẽ/ 'live', /yõ ~ ɲõ/ 'when, where')
/pǽdæpṍ.ɲámba/ 'He handed it over' (/pæ/ 'extend', /dæ ~ næ/ 'away from', /põ/ 'hand over', /dõ ~ nõ/ 'direction toward')

/kṍð/ 'kapok'

/bádã/ 'mother' (/dã ~ nã/ 'feminine with respect')

/bódæpóka/ 'ant-hill' (/bódæ/ 'ant', /po ~ mbo/ 'ground', /ka ~ ŋka:ŋga/ 'fastened')

Before passing to the next rule we raise the question: WHAT HAPPENS WHEN THE TWO WAVE TRAINS MEET AT THE JUNCTION OF STEM AND SUFFIX? Here is the most fascinating part of the entire study. Four separate types of phenomena are observed: (a) A special set of morphophonemic rules for stress comes into play. (b) A set of juncture phonemes and rules for their occurrence become relevant. (c) Intonational relations occur across the two halves of the total phonological unit – the phonemic phrase. (d) Special rules for sequences of vowels in relation to syllable nuclei and to alternating stresses must be set up. We consider these in turn.

RULE 3A: If the two wave trains are 'in phase' – i.e., if the stem train ends with a stressed syllable and the suffix train begins with an unstressed syllable, or vice versa – then no interference with either train is observed. Illustrations of this rule are given above, in formulas such as CáCaCá.Ca and CáCaCáCa.CáCa. Note also CáCa.-CáCa:

/kǽga.kǎmba/ 'His tooth hurts' (/kæ/ 'hurt', /ga ~ ŋa/ 'tooth')

RULE 3B: If the two wave trains are 'out of phase', special rules must be given. When the regular rules would cause the final syllable of the stem to be stressed, and the regular rules of the suffix train would cause the first suffix to be stressed, both stresses are retained. Note the formulas Cá.CáCa, CáCaCá.CáCa, and CáCaCáCaCá.CáCa:

/á.kǎmba/ 'He sees' (/a/ 'see')

/yíwæ̃mṍ.ŋǎmba/ 'He carves, he writes' (/yi/ 'cut', /wæ̃/ 'down', /mõ/ 'state of')

/tíkawódõnó.kǎmba/ 'He lights' (/tí/ 'touch lightly', /ka ~ ŋga/ 'fasten', /wo/ 'float, blow')

RULE 3C: When the regular stress rules would cause the final syllable of the stem to be unstressed and the regular rules of the suffix train would cause the first suffix to be unstressed, the final root of the stem becomes stressed as in the formulas *CáCa.Ca > CáCá.Ca, *CáCa.CaCáCa > CáCá.CaCáCa, and *CáCaCáCa.Ca > CáCaCáCá.Ca.

/wódṍ.ŋã/ 'She hangs up' (/wo/ 'float, blow')

/ẽ́ŋá.kãndápa/ 'He was born' (/ẽŋa/ 'to give birth, to be born')

/gǎnæǽmǽ.ŋã/ 'He raised up his arms' (/gã/ 'roll', /ræ ~ næ/ 'away from', /æ̃/ 'raise', /mæ̃/ 'arm')

Note that these various rules lead to phonemic contrast between stress patterns resulting from CáCaCá.CáCa vs. CáCá.CaCáCa, since the second syllable (a) is stressed if stem final but (b) unstressed if stem medial; and the third syllable is (a) stressed if it is stem final but (b) unstressed if it comprises the first of three suffixual syllables:

/ápǽné.kăndápa/ 'He speaks' (/apǽ/ 'speak', /re ~ ne/ 'mouth')
/dádő.ŋăndápa/ 'He fished' (/da/ 'fish')

On the other hand, no stress contrasts develop between three-syllable words which have, respectively, two-syllable and one-syllable stems, since in each case the first two syllables of the words would be stressed by the regular rules: i.e., CáCá.Ca and Cá.CáCa.

/tǽnő.mi/ 'You spear' (/tǽ/ 'spear', /bi ~ mi/ 'second person singular')
/bé.kĭmo/ 'I will drink' (/be/ 'drink', /bo ~ mo/ 'first person singular')

RULE 3D: In one special instance in which the stem is made up of three monosyllabic roots plus three following stem-formative syllables, the stem-formatives are all unstressed, and very rapid.

/yǽrakǽgĭnewa.kăndápa/ 'He licked' (/yǽ/ 'to stick out', /gĭnewa ~ ŋĭnewa/ 'tongue', /kæ ~ ŋæ/ 'verbalizer')

Elsewhere, these – and other – stem-formatives appear to follow the regular rules for root syllables and lead to no further contrastive patterns.

/kǽgĭnéwá.kă/ 'His tongue hurts' (/kæ/ 'hurt')

In Rule 4 we discuss juncture placement. Two juncture phonemes must be postulated for these rules. The first we call 'primary juncture'. It comes at the end of phonemic phrases, which in turn are co-terminous either with grammatical words or with grammatical words plus accompanying enclitics. Secondary juncture we shall symbolize with a lowered grave accent between syllables – i.e., as Ca͵Ca. It comes medially within phonemic phrases.

RULE 4A: Primary juncture occurs after phonemic phrases. It is phonetically marked by one or more subtle but audible cues. A phonemic phrase containing a single syllable usually has a decrescendo during that syllable, and often falling pitch. In other instances, slight differences of timing or pseudo-pauses (extra-weak but continued articulation of a sound) force the grouping of an unstressed syllable with a stressed one before or after it in the phonemic phrase to which it belongs. When two or more stresses occur within one phonemic phrase the last is often freely – not necessarily – weakened. (I have treated this as an allophone of the primary stress phoneme, weakened by its conditioning position in the phrase.)

In addition, intonation cues are relevant here (see Rule 5).

Note primary juncture in the following phrases, symbolized by space:

Cá CáCaCáCa: /wǐ pő́nĕmópa/ 'I do not believe it' (/wǐ/ 'negative', /põ/ 'come', /rẽ ~ nẽ/ 'causative')

CáCa CáCaCáCa: /bíwi tókãndápa/ 'younger brother laughed' (/bíwi/ 'younger brother', /to/ 'laugh')

CáCa áCáCa: /ɲówo éɲíɲa/ 'Now she understands' (/ɲówo/ 'now', /eɲi/ 'hear, understand')

RULE 4B: Secondary juncture occurs at the end of the stem following two stem stresses before suffixual nonstress.

CáCá.ˌCaCáCa: /ówó.ˌkãndápa/ 'He stayed at home (in his hammock)' (/o/ 'stay', /wo/ 'float')

RULE 4C: Secondary juncture follows an unstressed suffix syllable which is next to the stem, when the stem is totally composed of one stressed syllable.

Cá.CaˌCáCa: /mő́.ɲãˌndápa/ 'He slept' (/mõ/ 'sleep')

RULE 4D: Secondary juncture occurs at the end of the stem, following stem non-stress, before suffixual stress.

CáCa.ˌCáCa: /gówæ̃.ˌɲǎ́mba/ 'He fell down'

RULE 4E: Secondary juncture follows the second of three syllables of a stem which precedes a stressed suffixual syllable.

CáCaˌCá.CáCa: /époˌkáe. bópa/ 'I swim' (/e/ 'grab', /po ~ mpo:mbo/ 'hand')

RULE 4F: Secondary juncture follows the second and fourth syllables, nonstressed, of the stem before a stressed suffixual syllable.

CáCaˌCáCa.ˌCáCa: /tówæˌrǎ́nõ.ˌɲǎ́mba/ 'He spit' (/to/ 'straight', /wæ tã/ '?')

RULE 4G: In a chain of five suffix syllables, the secondary juncture occurs after the second suffixual syllable.

Cá.CáCaˌCaCáCa: /kǽ.ɲǽ dõˌmonmáĩmba/ 'We would have eaten' (/kæ̃/ 'eat')

RULE 5: The total phonemic phrase (i.e., the macrosegment including the sum of units between primary juncture, whether or not secondary junctures also occur) in unemotional speech has an overall intonation contour. This pattern has variants, of which the most frequent has high pitch on stressed syllables, with stressed syllables of the suffix train cascading a bit lower in a contour 'fade'. Occasional variants – especially in fast speech – have unstressed syllables on the same pitch level as the stressed ones.

More thorough study of pitch patterns in a variety of communicational and emotional contexts needs to be made, however, before the outlines of the intonational system are clarified, and contrastive pitch and quality contours identified.

RULE 6A: Within the stem, sequences of two like or of two diverse vowels act as sequences of two syllable nuclei in the mora count which affects the placement of stresses. An analog of CáCá.CaCáCa, with vowel sequences:

/őő.ŋãndápa/ 'He went blow-gunning' (/őő/ 'hunt with blow-gun')
An analog of CáCaCá.CaCáCa: /wóőő.ŋãndápa/ 'He blew his blow gun'

RULE 6B: Within the suffix train, however, sequences of diverse vowels act in the mora count as single-syllable nuclei – and morphologically-expected sequences of like vowels fuse to single ones. This rule heightens the contrast between the stem and the suffixual component of the phonemic phrase. Note:

Cá.Ca$_1$a$_2$ and Cá.CaCa$_1$á$_2$Ca: /á.boi/ (/a/ 'I see', /i/ 'subjunctive'), /wáe.kĩmoĩmba/ 'I will cry' (/wæ/ 'cry')
*Cá.Ca$_1$a$_1$ > Cá.Ca: /ǽ.mi/ 'Take!' (/ǽ/ 'take', /bi ~ mi/ 'second person singular', /i/ 'subjunctive')

BEYOND THE SENTENCE*

Underlying my views concerning the structure of language and experience are several beliefs:

THE OBSERVER ADDS PART OF HIMSELF TO THE DATA that he looks at or listens to. He hears more than impinges on the ear. His inner self adds to nonrandom eardrum rattle a restructuring conditioned by his private experience and his social-cultural setting. Whatever structure may reside in the data proper, it inevitably becomes moulded by the observer. An unbiased report is impossible.

Observers differ, and hence their reports differ. An author observing the action of people (or observing his own work), a critic observing the work of an author, the philosopher or critic of critics observing the critic, and the man in the street observing author, critic, and philosopher — each brings some structural bias to the data he sees.

A bias of mine — not shared by many linguists — is the conviction that BEYOND THE SENTENCE lie grammatical structures available to linguistic analysis, describable by technical procedures, and usable by the author for the generation of the literary works through which he reports to us his observations. The studying of these structures has thus far been left largely (but not exclusively) to the literary critic. But even a brief glance in this direction where the linguist still has so much to learn has enriched my own experience. Sheer delight awaits the linguist who sees the poem as linguistically a unique lexical event (an intricate 'idiom' as it were) with an interlocking (partially unique) phonological structure embedded in a high-level grammatical pattern (in a genre, that is to say, which is in part culturally determined and in part created newly).

COMPLEXITY CAN BE FRACTIONATED, but experienced wholeness must be reaffirmed as beyond the debris. Analysis of an object — like the dissecting of a rose — may give insight into structural detail, by tools allowing systematic description, while destroying almost everything about the rose which is of value — its beauty. As I see it, the literary critic should welcome the linguist as a low-level servant. But when the linguist is through with his fun and his mechanisms, the important problems of value permanence, esthetic impact, and social relevance must then be tackled by the literary critic.

* *College Composition and Communication* 15 (1964), 129-135. Reprinted by permission.

The tagmemic approach to linguistic theory (of which this article is an example) claims that certain universal invariants underlie all human experience as characteristics of rationality itself. Since I have discussed them elsewhere (See "A Linguistic Contribution to Composition", *CCC* [1964]), I merely list four sets of these characteristics so that I can refer to them in a moment, as I attempt to show how they can be brought to bear on language structures of types which may range beyond the sentence.

(1) Units as structures:
    (a) with contrastive-identificational features,
    (b) with variants, which include some physical component,
    (c) distributed as members of classes of items, functioning within slots (positions) in a temporal sequence (or spatial array), and distributed in cells of a dimensional system;

(2) Perspectives as complementary:
    (a) as particle,
    (b) as wave,
    (c) as field;

(3) Language as social behavior:
    (a) with form-meaning composites,
    (b) in a universe of discourse,
    (c) with impact or change carried over a bridge of shared components;

(4) Hierarchies as interlocking:
    (a) lexical,
    (b) phonological,
    (c) grammatical.

The observer brings to bear on experience a unitizing ability. Without segmentation of events into recallable, namable chunks, without abstraction of things as figure against ground, without reification of concepts manipulatable as discrete elements by our mental equipment, man would be inept. These unitizings are an observer imposition on a continuum. So, also, is the recognition of units as contrasting with one another; the ability to ignore irrelevant differences; and the possibility of experiencing one element as in relationship with other elements in a system.

The observer can change perspective. On the one hand he can study experience as made up of particles, or unit chunks. On the other hand he can use physical equipment to prove — on the supra-atomic level — that data occur in a continuous merging or flow. Or he can see an item as a point in a mesh of relationships. These perspectives, likewise, are imposed by the observer.

The understanding of a language involves the observer-linking of a linguistic form to an experienced meaning. This form-meaning integration takes place relative to a universe of discourse, a generalized field of observation, cut out by the observer from possible areas of interest to him. And when he wishes to communicate with others, to influence them by his writing, or to let them share an experience of his own, he must do so by getting to the reader on territory which they share psychologically, physically, or linguistically. This, too, reflects an observer characteristic.

The observer can fasten attention on larger or smaller units of a uniform series. He can also focus upon one of various types of uniform hierarchical series simultaneously present within a larger unit. The capacity for focus on these hierarchies or their various levels is an observer component. It allows for the studying of interrelations of words within a larger work, as these words make up lexical sets (*spring*, *summer*, *fall*) in a lexical hierarchy and universe of discourse, the study of phonological integration (alliteration within a phrase, meter within a poem), and the study of the function of formal segments of sentences, or of stanzas, or of formal parts of an essay (introduction, body, conclusion).

Evidence which to me brings an overwhelming reaction of wholeness to a language element — whether composed of one or many sentences — can be seen in jokes. In order to analyze one of them, it often becomes necessary to call on a large percentage of the theoretical apparatus which we have mentioned. For example: "Even worse than raining cats and dogs is hailing taxis" (from a collection by Robert Margolin, *The Little Pun Book* [1960]). (1)[1] This joke is a unit. (a) It contrasts with other kinds of language units — with a drama, a novel — by its briefness, its element of surprise, its highlighted pun. (b) It can be told in a variety of ways, not all equally efficient, (e.g. — with reversed order, "It is worse if it is hailing taxis rather than raining cats and dogs"). (c) This kind of joke is appropriate to a particular set of situations in our social structure; in other places — e.g., some formal ones — it would be unwelcome. (2) The joke (a) is a whole segment, a language particle. Included within it are smaller particles — words, sounds, grammatical parts. (b) Viewed as a wave composite, however, one sees within it sequences of articulatory movements merging within syllables (with vocalic nuclei) within stress groups, as elements of higher-level phonological waves. (c) Viewed as field, the joke is composed of the intersecting universes of discourse of weather and traffic, and the intersecting hierarchies (or conflation of hierarchies) of lexicon, phonology, and grammar.

(3) (a) As a composite of both form and meaning the joke is lost if the specific words are replaced by apparent synonyms, or if idiomatic expressions are replaced by explicit statement. If we wish to retain the joke, we must not replace *cats and dogs* with *hard*, or *hailing* with *calling*. To change the form — whether particular sounds, or words, or grammar — at a crucial point is to destroy the joke. Neither form nor meaning can survive by itself. (b) The joke switches from the universe of discourse of the weather, to that of traffic (or transportation), and back to weather, (c) turning on shared components of lexicon, phonology, and grammar.

The shared lexical set includes *rain* and *hail* from the universe of discourse of the weather. Phonological sharing includes the homophonous pronunciation of *hail*

[1] The parenthesized numbers and letters in this discussion and in the later discussion of Emily Dickinson's poem are keyed to the outline of tagmemic principles presented earlier in this article.

(as falling ice), and *hail* (as a calling act). The grammatical sharing involves the grammatical equating of the two contrastive forms with *-ing*.

(4) Hierarchical elements are involved. (a) The pun on *hailing* occurs phonologically at the word level. But (b) the pun works only because of its place in the higher-level lexical idiom *raining cats and dogs*. The influence of the phrase *raining cats and dogs* carries forward — with the help of the phonological homonymy and (c) the grammatical ambiguity of the *-ing* forms — to force the interpretation of *hailing* into the universe of discourse of *raining*. At the same time, the high-level lexical phrase *hailing taxis* — once it is interpreted as a participle plus its object — retrospectively forces the phrase *raining cats and dogs* to be interpreted literally within an imaginary universe in which the weather pattern can include taxis as also falling from the sky. Thus (d) the interpretation of the higher-level lexical idiom is broken down into an interpretation as a non-idiomatic sequence of lexical elements.

Other jokes build on these same theoretical components but in different proportions: "Why are a mouse and a pile of hay alike? — The cattle/cat'll eat it." The immediate attention here is focussed on the homonymity of *cattle* and *cat'll*. Each (provided one uses the contracted pronunciation of *cat will* needed here) is a single stress group with identical vowels and consonants. But it would be a serious error to assume that the pun could be described by phonology alone. As for lexicon, there is the contrast of the one word *cattle* with the lexical sequence *cat will*. As for grammar, there is the difference of the grammatical relation of *cattle* and *cat will* to the remainder of the sentence (as part of subject only, versus part of subject and predicate). As a unit, on the other hand, this joke contrasts with the first pun in that it has a grammatical structure beyond the single sentence — it has a question segment and an answer segment as its characteristic parts.

If jokes of various subgenres are short linguistic particles, yet so complicated that all available linguistic apparatus must at times be called on for explaining them, how can we conceivably expect to use anything less for the description of a sonnet, epic, or tragedy? And with all this complexity we must continue to expect — as for the jokes — that the observer will supply the intuition of the integration of the parts into a form-meaning whole, often beyond the sentence in size and intricacy of structure, and beyond the sum of separate words in meaning. So, with Murray Krieger (writing in *College English* 25:6 [1964], 408, 411), we may be "astounded with all that seems to happen at a stroke", during the "multiple levels of simultaneity which the acrobatic poetic context displays", as it arrives at meanings which "cannot be reduced" to assertions ABOUT the poem.

If, furthermore, we conclude with Robert Frost that the chief thing about poetry is that it is metaphor "just saying one thing in terms of another" so that college boys can be told "to set their feet on the first rung of a ladder the top of which sticks through the sky" (from his essay "Education by Poetry," reprinted in Robert A. Greenberg and James G. Hepburn, *Robert Frost: An Introduction* [1961]), then a continuity emerges between the kind of meaning found in a good poem and the meaning of a pun. Both deal with multiple, simultaneous meanings, with a crossing from one universe of discourse to another over the web of interwoven hierarchies of lexicon, phonology, and grammar — often, but not always, beyond the sentence.

My literary colleagues insist, however, that demonstration of the relevance of a set of analytical tools to a joke cannot automatically be assumed to transfer to the analysis of a poem. To test this relevance on a poem which was neither too simple to be interesting nor too long to be feasible (nor selected to fit the approach), I returned to a poem which had previously (1953) been selected for me by a colleague on the basis of literary interest, rather than on the basis of any prior judgment of linguistic form. The poem was by Emily Dickinson:

> The brain within its groove
> Runs evenly and true;
> But let a splinter swerve,
> 'Twere easier for you
> To put the water back
> When floods have slit the hills,
> And scooped a turnpike for themselves,
> And blotted out the mills!

At that time I had had the poem read aloud by various persons, and recorded. I marked these variant readings for the pitch of the voice (with three alternate readings published later in *Language in Relation to a Unified Theory of the Structure of Human Behavior* 3 [1960], 48-49). Now, however, I wanted to find out whether any of the points listed above would force me to ask questions about this poem which had not occurred to me when I was looking at it from the point of view of its pitch alone. What I now saw (as linguist, not as literary scholar) is this:

(1) Unit. (a) In form (rhyme, length) the piece contrasts as poem versus essay — and so on — or even with a more specialized poetic form such as the sonnet. Its overall meaning — contrasting with other possible messages — seems to be that the brain is delicate and can suffer drastic permanent damage.

(b) Variation occurs both in the form and in the meaning (interpretation of the form). Variants in the writing of the poem—i.e., alternative wordings of the author— have been published (in Thomas H. Johnson, *The Poems of Emily Dickinson* [1955], 425). Word alternates occur there (*a Current* and *the Waters* for *the water; trodden out* and *shoved away* for *blotted out*). When one selects a reader (rather than author) as observer, a further set of variants emerges. Different readers bring sharply-different intonations and dynamic phonological structures to the poem. They add meanings to the poem to whatever extent intonations themselves (or stress, voice quality, and so on) carry meaning. In my earlier recordings, referred to above, the reading by a graduate student occurred as a somewhat dull sing-song. The second reading, by a poet, attempted to prevent over-emphasis on rhythms, by using a quiet near-monotone. The third reading, by a literary critic, attempted to highlight individual words (since he felt that in Dickinson's writings the separate words were often highly meaningful), and did so by the use of extra pauses, emphatic stresses, high pitches, change of pitch direction, and sharp change of speed.

(c) Due to the contrastive characteristics already mentioned, the poem finds its place in a class of short poems as a member of the poetic genre filling its appropriate role in the larger system of literary types. Internally, the evidence that classes of alternatives are present has already been indicated in terms of the alternate words suggested by the author of the poem. These words do not occur at arbitrary places, but in reference to substitution in grammatical slots. The selection of a particular word as an alternate, however, is probable only if it fits the proper universe of discourse, and is a member of the class appropriate to a slot in that particular construction.

(2) (a) Among the particles whose interrelationships one would like to understand in this poem are the *brain, groove, splinter, water, dam, mills,* and others. What is the groove? or the splinter? It seemed to me that the analogy requires that the groove be thought of as guiding some kind of a moving door in its track — which would jump from the track if a splinter got in its way. This would allow for the analogy of the water going through the millrace turning the wheel, but causing chaos if it jumps over the bank and tears out the dam.

(b) Processes supply the wave component. The brain was represented as a process — a flowing (through the groove); the water also occurred as flowing (through the millrace). The swerving of the brain led, it seemed to me, to wreckage, just as the swerving of the water tore out the mills and ended in destruction. When I checked with my colleagues, however, I found that there was by no means agreement as to the meaning of the splinter or the groove. An indeterminacy of observer interpretation was certainly present. (One quick answer — that the groove was like those in a bowling alley — seems unacceptable within the context — field — of the poem, since there we prefer to have the ball stay out of the groove!)

(c) In searching for some type of presentation for field, in line with the preceding interpretation, I seemed to understand the poem better when I looked at it as showing states of health and illness intersecting with productive elements of brain and water. A healthy brain produces good thoughts; a sick one chaos. Controlled water produces work in the mills; swerved water leads to economic loss and damage of equipment. These can be shown in a two-dimensional schema:

	Well	*Sick*
BRAIN	good thinking	mental illness
WATER	mill production	valley disaster

(3) Yet a social component lay hidden in my judgment. I realized this only when someone raised a question as to whether the mills were to be considered good (as productive) or bad (as economic clutter of an ideal landscape). If the author had thought of them as bad, then the figure of speech of the mill (working backwards

through the poem), might force a change in the interpretation of brain movement. Instead of representing a process of becoming ill, mental change could be seen as growth of outlook, irreversible but desirable. An analytical-observer component could therefore not be left out of consideration here.

Similarly, an observer component is involved in the total meaning of the poem. The statement "Mental illness is bad" does not carry the same impact that the poem does. Thus (a) the poem is a form-meaning composite such that the meaning (as impact) will not remain unchanged if the poem is put into prose. Part of this impact, further, comes (b) by the use of pivot elements shared (c) by the two universes of discourse of brain activity and water activity for the mill. They share (in a metaphor) the concept of channel and they both can swerve from course. Without the sharing of these elements from the larger behavioral setting, the metaphor would be powerless.

(4) The linguistic elements can be analyzed hierarchically. (a) Sounds enter into syllables, the syllables into feet, the feet into the larger groupings. (b) The words enter phrases, the phrases into the clause or the total sentence. Some lexical sets — the rhyming ones, *true* and *you*, *hills* and *mills* — have their membership determined by phonological criteria. Other sets have other properties such as a kind of semantic hierarchy; the movement from micro-level (with *splinter*) to macro-level (with the *hills*) carries a special impact. (c) Grammatical entities (such as subjects and predicates and locatives) enter into larger and larger constructions within the poem, and an internal feature of the structure of the plot of the poem as a whole is seen in the shift of the section dealing with the brain, to the second which discusses the water in its parallel swerving and resultant chaos.

One further question arises: How do these considerations apply to the teaching of composition? I earlier suggested a list of exercises which might have some possible relevance at this point (*CCC* [May, 1964]). How do they in fact work out? And what implications do these results — in their first stages — have for the theory?

I asked some students to attempt brief, rapid drills in which they were to emphasize contrast, stating about a thing only what it is not (as part of the definition of the element as a unit). A sample: "Chalk is not a fountain pen because it does not have a metal point nor use ink. Chalk is not a pencil because it contains no lead and is not encased in another substance. Chalk is not a crayon because it contains no wax." The result proves unsatisfactory — as literature — precisely because it fails to take advantage of other components of a literary unit. It does not build a structure integrating the individual sentences, but merely piles them up like cordwood. The monotony experienced through the dull repetition of the one sentence type suggests that acceptable communication requires variety. But much more than sheer variety is involved. Rather, an interesting narrative or argument requires a multi-dimensional structure beyond the sentence. Exercises on contrast must be supplemented with further exercises to teach the person to reach complexity of sentence type and complexity of paragraph and essay structure as wholes. (A report of an attempt of this kind was given by Alton Becker at the *CCC* meeting in New York in March, 1964.)

Although my assumption has been that for some purposes it might prove useful to start with very simple drills, these must be followed by integrating exercises. Beyond all exercises, however, there will continue to lurk an observer element not prescribable or programmable. Among the students following the same set of instructions referred to above on contrast, some of them added more interesting, nonpredictable observations: "A horse ... is not a cat as it does not meow, nor eat birds, nor have claws. It is not a dog because it doesn't bark nor wag its tail nor climb up on people's laps."

To me — as one observer — it appears clear that there is a corollary to this intricate set of concepts: Just as no one complete success has ever been achieved in devising a mechanical procedure to ANALYZE a novel or sentence, so also we must not build our hopes on any mechanical procedure to GENERATE all possible useful and BEAUTIFUL sentences and sonnets. (For discussion of the capacity of the unconscious versus the conscious in composition, as an antidote to over-formalization of the composition curriculum, see articles by Janet A. Emig, William Stafford, and Margaret Blanchard in *CCC* [February, 1964].)

Beyond the linguist lives the artist.

ON SYSTEMS OF GRAMMATICAL STRUCTURE*

Extensive work through the Summer Institute of Linguistics is going on (often from a tagmemic point of view) in some 260 languages — largely those of preliterate tribes — of Peru, Mexico, New Guinea, the Philippines, and elsewhere.

Empirical data from these researches are being published as rapidly as possible.[1]

In order to explain these data, we have been forced to develop a number of theoretical concepts and new field procedures. Tagmemics is a theory growing out of empirical work. No component of the theory is allowed to remain if it does not prove fruitful under field test. This paper is a brief report to show the direction of progress of some of these concepts, and to indicate where the results can be found.

1. WELL-DEFINED UNITS

Tagmemic theory has so far been largely addressed to the problem of determining the nature of a unit of relevant human behavior. Units of all kinds of purposive behavior are within the scope of the theory, though stimulus for it comes from and tests thus far have been largely applied to linguistic behavior.

The basic assumption: Any unit of purposive human behavior is WELL-DEFINED if and only if one describes it in reference to (a) contrast (and resulting identification), (b) range of variation (with its essential physical manifestation), and (c) distribution (in class, in hierarchical sequence, and in systemic matrix).

Contrast: One does not know what an item is until one knows what it is not. Note the long-standing attention paid to phonological opposition by the Prague school. Once items are thus separated from others, the contrastive features in further environments sometimes allow for identification of items even under conditions where one of two members of a contrast does not occur.

Variation: Within tagmemic theory no unit is relevant to the behavioral system unless it has a physical component. (A mental entity would have a physical neuro-

* *Proceedings of the Ninth International Congress of Linguists, Cambridge, Mass., 1962* (The Hague, Mouton, 1964), 145-153. Reprinted by permission.
[1] For a recent listing, see *Twenty-Fifth Anniversary Bibliography* of the Summer Institute of Linguistics (Glendale, [Now Box 1960, Santa Ana] Calif., 1960). Special volumes on the languages of Ecuador, of Peru, and of New Guinea will be appearing soon in the Linguistic Series of the Summer Institute of Linguistics of the University of Oklahoma, Benjamin Elson, Editor. Just off the press is *Studies in New Guinea Linguistics* (= *Oceania Linguistic Monographs* 6) (Sydney, Australia, 1962).

logical component.) The manifestation — or realization — of the unit could vary substantially, leading to etic variants, or allo units.

Distribution: A well-defined unit is a member of a class of units APPROPRIATE to a particular SLOT in a construction. (A tagmeme is in grammar a unit comprising a slot with its appropriate emic class. An emic class must also be well-defined.)

A well-defined unit must be seen as a member of a hierarchy of units. An utterance therefore is multiply-segmentable — segmentable successively into units of various levels of a hierarchy, with smaller units entering larger units of the hierarchy. (As morpheme sequences are segmentable into larger word units, phrase units, clause units, discourse units, etc.)

The segmentation can be determined by boundaries of units, with nuclei indeterminate, or by nuclei of units with boundaries indeterminate[2] (as when /a/ and /i/ smear in /ai/). (A sharp-cut unit with both the nucleus and boundaries determinate should be treated as a special case of segmentation.) Such a view removes a number of the problems inherent in previous treatment of segmentation.

A unit must be seen as placed within a system. European scholars have long been interested in such matters, especially as related to phonology. Tagmemics[3] labels as a matrix an array of units as an intersection of contrastive features, in some such fashion as an articulatory chart of phonemes.

2. MULTI-HIERARCHICAL STRUCTURE

Implied in the previous section, but now made explicit, is the assumption that language is multi-hierarchical. A mono-hierarchical view, with progression from phoneme to morpheme to word to clause to sentence to discourse — or the reverse — is too thin. A richer theory is needed to accommodate the empirical data.

(a) In a lexical hierarchy, of specific lexemes, tagmemic theory treats morpheme at the lowest level, with specific units from word to phrase — or idiom — to clause to sentence to discourse (or sonnet, etc.) at the top.

(b) In the phonological hierarchy phones are the minimal etic segments — phonemes the minimal emic segments — with various larger etic (and emic) units of ascending[4] size.

---

[2]   For a discussion of indeterminacy of segmentation of stress groups, see my "Practical Phonetics of Rhythm Waves", *Phonetica* 8 (1962), 9-30.

[3]   If one equates contrast-identification with feature mode, variation-manifestation with manifestation mode, and distribution with distribution mode, one can then see that the thrust toward units, well-defined, represents the heart of my *Language in Relation to a Unified Theory of the Structure of Human Behavior* (Glendale, [Now Box 1960, Santa Ana] Calif., Part I, 1954, Part II, 1955, Part III, 1960); an edition of the work will be appearing with Mouton and Co.

For well-defined constructions see my "Dimensions of Grammatical Constructions", *Language* 38 (1962), 221-244. Here, also, is found the basic treatment of grammatical matrix.

[4]   For my attempt at an exhaustive etic treatment of medium layers see "Practical Phonetics of Rhythm Waves". For a brief emic sample, "Abdominal Pulse Types in Some Peruvian Indian Languages", *Language* 33 (1957), 30-35. See, also, an article on Marinahua Phonology by Eunice Pike and Eugene Scott, *Phonetica* 8 (1962), 1-8. For other layers, see my *Language ... Behavior*.

(c) In the grammatical hierarchy there is an interlocking of tagmemes with constructions. Tagmeme sequences make up constructions, which in turn enter slots of larger constructions,[5] etc.

Boundaries of units of one of the three hierarchies at times reinforce and at other times clash with borders of the other hierarchies. Without this fact of clash only one hierarchy could be maintained.

3. KERNEL OR DERIVED MATRIX (WITH ANTI-REDUNDANT PRESENTATION OF CONSTRUCTION RELATIONSHIPS)

Each of the tagmeme and construction units must be well-defined. It is not sufficient, from the viewpoint of tagmemic theory, to list in miscellaneous or arbitrary fashion various constructions in relation to a general typology — i.e., etic classification. Rather one must attempt to see constructions in contrast with each other — and answer concerning them the question: "What is a minimal pair?" Constructions, like phonemes, must be subject to analysis as well-defined units. Constructions contrast, in this view, only when there is a dual[6] structural difference between them. The etics and emics of grammatical constructions thus come to the fore. (An active versus passive clause shows contrast, for example, both by having a different subject tagmeme — subject as actor versus subject as goal — and a different predicate tagmeme, as well as by absence versus presence of a special agent tagmeme.)

Once constructions are well-defined, their symbols can be placed in the cells of a contrastive matrix. Note, in Table I, a very simple array of some Kanite[7] (New Guinea, Eastern Highlands) clauses.

Two advantages come from such a display. (a) The relationship between these clauses is implicitly defined and shown as the relationship between intersecting classes

TABLE I

Kernel Matrix of Kanite Clauses

	Neutral Transitive	Indirect Transitive	Direct Transitive	Intransitive	Equative
Independent Indicative	1	3	5	7	9
Dependent Indicative	2	4	6	8	10

Numbers in the cells refer to clause types, and will be illustrated below.

[5] See *Language ... Behavior*, §12.
[6] See Robert E. Longacre, "String Constituent Analysis", *Language* 36 (1960), 63-88, for the initial theory here; for more formal presentation, see "Dimensions".
[7] Kanite data here and below are from Joy McCarthy, Summer Institute of Linguistics. A somewhat different presentation — and more complete — will be seen in her *Kanite Clause Chains* (in preparation).

of clauses (which are grouped according to the implied presence or absence of certain contrastive components). (b) The redundancy of presentation is sharply cut, as over against a presentation which treats clauses one at a time. The intersecting classes of clauses are posited by the rows and columns of the matrix, and can be referred to by groups.

A further anti-redundancy advantage comes through matrix presentation when a simple chart like this one is treated as the nucleus — or kernel — of the system. From it a derived matrix can be obtained by 'multiplying' it by a further feature which affects each cell. Thus the formulas:

$$M \;.\; \text{Inter} \;=\; M_{\text{Inter}}$$
$$M \;.\; \text{Imp} \;=\; M_{\text{Imp}}$$

state that by suitable tagmemic modifications the constructions in the cells of the nuclear matrix can be transformed into interrogative and imperative clauses, etc. (Only the FACT of their occurrence is shown by this display — the structure of the derived constructions is given in tagmemic formula elsewhere in the description of the system.)

Such matrices have proved to be of substantial methodological importance, for two reasons: (a) They call attention to GAPS in a system. If a matrix implies a cell, but no illustration for it is present, one may be stimulated to look for the implied data which the language contains but which have escaped the analyst. Note that I happen to have no data to illustrate (8), implied by the system. Presumably a check with the informant would supply it.

In addition (b), the array can be used as a SEARCH MATRIX, for analysis. In many of the languages of the New Guinea highlands, a dependent clause has various ties (of subject, identity, or of time) with a following independent clause. If, on the basis of known language characteristics of the region, the possible concord components of the first clause are listed at the left of a matrix, and of the second clause along the top, bilingual elicitation often can locate many forms rapidly — to be checked later against text material. In reverse fashion, if in a particular language numerous morphs have been segmented out of the two clause positions but with meanings unknown, the two morph lists can be placed on the left and top of a search matrix, with systematic trial with a bilingual to seek for their semantic interrelations.

4. SYNTAX PARADIGM (UTILIZING CONTROLLED REDUNDANCY)

In the preceding section a matrix approach was used to cut redundancy in presentation. Now we take the opposite approach, utilizing a matrix approach in a manner which allows us to exploit redundancy of presentational material for rapid reading of unfamiliar material — material where the reader may be uninterested in learning to speak or read the particular language as such, but wishes merely to grasp its structure as quickly and easily as possible.

The data are presented in a SYNTAX PARADIGM[8] in CITATION FORM. Just as in the presentation of a morphological paradigm the choice of stem is kept constant,[9] with only inflectional changes, so in a syntax paradigm the same illustrative words and morphemes are used whenever possible. This leads to CONTROLLED REDUNDANCY as an aid to understanding — since an entire grammar can be read intelligibly on the basis of a few dozen (?) forms. Every new word or morpheme introduced into the citation paradigm warns the reader that the contrastive structure has somehow changed.

Accompanying the citation paradigm is a TAGMEMIC-NOTATION PARADIGM, in which each construction type is given with cut-down tagmemic formulas — not in citation form. These formulas are enclosed in braces { } to symbolize their emic status — as are morphemes as against morphs.

A TAGMATIC-NOTATION PARADIGM — in square brackets to show its etic status — then gives a breakdown of the constructions (a) to show, further, both slot function and class of filler of each slot (without which no tagmemic analysis can be checked for accuracy) and (b) to show variants of tagmemic order, or optional occurrence of included tagmemes. Variants of emic constructions can be shown by a tilde: {[ ] ~ [ ]}.

In Table II we now list as a citation paradigm illustrations of the six types of clauses implied by the matrix of Table I. For each dependent clause type two illustrations are given (marked as 2a, 2b, etc.). The first of the pair has as its subject the same as that of the following independent clause (not cited, but suggested by the three dots following the dependent clause). The second of the pair has a subject differing from that of the implied following clause. Ditto marks are used to allow faster recognition of some of the repeated forms.

TABLE II

Citation Paradigm of Kanite Clauses

(1)	naaki	eka	vie-mo-ʔa	———	maya	no-te-ka	—-ne-kah-i-e
(2a)	,,	,,	,,	———	,,	,,	—-'' -te-no ...
(2b)	,,	,,	,,	———	,,	,,	—-'' -t-e-ke-no ...
(3)	,,	,,	,,	neʔ-mo-na	,,	,,	a-mi-kah-i-e
(4a)	,,	,,	,,	,,	,,	,,	''- '' -te-no ...
(4b)	,,	,,	,,	,,	,,	,,	''- '' -t-e-ke-no ...
(5)	,,	,,	,,	,,	,,	,,	''-ke-kah-i-e

[8] For detailed presentation, see "A Syntax Paradigm", *Language* 39 (1963), 216-230; with illustration via Bilaan, of the Philippines.

[9] A morphological paradigm is therefore artificial. So is a syntax paradigm. Its elicitation is subject to all the dangers of morphological elicitation. Its results must, as in morphology, be checked against uncontrolled text. And, as in morphology, its value as a pedagogical or description device is sometimes substantial. Supplementary illustrations from text give support to and test the correctness and completeness of the analysis.

(6)	”	”	”	”	”	”	? ? ?...
(7)	”	”	”	————	———	”	--u-kah-i-e
(8a)	”	”	”	————	———	”	--u-te-no ...
(8b)	”	”	”	————	———	”	--u-t-e-ke-no ...
(9)	”	”	”	————	kanareʔ vie	”	--mai-kah-i-e
(10a)	”	”	”	————	”	”	--mai-te-no ...
(10b)	”	”	”	————	”	”	--mai-t-e-ke-no ...

Lexical Items:

naaki	'so'			*a-*	'it'
eka	'tomorrow'			*-mi-*	'give'
vie-	'man'	*ne-*	'eat'	*-ke-*	'see'
-mo-	equational	*-kah*	'will'	*u-*	'go'
-ʔa	'he'	*-i-*	'he'	*kanareʔ*	'good'
		-e	indicative	*mai-*	'to be'
neʔ-	'boy'				
-na	oblique	*-te-* ~ *-t-*	'first'		
maya	'sweet potato'	*-no*	'he₁₋₂' (when in structure 2a, etc.)		
no-	'house'		'he₂' (when in structure 2b, etc.)		
-te-	'at'	*-e-*	'he₁'		
-ka	locative	*-ke-*	transitional		

In Table III we give free translations of the citation components of Table II.

TABLE III

Translation of Citation Paradigm of Clause

(1)	So tomorrow the man will eat sweet potato at the house.
(2a)	So tomorrow the man will first eat sweet potato at the house. (Implying: and then he — the man — will ...)
(2b)	So tomorrow the man will first eat sweet potato at the house. (Implying: and then he — someone else — will ...)
(3)	So tomorrow the man will give sweet potato to the boy at the house.
(4a)	So tomorrow the man will first give sweet potato to the boy at the house. (Implying: and then he — the man — will ...)
(4b)	So tomorrow the man will first give sweet potato to the boy at the house ... (Implying: and then he — someone else — will ...)
(5)	So tomorrow the man will see the sweet potato at the house.
(6)	?
(7)	So tomorrow the man will go to the house.
(8a)	So tomorrow the man will first go to the house ... (Implying: And then he — the man — will ...)
(8b)	So tomorrow the man will first go to the house ... (Implying: And then he — someone else — will ...)
(9)	So tomorrow the man at the house will be a good man.
(10a)	So tomorrow the man at the house will first be a good man ... (Implying: And then he — the man — will ...)
(10b)	So tomorrow the man at the house will first be a good man ... (Implying: And then he — someone else — will ...)

We now give, in Table IV, the same paradigm in tagmemic notation. (We might have omitted here those optional tagmemes which serve no contrastive function between the clauses — introducer, time, independent subject, and location. They would then have appeared as expansions in the tagmatic paradigm.)

Each predicate type differs from the others. For a sample breakdown formula see Table V.

TABLE IV

Syntax Paradigm in Contrastive Tagmemic Form

	Intro	Time	Subj	IndirObj	Obj	Loc	Pred	
(1)	{± Intro	±Time	± Subj	——	± Obj	± Loc	+ $\text{Pred}_{\text{NeuTrIndep}}$}	'eat'
(2)	{ „	„	„	——	„	„	+ $\text{Pred}_{\text{NeuTrDep}}$ ..}	'eat'
(3)	{ „	„	„	± IndirObj	„	„	+ $\text{Pred}_{\text{IndirTrInDep}}$}	'give'
(4)	{ „	„	„	± IndirObj	„	„	+ $\text{Pred}_{\text{IndirTrDep}}$ ..}	'give'
(5)	{ „	„	„	——	„	„	+ $\text{Pred}_{\text{DirTrIndep}}$}	'see'
(6)	{ „	„	„	——	„	„	? }	'see'
(7)	{ „	„	„	——	——	„	+ $\text{Pred}_{\text{IntrIndep}}$}	'go'
(8)	{ „	„	„	——	——	„	+ $\text{Pred}_{\text{IntrDep}}$ ..}	'go'
(9)	{ „	„	„	——	+ Compl	„	+ $\text{Pred}_{\text{EquaIndep}}$}	'be'
(10)	{ „	„	„	——	+ Compl	„	+ $\text{Pred}_{\text{EquaDep}}$ ..}	'be'

The plus and plus-minus signs indicate obligatory versus optional occurrence. Subscripts indicate predicates with contrastive internal structure.

We could continue now[10] to give formulas — in etic brackets — amplified to symbolize the fillers of the tagmemic slots. Such formulas would thus show that specially marked noun expressions fill the time slot; that specially marked noun, pronoun, and verb expressions fill the location slot; and would show separate contrastive verb structures for each of the different predicate tagmemes.

In addition, the tagmatic notation would show the subject concord seen in the citation paradigm of Table II, above, where (2a) and (2b) would be related as {2} = [2a] ~ [2b], etc.

The neutral-transitive clause (1) contains (a) a class of neutral-transitive verb stems ("eat"), (b) optional independent object on a clause level, but (c) obligatory absence of a dependent object prefix in the verb, and (d) obligatory absence of an indirect object on a clause level; whereas the indirect transitive (3) contains (a) a class of indirect-transitive verb stems ("give"), (b) optional independent object on a clause level, but (c) obligatory indirect-object prefixal tagmeme in the verb, (d) and optional indirect-object on a clause level. The direct-transitive clause (5) contains (a) a class of direct-transitive verb stems ("see"), (b) optional independent object on a clause level, but (c) obligatory object prefixal tagmeme in the verb, and (d) obligatory absence of indirect-object on a clause level. The prefixal indirect- and direct-object tagmemes in the verbs are homophonous; the same set of pronouns fills the functionally contrastive slots of the respective tagmemes. I have chosen

[10] But shall not; see, rather, reference to Paradigm in fn. 8.

here to treat these various structural differences as sufficient to contrast, emically, {1} with {3} and {5} and {7}. If, however, an analyst were to feel that these differences are minor, it is conceivable that he might choose to treat the first three as subtypes of transitive. If so, his formulas would require that

$$*\{\text{Transitive Clause}\} = [\text{NeuTr}] \sim [\text{DirTr}] \sim [\text{IndirTr}],$$

and separate tagmatic formulas would then be required for the direct versus indirect alloconstructions.

Before one can see in formula the full structure, however, a breakdown formula must be given for the fillers of each of the predicate tagmemic slots. As a sample,

TABLE V

Internal Tagmemic Structure of Verbs

	±Aspect	±Neg						
(1)	±Aspect	±Neg	——	+NeuTrVbStem		+Subj$_i$	+Mood	'eat'
(2)	„	„	—— +	„	±TimeRel	±(Subj$_d$ +Transit)	+Subj$_c$	'eat'
(3)	„	„	+IObj	+IndirTrVbStem		+Subj$_i$	+Mood	'give'
(4)	„	„	+ „	„	±TimeRel	±(Subj$_d$ +Transit)	+Subj$_c$	'give'
(5)	„	„	+Obj	+DirTrVbStem		+Subj	+Mood	'see'
(6)	?	?						
(7)	„	„	——	+InTrVbStem		+Subj$_i$	+Mood	'go'
(8)	„	„	——	„	±TimeRel	±(Subj$_d$ +Transit)	+Subj$_c$	'go'
(9)	„	„	——	+EquaVbStem		+Subj$_i$	+Mood	'be'
(10)	„	„	——	„	±TimeRel	±(Subj$_d$ +Transit)	+Subj$_c$	'be'

note Table V. By this symbolization, fuller explanation is provided for the verbal-morpheme occurrences illustrated in Table II. In the verbs of independent clauses, the suffixal subject tagmeme Subj$_1$ has a different morpheme class (e.g., -i 'he') from that of the suffix tagmemes of the dependent verbs. The dependent verb has, obligatorily, a suffixal subject tagmeme in concord (see subscript in Subj$_c$) with the following independent clause (implied in Tables II, III, and IV by the three dots). When the subject of the dependent clause is the same as that of the independent clause, the concord subject in the dependent clause implies both the person of the dependent and the person of the independent clause (cf., -no as 'he$_{1-2}$' in the legend of Table II). When, however, the subject of the dependent clause differs from that of the independent clause following it, the concord pronoun of the dependent verb is retained unchanged, but a further dependent subject tagmeme Subj$_d$ is added (e.g., -e- 'he$_1$'). Between the two, a morph -ke- is placed called transitional (see Transit, in Table V) by McCarthy.

As implied earlier, the dependent object and dependent indirect-object tagmemes in the formulas (5) and (3) of Table V are manifested homophonously. The tagmemic difference between them — their functional difference — is determined by their relationship to the embedding clauses.

Some further tagmemes which the verbs may optionally contain — aspect and negation — are not illustrated in the data here but are symbolized by the formulas. Time Relation tagmeme — also not illustrated — may show time relations between clauses.

5. FIELD THEORY

The handling of language systems in matrix terms encourages us to believe that a field theory of language is well worth developing, with matrix as one component. Analysis of language behavior yields segmental units. Analysis of the system of units yields field structures — matrix units, matrix types, matrix hierarchies. Implications of this view are beginning to emerge.[11]

[11] See my *Language ... Behavior*, §12.1; "Language as Particle, Wave, and Field", *The Texas Quarterly* 2:2 (1959), 37-54; "A Note on System as Field", unpublished; "Matrix Rotation and Matrix as an Emic Unit", a paper to be presented to the December meeting of the Linguistic Society of America, 1962.

HYPERPHONEMES AND NON-SYSTEMATIC FEATURES
OF AGUARUNA PHONEMICS*

with MILDRED LARSON

INTRODUCTION

Aguaruna[1] has a number of very difficult problems in connection with skewing in its phonemic system, especially as concerns nasal components. Whichever of several solutions the analyst adopts leaves the system askew as to members of phoneme series, as to allophonic distribution, as to allophones crisscrossing over two or more contrastive series of phonemes, as to morphophonemics, or as to psycholinguistic responses of the native speakers of the language.

The hyperphonemic system involves special kinds of contrastive rhythmic types (contrastive abdominemic patterns), as well as the kinds of pitch-stress-juncture correlations which are less rare.

NON-NASALIZED PHONEMES OR ALLOPHONES OF PHONEMES

The oral vowel series is fairly straightforward in analysis. Speakers of Dialect A — which is the dialect referred to unless otherwise specified — have a system of three high vowel phonemes /i/, /ɨ/, /u/, and one low vowel phoneme /a/. When, in non-initial position in a stress group, /a/ precedes any of the other three vowels, it is actualized by an allophone which, in general, is moved to mid-position in the direction of the high vowel which it accompanies: i.e., /a/ may have the allophones

*   *Studies in Languages and Linguistics in Honor of Charles C. Fries*, ed. by A. Markwardt (Ann Arbor, Mich., English Language Institute, 1964), 55-67. Reprinted by permission.
[1]   Aguaruna is a member of the Jívaro language family. The Aguarunas populate the northern jungles of Peru and are scattered chiefly along the Upper Marañon River and its many tributaries, from the Pongo de Manseriche on the east to the Chinchipe on the southwest. No accurate census has been taken. The informant estimated that there are some 8,000 persons who speak Aguaruna. A very small minority of these are bilingual, speaking some Spanish.

Data were gathered by ML for the Summer Institute of Linguistics of the University of Oklahoma in various field trips during July 1954 to October 1955. The informant was Silas Cuñachí, a middle-aged, bilingual man living at Nasaret on the Chiriaco River. Other persons living in this same area were used for checking materials. In addition ML has had access to data gathered by Mr. and Mrs. Ray Wakelin for the same Institute in various field trips made during 1952-1954. The analysis of the phonemes is that of ML; the presentation of the data, and the analysis of the hyperphonemes, is by KLP.

[e], [ə], and [o] before /i/, /ɨ/, and /u/ respectively. Most speakers, however, retain the allophone [a] after labial consonants. The phoneme /i/ has an allophone lowered to [ɪ] in final unstressed closed syllables, and the phoneme /a/ has the raised allophone [ə] in the same position. Note the following examples: /bitáik/ [bitéik] 'orphan'; /wikáitatus/ [wikə́itatus] 'that he may walk'; /idáuk/ [iⁿdóuk] 'sweet potato'; /pínik/ [pínɪk] 'scaffolding'; /wɨ́tasan/ [wɨ́tasən] 'that I may go'.

Dialect B is spoken by a minority in the same household, with no predictable basis for determining which speaker will utilize Dialect A or B. In this second dialect voiceless vowels[2] are in phonemic contrast to voiced ones: note the following examples: kaápI 'vine' versus čápi 'palm'; dukúčI 'grandmother' versus kúči 'pig'; uhúkɨ 'tail' versus kanúki 'only canoe'; píšakA 'bird' versus píšaka 'a bird!'; kadáitU 'paddle' versus yumímitu 'sweet'; áincU 'people' versus múncu 'milk'.

Of the consonants, the sibilant-assibilant group entails the fewest problems of analysis. The phonemes /s/, /š/, /c/, and /č/ are clearly in contrast: sápi 'worm'; sáka 'a certain tree'; sampáp 'nettle'; šína 'a certain tree'; šíɣki 'hardwood trees'; šampíu 'lizard'; cápa 'bowl'; cákat 'a certain animal'; cakús 'mud'; čápi 'palm'; čáka 'bridge'; čínap 'hook'; číɣki 'game bird'.

The phoneme /r/, a voiced flap, is present in the system only through loans from Spanish and Huambisa (a language closely related to Aguaruna) which are thoroughly assimilated in the speech of monolinguals in a few words such as karápu 'nail' (< clavo), and in one or two words of an onomatopoetic type such as suákaraip 'frog', where the noise made by the frog is said to be karáip.

Voiceless stops /p/, /t/, /k/, and /ʔ/ are in general unaspirated and voiceless, but with one or two special allophones which are not systematic with relation to each other. The phoneme /t/, for example, has an allophone comprised of voiceless lateral fricative [ɬ] before /h/: note /aɣáthunta/ [aɣáɬhunta] 'write!'. The bilabial stop /p/ likewise has a voiceless fricative allophone before /h/, but of a flat type [ø] as in /haiphámu/ [haiøhámu] 'clean'. The phoneme /k/, however, is not analogous to these in that before /h/ no fricativization occurs.

Further perplexing non-symmetries occur in the stop allophones. The /k/ (in the

---

[2] Voiceless phonemic vowels in Dialect B are the result of a partial unvoicing in restricted grammatical contexts (leaving phonemic contrasts with voiced vowels in other grammatical contexts). This unvoicing is paralleled in Dialect A by a complete loss of the vowels concerned. The unvoicing in Dialect B occurs exclusively during the formation of the subject forms of nouns. The subject form is derived from the object form through the unvoicing or loss of the final syllable of certain stems of three or more syllables. If there is no consonant at the juncture of the final two syllables of the stem, the final stem vowel is subtracted in Dialect A and unvoiced in Dialect B. If there is a homorganic cluster at this juncture, the final CV is subtracted or unvoiced in the respective dialects. If non-homorganic clusters occur at this juncture, subtraction or unvoicing do not occur but metathesis takes place in both dialects and the stem final CV becomes VC. Note the following, in which -n is the objectivizing suffix: kuhapín 'leg (obj)', kukáp (or B: kuhápɨ) 'leg (subj)'; bačiɣkín 'monkey (obj)', bačíɣ (or B: bačíɣkI) 'monkey (subj)'; ičínkan 'cooking pot (obj)', ičínak 'cooking pot (subj)'.

For other instances of phonemic voiceless vowels note the paper on Comanche vowels written by Elliot Canonge, *International Journal of American Linguistics* 23, 63-67.

analysis of ML — but for alternate analyses see below) has a voiced allophone [g] after /m/ and /n/ as in /išámkatasan/ [išámgatasən] 'that I may be afraid' and /ain-káta/ [aingáta] 'stretch!'. The phones [b] and [d] are not sub-members respectively of /p/ and /t/, however, but are in contrast with the voiceless stops; note *pičáktawai* 'it will lay eggs' versus *bičáktawai* 'it will break', and *takáwai* 'he works' versus *dakáwai* 'he waits'. The phones [k] and [g] never contrast in this fashion. The phonemes /b/ and /d/, moreover, have further allophonic variants which we shall mention in connection with nasalization.

NASAL PHONEMES AND PHONEMES WITH NASAL ALLOPHONES

The principal difficulty in the analysis of the Aguaruna phonemic system centers about the nasal components of phonemes — components which are present in all allophones of the phoneme or only in some of the allophones. Thus for /b/ and /d/ there is free variation in utterance-initial position from [b] and [d] to [^{m}b] and [^{n}d] respectively. There is a non-symmetrical feature here in the stop series as a whole, however, in that the velar stop phone [g] (in the /k/ phoneme) does not occur in utterance-initial and hence does not have the corresponding free variation to a nasal-plus-stop allophone in utterance-initial position. For illustrations of the variation of the bilabial and alveolar phones note illustrations of [^{m}b] and [^{n}d]: /báku/ [^{m}báku] or [báku] 'thigh'; /dúku/ [^{n}dúku] or [dúku] 'mother'.

A further analytical problem arises in this area of the system in that /b/ and /d/ sometimes appear to be in free variation with /m/ and /n/ with which they are said by this analysis to be in phonemic contrast. For illustrations of consistent contrast of [m] and [n] versus [^{m}b] and [^{n}d] note /wíčami/ [wíčami] 'let's not go' versus /wí-čabi/ [wíča^{m}bi] 'we did not go'; /inák/ [inák] 'a certain tree' versus /idáuk/ [i^{n}dáuk] 'sweet potato' and /nántu/ [nántu] 'moon'. Compare these with /makičík/ or /ba-kičík/ [makičík], [^{m}bakičík], or [bakičík] 'one'; /nápa/ or /dápa/ [dápa], [^{n}dápa], or [nápa] 'bee'. In these two latter illustrations we assume that the fluctuation of [m], [b], and [^{m}b] is a combination of free fluctuation between the full phonemes /m/ and /b/ and free fluctuation between the allophones [^{m}b] and [b], and that the fluctuation of [n], [d], and [^{n}d] is a combination of free fluctuation between the full phonemes /n/ and /d/ and free fluctuation between the allophones [^{n}d] and [d]. The free variation between full phonemes is limited to the initial position in a sporadic arbitrary list of words.

Two nasalized assibilants occur, /^{n}c/ and /^{n}č/: note *yú^{n}čmata* 'dive!'; *haá^{n}č* 'clothes'; *iwa^{n}č* 'devil'; *ai^{n}cšakam* 'people also'; *cúncu^{n}c* 'a stream'; *ai^{n}ckawai* 'he put cargo on'. These are not analogous to the series including [m$_b$] and [n$_d$] in that the assibilants have their second segment voiceless, not voiced, and in that there is no parallel non-nasal series such as a voiced sibilant series to parallel the voiced stop series. This constitutes another non-symmetrical feature of Aguaruna.

As a further non-symmetry we note that phone [ŋ] (limited to syllable-final oc-currence) is in complementary distribution with the voiced velar fricative [γ] (lim-ited to syllable-initial occurrence between vowels), so that we treat the two phones as members of the same phoneme /γ/. Here, as with the stops, the velars are not analogous to the bilabials and alveolars, /m/ and /n/. The /m/ is in contrast with the bilabial semivowel /w/ (*wáki* 'stomach' versus *máki* 'enough'), and with the bilabial voiced fricative [β] (*βíčakam* 'I also' versus *bíčatin* 'cold' and *βíki* 'I only' versus *bitáik* 'orphan') which occurs only before /i/ as a member of the /w/ phoneme, versus /b/.

With the alveolar nasal /n/ there is no close allophonic parallelism with either the velars or bilabials just discussed, since there is no [ð] to be united with it as [γ] is united with [ŋ], nor is there an [ð] which could contrast with it as [β] contrasts with /m/. Perhaps the closest analogy to these relationships would be the contrast of /n/ with palatal phoneme /y/, but the /y/ has no voiced fricative allophone to parallel the [β] allophones of /w/.

In previous paragraphs we have indicated the analysis chosen for the phones [k], [g], [ŋ] and [γ]. The complexities in this analysis are sufficiently great, how-ever, that it is difficult to see them all in the scattered form given, so that here we return to the analysis from a different point of view:

Phones [g], [γ], and [ŋ] are all in complementary distribution one with another. Phone [g] occurs only after /m/ and /n/; the phone [γ] occurs only between vowels; the phone [ŋ] occurs only syllable-finally before an initial consonant of another syllable, or utterance-finally. This distributional data, therefore, would not prevent the uniting of the three into a single phoneme.

On the other hand, the phone [k] contrasts with [ŋ] in syllable-final position (compare *šiwahúŋ* 'my enemy' versus *šiwahúk* 'Is it my enemy?'). The [k] contrasts with [γ] in intervocalic position (compare *aγátia* 'in that manner one writes' versus *takátia* 'in that manner one works'). But [k] is in complementary distribution with [g], since [k] never occurs following /m/ and /n/, whereas [g] occurs exclusively in this position. Since [k] contrasts with [γ] and [ŋ], but is in complementary distribu-tion with [g], one cannot unite [k] and [g] on the one hand, and unite [g], [γ] and [ŋ] into a second phoneme on the other, without running into a contradiction — since by this analysis [g] would be simultaneously a member of the two phonemes [k] and [γ].

Since this analysis, then, must be rejected, what possibilities remain open to us? We suggest the following, any one of which would avoid the contradiction men-tioned above. Hypothesis A (adopted by ML for this paper) unites [k] and [g] to /k/, and unites [ŋ] and [γ] to /γ/. Hypothesis B unites [k] and [g] to /k/ but treats [ŋ] and [γ] as separate phonemes /ŋ/ and /γ/. Hypothesis C treats [k] as the pho-neme /k/, unites [g] and [γ] into the phoneme /g/ and treats [ŋ] as a separate pho-neme /ŋ/. Hypothesis D treats [k], [g], [γ], and [ŋ] as each constituting separate phonemes /k/, /g/, /γ/, and /ŋ/. We will discuss each of these hypotheses separately.

Hypothesis A treats [k] and [g] as sub-members of the phoneme /k/ since they are in complementary distribution and because of observable native reaction on the part of informants having to write the language. These persons consistently write [g] with the letter 'k' even though they have not been taught to do so. Similarly, [ŋ] and [γ] are written as the phoneme /γ/ (with the orthographical sign 'g') since they are mutually exclusive in distribution and since here, likewise, native reaction of naive informants would suggest that these two are the same sound (since, in learning to write, informants use the same symbol for both sounds without having to be taught to do so). It should be noted that these informants have learned to write a small amount of Spanish, and could be affected by the Spanish phonemic system, though it is not apparent that Spanish bias should influence them in the direction indicated.

Hypothesis B unites [k] and [g] into a phoneme /k/ for the two reasons given under Hypothesis A. On the other hand, it separates [γ] and [ŋ] because the two phonemes are respectively members of two series which contrast at other points of articulation. That is, the bilabial members of the respective series are in contrast: [β] as an allophone of /w/ contrasts with /m/. (There is no fricative [ð] to make further contrasts at the alveolar point of articulation.) The chief disadvantage to Hypothesis B — but not a fatal one — is its ignoring of the psycholinguistic evidence which points to the phonemic unity of [γ] and [ŋ].

Hypothesis C treats /k/ as the sole prominent member of the phoneme /k/. It separates [k] and [g] on the ground of their being members of a contrastive series: [t] contrasts with [d] and [p] contrasts with [b], as illustrated above. Similarly, in Hypothesis C, [γ] is separated from [ŋ] because of a similar contrast in the nasal versus voiced fricative series as was indicated under the discussion of Hypothesis B. Finally, under Hypothesis C, [g] and [γ] are united into a phoneme /g/ on the basis of complementary distribution. It should be noted, however, that this leaves the system highly askew: /k/ has a distribution which has a gap in it following nasals — a gap which is pertinent since /g/ under Hypothesis C has a distribution limited to this position and to intervocalic occurrence — and /ŋ/ has a very small postulated distribution. In addition, Hypothesis C ignores the psycholinguistic evidence cited under the discussion of Hypothesis A.

Hypothesis D, which treats [k], [g], [γ] and [ŋ] as separate phonemes, does so by the argument that each of these phones is a member of a contrastive series. The contrastive series data is mentioned in the discussion of Hypothesis C for [k] versus [g], and under Hypothesis B for [γ] versus [ŋ]. We note, further, that [b] contrasts with [β] in illustrations given above and that this contrast might serve as a pattern to extrapolate the contrast to further members of the series, i.e., to the velars [g] and [γ]. This hypothesis entails the skewed distribution as mentioned under Hypothesis C, and ignores the psycholinguistic evidence mentioned under Hypothesis A. Probably no one would seriously consider adopting Hypothesis D. Its usefulness here is to demonstrate the problem involved if one gives consistent priority to the criterion of separating phones belonging to contrastive series of phones without restricting such a principle by other principles.

The phoneme /ʔ/ is in contrast with /h/ and other phonemes. Note *áiʔain* 'a certain animal' versus *áham* 'when cutting trees' and *tuntúh* 'neck' versus *apawáʔ* 'father' (form used for calling). Its distribution, however, is highly non-systematic in that it is extremely limited as to the consonant position it can occupy and as to lexical frequency of occurrence. It approaches extra-systematic status in that, apart from the word just cited and the word *aiʔait* 'midnight', it occurs only in interjectional items such as *čaʔ* 'Oh!', *iʔí* 'yes', and in utterance-final position as one of numerous lexically-determined segmental signals of a question as in *dukušáʔ* 'where is your mother?'. The phoneme /h/, however, does not have such distributional limitations.

An alveolar voiceless click occurs occasionally as a signal of interest, approval, or satisfaction. It constitutes part of no lexical item, is completely extra-systematic in distribution, therefore, and is accordingly not listed among the regular phonemes.

A further phone [l] is extra-systematic as regards normal speech but occurs in nonsense-syllables in a congruent system of song, where it is extra-systematic to the phoneme distribution in regular morphemes there.

Each of the four vowel phonemes, or their respective allophones, may be paralleled by a nasalized counterpart which is phonemically distinct from it. The alternatives here are either to treat the nasalized vowels as distinct phonemes in contrast with the oral ones (note *patą́ą́čuʔ* versus *takaáču* 'not working'; *sumákį* 'he buys' versus *pišáki* 'only a bird'; *ahį́t* 'to make sparks' versus *apijít* 'to double rope'; *takú* 'carried' versus *takų* 'carrying'), or to treat them as comprised of two phonemes, namely an oral vowel plus a componential phoneme of nasalization. The alternative chosen by ML is the latter, so that [ą] appears in the analysis as the sum of the two phonemes /a/ and /ˏ/. Various phonemic, allophonic, lexical, and morphophonemic consequences follow from this choice.

Nasalized counterparts of [w], [β], [y], [γ], and [h], since they occur only adjacent to the phoneme /ˏ/ on a neighboring vowel, are members of these consonant phonemes respectively, except that nasalized [w̨] and [β] are both members of the phoneme /w/, as are [w] and [β].

The lexical distribution of /ˏ/ is often determinate only within a statable range, since the nasalization phoneme may 'float' over a range covered by one, two or three vowels separated by /h/, /w/, /y/, or /γ/ (with these consonants non-phonemically nasalized at the same time). For some such words the nasalization alternately but freely appears on the first, the last, the central, or all of the three vowels, or either the first two or last two of the sequence. For example, note *tųwíyą*, *tųwíyą*, or *tuwíyą* 'where to?'; *kíhųą*, *kįhua*, or *kíhuą* 'toucan'; *kąhį́átatus*, *kąhįátatus*, or *kajįátatus* 'that it may ferment'; *įhúktatui*, *įhúktatui*, or *ihúktatui* 'he will add to'.

Note, furthermore, that this 'domain' of the 'floating nasalization' never crosses over voiceless stops, or other consonants than those mentioned.

Some lexical items, on the other hand, are completely or usually consistent in their placement of the phoneme /ᴗ/. Among the most stable of such words seem to be the following: *uhuhú̧* 'dry'; *ku̧hu̧* 'a certain animal'; *uwáhu̧* 'drank'; *himpi̧łhi̧* 'his gray hair'; *kuwáuhi̧* 'his lunch'. (Historically many of these more stable, localized nasals seem to be a reflex of an old *-*ŋ* since *ŋ + *V > *h*Ṽ. The nasalization of the vowels, in these instances, does not spread backwards past *h*, even as it would not past the *ŋ*.)

Morphophonemically, the nasalization problem is somewhat complicated. Full development of its presentation must await a paper on the morphophonemics as such, but a few bits may be mentioned here:

(1) Some suffixes have a form in which the segmental part is a clear CV sequence following the stem, but in which a further nasalization phoneme or sequence of such phonemes is actualized on the stem to which it is added. The suffix meaning 'during', for example, can be symbolized as {ᴗ...ᴗ... a̧i̧}. Allomorphs of this suffix include the minimum-form /a̧i̧/, with expansions by one or more nasalization phonemes before the minimum-form actualized on the stem phones. The number of such nasalization phonemes present will be determined by the potential domain of the spread of the nasalization, as defined for 'floating nasalization' in the preceding paragraphs. Note, for example, the following: *taká̧a̧i̧* 'while working'; *ka̧hí̧a̧i̧* 'while chewing' or 'while fermenting'; *išámą̧i̧* 'while being afraid'.

Note, further, that stems which are not homophonous on some occurrences may become part of homophonous words as a result of the nasalization of parts of the stem; compare *ihu-* 'to bump into', *ihútatui* 'he will bump into'; *i̧hu-* (or *i̧hu̧-*) 'to contribute', *i̧hútatui* (or *i̧hú̧tatui*) 'he will contribute', but *í̧hu̧a̧i̧* 'while bumping into' or 'while contributing'. A further allomorph of this morpheme or of others analogous to it involves a fusion of one of the nasalization-component phonemes with the initial voiced stop of the stem, so that /ᴗ + /d/ > /n/, just as *dii-* 'to see' plus /...ᴗ... a̧i̧/ becomes *ni̧á̧i̧* 'while seeing'; *dáwi* 'foot' plus /...ᴗ.../ 'third person possessive' becomes *ná̧wi̧* 'his foot'; *uba-* 'sister' plus -*yi̧* 'his' becomes *umáyi̧* (or *umayi̧*) 'his sister'; *dai* 'tooth' plus /...ᴗ.../ becomes *ná̧i̧* 'his tooth'.

Compare also the action of a morpheme which is entirely comprised of a nasalization phoneme manifested on the stem; *sumáka* 'buying' plus /...ᴗ.../ 'later time' becomes *sumáka̧* 'after buying'; *kuhápi-* 'leg' plus /...ᴗ.../ 'third person possessive' becomes *kuhapi̧* 'his leg'.

(2) The reverse of this phenomenon also occurs. Here, the suffix has a nasalization-cancelling component (written in our formulas as /...-ᴗ.../) which causes the deletion of the /ᴗ/ phoneme or phonemes from the stem, and/or the loss of nasalization from a nasal consonant. Note that *mú̧ha̧* (or *mú̧ha̧*) 'mountain' plus -γ 'my' becomes *buháγ* 'my mountain'; *ya̧wá̧a̧* (or *yawá̧a̧*) 'dog' plus -γ 'my' becomes *yawaáγ* 'my dog'.

(3) In other instances, the component /ᴗ/ actualizes as a full phoneme /m/, /n/, or /γ/ before a stop of these points of articulation respectively: *yawá̧a̧* 'dog' plus -*ki* 'only' becomes *yawaáγki* 'only a dog'; *takastí̧* 'he will work' plus -*paš* 'maybe' becomes *takastí̧mpaš* 'maybe he will work'; *piákhi̧* 'his bed' plus -*čau* 'negative' be-

comes *piákhinčau* 'not his bed'. However, there are also instances in which the nasalization does not actualize in this manner, as in the following: *patą́ą* 'family' plus *-ču* 'negative' becomes *patą́ą̌ču* 'not family'; *yąwą́a* 'dog' plus *-či* 'diminutive' becomes *yąwą́ą̌či* 'little dog'.

CHART OF ALLOPHONIC ASSIGNMENT OF CERTAIN PHONES
TO CONSONANTS AND VOWELS

In order that the reader may see more readily the asymmetry in the allophonic assignment of certain phones to phonemes, Chart I is provided. Parentheses enclose allophones of phonemes; a horizontal row of symbols indicates the members of a phonetic series; sets of parentheses which are non-symmetrically distributed in reference to horizontal rows of symbols indicate some of the non-symmetries in the system. In reference to the problem of the phones [k], [g], [ŋ], and [γ], Hypothesis A is represented on the chart. To obtain Hypothesis B eliminate the parenthesis joining [ŋ] with [γ]. To obtain Hypothesis D eliminate the parentheses joining [ŋ] with [γ] and [k] with [g]. To obtain Hypothesis C eliminate these two parentheses and join with another pair, [g] and [γ].

CHART I

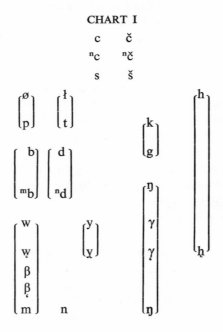

HYPERPHONEMES

In Aguaruna the relevant distributional matrices include the syllable, the stress group, and the pause group.

The peak of the emic syllable is constituted of a syllabic — the vowel. The peak of a stress group is constituted of a stressed syllable, symbolized by /'/. The peak of a pause group is constituted of a stress group whose accented syllable may be extra-strong, symbolized by /'/ before the peak syllable.

The borders of a pause group are, as the name implies, phonologically marked by pause. The borders of a stress group are phonologically marked by a slight break in the rhythm, without pause. The borders of a syllable are marked by a lesser break in the even flow of speech. It is assumed here that the syllable has a chest pulse as one of its contrastive features, that the stress group has an abdominal pulse as a contrastive feature, and that the pause group is a higher-layer in the hierarchy of abdominal pulses. The borders in connection with the joints between syllables, stress groups, or pause groups are treated here as contrastive features of the units concerned, rather than as constituting juncture phonemes in themselves.

The phonological shape-types of the syllable include CV, V, VC, and CVC. Within any one stress group, combinations of any two of the syllable types in sequence may occur with the one restriction that syllables of type VC or CVC may not precede syllables of type V or CV. One to seven syllables may occur in a single stress group. Note the following illustrative combinations of syllable patterns: CV.CV.V.CV.CV *hįγá.u.či.ču* 'it isn't a little house'; CV.VC.CV. *wí.aγ.mį* 'they went'; V.CV.V.CVC *a.kí.a.mun* 'those who pay'; CV.CVC.CV.CVC *pi.šák.hu.mik* 'Is it your bird?'; V.V *á.u* 'it was'.

Within pause groups, however, sequences of VC (or CVC) and of V (or VC) occur at the borders of stress groups such that a syllable ending in a consonant may end a stress group preceding a stress group which begins with a vowel. Note the following illustration in which space symbolizes the rhythm break between stress groups: CV.CV.CV.CVC V.CV.V *mi.ná.ša.kam a.'cá.u* 'mine also isn't'.

Stress groups, in addition to the characteristics mentioned above, have a pitch contour which steps up gradually to the stressed syllable and steps down gradually on the remainder of the syllables of the stress group. Stress groups are of several contrastive types depending on the lexically-controlled placement of the stress, which may appear on any syllable of a sequence: e.g., *aykų* 'late' versus *áykų* 'spider web'; *ukuák* 'leaving' versus *ukúák* 'boiling'; *tákamčau* 'total' versus *takámčau* 'hidden' versus *takamčáu* 'one who touches the things of others'.

There are two kinds of contrastive pause groups, one tentative and one final, symbolized by single and double vertical bars respectively, at the end of the group: e.g., *icíγkathai 'wi učiúč ása | tikíma a'ší hintiáhą | muúmpahą anin'táimtąyąma núnika anintáimčau asán | mun yuháinakuį wikáisan | waki'γá wahakbáun‖wí íkam číγkín tukutátus 'wínakuį yacú įįmkau 'wínakuį kuáčat wítasan wakįyin áyahai ‖* 'I am going to tell of when I was a small child — all the ideas of grown-ups that I think now, which at that time I did not think. When the grown-ups walked I also walked; they are the ones who walked before. When my older brother went to the jungle to hunt birds I very much wanted to go'. Otherwise the overall pitch of a pause group has a general contour of rising and falling pitch, modified by the included pitch curves of the stress groups; the highest pitch of the pause group is at the point of its loudest stress.

Certain other hyperphonemic units occur. There are many songs, for example, which have song voice-quality and, as a further contrastive phonological feature, have regularly recurring rhythm sequences comprised of abdominal pulses or pause groups and/or pause groups of a 'controlled' type.

This song rhythm, however, is in very strong contrast to the formalized antiphonal responses between a group host and a group of visitors which has the same number of speakers.[3] These responses may be carried on for an hour or two to a regular sharp rhythmic beat. The abdominal pulses constituting these equally spaced beats are extremely sharp and short like a shouted army "hup-two-three-four". In this style there is very rapid sharp crescendo and very rapid decrescendo on each abdominal pulse. With a pause between each such ballistic pulse, the separate pulses of the rhythm are usually of one word, with any unstressed syllables before or after the peak of the abdominal pulse jammed together, in spite of allophonic distortion, in order to preserve the sharp short beat. Special lexical or syntactic omissions or repetitions or rearrangements are also occasionally utilized in order to preserve the beat uninterrupted, and 'hesitation' pulses constituted of the syllable *ma* fill any gap left while speakers are thinking of what they are going to say.

At the opposite pole of rhythm types in this language is the chanting of the shamans, which makes very 'long' and 'smooth' breath groups, with many stress groups slurred together in the breath group for the pattern — a pattern which is in contrast to the moderately long and more sharply accented breath groups of normal song. Between the long breath-group-units and the shorter stress-group-units of the chant is an intermediate hyperphonemic unit which we may call a PHRASE since it is not marked by pause but rather by an elongated final syllable. Lexically, these shaman chants are largely comprised of nonsense-syllables, whereas their ordinary songs utilize nonsense-syllables only for the introduction of a line or two, or for setting the tune at the beginning of a song or stanza which otherwise has normal syntax.

These formal songs, antiphonal responses, and chants differ in form from the pitch and rhythm of the informal ditties used by the women for commenting on pictures as they look at them, or for occasions of special excitement — e.g., the sighting of an airplane, or the departure of a friend. In these ditties the pitch and rhythm are distinctive, but need further analysis before being described. Sung ditties follow the spoken syntax but have a special sung-quality.

Children about three years and over have a further stylized rhythm pattern in

---

[3] For a description of some related characteristics of visitation as well as warrior antiphonal responses among the Jívaros of Ecuador — which also occur among the Aguarunas but are not in our recorded materials — see Rafael Karsten, "The Head-Hunters of Western Amazonas", *Commentationes Humanarum Litterarum* 7:1 (Helsingfors, Societas Scientiarum Fennica, 1935), 246-247, 283-285. Many Jívaro chants and dance songs are also described there: e.g., 127-137, 198, 200, 321-325, 340-341, 348-349, 465, 496-497, 501.

crying; the words of the weeping, if any, or the wailing without words, is carried on to regular rhythm, its peak on a rising pitch. Women in wailing for the dead use the same pattern. Occasionally at the end of a song, a shouting pattern replaces song-quality and rhythm, reminding the American listener of the pattern of a college yell at a football game.

A further informal hyperphonemic musical type is the lullaby. The special phonetic characteristic here is the presence of a voiced bilabial trill which is utilized by the mother throughout the entire song as she trills her way through it without words. This trill phone, not mentioned in our earlier discussion of sounds, is extra-systematic to speech.

The hyperphonemic units mentioned above constitute three general types differing according to relationship in terms of the number of participants. The antiphonal responses necessarily involve several persons of one 'team' speaking in unison. All the other song types are solo. The sung music of a dance pattern, however, is an interlocking of individual and group characteristics. Here, every person at the dance sings his song to his own tune and with his own words. On the other hand, each of these persons is singing a song simultaneously and in unison as regards abdominal pulse type and pause groups; they sing the individual songs simultaneously to the beating of drums.

Whistle talk also occurs. Here, communication by whistle utilizes contrastive stress groupings and pause groupings, since pitch as such has no lexical function in the language separate from stress, which conditions the occurrence of high pitch. A contrast of high and low pitch, however, is perhaps significant to the whistle talk system, although it is not yet clear how this pitch is correlated with the pitches of regular speech. Possibly some articulatory characteristics (degrees of labialization, etc.) are also relevant, as they are for whistle talk in Tepehua, which is a non-tone-language of Mexico.[4]

Returning to the more specific distribution of sound groups, we note that vowels in sequence of two — each constituting a syllable nucleus — may occur in any order in respect to each other, except for the one non-systematic feature comprised of the restriction that /i/ does not precede /i/, and /i/ does not precede /i/. For examples, note the following: *diismí* 'let's see'; *iímkau* 'oldest'; *puhuúmata* 'you stay'; *paámpa* 'plantain'; *híu* 'whistled'; *hintiáhạ* 'ideas'; *wíu* 'he went'; *piák* 'bed'; *duík* 'before'; *dákuiyi* 'he extended'; *kuášat* 'many'; *dái* 'tooth'; *saipín* 'skin'; *aúⁿc* 'wild turkey'. In a series of three vowel nuclei, the third is restricted non-systematically to the high vowels /u/ and /i/. Note the following illustrations: *inkíau* 'he put'; *tukụáị* 'when he shot it'.

Consonants are an emic class of sounds which contrast with the emic class of vowels. At no point in the structure of hyperphoneme patterns can every consonant occur. An alloclass composed of all the consonants except the nasalized affricated

[4] George M. Cowan, "El idioma silbado entre los Mazatecos de Oaxaca y los Tepehuas de Hidalgo, México", *Tlatoani* I (1952), 31-33.

/ⁿc/ and /ⁿč/ occurs initially in the CV pattern. A further alloclass containing the voiceless stops /p/, /t/, /k/; the assibilants /c/, /č/, /ⁿc/, /ⁿč/; the sibilants /s/, /š/; the nasals /m/, /n/; and the phonemes /γ/, /h/, and /r/ occurs syllable-final in the pattern VC (i.e., this alloclass lacks the voiced stops /b/ and /d/, as well as /w/ and /y/). In addition, there is a sub-alloclass of the syllable-final consonant in the middle of a stress group: in addition to the restrictions already mentioned for syllable-final consonants at this point (the first C spot in VC. CV), none of the assibilants /c/, /č/, /ⁿc/, /ⁿč/ appear before the assibilants, sibilants, or /p/; sibilants /s/ and /š/ do not appear before /s/ or /š/; assibilants /ⁿc/ and /ⁿč/ do not appear before voiced stops /b/ and /d/. A few further non-systematic gaps appear in the data but may later be filled or may prove to constitute permanent asymmetries in the system. The following have not yet appeared: /p/ before /b/; /s/ before /b/ or /c/; /h/ before /p/, /d/, or /m/. In the CV pattern, furthermore, /i/ never follows /š/, while /i/ and /ɨ/ never follow the loan phoneme /r/. In the VC pattern /ɨ/ never precedes /r/, since /ɨ/ never occurs in loans whereas /r/ occurs only in such words.

TONGUE-ROOT POSITION IN PRACTICAL PHONETICS*

(1) This paper is intended as a companion to J. M. Stewart's "Tongue-Root Position in Akan Vowel Harmony".[1] Stewart has given powerful arguments for relating the articulatory basis of West African vowel harmony to the position of the root of the tongue. The vowels /i, e, o, u/, for example, are described as having the root of the tongue more advanced than the otherwise-comparable /ɪ, ɛ, ɔ, ʊ/. The parameter of advanced versus unadvanced root position is utilized in place of a (rejected) description in terms of tense versus lax, or close versus open. Stewart discusses the phonetic, the morphophonemic, and the historical evidences for this judgment, and surveys the relevant literature.

The task I have taken on is not to duplicate his arguments, but to discuss the implications of the data for a general framework of articulatory phonetics, and for the classroom utilization of this framework. These newer data, that is, should be integrated with my articulatory framework of 1943, the voice-quality framework of 1945, and the throat drills of 1947.

(2) In my first approach to the problem of pharyngal openness, I treated the tongue-root as an articulator, in reference to the pharyngal wall as point of articulation (1943: 120, 123). A stricture at this point was tertiary (1943: 133) in reference to secondary nasal stricture, or primary oral stricture. Yet the relation of fronting and backing of the tongue-root played but small part in the treatment, except for certain pharyngal spirants (1943: 63).

Two years later, however, a more general function was assigned to the openness of the throat. In a scheme to describe possible parameters of voice-quality, I set up openness of the throat as one of the articulatory characteristics — with five arbitrary degrees from closeness to openness (1945: 101). There was a brief suggestion as to the way in which a change in throat openness could affect voice-quality during a drama (1945: 102-103) in symbolizing personality differences. In addition, the degree of openness of the throat was differentiated from the degree of tenseness of the vocal chords (101).

* *Phonetica* 17 (1967), 129-140. Reprinted by permission of the publishers S. Karger, Basel. This paper was in part supported by a grant from the United States Office of Education, Contract OE-5-14-065.
[1] Which appeared earlier in *Phonetica* 16 (1967), 185-204.

After a further two years I commented on specific kinds of voice-quality change which may be observed when changes occur in the size of the throat cavity: "All of the vocoids (that is, vowels viewed apart from their relation to a particular phonemic system, and defined in phonetic rather than phonemic terms) previously described can be modified by amplifying the throat cavity to make them have a different type of resonance — one which sounds 'fuller' or 'deeper'. This amplification may occur (1) by the lowering of the larynx (which can be seen by observing the lowering of the Adam's apple), or (2) by the fronting of the tongue so that the root of the tongue is farther from the wall of the throat" (1947: 21b).

This hollow or deeper quality is in contrast with that quality which comes from the fronting of the tongue root: "Move the back of the tongue further back into the mouth until the vocoid becomes somewhat 'choked-up' but is still discernibly [a]. This type may be called *Pharyngealization*" (1947: 22a). By this time, therefore, I was introducing specific drills to exploit such differences. Note, for example, instructions to "Try to pronounce some of the vocoids with the larynx lowered and with the root of the tongue relatively far front in the mouth" (1947: 22b). This exercise was designed to elicit the hollow type of voice-quality, in contrast with the choked-up quality produced by the backing of the tongue-root.

On the other hand, I had not yet correlated in my thinking the throat positions with the tense versus lax contrast of articulatory mouth position (i.e., of the 'vowel triangle'), nor with close versus open terms representing some of the same (or related) acoustic results. These I continued to treat as oral components in terms of degree of mouth opening (1943: 137 — and narrow versus wide in reference to the opening from side to side), or in terms of tenseness of muscular formation (1947: 25a, and 17b). In the latter I did point out that during a slur from [ɪ] to [ɛ] one did not necessarily pass through [e] (1947: 17b); this problem, however, did not appear to me in the guise of relation to throat openness — although I did suggest a possible throat tenseness for [æ].

(3) I was startled, therefore, when in listening to Twi a hollow quality reminded me of the fronted (= advanced) tongue-root position of these former drills. Dr. Stewart then pointed out to me, when I mentioned this voice-quality possibility, that for some time he had been suggesting that internal opening of the throat could be seen externally on informants by the marked lowering of the under side of the chin. With Mr. Denteh, an Asante-Twi speaker, this throat movement was vigorous — a strong muscular down-thrust under the chin could be seen and felt. On the other hand, his larynx barely lowered. This latter fact was of considerable importance, since — in the drills of 1947 — I had elicited related acoustic phenomena by the lowering of the larynx.

Stewart also called my attention to some of the literature which I had not seen, including the important note by Sweet (1906 in Ladefoged 1964: 40), who many years earlier seems to have been aware of the "'bunching-up' lengthways" of that part of the tongue with which some sounds are formed. 'Narrowness' may have meant the bunching from front to back — not the opening at the palate, nor the lateral shape of the palatal opening — and is perhaps related to the muscular activities needed to push and maintain the tongue-root front-ward — with that tenseness and movement which could be easily felt on the outside of the upper part of the throat, or under the chin, as it is seen to expand during this process in Twi.

(4) I was definitely surprised to find the close relationship between 'tense' articulation and 'hollow' acoustic character. I would have expected them to be independently variable. This uniting of a certain tenseness with the front tongue-root position then forced a crucial question: WHAT PEDAGOGICAL IMPLICATIONS GROW OUT OF AN ANALYSIS OF THE VOWEL-HARMONY SETS AS CONTRASTING BY POSITION OF THE TONGUE-ROOT?

First: It is clear that the root of the tongue (or the front of the pharyngal wall) needs to be treated seriously as an articulator relevant to the basic vowel system of many score languages of Africa, rather than being relegated to a minor role as affecting voice-quality in general, or as limited to a few pharyngal spirants. Drills for throat movement need to be given a degree of attention comparable to that of other articulatory variables.

Second: Since the throat change can be made while any one vowel position, in its normal blade contour, is held approximately constant, the range of variability of throat openness needs to be treated as a parameter PARTIALLY (to some degree yet to be determined) INDEPENDENT OF THE BLADE OF THE TONGUE. In any attempt to exhaust the kinds of sounds which the human voice can make, it no longer can be sufficient to deal with some 'practical composite' of vowel qualities which inter-

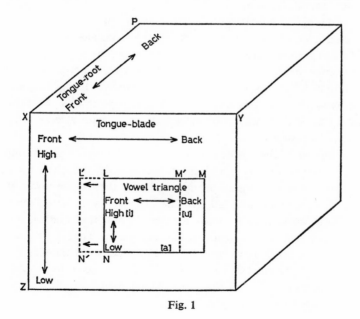

Fig. 1

lace blade position with root position on a single two-dimensional chart. The placement of close versus open varieties on the same chart in a language like Twi, that is, does not reflect the three dimensional structure.

In Fig. 1, I have given a schematic four-dimensional display of the problem. From L to M is the normal position, from front to back, of a vowel triangle, contrasting [i] with [u] in terms of tongue-blade position (or highest part of the tongue). From L to N the normal triangle shows the comparable dimension of high to low — [i] to [a].

The range from X to Y symbolizes the potential shift of the entire vowel system toward the front — as seen in the shift of L to L': M to M'. The lowering or raising of the triangle occurs from X to Z.

Added to these changes is the further tongue-root dimension. From X to P the tongue-root is fronted or backed.

Third: Drills for variability of the placement of the 'vowel triangle' in the oral cavity need, therefore, to be treated separately from drills for degree of openness of the throat. Then the two drill types need to be combined.

For classroom training I have for many years had students practice moving the vowel triangle AS A WHOLE frontwards, backwards, upwards, and downwards in the mouth during connected speech. The auditory effects are startling, and easy to achieve. With the whole blade of the tongue thrust somewhat forward in the mouth (and retained there, relative to normal position), all vowel qualities come closer to that of a language such as Spanish. In addition — automatically — many consonants are modified appreciably. Sibilants, for example, are likely to become dental, with a sharper hissing quality. A single 'shifting of gears' of this type results in enormous amounts of allophonic change.

The great pedagogical advantage: The student is required to focus on ONLY ONE articulatory characteristic, in order to obtain MANY simultaneous results. Pedagogically, therefore, it proves a great deal easier to achieve the desired SET of articulatory allophonic varieties, in this way, than it does by having the student attempt to build a SUM of a large number of separately-intended changes. In my judgment, no other single drill is as useful in getting quick, useful, extensive results. (A close contender, however, has to do with dynamics of syllable-timing versus stress-timing, but is not relevant to this discussion.)

Similarly, a raising of the whole triangle toward the top of the mouth introduces a rather 'thin' childish quality — reflecting, presumably, the small mouth cavity of the child. When the vowels are all pronounced with the tongue lower in the mouth, on the contrary, — so that the blade (or the highest point) of the tongue for [i] or [u] is substantially lower than normal-, a rather 'sepulchral' quality is heard. When in a further change, the tongue-blade is backed, a somewhat 'dull' quality is given. (These classroom exercises have also been combined with changes of other types towards which student-focus can be easily directed: degree of lip rounding, nasality, changes in decrescendo type, and the like.) Along with these drills, I have included position of the tongue-root.

TABLE I

Schematic representation of semi-independent parameters of movement of tongue-blade and tongue-root

	Tongue-blade fronted	Tongue-blade neutral	Tongue-blade backed
Tongue-root fronted	(A) (1) root fronted (2) blade fronted (3) throat open (4) tongue slightly bunched lengthwise (5) auditorily hollow, with clean-cut articulation (relatively simple)	(B) (1) root fronted (2) blade neutral (3) throat open (4) tongue somewhat bunched lengthwise (5) auditorily hollow (Cf. Twi tense vowels)	(C) (1) root fronted (2) blade backed (3) throat open (4) tongue extremely bunched, with minimum extension lengthwise (5) auditorily hollow, and with muffled articulation (very difficult)
Tongue-root neutral	(D)	(E) (1) root neutral, relaxed (2) blade neutral, relaxed (3) throat neutral, relaxed (4) tongue neutral, relaxed (5) auditorily clear quality and articulation (Cf. the majority of Twi lax vowels)	(F)
Tongue-root backed	(G) (1) root backed (2) blade fronted (3) throat closed (4) tongue maximum extension lengthwise (5) auditorily choked, but with clean-cut articulation (very difficult)	(H) (Sometimes the Twi lax vowels may come here)	(I) (1) root backed (2) blade backed (3) throat closed (4) tongue somewhat bunched lengthwise (5) auditorily choked, and with mushy articulation (relatively simple)

(5) Now, however, the importance of the distinction between general changes of tongue-blade and tongue-root requires a more explicit attempt to combine extremes of the two types of drills.

In order to test the possibility and feasibility of building such exercises, I constructed Table I as a schematic representation of the way the semi-independent parameters of tongue-blade and tongue-root could be expected to work together. The first row shows the tongue-root fronted. Intersecting this row are columns showing the position of the vowel triangle in general, by way of the position of the tongue-blade. The first column has the tongue-blade far front (as we indicated it might be, say, for Spanish). The middle column has the tongue-blade in a neutral position. (In Box B, where the first row and second column intersect, one presumably finds the Twi 'tense' vowels /i, e, o, u/.) The second row leaves the tongue-root in neutral position. (When it intersects with the second column, where the vowel triangle is also in neutral position, in Box E, one presumably is most likely to find the Twi lax vowels — the 'open' set /ɪ, ɛ, ɔ, ʊ/ of the vowel harmony pairs.) The third row backs the root of the tongue, introducing the choked quality. (Occasionally Stewart hears the Twi vowels with a quality — indicated in his article as — "choked or even strangled". These would presumably, therefore, come in Box H.)

Preliminary results of the drill scheme: I was able to artifically pronounce words or sentences in these indicated styles. But a chart this complicated is definitely not feasible as the base for practical phonetic drills, for two reasons. The first problem is an auditory one: In the early attempts at least, the differences between some of the boxes were not great enough; beginners could not be expected to differentiate them. The difference between B and E (or B and H), however, was very clear and adequate as the basis for a feasible drill on tongue-root position. Similarly, the difference between D and E is very clear — as the basis for a feasible drill between front triangle and neutral triangle. (As we indicated, it is a good preliminary drill to prepare people for listening to Spanish.) But some of the boxes on the extreme corners of the chart were not as clearly different as one might have expected.

There is, however, a second difficulty, one of articulatory feasibility. We have long known that certain parameters otherwise independent could be combined only with extreme difficulty, if at all, in particular instances where muscles of the throat and muscles of the tongue were instructed to operate in opposite directions. It has been relatively simple, for example, to make implosive clicks (ingressive pharynx air combined with simultaneous ingressive oral air) in which a voiced velar implosive was pronounced simultaneously with some type of oral click (1943: 98-99). It is also relatively simple to pronounce the reverse — a glottalized egressive click (egressive pharynx air plus egressive oral air) — even though this is not a speech sound. It is extremely difficult, on the other hand, to crisscross these — i.e., to produce an ingressive pharynx movement simultaneously with an egressive oral movement; or an egressive glottalization of an ingressive oral click.

Similarly, here, Box A is relatively simple to pronounce, inasmuch as the position of the tongue-blade is fronted while the position of the tongue-root is also fronted. On the other hand, Box C is exceedingly difficult to pronounce: The tongue-root is pushed front, while the tongue-blade is pulled far back. The result is a very bunched-up tongue in the middle of the mouth, in an unnatural position.

Likewise, it is relatively simple to pronounce Box I, where the tongue-root is back in the mouth while the tongue-blade is also back. But it is extremely difficult to pronounce Box G, where the tongue-root is back in the mouth but the tongue-blade is front in the mouth. Here the tongue is stretched out lengthwise trying to get the front fronter but the back backer.

The abnormality of Box C and of Box G make each of them difficult, even though the articulatory difficulties are of opposite types. The abnormality of the two perhaps contributes to the blurring of the auditory differences, referred to above, which might otherwise have been more clear-cut. These muscular restrictions on the ease of combining extremes of tongue-blade and tongue-root movements, furthermore, place a limit on the independence of the two parameters. It is obvious, once one has attempted to utilize Table I, that the elements are only partially independent, not completely so.

(6) What, then, are the theoretical implications for phonemics of this articulatory restriction, growing out of interference of the muscular requirements? It would seem that if one were to move the tongue-root forward, for purposes of phonemic contrast, that the tongue-blade would be likely to go forward at least a little bit at the same time. How would this be expressed in phonemic terms? If the backing of the tongue-root has some implication of pharyngealization, the fronting of the tongue-root (to the degree that it pushes the tongue-blade in front of it) might be accompanied by some degree of conditioned PALATALIZATION. It might be expected, therefore, that vowels which involve a front tongue-root position might occasionally develop palatal allophones. We note in Stewart's article that this has, in fact, occurred, and can be demonstrated historically in the development of certain palatalized consonants.

It will also be interesting to check to see whether some restrictions on frequency of certain consonant sets in relation to front and back vowels might also be related ultimately to this problem of articulatory restrictions. Not only the POSSIBILITY of occurrence in a particular environment, but also the FREQUENCY of occurrence in such environments might conceivably be affected by these articulatory characteristics.

Since tones have long been known to be allophonically affected by consonants, or themselves to affect the distribution of consonants, perhaps these problems should also be re-investigated to see if a hypothesis of tone variants conditioned by tongue-root position might sometimes be useful; with frequency of vocal-chord vibration involving tenseness, and tongue-root fronting also affecting tenseness, perhaps there could be some correlation.

Could the same parameters be useful in handling certain characteristics of English? Probably every phonetician has repeatedly had the experience of learning a phonemic contrast in a 'strange' language, only to hear, then, the same elements as allophonic in his own. Analytical recognition most easily comes in phonemic contrastive contexts; its phonetic recognition may then spread to nonphonemic ones. This happened to me. Dr. Stewart, with a Scotch accent, suddenly appeared to me to have used a very markedly 'hollow' [u] in, for example, a word like *two* spoken emphatically in isolation. I have also heard what appeared to me to be an exaggerated hollow quality — perhaps now to be attributed to tongue-root position — in the English of certain native speakers of Danish. The implication would be that some dialects of Danish might have, for certain vowels, a tongue-root position which would be farther front than my own.

(7) Such questions need instrumental investigation. Some preliminary samples of Twi contrastive pairs were analyzed by Dr. Ruth Brend from spectograms made of my recordings by Charles Peck of the Communications Sciences Laboratory of the University of Michigan. The amount of data handled was insufficient to reach positive conclusions, but the preliminary sampling strongly suggested the probability that the auditory analyses in this paper and in the one by Stewart are on solid foundation in so far as throat openness is concerned.

The opening of the throat does, in each pair of vowels contrasted, produce a lowering of the first formant. The partial correlation of wider throat opening with the lowering of the first formant has been suggested by Gunnar Fant.[2]

See Table II for some measurements of contrasting sets of vowels produced by the Twi informant, in both artificial and real language sequences. (Various utterances were measured; the figures cited suggest the range of variability.)

TABLE II

Measurements of formants one and two for Twi vowels

	F_1	F_2
ɪ	250-300 cps	1750-1850 cps
i	175-200	1750-1850
ʊ	300	600- 700
u	200	600- 700
ɔ	400-500	800- 950
o	200-300	800- 900
ɛ	400-450	1600-1800
e	200	1800-1850

Measurements on the lower vowel set which included [a] were less conclusive. A preliminary check of some artificial sequences pronounced by me in accordance

---

[2]   He gives, however, the following caution: "... it is generally proposed that the first formant is associated with the resonance of the back cavity and the second formant with the resonance of the front cavity. One of the purposes of the present publication is to show the considerable limitations of this rule ... all parts of the vocal tract contribute to the determination of all formants but with varying degrees ..." (1960), 20-21.

with Table I seem to confirm the lowering of the first formant when the tongue-root is in the fronted position, as expected. Data concerning the sharply-backed position of the tongue-root, however, were far less convincing. Whether lack of clear-cut differences in the acoustic records in the backed position of the tongue-root versus its neutral position is due to articulatory factors (such as compensatory changes which were not intended) or whether some other explanation will eventually be forthcoming is unknown. In any case, however, the difficulty of finding clean-cut acoustic differences in the far-backed, tongue-root position is perhaps correlative with the auditory difficulty of distinguishing the results of some of the extremes in such an exercise as I have mentioned above in the discussion of Table I. Further practical and theoretical work, both articulatory and acoustic, is needed in these areas.

SUMMARY

This is a companion article to the earlier one in which Dr. Stewart related West African vowel harmony to the (advanced or unadvanced) position of the root of the tongue.

In previous publications I had set up drills to induce control of the openness of the throat, with resultant voice-quality changes ('hollow' when tongue-root is fronted; 'choked' when backed). Here I develop further the integration of such drills with others which change the general position of the blade of the tongue — i.e., of the 'vowel triangle' as a whole.

The two kinds of changes — of root versus blade — are in general independent. Some restriction, however, occurs: it is difficult to crisscross direction of the movements of root and blade, but simple to have them move in the same direction. This leads to some conditioning of phoneme variants.

Pedagogically, it is more efficient to use drill types which teach general kinds of articulatory changes which lead to sets of allophones than it is to attempt to induce the same result through a conscious summation of many (apparently) distinct allophonic rules.

ZUNGENWURZELSTELLUNG UND ANGEWANDTE PHONETIK

Zusammenfassung

Dieser Beitrag steht im Zusammenhang mit einem früher von Dr. Stewart publizierten, in dem die westafrikanische Vokalharmonie mit der Stellung der Zungenwurzel in Verbindung gebracht wurde.

In früheren Veröffentlichungen hatte ich Übungen ausgearbeitet zur Kontrolle der Offenheit der Kehle und der damit zusammenhängenden Stimmqualität ('hohl' bei vorderer Zungenwurzellage, 'erstickt' bei hinterer). Hier werden nun solche Übungen mit anderen verflochten, bei denen die allgemeine Lage des Zungenblattes verändert wird, d.h. wo das Vokaldreieck als Ganzes verschoben wird. Beide Arten der Veränderung sind an sich nicht voneinander abhängig. Immerhin begegnen einige Einschränkungen. Es ist schwierig, Zungenwurzel und -blatt in entgegengesetzter Richtung zu bewegen. In gleicher Richtung ist das leicht. Dies bedingt einige Phonemvarianten.

Pädagogisch gesehen, ist es wirksamer, solche Übungen zu benutzen, die allgemeine Arten der Veränderungen artikulatorischer Art lehren und dadurch zu Reihen von Allophonen führen, als zu versuchen, die gleichen Ergebnisse zu erzielen durch bewußte Summierung vieler (offensichtlich) verschiedener allophonischer Regeln.

POSITION DE LA RACINE DE LA LANGUE DANS LA PHONÉTIQUE PRATIQUE

Résumé

Cet article est un complément à celui rédigé par le Dr Stewart antérieurement dans lequel il met en rapport l'harmonie vocale de l'Afrique occidentale avec la position de la racine de la langue (avancée ou retirée).

Dans les publications précédentes, il proposa des exercices de contrôle pour l'orifice de la gorge et les changements survenant dans la qualité de la voix ('creuse' si la racine de la langue est avancée, 'étouffée' si la racine de la langue est retirée). Dans le présent article, il intègre de tels exercices dans d'autres qui changent la position générale de la pale linguale, du triangle lingual proprement dit.

Les changements — de la racine vers la pale — sont dans les deux cas en général indépendants. Bien entendu non sans quelque réserve: il est difficile de croiser la direction des mouvements de la racine et de la pale linguale par contre il est facile de les mouvoir dans la même direction. Ceci implique quelques variantes phonémiques. Pédagogiquement, il est plus efficace d'appliquer des exercices généraux pour modifier l'articulation — pour ainsi être mené aux séries des allophones — que de tenter d'atteindre ce but par une sommation consciencieuse de beaucoup de règles allophoniques distinctes.

REFERENCES

Fant, G.
  1960   *Acoustic Theory of Speech Production* (The Hague, Mouton).
Ladefoged, P.
  1964   *A Phonetic Study of West African Languages* (Cambridge, University Press).
Pike, K.L.
  1943   *Phonetics* (Ann Arbor, University of Michigan Press).
  1945   *The Intonation of American English* (Ann Arbor, University of Michigan Press).
  1947   *Phonemics* (Ann Arbor, University of Michigan Press).

GRAMMAR AS WAVE*

When one is studying phonology from the perspective of phones, phonemes, syllables, and stress groups as in some sense comprising items or units, one is studying phonology as 'particle'. Similarly, grammar is studied as particle when one partitions the universe of discourse into noun phrases, clause types (e.g. transitive), or word classes (e.g. an animate subclass of nouns), and so on. Lexicon is studied as particle when one treats words or specific phrases (e.g. *these* or *this boy* or even *the boy I know*) as in some sense isolated. In each of these instances the particles are segmented from continua and then treated as chunks of structure.

Much of the best in linguistic analysis has concentrated on language as made up of particles. For hundreds of years, however, the literature has contained indications that language also includes elements which need to be viewed as 'field'. One of the most common of these is the traditional phonetic chart:

p	*t*	*k*
b	*d*	*g*
m	*n*	*ŋ*

Curiously enough, however, although such materials have a long practical history and have often been utilized by competent analysts, these same persons speaking as theoreticians have repudiated[1] from their basic theoretical constructs any such field component.

---

* *Monograph Series on Languages and Linguistics* 20 (*18th Annual Round Table*), ed. by E.L. Blansitt Jr. (1967), 1-14. Reprinted by permission.
[1] For references to very early treatment of phonetic charts, and to the utilization but theoretical repudiation of them by Bloomfield (versus my insistence upon treating such elements as structurally relevant to linguistic theory), see my *Language in Relation to a Unified Theory of the Structure of Human Behavior* (The Hague, Mouton, 1967), 8.623, 8.82, 8.61.

Lexicon has also been treated as field. One can, as with phonetics, note intersecting vectors (or distinctive features) as in the following:

tiger	tigress
king	queen

Studies of Kinship systems have vigorously exploited this area recently; for references to Lounsbury, Goodenough, and others see my *Language* ... 16.825. For other references to field in semantics, see 16.81.

More recently I have attempted to exploit grammar as field, parallelling phonology as field.[2] A minimum table suggesting such a field for clauses might be something as follows:

	Transitive	Intransitive
Independent:	IndepTrans	IndepIntrans
Dependent:	DepTrans	DepIntrans

The present article wishes, rather, to emphasize that grammar can be viewed as 'wave'. The attention to wave in phonology is not new for me. I have emphasized nucleus and margin (of waves) for syllables and for stress groups on many occasions.[3]

Attention can be directed to the nucleus of a stress-group wave — as in *I want the réd dress* in which attention is on *red*. The premargin may often be fused — as when *Did you enjoy it*? becomes /jɪnjóɪt/. Here the phonological nucleus places semantic attention on [en]jóy, whereas the premargin *did you* (out-of-focus) is fused. On the other hand, lexicon as wave has not been treated as extensively, though description of central (= nuclear) and marginal meanings indicates the relevance of this concept here.[4]

In treating grammar as wave, therefore, we are interested in analogous kinds of components of a unit: attention is directed especially to the structural distinction between nucleus and margin; semantic attention may often be directed to the nucleus of the grammar wave; and fusion or loss may occur on morphemes at the periphery.

We begin with data from Kasem of the Grusi subfamily within the larger Gur (Voltaic) languages of northern Ghana. Data are from Mrs. Kathleen Callow.[5] Callow points out that in Kasem a sentence may begin with an optional dependent clause followed by an obligatory independent clause and a further optional dependent clause. Within each of these three sections of a sentence there can be amplification in the detail of the clause structures; each of the three sections may be amplified to a clause-cluster (a series of clauses interrelated).

---

[2] The first attempt is in my "Dimensions of Grammatical Constructions", *Language* 38 (1962), 221-244. For an annotated bibliography treating related material through early 1964, see my "Guide to Publications Related to Tagmemic Theory", in *Current Trends in Linguistics* 3, ed. by Thomas A. Sebeok (The Hague, Mouton, 1966), 365-394; and my "Non-Linear Order and Anti-Redundancy in German Morphological Matrices", *Zeitschrift für Mundartforschung* 32 (1965), 193-221.

[3] For theoretical discussions, see my *Language* ... 3.2, 9.312, 11.51. For pedagogy, see "Practical Phonetics of Rhythm Waves", *Phonetica* 8 (1962), 9-30. For extensive discussion of English, in which the nucleus is marked with a degree sign and various pre-contours and post-contours (i.e. margins) are described, see *The Intonation of American English* (Ann Arbor, 1945). For an annotated bibliography of recent materials, see "Guide".

[4] See my handling of orbiting, in 16.13 of my *Language* ....

[5] For more specific details one may consult my final report to the United States Office of Education, Contract OE 5-14-065, on *Tagmemic and Matrix Linguistics Applied to Selected African Languages* (1966). Published version forthcoming.

A Kasem clause-cluster has various restrictions such that not all clause types can precede or follow one another within such a cluster (which in turn fills one of the slots in a sentence). These particular restrictions are important, but need not concern us for our present purposes. Rather we are interested in certain of the more general rules by which clauses are combined into a clause-cluster within one of the larger slots of the sentence.

When two clauses are combined in Igede,[6] they share the same subject and the same object; the second occurrence of the same subject and the same object are deleted:

Igede: *àhì   hû   ólō*
            we   take load

plus: *àhì chū   ólō*
         we put-on-head load

yields: *àhì hû ólō chū*
         we take load put-on-head

Similarly, if there is a locative phrase which is repeated in the separate clauses, one of these is deleted in the combination; in this instance, however, it is the first rather than the second element which is lost:

àhì hû   ólō í-ìhì
we take load in-market

àhì chū   ólō í-ìhì
we put-on-head load in-market

àhì hû   ólō chū   í-ìhì
we take load put-on-head in-market

The words /alé/ 'today' and /ínyínyì/ 'similarly' act comparably.

This kind of deletion is by no means pointed out here for the first time — it has long been known.[7] Now, however, we wish to indicate how a specialization developed which can be treated as a kind of grammatical fusion: a loss of freedom of parts of the first clause such that it develops a special function modifying the second part of the clause-cluster. Specifically, we find in Vagala that one is unable to say in a single clause 'He cuts meat with a knife'. No single, simple clause allows

---

[6] Data from Igede gathered by Richard Bergman; from Vagala by Miss Marjorie Crouch. These investigators, like Callow, are members of the Summer Institute of Linguistics. For fuller details on certain of these materials, see the report referred to in the previous footnote.

[7] See John M. Stewart, "Some Restrictions on Objects in Twi", *Journal of African Languages* 2 (1963), 145-149, for a particularly clear and helpful discussion.

the requisite tagmemes to state 'He x'd y with z'. This at first appears astonishing. We would have assumed that among the universals of culture is the capacity to speak of something being done WITH something. Surely we cannot drop our belief in the universality of human nature to the degree that we would assume that any group of people would be unable to communicate such an element of a cultural situation. How, then, can we account for this situation in much of West Africa, where an instrumental tagmeme does not occur within a simple clause? The cultural solution — finding its way through the linguistic structures available here — is to achieve the same semantic result with a special kind of clause-cluster:

> *ù   kpá   kíyzèé   mòng   ówl*
> he took knife   cut   meat
> 'He cut the meat with a knife'

Here the meaning of 'with a knife' is covered by the included clause 'he took knife'; and the total meaning of 'He cut the meat with the knife' is covered by the total clause-cluster of 'He took knife cut meat'. The cultural universal is therefore satisfied even in the face of the gap in expected tagmemic content of simple clauses.

A crucial question now arises: How can we analyze the semantic relationships which are obviously being communicated within the clause-cluster? Our tagmemic solution is to suggest that the first clause is itself, as a whole, filling a newly-developed tagmemic slot: a new tagmemic slot within the old clause-cluster. The old clause-cluster has developed into a special subcluster of which the first included clause is instrumental, filling a newly developed 'instrumental' slot followed by a new tagmeme which means 'the utilizing act'. This can be diagrammed:

$$+ \text{ Instrumental tagmeme} \qquad\qquad + \text{ Utilizing-act tagmeme}$$
$$+ \text{ Subject} + P_{tr} + \text{Object} \qquad = P_{tr} + \text{Object}$$
$$NP_1 \qquad kpá \quad NP_2 \qquad\qquad V_{tr} \quad NP_3$$

'He took knife', as the first of the old clusters, has developed an instrumental overtone to be translated 'he, with a knife'; and the old 'cut meat' implies not only the act, but an act BY the prescribed instrument. This entire complex can now serve as if it were one of the single clauses of a larger clause-cluster. We can call the specialized instrument pair, therefore, a subcluster (within any regular larger clause-cluster).

A new problem arises here. At times one cannot be sure whether one is hearing a specific specialized instrumental subcluster or rather the normal nonspecialized clause-cluster. This can be restated as follows: Tagmemes may be homophonous in some of their manifestations; just as two morphemes may be pronounced alike but have different meanings and different functions, so two tagmemes may occasionally be ambiguous if they happen to share the possibility of being manifested by one or more of the same morphemes. The situation here is that the instrumental tagmeme in the specialized subcluster is limited to the word *kpá* 'take'. Thus if in a normal cluster of two clauses any other verb occurs, we do not have to have any doubt as to whether or not it is instrumental. Since, however, *kpá* 'take' can also on occasion be used as a regular verb, in the first clause of a regular clause-cluster, ambiguity sometimes develops.[8]

A second kind of specialization should also be mentioned as illustrative of the probability that many semantically-specialized subclusters may have developed, even though only a few have been studied. Note, for example, that the second clause of a regular cluster may become specialized and modify the first — the reverse of the earlier situation. One can, for example, use the Vagala verb for 'give' in the second slot of a cluster with specialized benefactive meaning:

> Benefactive:
> *ù   wà   sá   ígyò tè   ù   bówl*
> he   came danced igyo give his village
> 'He came and danced the igyo dance *for* his village'

Here, once more, a clause sequence in a cluster has become specialized as a semantically distinct subcluster — which can in its turn operate as a single unit in still larger clusters. Specialization of particular structures, we conclude, can be synchronically detected as the end product of a historical development.

We now turn to an especially-attractive instance related to the clause-cluster problem, and which, in my view, confirms the judgment very strongly. In this latter instance we wish to indicate (1) that a class of auxiliaries can be developed from a class of verbs, by specialization within a clause-cluster; and (2) that this class of auxiliary verbs in the single tagmemic slot is synchronically visible as being in a state of change, because of the sharply-different characteristics of the specific members of that class.

Vagala has a clause-cluster in which the first verb is of a motion type. Note:

> *ù   wà   á   ¹ló   ká¹bílà*
> he   came imperfective pound food

> *ù   gà   á   ¹sow kàrá ní*
> he   went imperfective sit chair on

The verbs for 'come' and 'go' — *wà* and *gà* — appear to be the first verbs in a regular clause-cluster, if one gives them only a quick glance. Nevertheless, they differ from free verbs (non-auxiliaries, which would come in a regular cluster) in five ways:

---

[8]   Here, also, for the data indicating how this is ambiguous we refer the reader to the fuller report.

(1) Neither *wà* nor *gà* take suffixes here (but compare *bà dáálí dó'zí* 'They cooked soup' and *bà dááló* 'They cooked').

(2) They cannot be preceded by the imperfective form *ra*.

(3) They do not occur alone as verbs in a single one-verb clause.

(4) They have different tone rules from those occurring as a free verb.

(5) They cannot be immediately followed within the first clause of the cluster by tagmemes of location, etc.

These reasons would at first make one suspect that the auxiliary verbs — as I am calling them here — could just as well be treated as simple particles, without attempting to relate them to verbs at all. We turn, therefore, to another member of the same distribution class of items (i.e. occurring in the same tagmemic auxiliary slot), but one which is more like a free verb even though still restricted. The verb is *kuàri* 'make, fix'. It has greater freedom:

(1) It can occur as the only verb of a simple clause: *ù kuáró* 'It is-fixed'.

(2) It may be accompanied by a peripheral tagmeme (e.g. a locative element) as can other simple verbs.

(3) Verbs after it act like the second verb of a regular cluster rather than like the first one.

Nevertheless, this same verb, in spite of the freedom mentioned, has several special restrictions as an auxiliary:

(1) It has a special meaning in its auxiliary function as over against when it is free. As an auxiliary it means 'again' as in *ù kuàri là diá* 'He again went home'.

(2) It has no perfective ending in the auxiliary slot (but compare the suffix *-o*, which is found in an illustration previously given, attached to the main verb of the clause).

As a further member of the same auxiliary distribution class we take the word for 'to turn', seen as *bìr* (in isolation) and as *bítò* (in *ù bítò bà* 'he turned came' in a clause-cluster where the verb serves as an ordinary full verb, even in the first — primary — slot in the cluster, as evidenced by the perfective suffix *-o*).

The primary usages contrast with its secondary use (where the two clauses are separated by *dì* 'and' — not relevant to our problem here) as in:

> *ù   ízô   dì   bìr   ù   hár*
> 'He got up and turned his back'

In such a 'free' instance the verb for 'to turn' may have a peripheral tagmeme, as can *kuàrì* 'make'.

On the other hand, when *bìr* occurs as an auxiliary, it has restrictions:

(1) A peripheral tagmeme is not allowed with it.

(2) It has the special meaning of 'again' as: *ù bìr ngó* 'He said again'.

The verb is not allowed to occur in isolation — nor as the sole verb in the clause — when it carries this specialized meaning.

We turn to a final set of members of the class, with still further specialization: *wèyr* 'be able'; *kútì* 'do purposely'; *fúúrì* 'do unintentionally'. In several ways they act like main verbs; e.g. *wèyr*:

(1) It takes a perfective ending as in *ù wéytò ló ká'bílá* 'he is-able pound food' (note the suffix *-o* on the verb).

(2) The following verb is in its secondary form.

(3) It can in fact stand alone as the main verb of a clause as in *ù wéytò* 'He is-able'.

Nevertheless, in certain senses it acts as specialized when in auxiliary function:

(1) Its ability to stand alone as just illustrated above is in turn specially limited and rare. If it occurs in response to a question (such as *ì wéytò èè gúng* '[Are] you able [to] do that?', to which the reply then may be *ǹ wéytò* '... I am-able ...'), the clause in which it occurs by itself as a main verb is a dependent sentence, in the answer slot of a conversation composed of question and answer. Thus even its apparent freedom to occur as a main verb is an exaggeration; it occurs as a main verb only in a response slot in which there is an 'implicit' deletion of a following main verb of an implicit cluster. It continues, therefore, to have certain of the characteristics of an auxiliary.

Our summary of the data about the auxiliary: We can see by the synchronic data that there is an emerging class of auxiliaries. The evidence of the emergence of this class within the clause-cluster is grammatical (by restrictive distribution in construction), lexical (by specialization of meaning), and phonological (by special minor rules for usage of tone, which we have not attempted to describe here).

Were this direction of change to be completed, with complete specialization in all instances, we would then end up with the entire class as being made up of particles which could not be isolated like verbs, could not be inflected as verbs, could not take the peripheral elements of regular predicates, could not be the head of verb phrases, could occur only in special places in verb phrases, and have no clear relation to free verbs. They would be particles.

It would appear, further, that these developed auxiliaries occurring before a verb may in turn be preceded by a further set of elements which have already arrived at this stage of verbal degeneracy. We do not cite the data here. Rather we suggest that a fuller treatment would show that a verbal phrase—developed out of a clause-cluster or clusters — may include three (or more) tagmemes: (a) a preliminary slot, filled by a distribution class of particles which synchronically are no longer relatable to verbs, but with a possible guessed-at relation of this type, (b) an auxiliary tagmeme with its set of fillers obviously in a state of transition (and not consistently at the same point in transition), and (c) the nucleus of the verb phrase, filled by a main verb which was once a second (or third) verb in a (reconstructed) clause-cluster.

We now return to our main theme: that grammar can be viewed as a wave. Notice how much the movement from verb to auxiliary to particle looks like the phonological fusion in which *let us go eat* becomes /skuít/: the nuclear morpheme *eat* is preserved, unmodified; other morphemes, in the margin of the stress group (= syllable cluster), are phonologically changed almost beyond recognition. So, also, in the grammar wave the main verb, at the nuclear point of the clause, remains unchanged and unrestricted, whereas the peripheral verbs of the clause undergo successive (phonological) compression (distributional) restriction, and (semantic) specialization.

It is important to see that these changes are not exclusively phonological. If phonology alone had been involved, one would find no need to treat this as a grammatical wave — one could rather attribute everything to the phonological processes themselves. It is the fact that special grammatical distributional restrictions, as well as semantic specialization of the lexemes, are involved which forces us to treat this as something other than pure phonological process.

The change does not lead exclusively to the first item being specialized (as auxiliary). The second may in certain instances be specialized. The Vagala word *hùnzì* 'to fail' acts as a post-auxiliary:

(1) It does not serve as the sole member of a Vagala clause;
(2) It shares with the preceding verb the periphery which follows the two of them.
Compare:

> ù   kuár-û   hùnzì
> he fix-it   fail
> 'He wasn't able to fix it'

with:

> ù   kuár-û   hùnzì   dèèlà
> he fix-it   fail   yesterday
> 'He wasn't able to fix it yesterday'

in which the periphery ('yesterday') applies both to the auxiliary and to the main verb.

The extraordinary interest of this grammar-wave phenomenon is not that it occurs at one particular point, but that it occurs as a synchronically-living dynamic on various levels of structure of a system. We have already seen it (a) with auxiliaries within verb phrases, developing from clusters of clauses, and (b) with subclusters of clauses as specialized within larger clause-clusters. Now (c) we show evidence that sentence-clusters themselves may develop in which certain initial sentences have primary (nuclear) function in a sequence, with special marks on these sentences. The end result of this sentence clustering implies the development of emic, structural paragraphs.

A sentence-cluster — a paragraph[9] — differs from a clause-cluster, inasmuch as any one sentence in a paragraph may have all of the kinds of sequences of clause-clusters mentioned earlier for any one sentence: A sentence may have a dependent

---

[9]   Defined, of course, for one language at a time, as any empirical term must be in language.

clause-cluster, an independent clause-cluster, and a following dependent clause-cluster. In the light of these evidences, we conclude that we are not dealing with the same level of structure which we discussed above, but are dealing on a higher level.[10]

The primary, nuclear sentence of the sentence-cluster may be specially marked. The marking may be by tone. Compare, for example, the difference between in-dependent:

> *ù   kyìgó   níí   bà*
> she   carried water   came

in which the verb begins with a low tone and carries a suffix, as over against its high tone when in a dependent sentence (of the same meaning) later in a marginal posi-tion of the paragraph:

> *ù   kyí   níí   bà*
> she   carried water   came

The difference between independent and dependent sentences (I repeat: we are not talking about dependent and independent clauses here) leads to the contrast between 'topic sentence' (as a term of rhetoric), i.e. a nuclear sentence, versus marginal sen-tences which are commenting on items which the topic has introduced.

A second marker (i.e. other than tone) of the first sentence only (of the topic sen-tence of the sentence cluster) is sometimes the occurrence of a tense morpheme in the first, but not in later, sentences:

> *ǹ níy ǹ   hááng né   de   rá*
> I and my wife emphatically yesterday imperfective
>
> *náà ǹ   háàng kyàg ǹ   kyàgá bél.*
> fight. my wife   insult me insult one.
>
> 'Yesterday I and my wife had a quarrel. She insulted me with a certain insult.'

Note that the imperfective form occurred only in the first of the two sentences of the paragraph.

Sentences within a paragraph then — within sentence-clusters — may be formally differentiated as to whether they are at the nuclear or post-margin points.

It is also true, however, that sentences of a paragraph may form certain subclus-ters of sentences which fill special tagmemic slots in paragraphs. This is similar to the semantic specialization of subclusters of clause-clusters (see the specialization

---

[10]   For the data supporting this argument, we must refer the reader to the fuller report.

of instrumental and benefactive above). It would appear that, in general, many of the paragraphs of Vagala could be treated as beginning with a proclamation tagmeme (filled by the topic sentence), followed by a commentary class of tagmemes (in which a sequence of sentences manifests the commentary). It is quite possible, furthermore, that the commentary section will have to be further subdivided.

The proclamation section, however, is by no means uniform. There are contrastive tagmemes within this class of tagmemes. As one example, notice a 'request' tagmeme of the proclamation followed by a 'carrying out' tagmeme of the commentary:

Request: *ǹ dá nyíyngì í kuárì ǹ dìá ¹te ṅ*
            'I want you   to fix   my house for me'

Carried out: *u kuàrì u dìá té ú*
            '[So] he fixed it   for him¹'

Yet a still higher wave element than the paragraph can be seen in Vagala. This includes — among other possible structures — a story viewed as a grammatical wave. It begins with an opening tagmeme and ends with a closing one:

Opener: *ǹ múr té kéng*
           my story emph. this
           'This is my story¹'

End: *ǹ tú nò*
           'I finish'

In Vagala we do not yet have a further breakdown of the wave structure within the discourse itself. For this I turn to Sisala.[11]

Rowland in attempting to study tagmeme sequences within clauses observed first of all that the time element sometimes came early and sometimes came late. He wishes to determine the specific situation which might control the (apparently optional) occurrence of the time tagmeme. Since he had available concordance[12] material, he was able to take specific temporal words and find their sources in contexts of the larger narratives in which they occurred. To his surprise he found that the discourse itself seemed to have topic paragraphs (nuclear paragraphs). These outlined the special settings for the narrative. Once delineated, they were more or less ignored. Specifically, early in the discourse the temporal setting might be given — and thereafter time would scarcely be mentioned (either overtly or through affixes) unless a change in episode (a further grammatical level?) demanded it. Thus a

---

[11] Closely related to Vagala; data from Ron Rowland.
[12] Produced from Rowland's texts at the University of Oklahoma by the linguistic retrieval project for aboriginal languages, partially supported by the National Science Foundation grant GS-270 and GS-934. Input data are archived on magnetic tape at the University of Oklahoma.

narrative, as a whole, could be viewed as a sequence of the following tagmemes:

± preview, ± narrative setting, ± sequential,
± focus change, ± climax, ± comment by narrator,
± summary application.

It is within the narrative setting that certain of the temporal matters are mentioned. The dots suggest possible change, especially, perhaps, through episode change.

In order to show the time position within the narrative, we now give two further formulas. The first of these is an expansion of the filler of the second slot indicated above for the narrative as a whole — the narrative setting:

(a) $\pm\ {}^f\text{TP}_1\ +\ \text{S:NP}\ \pm\ {}^f\text{Part}\ +\ \text{Pr}_{tr}\ [?]\ \text{O:NP}\ \pm{}^f\text{LP}\ \pm[?]\text{AdvP}$

The time particle occurs at the beginning of the sentences produced according to this formula, (in which the superscript f implies fixed order in this discourse slot; subscript 1 labels the subclass of expressions allowed here; other symbols refer to time phrases, nominal phrases, particular particles, transitive predicates, locative and adverbial phrases, etc.).

In contrast, if the time must be mentioned in a sequential slot — that is, in a paragraph which follows up the sequence of discussion but is not setting the topic of the discourse —, a different allo-construction of the transitive clause occurs. Note, therefore, the following transitive-clause, allo-formula as it might be found in a sequential slot:

(b) $+\ \text{S:NP}\ \pm\ \text{O:NP}\ \pm{}^f\text{LP}\ \pm[?]\text{AdvP}\ \pm\ {}^f\text{Part/TP}_{1/3}$

In this instance the time phrase occurs at the end of the clause — and has certain other restrictions indicated by the subscripts (whose details do not interest us here).

In summation, grammatical constructions may be viewed as waves.[13] The nucleus of the wave often suggests the point of attention elicited by the speaker from the hearer. Wave characteristics may appear throughout the whole hierarchical sequence of units of the grammar. They occur not only within the word (stem versus affix), but within the phrase (auxiliary versus head), the clause-cluster (with specialized instrumental tagmemes modifying the nuclear tagmeme of the developed subcluster), within the paragraph — the sentence-cluster — level, and on the level of discourse itself.

---

[13] Since this material was prepared, I have seen Richard Watson's "Clause to Sentence Gradations in Pacoh", *Lingua* 16 (1966), 166-189. There appears to be a number of interesting points of contact with this data from Vietnam.

MATRIX PERMUTATION AS A HEURISTIC DEVICE IN THE ANALYSIS OF THE BIMOBA VERB*

with GILL JACOBS

The purpose of this paper is to show, by an extended example, the way in which the simple but repeated operation of exchanging one row with another in a table, and of one column with another, can stimulate insight into the underlying rules of a language. This matrix permutation is especially valuable when the patterns involved result from rules which are partially independent and partially dependent, but criss-crossing one another in a way which leads to bewildering complexity. Whereas the experienced scholar may intuitively pick his way through the morass, the beginner can profit from a systematic search. By appropriate heuristic techniques he may discover bits and pieces of patterns which otherwise could elude him for many years.

Human nature can be blinded by expectation. One's focus often determines what one is capable of seeing. This human restriction on perception in general is no stranger to linguistic analysis. The matrix technique presented here, by the forced changing of focus through deliberate mechanical rearrangement of tabular elements, helps the analyst to overcome such bias by setting the stage for him to see elements of pattern which have previously been overlooked. It is with a feeling of astonishment, oftentimes, that one sees the new pattern — astonishment that one could have been so blind. That which is now 'obvious' was previously completely unobserved — or its significance unrealized even if the physical data had come to attention.

The fact that these techniques have, in some sense, been implicit in the work of scholars for a long time should not deaden us to the value of making them explicit. The explicitness of some recent formulations of linguistic presentation has been a great contribution; explicitness allows gaps in theory, presentation, and analysis to become glaringly apparent. Our claim is that PRECISION IS AS DESIRABLE IN HEURISTIC PROCEDURES AS IT IS IN PRESENTATIONAL ONES.

There is of course a difference — heuristic procedures require intuitive leaps, whereas presentation may be validated mechanically. But the presence of a heuristic leap, essential to the search process, should not blind us to the fact that search can be partially systematic, even though insight cannot thereby be guaranteed. Trial and error can be guided, even when profitable lines of search cannot be certified in

* *Lingua* 21 (1968), 321-345. Reprinted by permission of the North-Holland Publishing Co., Amsterdam.

advance. Individuals will differ at the point in time at which a particular fact will strike them as being important, even though using the same general search techniques. This, also, must be accepted as inherent in the nature of insight, conditioned by expectancies, by capacity, and — we add here — by adequate search procedures.

The Bimoba[1] material proved valuable for our demonstration because of certain characteristics of the data: (1) Even after the analysis is finished, no clean-cut simple morphemic solution of a classical type can be obtained. The end result of historical change has left such a messy conclusion — cluttered, relative to any expected morphemic segmentation — that it resists simple description in classical terms. The resistance to description is reflected in the difficulty of recognizing pattern. (2) It turns out that two or more sets of conflicting patterns result in waves of fusion such that, at any one particular point of fusion, the pattern can no longer be seen. It is only by standing back and looking at the broader sweep of fusion as a whole, and observing it from different vantage points, that the points of intersection of the patterns emerge as such. (3) No one standpoint allows one to find certain very specific regularities which are opaque from that viewpoint. Insight gained from one vantage point by no means leaves certain other elements in view.

The strength of the heuristic approach is precisely the fact that even after one gets the excitement of insight into pattern from one viewpoint, a mechanical insistence on further search — for a little while at least — helps to force a person to look from other vantage points. From these other perspectives, some further residues of pattern can then be seen clearly.

Central to the problem as it arose in Bimoba, was the slowly emerging insight that the list of conditioning features had to be set up in a priority sequence. Yet, according to the choice of priorities, different patterned elements emerged. Note clearly, however, that the result of the search was not merely that there was an ordering of rules — a set of priorities of statements about pattern — but that rather there were ALTERNATIVE SETS OF PRIORITIES (ALTERNATIVE ORDERINGS), EACH OF WHICH BROUGHT A DIFFERENT SET OF PATTERNS INTO VIEW.

Leaving, for the moment, the heuristic search which is the point of this paper, allow us to make a major theoretical point about matrix linguistics in general. A matrix display is to some extent like a general map — let us say a Mercator projection. A single ordered set of rules is more like a strip map[2] obtained through an automobile club.

The strip map gives us a single near-straight line from one city to the next, with specific warning posts telling how to keep on the road. But distortion of the points

[1] From the Gurma group of the Niger-Congo family of Ghana. (An earlier form of this paper was written as part of research performed under a grant by the United States Office of Education, Contract OE 5-14-065.)
[2] For a discussion of reaction to maps, see Michael Polanyi, *Personal Knowledge* (New York, 1964 [1958]), 83, 94, 119.

of the compass is extreme; in general, the strip map is a near-straight line, and north, south, east, and west disappear. Only the occasional sharp corner at a change of route or in working through a city is likely to be relevant. Nevertheless, as long as one is on route, this strip map is enormously valuable — it allows one to go rapidly and directly from point of origin to end point. The difficulty is that, if one is once off the trail, off the marked set of rules, he is lost and his orientation disintegrated. He does not know which way is up or down. He has no idea how far he is off the trail, nor which direction he must turn to get there — nor whether it is worthwhile to retrace his steps to get on the trail once more as over against plotting a new journey. Bafflement in this case is overwhelming.

With a regular map, on the other hand, he has the great advantage that if he can find the name of the spot where he is, plus direction of the compass, he can orient himself as to his theoretical and practical position — to the direction in which he wants to go. He can plot a new course — of fifty new courses — to bring in interesting side trips. Something of this characteristic differentiates the presentation of some kinds of matrix material from a derived-rule representation of that material.

Matrix heuristics takes a general map, as it were, and deliberately plots on the map various alternate paths across it to see what various interesting points may be picked up on the way. If one is in a hurry, and does not get off the trail, the strip map is more efficient; if one wishes freedom to look around at other points of interest, the general map is the more profitable.

Implications for pedagogy (as well as for analysis which is in focus) abound here. Drills need to be set up for exploiting the sub-patterns. In such surface chaos, each bit of hidden regularity needs to be separately exploited. The development of this principle, however, must wait for further publication elsewhere.

In this article we take alternate sectors of an implicit large map, and trace different kinds of paths through them — that is, we rearrange the data according to different criteria. We then see various subsystems interlocking but partially separate: one for the segmental components of suffixes, a different one for the tone of the word as a whole, and another one for the stem. The systems only partially merge into a single simple pattern; substantial apparent arbitrariness remains. We retrace our journey, except for eliminating some parts in order to hold the material to a manageable size. The particular elements which had to be handled in some order of priority (although we did not realize this at the start of the search) include the first tone of the imperfective, the second tone of the imperfective, the tone of the perfective, the first tone of the imperative, the segmental CV shape of the stem, the relation between perfective, imperfective, and imperative affixes, and the phonological structure of the word as a whole. Undoubtedly other factors are still escaping us.

We realize full well that such a step-by-step description of an analysis appears unordered — since the ordering is in fact one of successive insights, hunches, etc., which cannot be set up by rule. Nevertheless we have thought that some readers may chose to see our particular oversights and insights as illustrative of the advantages and limits of this search technique.[3]

We now present the data and comments in relation to matrices which show various stages of the analysis as it, in fact, did develop. This is not an idealized pseudo-procedure suggesting how one OUGHT to act or where one should have found insight, but an abbreviated report of some of our actual work.

We began with Matrix 1, taken from prior work by Miss Jacobs. Miss Sonia Hine had also worked on the data, and provided us with Matrix 4, our starting place for tone (which may still need later revision; e.g., the reinterpretation of some of the data in terms of a down-step). Matrix 1 abstracted consonantal suffixes from certain verbs. Tone was temporarily ignored, since no simple correlation with the consonantal suffixes appeared on the surface.

COMMENTS ON MATRIX 1

(1) A study of this display showed an inconsistency underlying the subdivision of its stems (the rows). Usually stems were grouped together (in rows at the top of the matrix) if they had zero as their perfective suffixal form (first column). At the bottom of the matrix, however, this priority was overridden by the presence of an *i* (or *li*) suffix in the imperfective (second column).

(2) The first reworking of the same data showed the matrix in a better display, rigorously grouping together all rows with the same form in the perfective. This appeared to reflect a single priority, rather than a double priority as in Matrix 1. This matrix is not reproduced here.

NEW AIM: In a search for further pattern — since these matrices had still not shown any particularly interesting groupings, although they could be used if necessary for a routine description of stem subclasses — we tried a substantial number of re-arrangements, searching for further contrastive characteristics according to nasalization, specific stem-final consonants such as *-b, -t*, etc. These matrices, also, are not given here, but revealed some patterning (see Matrix 2).

We then decided to subdivide stems according to syllable pattern, CV, CVV, CVC, CVCV, etc., in an attempt to see if the syllable structure of the stem was conditioning pattern in a way which had been escaping us. These materials are seen in Matrix 2.

[3] For another specific illustration of pattern emerging by manipulation of rows and columns — a description especially useful for introducing beginners into the technique, since it leads one to see intuitively elegant patterns which have previously not been described nor well worked over — see Kenneth L. Pike and Barbara Erickson, "Conflated Field Structures in Potawatomi and in Arabic", *International Journal of American Linguistics* 30 (1964), 201-212. For a contrary view, see Charles Hockett, "What Algonquian is Really Like", *IJAL* 32 (1966), 59-73, which attempts a restatement in more classical morphemic terms.

MATRIX 1

Starting data on shapes of verb suffixes, which accompany (in rows) various sets of stem types

Perfective	Imperfective	Imperative
ø	ø	n
ø	ø	l
ø	ø	t
ø	loss[a] ø	loss n
ø	loss ø	n
ø	gain ø	n
ø	gain *l* R[b]	l
ø	t	t
ø	t	n
ø	l	l
ø	n	n
ø	kt	n
l	ø	t
l	gain ø	t
l	loss ø	t
n	loss ø	nt
n	ø	nt
l	t	t
l	n	t
l	l	t
l	l	n
n	i	nt
l	i	t
ø	i	n
ø	*li* R	l
ø	loss i	t

[a] For loss and gain, see Comment (1) after Matrix 3.
[b] R = replacive; stem-final consonant *t* replaced by suffix.

COMMENTS ON MATRIX 2

(1) CV, CVCV, CVV, CVC, etc. were given as the basic classification. Within this group, it had already been observed (see comment on Matrix 1) that a special set of rows resulted when the final stem consonant was -*t*. These were therefore listed separately from the other final consonants.

(2) On the other hand, there was only a partial consistency given to the grouping of suffixal consonants. It was evident that a further re-arrangement, making explicit a second priority (the consonantal suffix characteristic), would bring further order into the picture. This is suggested in Matrix 2 by [a]'s, which indicates which rows

MATRIX 2

Suffixes of stem patterns subdivided according to CV shapes

Stem Pattern	Perfective	Imperfective	Imperative
CV CVCV	∅	∅	*n*
CVV	∅	∅	*n*
	∅	loss ∅	*n*
	∅	loss ∅	loss *n*
	∅	*n*	*n*
	∅	*t*	*n*
	∅	loss *kt*	*n*
	l	∅	*t*
	l	loss ∅	*t*
	n	∅	*nt*
	n	loss ∅	*nt*
	l[a]	*t*	*t*[a]
	l[a]	*n*	*t*[a]
	l[a]	*l*	*t*[a]
CV*t*	∅	∅	*l*
	∅	gain *l* R	*l*
	∅	*li* R	*l*
CVV*t* CVC*t* CVVC*t*	∅	*l*	*l*
CVC	*l*	∅	*t*
	∅	∅	*t*
	∅	∅	*n*
	∅	gain ∅	*n*
	∅	*n*	*n*
	∅	*t*	*n*
	l	*t*	*t*
	l	*n*	*t*
	l	*l*	*t*
	l	*l*	*n*
	n	*i*	*nt*
	l[a]	*i*	*t*[a]
	∅[a]	*i*	*n*∅[a]
CVVC	∅	∅	*n*
	∅	∅	*t*
	∅	loss *i*	*t*
	∅	*t*	*t*
CVCC	∅	∅	*n*
	∅	∅	*t*
	∅	*t*	*t*
CVVCC	∅	∅	*n*

[a] Needs to be moved upward, to join its particular subgroup.

could be moved upward to get these groupings together. The result here was to show some further subdivision, but no pattern seemed to be especially striking.

NEW AIM: An observation was made, however, that in the imperfective there was a wider variety of forms than in the other columns. In general, in seeking basic forms one chooses the more diverse set since it is easier to predict the coalescence of forms than the split of forms. Hence it was decided to set up the imperfective as basic — i.e., to be given priority over the other columns — and to concentrate on the CVV and CVC sets. The result is seen in Matrix 3, with imperfective in the first column.

COMMENTS ON MATRIX 3

(1) We see that all but one of the stem sets marked 'loss' in the imperfective column have been brought together by giving priority to the imperfective ø. Here 'loss' implies that the basic starting stem shape of consonant-vowel-vowel has lost the second of the two vowels; CVV > CV. Similarly, 'gain' listed in the cell meant that an extra vowel was added to the stem; CVC > CVVC. Loss is confined to pattern CVV; gain is confined to pattern CVC.

MATRIX 3
Re-arrangement of CVC and CVV sections of Matrix 2, with imperfective as basic

CVV Stems			CVC Stems		
Imperfective	Perfective	Imperative	Imperfective	Perfective	Imperative
ø	ø	n	ø	ø	n
loss ø	ø	n	gain ø	ø	n
loss ø	ø	loss n (of v)			
ø	l	t	ø	l	t
loss ø	l	t	ø	øª	t
ø	n	nt	ø		
loss ø	n	nt	ø		
n	ø	n	n	ø	n
n	l	t	n	l	t
t	ø	n	t	ø	n
t	l	t	t	l	t
			l	lª	n
l	l	t	l	l	t
			i	ø	n
			i	l	t
			i	n	nt
loss kt	ø	n			

ª Rare; probably irregular.

(2) After the imperfective is treated as basic, the perfective is then subdivided according to its suffixal consonant. The perfective suffix sets with the CVV stems included ø, *l*, or *n*. The imperative, similarly had a set of three: *n*, *t*, or *nt*.

(3) There are CO-OCCURRENCE RESTRICTIONS between the perfective and the imperative sets, so that if one knows the perfective form the imperative is predictable; or, knowing the imperative, the perfective is predictable.

(4) Main conclusion and insight gained from this matrix: imperfective is well treated as having basic priority over the other aspects, since, with this as a basic starting point, a co-occurrence pattern subdividing the other aspects becomes evident. The data had been there all the time, of course, but it was not until this matrix that there appeared to be any significant order to the data. It lent the first bit of excitement to the search.

NEW AIM: The question was raised: Can anything be found to predict any of these consonantal subsets ø, *l*, *n*; or *n*, *t*, *nt*? At this stage, and even in spite of further matrices attempting to answer this question, no such rule could be found. The differences in the sets — shown by the rows — must be attributed to basic subclasses of stems; membership in the subclasses is arbitrarily determined, and must be listed in lexicon.

Since work on the consonants was at a standstill, we turned temporarily to the study of tone. See Matrix 4.

MATRIX 4
Starting data on tonal shapes of verbs (= stem plus suffix)

Perfective	Imperfective	Imperative₁ with *t, l, nt*	Imperative₂ with *-n*
(/)/[a]	//	/⌐	//
(/)/	/\	/⌐	//
(/)/	-/	/⌐	[/ ⌐\][b]
(/)/	-\	/⌐	
(-)-	//	/⌐	//
(-)-	/\	/⌐	//
(-)-	-/	/⌐	-\
(-)-	-\	/⌐	-\
(\)\	\-	\⌐	[\\J√][b]
(\)\	\\	\⌐	\\
(\)\	√/	\⌐	\\

[a] The perfective forms, though written with a single tone mark, should be interpreted as applied either to single vowels or to vowel sequences with or without intervening consonants. In this respect they are like the high-high, mid-mid, and low-low of the imperfective, which are written as double tones for convenience in showing contrast with mid-high, etc. (In utterance-final position a single-vowel imperfective seems to be extended by a dummy clitic *-e* which carries the tone; elsewhere, the single-syllable imperfective may omit the second tone.)

[b] Possibly an error?

COMMENTS ON MATRIX 4

(1) This matrix was provided for us by Sonia Hine. The tone sets represented, and the prior tone analysis, are taken from her work.

(2) We now went through procedures of matrix permutation similar to those we had used for the consonants of the suffixes, but applied to the tones of THE WORD AS A WHOLE. The tone pattern extends over the stem and the suffix, making a single-word pattern.

(3) The perfective is treated as basic, with its high, mid, and low giving the crucial priority subdivisions. Comparable groups appear in the first of the two imperatives (the one which ends in *t*, *l*, or *nt*, rather than in *n*).

NEW AIM: The question arose, however, whether the patterning observed in reference to the suffixal consonant and vowel, with imperfective being treated as basic (Matrix 3), would throw any new light on the tone system as well. If so, it would imply a basic characteristic of the imperfective which carried throughout the system. If it did not show such pattern, then it would imply that the tone systems and the segmental systems crisscross in some independent way — and that the verb stems would have to have a double classification. We decided, therefore, to re-arrange Matrix 4 by putting the imperfective first, treated as basic, in order to see if we could exploit the pattern breakthrough gained by the study of the consonants.

MATRIX 5

First tone of imperfective as basic

Imperfective	Perfective	Imperative₁	Imperative₂
// //	(/)/ (-)-	/⌐	// //
∧ ∧	(/)/ (-)-	/⌐	// //
-/ -/	(/)/ (-)-	/⌐	[/⌐] -\
-\ -\	(/)/ (-)-	/⌐	-\
V/ \- \\	(\)\ (\)\ (\)\	\⌐ \⌐ \⌐	\\ V[\\] \\

COMMENTS ON MATRIX 5

(1) Note that classificatory priority is given not merely to the imperfective as such, but to its FIRST tone-high, mid, or low. This leads to three sections of the matrix, with forms of imperfective beginning with high, mid, and low respectively.

(2) On the other hand, it was suddenly possible to see that the chart divided also into two parts: The lower three rows formed a group because in the perfective there was uniformly low tone; the other two sections of the perfective were not uniform in this way.

(3) In the upper part, there was a pairing; for each pattern of the imperfective (separated by dotted lines), two and only two patterns occurred in the perfective — the first high and the second mid. For the first imperative, on the other hand, the tone of the imperative corresponding to the perfective high became high followed by a mid fall; but the first imperative had no occurring form to parallel the perfective mid set.

NEW AIM: We next wanted to see if any further pattern would emerge by taking the SECOND tone of the imperfective as basic, rather than the first one. This was a routine way of exploring various possibilities, as a trial and error method. It might prove relevant (especially since the second tone comes physically closer to the suffixes — whose consonants had already proved relevant). See Matrix 6.

MATRIX 6

Second tone of imperfective as basic

Imperfective	Perfective	Imperative₁	Imperative₂
//	(/)/	/⌐	//
//	(-)-		//
-/	(/)/	/⌐	[/⌐]ᵃ
-/	(-)-		-⌐
\//	(\)\	\⌐	\\
\-	(\)\	\⌐	[\\]\/
∧	(/)/	/⌐	//
∧	(-)-		//
-\	(/)/	/⌐	
-\	(-)-		-⌐
\\	(\)\	\⌐	\\

ᵃ Possibly an error?

COMMENTS ON MATRIX 6

(1) Matrix 6 divides into three parts, as the result of choosing the second tone of the imperfective as basic.

(2) The first and third sections are identical in the perfective. This was quite unexpected. Similarly, the first sections of the imperative columns are nearly identical with the comparable elements of their third sections. (One exception in the third row of the imperative₂ might conceivably be due to error in the data, and should be checked.)

NEW AIM: At this point a comparison was made of Matrices 5 and 6. Here there came to our attention a possible element of pattern relevance in the two main upper sections of the perfective column of Matrix 5: For every pair of imperfective stem sets there was a split into high and mid in the perfective. (In retrospect, we NOW show these by the dotted lines in Matrix 5.) What would happen if one were to make a matrix by pulling out the comparable rows of the perfective and grouping them together? This is done in Matrix 7.

MATRIX 7
Re-arrangement of Matrix 5

Imperfective	Perfective	Imperative₁	Imperative₂
//	(/)/	/⌐\	//
∧	(/)/	/⌐\	//
-/	(/)/	/⌐\	[/⌐\]
-\	(/)/	/⌐\	
//	(-)-		//
∧	(-)-		//
-/	(-)-		-\
-\	(-)-		-\
∨/	(∨)\	\⌐	\\
\-	(∨)\	\⌐	∨[\\]
\\	(∨)\	\⌐	\\

COMMENTS ON MATRIX 7

(1) It was very obvious, once this permutation was seen, that the perfective had been treated as the controlling, priority, pattern — with high, mid, and low tones giving the basic sections.

(2) It startled us, however, to find that, in terms of the groupings of the rows, this was identical with Matrix 4 above! We had unwittingly returned to Matrix 4 by a circular chain of perturbations. (This was not at first obvious, because of the interchange of columns, from perfective being first in Matrix 4 to second in Matrix 7.)

(3) This raised an important question: Why was the circle complete? How could it possibly be completed as a result of these permutations? Some kind of patterning-principle had to be concealed here; this result could not have been obtained otherwise.

The hypothesis: perhaps the system of priorities was more complex than we had articulated above; instead of there being a single priority — as to a particular tone, for example — necessary to describe the system, perhaps two, three, or even four priorities need to be specified. This was now done retroactively for each of the matrices in turn:

EXPLICIT RANKING OF PRIORITIES APPLIED TO TONE MATRICES ABOVE:

Matrix 4 priorities:
 (i) Tone of perfective
(ii) First tone of imperfective
(iii) Second tone of imperfective

Matrix 5 priorities:
 (i) First tone of imperfective
(ii) Second tone of imperfective
(iii) Tone of perfective
        (Tones of imperatives, in addition, lead in two columns.)

Matrix 6 priorities:
 (i) Second tone of imperfective
(ii) First tone of imperfective
(iii) Tone of perfective

Matrix 7 priorities:
 (i) Tone of perfective
(ii) First tone of imperfective
(iii) Second tone of imperfective

It was only now evident that it was an underlying implicit ranking of priorities, changing from one ordered ranking to another, which made it possible by continued shuffling to arrive back at the point of origin.

NEW AIMS:

(1) At this point there seemed to be no further profitable way of permuting these particular data. We decided to expand them by adding certain future particles before the verb. Special sections of the combined particle plus verb suggested that there were small SUBPATTERNS WITHIN THE LARGER COMPLEX. None of these can be shown here — but were visible, for example, as a single large cell of a matrix uniformly filled with a single pattern of tone sequences which did not occur elsewhere in the matrix. The intersection of priorities — or of rules — led to the special pattern for that cell.

(2) Now, however, that we had looked separately at the patterning of the seg-mental character of the suffixes and the tonal characteristic of the word as a whole (stem plus suffix), we were interested to see if the pattern-groups of the tones coin-cided with those of the segments. If they were to do so, it would prove that we had basically only one system, composed partly of segmental materials and partly of tone. If, on the other hand, there were no neat, patterned, correlation between the

two, then this would be evidence that we were dealing with two systems, each of which would lead to a different classification of those stems.

In order to try this conflation we had to keep the parameters constant (that is, we had to keep the columns in the same order beginning with our best basic set, the imperfective), and we had to keep the rows of stems in the same order, again using a sequence which was previously useful. We first added the consonantal suffixes of Matrix 3 (arranged with segments of the imperative given priority) to Matrix 5 (which had been arranged according to the first tone of the imperfective). We did not see significant correlation of these patterns. We therefore did not reproduce that matrix.

(3) We next wanted to see what would happen if we conflated the consonantal groupings of Matrix 3 (arranged, as before, with priority on imperfective consonants) with the tones of Matrix 7 (arranged with priority according to the tone of the perfective). The result can be seen in Matrix 8.

MATRIX 8

Matrix 3 combined with Matrix 7

Imperfective	Perfective	Imperative₁	Imperative₂
//ᵃ ø	(/)/ ø	/⌐\ t	// n
ø	l	t	
ø	n	nt	
n	ø		n
n	l	t	
t	l	t	
l	l	t	
l	[l]		n
i	l	t	
i	n	nt	
∧ ø	(/)/ ø	/⌐	// n
loss ø	l	t	
loss ø	n	nt	
-/ ø	(/)/ ø	/⌐	[/⌐\] n
ø	[ø]	t	
t	l	t	
l	l	t	
i	l	t	
-\ ø	(/)/ l	/⌐\ t	
loss ø	l	t	
ø	n	nt	

ᵃ   The tone pattern in a cell occurs with each row of the cell.

MATRIX 8 (*continued*)

Imperfective		Perfective	Imperative₁	Imperative₂	
//	*n*	(–)–øᵇ		//	*n*ᵇ
	i	ø			*n*
∧	ø	(–)–ø		//	*n*
–/	*n*	(–)–ø		–\	*n*
	t	ø			*n*
–\	ø	(–)–ø		–\	*n*
gain	ø	[ø]			*n*
loss	ø	ø			*n*
loss	ø	ø		loss	*n*
∨/ᶜ	ø	(∨)\ø	\⌐	\\	*n*
	ø	ø	*t*		
	t	ø			*n*
	i	ø			*n*
	i	*l*	*t*		
	i	*n*	*nt*		
\–	ø	(∨)\ø	\⌐	[\\]∨	*n*
	ø	ø			*n*
	n	ø			*n*
	t	ø			*n*
	t	*l*	*t*		
	l	*l*	*t*		
loss	*kt*	ø			*n*
\\	ø	(∨)\ø	\⌐	\\	*n*
gain	ø	ø			*n*
loss	ø	ø		loss	*n*
	ø	*l*	*t*		
gain	ø	*l*	*t*		
loss	ø	*l*	*t*		
	ø	*n*	*nt*		
loss	ø	*n*	*nt*		

ᵇ   See comments (1) and (2).
ᶜ   See also fn. 5.

COMMENTS ON MATRIX 8

(1) Note, especially, the particular grouping of zeros that completely fills the perfective consonantal column in the middle section of the chart. Note further that the CONTROLLING FACTOR pulling these together is the presence of a mid tone in the perfective.

(2) Similarly, in the same stem sets where mid tone and zero consonants occur in the perfective, there occurs, in every instance, an *n* as the consonantal part of the imperative suffix.

(3) Up to this point, this small subpattern had completely escaped our notice. It was camouflaged by the many occurrences of ø and n elsewhere, so that the small point of regularity and predictability at intersections of consonant -ø and tone was not easy to find. It is precisely the presence of such sub-rules, or subpatterns, which prevents the language from being completely irregular in the formation of its aspects.

But it is the complexity of the interlocking of these rules which makes it difficult to analyze the system by any classical morphemic segmentation techniques. Here one begins to see the value of a 'field' theory of language (as over against one of morphemic particles). By it, the conflation of pattern components can be presented (in an emergency) without the required apparatus of morphemic identification of particles.

Irregularity — from one view — is seen as deep field structure from another.[4]

(4) Note, further, that predictability is not reciprocal for the elements of this subpattern. If one knows (a) that the perfective is involved and (b) that it has mid tone, he can know that the suffix will be consonantally zero. But knowing (a) the presence of zero suffix, and (b) the involvement of perfective aspect, one still does not know the tonal class from which the stem must be chosen. Matrix displays of this type, therefore, show the DESCRIPTIVE ORDER (or priority of ORDERED RULES) for useful presentation of such a subpattern.

(5) The greater number of rows in Matrix 8 than in Matrix 3 arises from the cross-cutting of some segment blocks of 3 by tonal subdivisions introduced by 8. This indicates that the two systems are partially independent of one another, in spite of subpatterns like those just mentioned in (2).

NEW AIM: Within this crisscross we wondered whether further ordered rules might be found, leading to further subpatterns based on different sets of priorities, if the conflation of consonantal and tonal data were handled by different sets of permutations. We decided, therefore, to try the conflation of the segmental elements of Matrix 3 combined, this time, with the tonal permutations carried by Matrix 6. See, for the result, Matrix 9.

COMMENTS ON MATRIX 9

(1) We have already mentioned some clustering of sets of stems with loss of vowel, in Comment (1) on Matrix 3. Now we observed a further compacting of these sets which was not visible earlier: all gains and losses occur in the two lower major sections of Matrix 9, (i.e., after an imperfective tone which is mid or low); all gains, and all but two of the losses, are in the imperfective column.

Here, again, a nonreciprocal is present: loss occurs only if the imperfective ends

[4] For a discussion of a theoretical view of a postulated historical oscillation between the two pattern types, see my "Non-Linear Order and Anti-Redundancy in German Morphological Matrices", *Zeitschrift für Mundartforschung* 3 (1965), 193-221.

MATRIX 9

Matrix 3 combined with Matrix 6

	Imperfective	Perfective	Imperative₁		Imperative₂	
//	1	ø	(/)/ ø	/⌐\		//	n
	2	ø	l		t		
	3	ø	n		nt		
	4	n	ø				n
	5	n	l		t		
	6	t	l		t		
	7	l	l		t		
	8	l	[l]				n
	9	i	l		t		
	10	i	n		nt		
//	11	n	(–)– ø			//	n
	12	i	ø				n
–/	13	ø	(/)/ ø	/⌐\		[/⌐\]	n
	14	ø	[ø]		t		
	15	t	l		t		
	16	l	l		t		
	17	i	l		t		
–/	18	n	(–)– ø			–\	n
	19	t	ø				n
\/	20	ø	(\)\ ø	/⌐		\\	n
	21	ø	[ø]		t		
	22	t	ø				n
	23	i	ø				n
	24	i	l		t		
	25	i	n		nt		
\–	26	ø	(\)\ ø	\⌐		[\\]\/	n
	27 gain	ø	ø				n
	28	ø	ø				n
	29	t	ø				n
	30	t	l		t		
	31	l	l		t		
	32 loss	kt	ø				n
∧	33	ø	(/)/ ø	/⌐\		//	n
	34 loss	ø	l		t		
	35 loss	ø	n		nt		
∧	36	ø	(–)– ø			//	n
–\	37	ø	(/)/ l	/⌐\	t		
	38	ø	n		nt		

MATRIX 9 (*continued*)

Imperfective	Perfective	Imperative$_1$	Imperative$_2$
–\ 39 ø	(–)– ø		–\ n
40 gain ø	ø		n
41 loss ø	ø		n
42 loss ø	ø		loss n
\\ 43 ø	(\)\ø	\⌐	\\ n
44 gain ø	ø		n
45 loss ø	ø		loss n
46 ø	l	t	
47 gain ø	l	t	
48 loss ø	l	t	
49 ø	n	nt	
50 loss ø	n	nt	

with mid or low tone, but one cannot predict, from this matrix, that all verbs of these tone sets will lose a vowel.

(2) In the last minor section of the imperfective column another uniform grouping occurs: all of the suffixes are represented by zero segments. Here, the zero is predictable whenever the imperfective of the VERB has a low-low tone pattern — but the predictability is not reciprocal.

(3) A mid-low glide occurs on all columns of the forms of imperative$_1$; no unquestionable glide occurs in imperative$_2$. Suffixes *t* and *nt* occur in imperative$_1$; only *n* with imperative$_2$. It is clear, then, that here reciprocal relations join segment and tone, and that they had been responsible for the basic split of the imperatives in the two columns of Matrix 4.

One is likely to feel, in retrospect, that one should have sensed much earlier the significance of such correlations. Different observers will see the relevance of an element at different points in the process of inquiry. Yet self-recrimination here is futile — no technique can guarantee the necessary burst of insight. We can, however, cultivate heuristic procedures which are more likely to invite this insight.

In Matrix 9 the relation between the tone and the *n* in the second of the imperative columns became startlingly obvious. In earlier matrices, such as 4, the presence of the *n* in the second imperative column was indicated — but its function in relation to our QUESTIONS about it was quite different. Earlier we had been asking what the tone groups were — and the consonant marking was incidental to getting the tones into groups. Now, however, our focus was taken away from the tones as such, and placed squarely upon the co-occurrence restrictions, if any, between the tones and the consonants. We were SPECIFICALLY looking for groupings, conditionings, or conflation across the systems. When, therefore, all the consonants were specifically written out, as for Matrix 9, the sharpness of the clean-cut occurrence of *n* in the second imperative column was made the more striking in contrast to the diversity of consonants in — for example — the perfective column.

The general principle here is important — although it sometimes leaves one feeling a little astonished that one can be so blind: One's expectancies in part determine what one can see. When looking for one item or one type of item, another may be present but completely unobserved; or its presence may be seen but its significance may be totally unnoticed. The matrix technique, by forcing a change of focus through deliberate mechanical re-arrangements, helps one to notice such matters which one has previously overlooked.

(4) No further major co-occurrence relation of tone to suffixal consonant appeared either in Matrix 9 or in supplementary permutations of it. We concluded that in the imperfective there are THREE SEPARATE SYSTEMS — one for the SEGMENTAL components of the suffixes and a different one for the TONE of the word as a whole, which in turn is determined by the particular STEM chosen. The systems are arbitrarily related. Presumably they had different historical sources. In any case, at the moment, no clean-cut coordinating pattern has emerged. One must list two sets of arbitrary subclasses of verb stems, which intersect each other — one set determining the basic tone pattern, and the other determining the basic segmental pattern of the suffix. (Once this has been done for the imperfective, however, many of the remaining characteristics of word tone and suffix can be determined by the groupings which we have discussed above.)

(5) The following data, taken from a corpus of over 500 verbs, corresponds with the numbers of the rows in the imperfective column of Matrix 9. Where possible, two examples of each row are given, showing both transitive and intransitive, and both CVV and CVC patterns. (This matrix is for CVV and CVC patterns only.)

//	1.	*bui*	'weep'			*buu-t*	'get better'
		lik	'mend'	-/	16.	*bii-l*	'spoil'
//	2.	*guu*	'wait'	-/	17.	*yeb-i*	'choke'
//	3.	*taa*	'be one and the same'			*kɔn-i*	'break'
		saa	'go'	-/	18.	*bal-n*	'hang over shoulder'
//	4.	*kpo-n*	'die'	-/	19.	*yek-t*	'shoot'
		bil-n	'put (on ground)'	\//	20.	*kɔi*	'sell'
//	5.	*gaa-n*	'agree'			*foi*	'rest'
		yek-n[a]	'sieve'	\//	21.	*yab*	'abound'
//	6.	*kaa-t*	'finish'	\//	22.	*buk-t*	'put over shoulder'
		bia-t	'remain'			*job-t*	'bump'
//	7.	*pia-l*	'wipe'	\//	23.	*bɔl-i*[a]	'hide'
		mii-l	'joke'	\//	24.	*ban-i*	'interfere'
//	8.	*nub-l*	'smell'			*sok-i*	'wash (dishes)'
//	9.	*ŋman-i*	'twist'	\//	25.	*duk-i*	'think'
		tik-i	'gather together'	\-	26.	*aa*	'cook'
//	10.	*puk-i*	'add'	\-	27.	*teeb*	'heal'
		bik-i[a]	'taste'	\-	28.	*fib-n*	'faint'
//	11.	*sɔb-n*	'write'			*sii-n*[a]	'touch'
		ŋak-n	'shake'	\-	29.	*jak-t*	'attack'
//	12.	*tɔk-i*	'accompany'			*too-t*	'drip'
-/	13.	*koi*	'learn how to'	\-	30.	*baa-t*	'come'
-/	14.	*man*	'perform'	\-	31.	*jek-l*	'shiver'
-/	15.	*sub-t*	'become wise'			*bii-l*	'slice'

\‒	32.	*ji-kt*	'take'	‒\	41.	*da*	'buy'
		yo-kt	'wear'			*nyi*	'come out'
/\	33.	*sii*	'vomit'	‒\	42.	*di*	'eat'
/\	34.	*fa*	'lie'	\\	43.	*bɔk*	'crawl'
		to	'pound'			*boi*	'ask'
/\	35.	*lu*	'fetch water'	\\	44.	*kaal*	'sit'
		yi	'call'			*kaan*	'count'
/\	36.	*kɔɔ*	'enter'	\\	45.	*do*	'climb'
		pull	'roast'			*kpi*	'kill'
‒\	37.	*dɔɔ*	'lie down'	\\	46.	*yee*	'break'
		bɔɔ	'slice'			*gbii*	'dig up'
‒\	38.	*tee*	'make'	\\	47.	*siin*	'fry'
‒\	39.	*kaa*	'not be'			*nuun*	'drive (a car)'
		tab	'stake out'	\\	48.	*fi*	'get up'
‒\	40.	*jaan*	'steal'			*pɔ*	'pluck'
		tiin	'run'	\\	49.	*tii*	'lean against'
				\\	50.	*mɔ*	'pour away'

---

* With alternative suffixal form in the imperative.

(6) This complexity of Matrix 9 represents only a part of the larger intricate problem; only stems of shapes CVV and CVC were included in Matrix 3, and — as a result — in Matrix 9. If, from Matrix 2, the other stem shapes were now to be taken, further complexity would result. If, further, particles were to be added before the verb — see New Aim (1), just before Matrix 8 — more tonal problems would appear.

The following data illustrate the imperfective form of the remaining rows of Matrix 2 (i.e., except the CVV and CVC sections, for which data have just been given). Where possible, two examples are chosen, of different tone pattern, and showing both transitive and intransitive form. When the shape-type may occur with more than one suffixal pattern, these are given at the right of the cited stem. For the others,[5] see Matrix 2.

				Perfective	Imperfective	Imperative
CV	‒\	*tɔ*	'shoot (arrow)'			
	‒\	*mɔ*	'weep'			
CVCV	//	*duli*	'limp'			
	\/	*puki*	'worship'			
CVt	//	*kpet*	'grow old'	ø	ø	*l*
	\\	*gat*	'answer'	ø	ø	*l*
	‒\	*bee-l*	'tell'	ø	gain *l* R	*l*
	‒\	*daa-l*	'pull'	ø	gain *l* R	*l*
	‒/	*ŋa-li*	'be slimy'	ø	*li* R	*l*
	/	*ce-li*	'meet'	ø	*li* R	*l*
CVVt	//	*yaat-l*	'depart'			
	\/	*caat-l*	'remove'			
CVCt	\/	*wɔkt-l*	'be light in weight'			
	//	*ŋmant-l*	'turn something'			

[5] A year or so after this was written, Jacobs reports also CVVT with *bilnt-l* 'roll' in high tone pattern' and *kabnt-l* 'beckon' in low high.

To Matrix 8 and Matrix 9 she would now add *bal-n* 'stroke' with low-high high tone, and with *n*, ø, ‒, *n* endings; *wen-t* 'soak' and *dun-t* 'take out' with these same tones, but with endings *t*, *l*, *t*, ‒.

CVVCt	//	gbiint-l	'listen to'			
	\/	dɔɔnt-l	'peep into'			
CVVC	-/	waal	'hunt'	ø	ø	n
	-/	koon	'cough'	ø	ø	n
	//	kpaan	'exhort'	ø	ø	t
	-/	tian	'shout'	ø	ø	t
	//	nɔb-i	'take'	ø	loss i	t
	//	jɔb-i	'use'	ø	loss i	t
	\-	biin-t	'cover'	ø	t	t
	\-	gbaan-t	'kneel'	ø	t	t
CVCC	\\	kaln	'read'	ø	ø	n
	//	butn	'become stunted'	ø	ø	n
	//	kpann	'deceive'	ø	ø	t
	\/	punn	'be lying across'	ø	ø	t
	\-	kpakn-t	'rest (head)'	ø	t	t
	\-	dɔkn-t	'cause to vanish'	ø	t	t
CVVCC	\-	foont	'greet'			
	\-	muuks	'cause trouble'			

FINAL AIM: Only at this point did we at last raise seriously a question which would have been one of the first under a classical, particle approach: Are there morphemes carrying these imperfective, perfective, and imperative meanings; if so, what is the list of their allomorphs, and what are the distributional constraints on the occurrence of these variants? As a step towards answering this question, we sharply re-ordered the conflated data of Matrix 9. The imperfective, perfective, and imperative meanings were transposed from the columns to the rows. All tone patterns were taken from the larger included cells and placed at the head of the new columns. The separate consonants (and *i*) scattered widely throughout Matrix 9, were gathered together somewhat, in the cells of Matrix 10, and placed at the points where meaning and tone intersected with the occurrence of the particular consonant.

MATRIX 10
Re-arrangement of Matrix 9 — segmental and tonal correlation with CVV and CVC stems

	//	∧	-/	-\	∨/	\-	\\	-	/⌐	\⌐
Imperfective	n		n			n				
	ø	ø	ø	ø	ø	ø	ø			
	t		t		t	t				
	l		l			l				
	i		i			kt				
Perfective	n						n			
	ø						ø	ø		
no *i*										
no *t*										
	l						l			
Imperative	n			n		n			n	
no ø									t	t
no *l*									nt	nt
no *i*										

COMMENTS ON MATRIX 10

(1) No allomorphically-simple classical morphemes can easily be found for imperfective, perfective, and imperative. Some of the tonal patterns occur in all three; so also do some of the consonants; and so, to a lesser extent, do combinations of tone and of segment. It is embarrassing, for example, to suggest that a phonemic shape made up of suffixal *n* plus word-tone high-high can ambiguously be three allomorphs, one for each of the three morphemes.

(2) On the other hand, the presence of *t*, *i*, or *kt* with tone patterns high-high, mid-high, rising-high, or low-mid is unambiguously a signal of imperfective, PROVIDED that the stem is of pattern CVV or CVC (the only ones represented in this matrix).

(3) This AMBIGUITY would have to be eliminated by relation to data from some HIGHER LEVEL,[6] such as phrase clause, sentence, or discourse.

(4) For the imperatives, however, a slightly more traditional answer can be given. The imperative$_1$ of Matrix 9 can be treated as derived from the perfective form by the addition of a mid-low glide, plus replacement of the perfective suffix by the imperative *t* suffixal consonant (with arbitrary variant of *nt* after certain stem subclasses). The imperative$_2$, as an arbitrary subset, is derivable from the imperfective form: the imperfective suffixal consonant is replaced by *n* (with two subclasses arbitrarily determined by stem sets which involve loss of a vowel). In addition there are some predictable tone relationships.

(5) For some purposes of linguistic analysis and of linguistic description, a theory of classical morphemes is enlightening — especially where segmentation of meaningful elements is clean-cut, and an easily-detectable relation between phonological form and lexical meaning is one-to-one on the level morphemic representation. When, however, no such simple, form-meaning relation is present, a field theory must be involved in which rigid requirement of a form-meaning relation is retained, but in which the meaning is the matrix of categories (meanings of rows and columns), and the form is the pattern (regular or irregular) of the distribution of phonological material within the cells of the matrix. The penalty for refusal to use a field view here is one of an enormously complex statement of a bewildering variety of allomorphic forms, distributions, homonymities and partial overlaps.

---

[6]   For this technique, see reference in fn. 4.

PRONOMINAL REFERENCE IN ENGLISH CONVERSATION AND DISCOURSE — A GROUP THEORETICAL TREATMENT*

with IVAN LOWE

0. INTRODUCTION

This investigation is an attempt to investigate formally a limited sociolinguistic situation — that of conversations between three individuals A, B, C. We find that the application of finite permutation groups enables us to arrive at a formulation which is sociologically relevant and this formulation is capable of generating and specifying all cases of pronominal reference within the rubric 'given' of section 1.1. In particular we are able, because of the peculiar properties of finite groups, to arrive at a general theorem which takes into account an indefinite number of embeddings of quotative margins and reduces the pronominal reference determination for such a problem to that for a single quotative margin. We have purposely limited our problem (as in "Given" section 1.1) in order to keep the mathematical detail simple without, however, losing any generality of principle. This ensures that the solutions and their underlying principles will be accessible to the linguist and not be obscured by excessive algebraic complexity. We believe that the particular algebraic formulation chosen (from among several possibilities which we have experimented with) has the advantage of sociological relevance at each step of its reasoning, and we have tried to present our conclusions in such a way that the linguistically-oriented reader will be able to follow these sociological implications. Our goal, then, is not formalism for formalism's sake, but rather formalism for the purpose of displaying sociolinguistic phenomena explicitly and generatively.

1. THE PROBLEM

1.1 *Given*

A group of three men A (Abe), B (Bill), C (Charlie) are in conversation, speaking to each other about various topics. Each person is allowed to speak to either of the others, only, and no plural references or reflexives, nor special forms such as editorial 'we', are allowed within the chosen limits of our restricted problem.

* *Folia Linguistica* 3 (1969), 68-106. Reprinted by permission.

1.2 *To Find*

In the sociological situation defined in 'Given' to pick out some simple kinds of utterance which can be used in conversation and, for each kind of utterance chosen, to formulate rules which will link any pronoun to its correct referent.

1.3 *General Remarks*

That this problem is non-trivial can be seen by considering a not-too-complicated case:

A (Abe) says to B (Bill): '"*I said to you "You said to me 'I saw you'"*"'

In the above utterance, who do the various pronouns refer to? It is true that with a certain amount of 'brute hack work' one can determine empirically the referents of each pronoun in the above utterance, but clearly such an approach is unsatisfactory. We need to ask ourselves questions like the following:

(i) What sorts of pattern are involved that connect pronoun with referent?

(ii) What sorts of generalization can be made as we successively embed an utterance or as we go from one kind of discourse to another (e.g., conversation to monologue)?

What remains invariant and what varies as we make such changes?

(iii) What general principles are applicable for the treatment of this and similar problems? What is likely to remain invariant as we pass from one language to another?

In an attempt to answer such questions, we treat exhaustively the simple sociolinguistic situation defined in 'Given' (1.1), and from this we expect to derive certain theorems and principles of more general application and interest.

2. SOME GENERAL PRINCIPLES

2.1 *Preamble*

In the situation given (1.1) with three people A (Abe), B (Bill), C (Charlie), some of the simple (non-recursively quoted) utterances would be as follows:

(i) *A (Abe) says to B (Bill) "I see you."*

(ii) *B (Bill) replies to A (Abe) "I see you too."*

(iii) *C (Charlie) says to B (Bill) "Do you know what he did to me last night?"*

(iv) *C (Charlie) says to B (Bill) "He rang you last night. Did you know?"*

(ia) In the 'quotation content' of (i), *I* refers to Abe and is FIRST PERSON SURFACE

SUBJECT — we denote this by SA1; *you* refers to Bill and is SECOND PERSON SURFACE OBJECT — we denote this by OB2.

(iia) In the 'quotation content' of (ii) we have similarly, *I* refers to Bill and is FIRST PERSON SURFACE SUBJECT, denoted by SB1; while *you* refers to Abe and is SECOND PERSON SURFACE OBJECT, denoted by OA2.

(iiia) Similarly in the 'quotation content' of (iii) we have: *you* denoted by SB2, *he* SA3 (in embedded clause), *me* OB1.

(iva) In the 'quotation content' of (iv): *he* SA3, *you* OB2 (first occurrence), *you* SB2 (second occurrence).

The important thing to notice here is that we have three vectors:

(a) A vector of case K with components the indexed triple $[\alpha, \rho, \chi]$,

(b) A vector of cast C with components the indexed triple $[A, B, C]$ (where A = Abe, B = Bill, C = Charlie),

(c) A vector of person P with components the indexed triple $[1, 2, 3]$.

It should be clear from the utterances (i-iv) above, that depending on the utterance, ANY individual in the cast can be agent α or recipient ρ or undefined χ (which in the simple case that we treat would map unto surface structure as surface subject S, surface object O, surface undefined function X, respectively). We noticed that our rules are more general in application if they operate first on a case vector and then on the surface grammar functions derived from this. Therefore, in the theoretical part of the treatment we shall use case vectors, but in concrete applications, surface function labels will be found much more convenient for some purposes.

2.2 *The Group of Permutations*

Thus the problem of finding all the possible combinations of ordered triples like SB2, should be intimately related to the problem of the possible permutations of the components of the 3-vector $[\alpha, \rho, \chi]$ of case, and of the possible permutations of the components of the 3-vector $[1, 2, 3]$ of person.

It is common mathematical knowledge that the permutations of n objects form a GROUP, called the SYMMETRIC GROUP P_n.[1] That is to say, for our problem, we need to involve ourselves in a study of the SYMMETRIC GROUP P_3 — the group of permutations of 3 objects — (whether these be $[1, 2, 3]$ or $[\alpha, \rho, \chi]$ or $[A, B, C]$).

In this simplified, restricted problem that we have chosen to tackle first, ALL the vectors (i.e., the case vector K, the person vector P, the cast vector C) each possess three components. Or in other words, we have chosen to deal with the limited problem of THREE cases (Agent, Recipient, Undefined), THREE persons (first, second, third), and THREE cast members $[A, B, C]$. Because of this arbitrary limitation, we need only ONE group, namely the symmetric group P_3, to describe all our permutations.

---

[1] See for instance, I. Grossman and W. Magnus, *Groups and Their Graphs* (New York, Random House, 1964), 30ff.; or Saunders MacLane and Garrett Birkhoff, *Algebra* (New York-London, MacMillan, 1967), 73-74.

Although the problem is limited in extent, its solution will be found to exhibit many of the general properties needed in a more general solution. In a more extended treatment, we must expect the different vectors to have different numbers of components — i.e., a yet undefined but finite set of cases $[C_1, C_2, ---, C_m]$, a person set $[1, 2, 3, - n]$ where n is probably no greater than four, and a cast $[A, B, C, - N]$ which is arbitrary but finite. Plural, gender, reflexivity, editorial 'we' and the like will also be involved. This more general solution will clearly involve more general permutations, but we expect that many of the characteristics of the limited problem will be recognizable in the more general solution.

It is intuitively obvious that within a sociological setting of three individuals A, B, C (and more generally N) in conversation with each other, the same situation can maintain itself indefinitely, provided there is neither any external interruption nor a mutual internal agreement to quit. This is expressible as a closure property (i.e., such that all operations stay WITHIN the situation, and so it is appropriate that our mathematical representation should be a group which is an algebra with closure).

Coming back to our sociological situation with A (Abe), B (Bill), C (Charlie) in conversation, any one of A, B, or C can take on first, second or third person. That is to say, all possible permutations of the basic ordered set $[1, 2, 3]$ can be associated, element by corresponding element, with the set $[A, B, C]$ to produce combinations of letter and number.

2.3 *Permutations of the Person Set*

For instance, the ordered set $[3, 1, 2]$ is a permutation of the basic set $[1, 2, 3]$ and if we now 'match' this permuted set $[3, 1, 2]$ with the cast set $[A, B, C]$, we get the 'matching array'

$$\begin{bmatrix} A & B & C \\ 3 & 1 & 2 \end{bmatrix}$$

Now, pairing off element with corresponding element from these two vectors — i.e., associating each letter with the number directly beneath it in the array — we get the combinations

A3, B1, C2

with the interpretation that A is third person, B is first person and C is second person. This is clearly a sociologically relevant combination and so also is any similar combination formed by 'matching' the cast set $[A, B, C]$ with any other permutation of the basic person set $[1, 2, 3]$.

2.4 *Permutations of the Case Set*

Similarly, taking the basic ordered set of grammatical case $[\alpha, \rho, \chi]$ where α = agent,

ρ = recipient, χ = unspecified, we can permute this basic ordered set to another new ordering, and then again we 'match' this newly ordered case set with the basic ordered set [A, B, C] of cast, element by corresponding element.

For instance, $[\chi, \alpha, \rho]$ is a permutation of the basic ordered set of grammatical case. Matching this with the basic cast set we get the array

$$\begin{bmatrix} A & B & C \\ \chi & \alpha & \rho \end{bmatrix}$$

and pairing off by columns, we then get combinations

Aχ, Bα, Cρ

with the interpretation that A is unspecified case, B is agent case, and C is recipient case.

2.5 *Mappings of the Case Set unto the Surface Structure*

The case labels $[\alpha, \rho, \chi]$ for agent, recipient, unspecified are deep-structure labels and can be mapped out unto surface structure in several different ways. If we let [S, O, X] be surface labels of subject, object, unspecified respectively, then one such mapping could be represented by the array

$$\begin{bmatrix} S & O & X \\ \alpha & \rho & \chi \end{bmatrix}$$

and reading down column-wise, we would get the pairs

Sα, Oρ, Xχ

with the interpretation: Subject as agent, Object as recipient, Unspecified as unspecified.

Such an interpretation would be satisfied in sentences like

I hit Bill
John said to me

i.e., in the commonly called active-sentences in English. In our discussion we shall limit ourselves to pronominal reference in active-sentences. From the point of view of group theoretical derivations of pronominal reference, all the necessary principles are invoked, and it is a simple matter to extend the treatment to cover the problem for non-active sentences by specifying the deep-surface mappings involved.

On the other hand if we were to match according to the array

$$\begin{bmatrix} S & O & X \\ \rho & \alpha & \chi \end{bmatrix}$$

we would have pairs like

Sρ, Oα, Xχ

realized in such sentences as

I was told by John etc.

Of the four vectors of CAST, PERSON, CASE and surface FUNCTION, the first three can be permuted freely with regard to each other. The last two, however, have more restricted mappings on each other — i.e., not all possible permutations of the components of the case vector will match with the surface function vector to give function-case combinations which will result in acceptable sentences of English.

2.6 *Some Special Permutations*

Let us look now at the linguistic significance of some special kinds of permutation of the three INDEPENDENT vectors, i.e., CAST, PERSON, CASE with respect to each other.

If we take the CAST vector [A, B, C] and match it up against some arbitrary permutation of the PERSON vector [1, 2, 3] and HOLD THIS MATCHING CONSTANT, then one individual of the cast stays fixed in the role of speaker, (i.e., of 1st person) and another individual of the cast stays fixed in the role of addressee and so on. This, then, is realized as a monologue.

To illustrate, we can, without loss of generality, take the (identity) permutation [1, 2, 3] of the basic person vector [1, 2, 3] and match this against the basic CAST vector [A, B, C] to give us the array

$$\begin{bmatrix} A & B & C \\ 1 & 2 & 3 \end{bmatrix}$$

which yields us the fixed pairs

A1, B2, C3

which, interpreted, tell us that A (Abe) is always first person, B (Bill) is always second person, and C (Charlie) is always third person. That is to say, we are in a monologue situation in which A (Abe) talks to B (Bill). (It is understood that any possible permutation of the case symbols [α, ρ, χ] matches with the fixed pairs [A1, B2, C3], now regarded as our indexed triple. Thus a complete representation in terms of person, cast, and case of all that can be said in this monologue (subject to the restrictions in 'Given', section 1.1) would be given by the array

$$\begin{bmatrix} A1 & B2 & C3 \\ \omega\,(\alpha, & \rho, & \chi) \end{bmatrix}$$

where ω is any arbitrary permutation of three objects and ω [α, ρ, χ] is the result of this permutation on the basic case set [α, ρ, χ].)

Similarly, matching each of the other possible permutations of the person vector [1, 2, 3] against the cast vector, we have each of the monologue possibilities with A or B or C as speaker, etc., provided that for each monologue we regard the permutation of [1, 2, 3] as fixed.

2.7 Permutations Corresponding to Possible Conversation Exchanges[2] in a Cast of Three Individuals A, B, C

(By 'possible' here, we mean ALL possible conversational exchanges under the re-strictions of 'Given' section 1.1.) Suppose now we match the unpermuted cast vector [A, B, C] against an arbitrary permutation ω_1 [1, 2, 3] of the unpermuted person set and, at the same time, against another arbitrary permutation ω_2 [α, ρ, χ] of the unpermuted case set, giving us the 'matching array'

$$\begin{bmatrix} A & B & C \\ \omega_2 \, [\alpha, & \rho, & \chi] \\ \omega_1 \, [1, & 2, & 3] \end{bmatrix}$$

and now combinations are gotten from this matching array by all the elements of one particular column — and repeating the same process for all columns.

We observe that if we FIX the permutation ω_1 of the components of the person vector [1, 2, 3] and allow the permutation ω_2 to range over all the possible permu-tations of the set of 3 case entities [α, ρ, χ], our sociological interpretation is that of one particular monologue, (with someone of the individuals A, B, C of the cast, holding the floor).

If now we allow BOTH the permutation ω_1 of the components of the person vector and the permutation ω_2 of the components of the case vector to vary simultaneously, then we get as interpretation all possible conversations in the social situation in-volving three individuals as participants, speaking one to one only. (See restrictions under 'Given', section 1.1.)

There is still one thing lacking, however, in our account. We cannot jump hap-hazardly from one arbitrary monologue to any other arbitrary monologue. Social conventions will not allow it. We need to include in our account, then, the condi-tions under which the 'initiative' can pass from one individual in the cast to another.[3] If these conditions can be built into the formalism itself, this will be all to the good — it will show the sociological relevance of the formalism. Our task, then, becomes clear. We need an algebra which will describe formally the set of all permutations

---

[2] A fairly rapid study of some conversations in the form of one-act plays and children's fairy tales etc., has already yielded some interesting results which have also been confirmed by observation of live social situations. For instance if A is holding the floor and speaking to B (group index I), this can be followed by either B replying to A (group index r) or by A switching and speaking to C (group index s). If A speaks to B (group index I), this CANNOT be followed immediately by C speaking to A (group index sr), unless C interjects or is rude or unless there is some external intervention of some sort. And so on. There is a relevance to the use of r and s. (In all conversation we need to assume at least one quotative margin — the 'identity margin' corresponding to *I* (Abe) *say to you* (Bill).) — The identity margin, i.e. the 'I-you' invariant role relationship underlies all other roles in conversa-tion, and this at least MUST always be assumed. In many conversations we need to assume others. Not infrequently — in fact far more frequently than we realise — we need to deal with embedded quotative margins.

[3] See note 2.

of 3 objects, and then we shall apply our permutation-algebra to triples like the cast triple, the person triple and the case triple and combine our results by a matching technique. We need, furthermore, to construct our algebra in such a way that its abstract operations will correspond to sociologically-relevant, concrete processes.

2.8 *Abstract Properties of the Permutation Group*

Let us take any three abstract objects 1', 2', 3'. (We will show how to use them concretely later.)[4]

It is well known that the permutations of any three abstract objects[5] like 1', 2', 3' form a finite group of order 3' = 6, called P_3, the symmetric group of degree 3.[6] This symmetric group has been treated in many standard texts on abstract algebra[7] but such formulations are oriented towards physical problems.[8] We shall instead formulate the same group in a slightly different way, so as to have sociologically-relevant operations.

Let us take then, our three abstract objects 1', 2', 3' taken as an ordered set [1', 2', 3'], which we can call the OPERAND, and define three OPERATORS, I, r, s, on this operand in the following way.

$I \equiv (1') (2') (3')$ ___ i.e., leave 1', 2', 3' each as they are.

$r \equiv (1'\ 2') (3')$ ___ i.e., interchange 1' & 2', leave 3' as it is.

$s \equiv (1') (2'\ 3')$ ___ i.e., interchange 2' & 3', leave 1' as it is.

---

[4] Our choosing the labels 1' 2' 3' for the three abstract objects of our set is deliberate because our purpose is first to study the general properties of the permutations of any three objects whatsoever and then later to apply these general properties to the permutations of specific sets of 'objects' such as [1, 2, 3], [α, ρ, χ], [A, B, C], etc. So we start off being general with our abstract objects 1' 2' 3' and only later do we become specific by equating our abstract objects to more specific ones, i.e., 1' = α, 2' = ρ, 3' = χ would refer specifically to all permutations of the case set, 1' = A, 2' = B, 3' = C would refer to all permutations of the cast set, etc. etc.

[5] We have, unfortunately, been compelled to use the term 'object' in two completely different senses: (a) as an abstract entity denoted generally by 1' or 2' or 3', etc., and (b) as the term generally used for a surface grammatical function. It is to be hoped that the context is sufficient to determine unambiguously which sense of the term is meant in any given case. We note also that O is surface indirect object in verbs of 'telling or giving', and is surface direct object in most verbs of action. Ditransitive verbs have not yet been dealt with.

[6] It is important here for us to distinguish clearly between the terms ORDER and DEGREE. ORDER of a symmetric group, as of any group, is simply the number of distinct elements in the group and this is, in our case, six. The DEGREE of a symmetric group is the number of abstract objects which are subject to permutation, in our case, three.

[7] See note 1.

[8] The treatments of P_3 in terms of generating elements r = rotation of 120° about an axis perpendicular to the plane of the triangle and passing through its centroid, and f a rotation of 180° about an axis in the plane of the triangle and joining any one vertex with the triangle's centroid, is given in many standard texts on algebra including the ones cited above in footnote 1. Such a formulation is quite convenient for problems of physics but does not suit our problem since it is difficult to find a sociologically relevant interpretation for the operator through 120°. We have thus decided on the alternative formulation given in the body of the text. — It is a matter of no difficulty to prove that the groups generated by the r, f, of Grossman-Magnus is isomorphic to the group generated by our generators r, s.

From these three 'generating operators' we can derive three more, namely:

rs $\equiv$ (1' 3' 2') ___ i.e., change 1' to 3', 3' to 2', 2' to 1'.

sr $\equiv$ (1' 2' 3') ___ i.e., change 1' to 2', 2' to 3', 3' to 1'.

rsr $\equiv$ (1' 3') (2') ___ i.e., interchange 1' & 3', and leave 2' as it is,

where the complex operator rs is interpreted to mean that we operate on the operand set first with r and then on the result of this with s, and similarly for sr and rsr. Taking the first three operators, I, r, s, as generators, with the definitions given above, it is easy to establish that the permutations corresponding to rs, sr, rsr are as given above also.

From these definitions, it is easy to establish the truth of the multiplication table:

TABLE I

	I	r	s	rs	sr	rsr
I	I	r	s	rs	sr	rsr
r	r	I	rs	s	rsr	sr
s	s	sr	I	rsr	r	rs
rs	rs	rsr	r	sr	I	s
sr	sr	s	rsr	I	rs	r
rsr	rsr	rs	sr	r	s	I

This table is to be read as follows:

The table proper is that enclosed within the double lines. We number the rows of the table from top to bottom and starting from the first row immediately below the top double line. We number the columns from left to right and starting from the first column immediately to the right of the left double line. The direction of the arrow tells us which factor must come first and which must follow, and this ordering MUST be obeyed because 'multiplication' is non-commutative. Then the element in row i and column j of the table proper is the 'product' of the element in row i of the left-flank column vector and the element in column j of the top-flank row vector taken in that order — that is to say, this element in row i and column j of the table is the operator which is equivalent to the successive application first of the element in row i of the left-hand flank column vector followed by the element in column j of the top-flank row vector, STRICTLY in that order.

For example, if we take row 3, column 5 from the respective flank vectors, the flank elements are s and sr — then the table says that the 'product' of s.sr in that order, is identically equal to r (i.e., no matter what the operand). From the table it is easy to see that the axioms of closure, unity and inverse are satisfied for all operators of the set $G \equiv \{I, r, s, rs, sr, rsr\}$. Associativity can also be established.[9] Thus the four group axioms of closure, associativity, unity and inverse are established for the set G of operators as we have defined them, and thus G is a group, which is indeed none other than the symmetric group P_3.

We can also look upon our group as being generated from the generating elements $\{I, r, s\}$, subject to the restrictions of $r^2 = s^2 = (rs)^3 = I$. From these restrictions we can derive

$$\text{(i)} \quad rsr = srs$$
$$\text{(ii)} \quad (rsr)^2 = (srs)^2 = I$$
$$\text{(iii)} \quad srsr = rs$$
$$\text{(iv)} \quad rsrs = sr$$
$$\text{(v)} \quad rsrsr = s$$
$$\text{(vi)} \quad srsrs = r$$
$$\text{(vii)} \quad (rs)^3 = (sr)^3 = I$$
$$\text{(viii)} \quad r = r^{-1}, s = s^{-1}, (rs)^{-1} = sr,$$
$$(sr)^{-1} = rs, (rsr)^{-1} = rsr$$

as has been done in Appendix 1. With these results (i)-(viii), we can again set up the same multiplication table as before and from there, proceed to verify the satisfaction of the group axioms pretty well as in footnote 9. This point of view also has its advantages as it centers our attention on the interpretation of the operators I, r, s.

2.9 Sociological Interpretations of the Generating Operations of the Group

We wish here to justify our choice of r, s as generating operators of the group (rather than the more usual ways of generating the same group, see for instance footnote 8).

---

[9] The four group axioms can be established as follows: (i) 'closure' can be established from the multiplication table by noting that the 'product' of any two elements of the set G is still an element of G, and moreover that this product element is unique. We simply check the multiplication table. — (ii) 'Associativity' can be established in at least three ways: (a) by sheer brute force by taking all possible triples λ, μ, υ (where λ, μ, υ, are each elements of G) and showing from the multiplication table that $(\lambda \mu) \upsilon \equiv \lambda (\mu \upsilon)$ in every case; (b) by noting that the multiplication table makes our group isomorphic with the symmetric group P_3 which obeys the associativity axiom; (c) by realizing that any permutation of a set of objects on itself is an automorphism of that set and invoking the theorem that any set of automorphisms of a set obeys the associative law. — (iii) 'Unity' can be established because the element I whether used as a right operator or as a left operator on any arbitrary element ω_1, gives us always the same result ω_1. This can easily be checked by the table. — (iv) 'Inverse' can be established by noting that in the multiplication table EACH row and EACH column has ONE AND ONLY ONE I. Thus every element has a unique left inverse, and also a unique right inverse, and we can check to see that in each case the right inverse always is identical with the left inverse. Thus each element has a unique inverse.

Our justification is based on a claim of sociological relevance.[10] We have

$$I \equiv (1')\ (2')\ (3')$$
$$r \equiv (1'\ 2')\ (3')$$
$$s \equiv (1')\ (2'\ 3')$$

Consider our basic vectors of cast [A, B, C], person [1, 2, 3], and case [α, ρ, χ]. If we match them against each other with their components in this particular order, we get the array

$$\begin{bmatrix} A & B & C \\ \alpha & \rho & \chi \\ 1 & 2 & 3 \end{bmatrix}$$

and combining elements in the same column to form the set of triples αA1, ρB2, χC3 which represent utterances like

I (Abe) saw you (Bill)
I (Abe) told you (Bill) about him (Charlie).

Such utterances we regard as belonging to the 'identity' set.

Consider now the application of the permutation operator $r \equiv (1'\ 2')\ (3')$. We have purposely defined r in terms of general objects 1' 2' 3', so that we can use this operator to permute the components of whichever vector we please.

Looking at the basic array, let us leave the person vector untouched and apply r to the case vector. This gives us

$$\begin{bmatrix} A & B & C \\ \rho & \alpha & \chi \\ 1 & 2 & 3 \end{bmatrix}$$

which yields triples αB2, ρA1, χC3 corresponding to such utterances as

You (Bill) saw me (Abe)
You (Bill) told me (Abe) about him (Charlie).

Notice that, here, A (Abe) is still speaker and therefore still in control of the situation. The r permutation of the case vector just gives us something else that A (Abe) can say, i.e., specifically, utterances that Abe can say with him (Abe) as recipient (usually surface object).

Similarly, reverting to the basic array and applying the permutation operator $s \equiv (1')\ (2'\ 3')$ to the case vector components, we get as result

---

[10] We could also quite easily and relevantly define our group in terms of three generators

$$r \equiv (1'2')(3'),\quad s \equiv (1')(2'3'),\quad q \equiv (1'3')(2')$$

with the 'redundancy relations'

$$q \equiv rsr,\quad r \equiv sqs,\quad s \equiv qrq$$

This formulation is also sociologically relevant and has the advantage of making q, r, s, more symmetrical with respect to each other but still ordered and we would expect them to be from a 'real world' standpoint.

$$\begin{bmatrix} A & B & C \\ \alpha & \chi & \rho \\ 1 & 2 & 3 \end{bmatrix}$$

yielding us triples αA1, ρC3, χB2 corresponding to such utterances as

I (Abe) saw him (Charlie)

I (Abe) told him (Charlie) about you (Bill).

Thus A (Abe) still holds the floor as first person but now he addresses Bill.

Quite a different thing happens, however, if we apply a permutation operator to the PERSON vector components, keeping everything else constant. Suppose, for example, we put $1' = 1$, $2' = 2$, $3' = 3$ and apply the permutation operator $r \equiv (1'\ 2')$ $(3')$ to the person vector of the basic array

$$\begin{bmatrix} A & B & C \\ \alpha & \rho & \chi \\ 1 & 2 & 3 \end{bmatrix}$$

We then get as result, the array

$$\begin{bmatrix} A & B & C \\ \alpha & \rho & \chi \\ 2 & 1 & 3 \end{bmatrix}$$

yielding triples

αA2, ρB1, χC3

corresponding to such utterances as

You (Abe) saw me (Bill)

in which now B (Bill) holds the floor as first person.

Thus permutation on the PERSON vector leads to a permutation of roles (of speaker, addressee, background) among the individuals of the cast (A, B, C). Notice now what happens when starting with the basic array

$$\begin{bmatrix} A & B & C \\ \alpha & \rho & \chi \\ 1 & 2 & 3 \end{bmatrix}$$

we simultaneously permute the components of both the case vector $[\alpha, \rho, \chi]$ and the person vector $[1, 2, 3]$ with the same permutation operator. Suppose, for example, we permute with $r \equiv (1'\ 2')\ (3')$, then our new array after both permutations have been made will be

$$\begin{bmatrix} A & B & C \\ \rho & \alpha & \chi \\ 2 & 1 & 3 \end{bmatrix}$$

yielding us triples

αB1, ρA2, χC3

corresponding to utterances like

I (Bill) saw you (Abe).

What has happened? The grammatical form of the utterance is exactly the same as what would have been derived from the basic array, but the individuals in the cast have changed. Now, Bill is holding the floor as first person, and Abe is the addressee as second person.

Notice the same result could have been achieved by starting with the basic array and permuting the components of the CAST vector [A, B, C] with the INVERSE PERMUTATION TO r. (But since $r = r^{-1}$, the same effect is obtained by permuting the cast vector with r.)

However, there is a trap here for the unwary, since the operators (rs) and (sr) are NOT equal to their own inverses, although the operators r, s, rsr ARE equal to their own respective inverses. In fact we have $(rs)^{-1} = (sr)$, $(sr)^{-1} = rs$ while $r^{-1} = r$, $s^{-1} = s$, $(rsr)^{-1} = rsr$.

We will show how to deal with the problem in the rs case. (The sr case is exactly the same in principle.) We have $rs \equiv (1'\ 3'\ 2')$ and so $(rs)^{-1} \equiv sr \equiv (1'\ 2'\ 3')$.

Starting from the basic array

$$\begin{bmatrix} A & B & C \\ \alpha & \rho & \chi \\ 1 & 2 & 3 \end{bmatrix}$$

EITHER we permute BOTH the case AND the person vector components with $rs \equiv (1'\ 3'\ 2')$ to give

$$\begin{bmatrix} A & B & C \\ \chi & \alpha & \rho \\ 3 & 1 & 2 \end{bmatrix}$$

yielding us triples

αB1, ρC2, χA3

OR we permute simply the cast vector of the basic array with the INVERSE PERMUTATION $(rs)^{-1} \equiv sr \equiv (1'\ 2'\ 3')$ to get

$$\begin{bmatrix} B & C & A \\ \alpha & \rho & \chi \\ 1 & 2 & 3 \end{bmatrix}$$

yielding us triples

αB1, ρC2, χA3

which are the same as before.

We can now easily deduce, by going through the algebra, the following results concerning change of role amongst individuals of the cast (Table II).

TABLE II

Operation or basic array		Interpretation
EITHER SIMULTANEOUS operation on both case and person person with	OR SIMPLE operation on cast only with	for same surface utterance
I	I	A1, B2, C3
r	r	B1, A2, C3
s	s	A1, C2, B3
rs	sr	B1, C2, A3
sr	rs	C1, A2, B3
rsr	rsr	C1, B2, A3

3. A VERY SIMPLE SOCIAL SITUATION — A MONOLOGUE

In this short section we take a very simple case and from it, try to discover some guiding principles. Suppose that there are three individuals A (Abe), B (Bill), C (Charlie) sitting around a table together and suppose A (Abe) talks to B (Bill).[11] Some of the things that A can say are represented in Table III.

TABLE III

I see you SA1 OB2	I
You see me SB2 OA1	r
I see him SA1 OC3	s
You see him SB2 OC3	rs
He sees me SC3 OA2	sr
He sees you SC3 OB2	rsr

[11] There is a sense in which the actual composition of the cast is irrelevant. The plot of the play stays the same, irrespective of the composition of the cast, so long as the number of individuals in the cast does not change. It is only in problems of reference that cast becomes important. — It is rather surprising to us that pronouns are more closely related to ultimate language-social situation interplay than the names of individuals in a cast. That is to say, the basic roles to be filled in con-

Underneath each of the various pronouns in the different utterances we have written a three letter symbol (like SA1, OB2). The first letter of the symbol gives the surface grammar function (S = subject, O = object, X = unspecified) of the pronoun in the utterance under consideration, the second letter of the symbol gives the individual (A or B or C) to whom the pronoun refers, the third letter (or really number) of the symbol gives the person (1st or 2nd or 3rd) of the pronoun as it occurs in the utterance. We could conveniently call this the function-cast-person triple. We restrict ourselves to one particular mapping of case onto surface grammar function and we choose the surface grammar symbols S, O, X for typographical convenience. Some of the cast symbols (in our case the C's) are underlined (viz. in OC3, SC3). This underlining is to indicate that our reference is at least partially indeterminate — in our specific examples the 'him' labelled by the symbol OC3 COULD refer to Charlie but could also refer to some other individual (so long as it isn't either Abe or Bill) and the same applies to the 'he' labelled by the symbol SC3.

To the right of each of the utterances is one of the elements of our permutation group (i.e., one of I, r, s, rs, sr, rsr). We call these the GROUP INDICES[12] of their respective utterances. We get these by regarding *I see you* as basic and so this corresponds to the identity operator I, and then the other utterances of the set have their group index assigned by considering the permutation of the function set [S, O, X] (or equivalently the case set [α, ρ, χ]) with respect to either the cast set [A, B, C] or the person set [1, 2, 3]. Thus in the identity configuration for all three vectors[13] we have

---

versation are those of speaker, addressee and background. It is these roles which are the ultimate conversational invariants, while the identification of any particular cast is almost a secondary variable. The SAME drama (invariant) can be played by many, many different casts.

[12] We shall find the idea of a GROUP INDEX extremely important for further extensions to the work. It is based on the relative permutation of function (or case) with respect to person, cast not being taken into consideration (see footnote 11), so that

$$I \Leftrightarrow \begin{bmatrix} 1 & 2 & 3 \\ S & O & X \end{bmatrix} \quad \begin{matrix} \text{index of } \textit{I said to you} \\ \text{or: } \textit{I see you} \end{matrix}$$

$$r \Leftrightarrow \begin{bmatrix} 1 & 2 & 3 \\ O & S & X \end{bmatrix} \quad \begin{matrix} \text{index of } \textit{You said to me} \\ \text{or: } \textit{You see me} \end{matrix}$$

$$s \Leftrightarrow \begin{bmatrix} 1 & 2 & 3 \\ S & X & O \end{bmatrix} \quad \begin{matrix} \text{index of } \textit{I said to him} \\ \text{or: } \textit{I see you} \end{matrix}$$

$$rs \Leftrightarrow \begin{bmatrix} 1 & 2 & 3 \\ X & S & O \end{bmatrix} \quad \begin{matrix} \text{index of } \textit{You said to me} \\ \text{or: } \textit{You see me} \end{matrix}$$

$$sr \Leftrightarrow \begin{bmatrix} 1 & 2 & 3 \\ O & X & S \end{bmatrix} \quad \begin{matrix} \text{index of } \textit{He said to me} \\ \text{or: } \textit{He sees me} \end{matrix}$$

$$rsr \Leftrightarrow \begin{bmatrix} 1 & 2 & 3 \\ X & O & S \end{bmatrix} \quad \begin{matrix} \text{index of } \textit{He said to you} \\ \text{or: } \textit{He sees you} \end{matrix}$$

where the double arrow ($\Leftrightarrow$) means 'refer to'.

[13] There is strong motivation for calling the particular ordered set of triples [SA1, OB2, XC3] basic and therefore associated with the identity I of the permutation group. This is because in every declaration, be it a business letter, a book preface, a political manifesto, a simple monologue or a quotation of someone else's speech, the 'I-you' type of declaration like *I tell you, I say to you* is implicit.

$$\begin{bmatrix} A & B & C \\ S & O & X \\ 1 & 2 & 3 \end{bmatrix}$$

from which we derive the triples

SA1, OB2, XC3

and *I see you* is a possible realization of this set of triples.

Now permuting the [S, O, X] basic function set with the operator r — i.e., putting $1' = S$, $2' = 0$, $3' = X$ and applying the permutation $r = (1' \, 2') \, (3')$ to the components of the function vector and leaving everything else unchanged, we arrive at a new array

$$\begin{bmatrix} A & B & C \\ O & S & X \\ 1 & 2 & 3 \end{bmatrix}$$

from which we derive the triples

SB2, OA1, XC3

and *You see me* is a possible realization of this set of triples.

To cover all the cases we proceed as follows: Calling $1' = S$, $2' = O$, $3' = X$, apply the permutation of the symmetric group of degree 3 (i.e., onto the ordered set [S, O, X]) to get the following results which are also in the form of ordered sets,

$$\begin{aligned}
\text{I} \,[\text{S, O, X}] &= [\text{S, O, X}] \\
\text{r} \,[\text{S, O, X}] &= [\text{O, S, X}] \\
\text{s} \,[\text{S, O, X}] &= [\text{S, X, O}] \\
\text{rs} \,[\text{S, O, X}] &= [\text{X, S, O}] \\
\text{sr} \,[\text{S, O, X}] &= [\text{O, X, S}] \\
\text{rsr} \,[\text{S, O, X}] &= [\text{X, O, S}]
\end{aligned}$$

where we have defined our group members as OPERATORS or permutations as in section 2.

If, now we combine, in turn, each of these permuted sets with the ordered triple [A1, B2, C3], element by corresponding element, we get exactly the triples with their CORRECT GROUP INDICES[14] as assigned to the utterances at the beginning of section 3, viz.

I corresponds to $\begin{bmatrix} S & O & X \\ A1 & B2 & C3 \end{bmatrix}$, i.e., SA1 OB2, XC3

r corresponds to $\begin{bmatrix} O & S & X \\ A1 & B2 & C3 \end{bmatrix}$, i.e., SB2, OA1, XC3

s corresponds to $\begin{bmatrix} S & X & O \\ A1 & B2 & C3 \end{bmatrix}$, i.e., SA1, OC3, XB2

[14]   See note 12.

$$\text{rs corresponds to} \begin{bmatrix} X & S & O \\ A1 & B2 & C3 \end{bmatrix}, \text{ i.e., SB2, OC3, XA1}$$

$$\text{sr corresponds to} \begin{bmatrix} O & X & S \\ A1 & B2 & C3 \end{bmatrix}, \text{ i.e., SC3, OA1, XB2}$$

$$\text{rsr corresponds to} \begin{bmatrix} X & O & S \\ A1 & B2 & C3 \end{bmatrix}, \text{ i.e., SC3, OB2, XA1}$$

4. MORE GENERAL CONVERSATION CASES IN A CAST OF THREE INDIVIDUALS

4.1 *Preamble*

In our restricted society of three individuals, we can look upon a series of conversational interchanges between the various individuals as a series of monologues with sociologically-acceptable transitions between any one monologue and the next.

We have seen in the preceding section how, by using purely group operations (i.e., permutations), we can distribute and redistribute roles of speaker, addressee and the background in all possible ways amongst the individuals of a cast of three people. Having now fixed the roles of speaker, addressee and background in a given way amongst the individuals in our cast of three, choice of utterance by the speaker will still include (amongst other things) a choice of possible case assignments to the various individuals in the cast (and probably to some individuals or things outside the immediately visible cast of A, B, C as well). The task in this section of the paper is to classify all such assignments in terms of our group operators (or if the reader prefers, to show how all possible assignments of this kind can be generated by application of our group operators). We begin with quotations within a single quotative margin, passing on later to embedded quotative margins. For each single quotative margin we can assign a group index, this group index being already defined in the monologue case and always equal to the group operator, which when applied to the case vector $[\alpha, \rho, \chi]$ will (after matching with unpermuted basic cast and person vectors) always give the right person, cast, case assignments for the quotative margin. Thus in sections 4.2.1-4.2.6 we shall consider successively single quotative margins whose group indices are respectively I, r, s, rs, sr, rsr, showing how, in each instance, we can arrive at the correct person-cast-case assignments and therefore at the correct pronominal references. In the following section (5), we shall then present in tabular form, each of the quotative margins together with some suitable 'quotation contents', i.e., what goes inside the quote, to demonstrate the correctness of our abstract generalizations.

In this tabulation, the cases of single quotative margins will be exhaustively presented. Only a limited selection of double quotative margins will be presented tabularly since the general theorem shows how in the case of an arbitrary number of n quotative margins, the problem of pronominal reference can be reduced to that of a single margin. In fact, all we have to do is to determine the group index of each individual quotative margin and then 'multiply' these group indices together with the factors in the same order as their corresponding margins occur in order to get the EFFECTIVE GROUP INDEX for the WHOLE EMBEDDING quotative margin. Then this EFFECTIVE GROUP INDEX, applied as if the WHOLE EMBEDDING MARGIN WERE REPLACED BY A SINGLE QUOTATIVE MARGIN OF THE SAME GROUP INDEX, will give the correct pronominal references (by referring to the tables in sections 4.2.1-4.2.6).

4.2 *Calculations for a Single Quotative Margin*

4.2.1 *Quotative Margin Group Index I*

When $I \equiv (1')(2')(3')$ is the group index for the quotative margin,

QUOTATIVE MARGIN

is represented by the basic array

$$\begin{bmatrix} A & B & C \\ 1 & 2 & 3 \\ \alpha & \rho & \chi \end{bmatrix}$$

which determines assignments $\alpha A1$, $\rho B2$, and $\chi C3$ for quotative margin. Since the individual who is agent α in quotative margin always goes to 1st person in quotation content, recipient ρ always goes to 2nd person in quotation content; then, the pairs A1, B2, C3 are invariant within the quotation content. Thus within

QUOTATION CONTENT

person reference is already fixed by quotative margin, i.e., we must have A1, B2, C3. However, case may still vary in what can be said within this quotative margin and we give in Table IV the possible permutations of the basic case vector components $[\alpha, \rho, \chi]$, its allowed combinations with cast and person, and then a very simple realization of this in surface structure.

TABLE IV

	A	B	C	Corresponding valid case-cast-person combination			One possible surface structure realization of this		
	1	2	3						
I	α	ρ	χ	$\alpha A1$	$\rho B2$	$\chi C3$	SA1	OB2	XC3
r	ρ	α	χ	$\alpha B2$	$\rho A1$	$\chi C3$	SB2	OA1	XC3
s	α	χ	ρ	$\alpha A1$	$\rho C3$	$\chi B2$	SA1	OC3	XB2
rs	χ	α	ρ	$\alpha B2$	$\rho C3$	$\chi A1$	SB2	OC3	AX1
sr	ρ	χ	α	$\alpha C3$	$\rho A1$	$\chi B2$	SC3	OA1	XB2
rsr	χ	ρ	α	$\alpha C3$	$\rho B2$	$\chi A1$	SC3	OB2	XA1

The group operators in the left-most column are the operators leading to the permutations of the case components in the same row of the chart. (The language data corresponding to this analysis will be found in section 5 under group index I for quotative margin).

4.2.2 *Quotative Margin Group Index r*

When $r \equiv (1'\ 2')\ (3')$ is the group index for the quotative margin,

QUOTATIVE MARGIN

is represented by the array

$$\begin{bmatrix} A & B & C \\ 1 & 2 & 3 \\ \rho & \alpha & \chi \end{bmatrix}$$

which determines assignments $\alpha B2$, $\rho A1$, $\chi C3$ for the quotative margin. Since the individual who is agent α in quotative margin always goes to first person in quotation content, etc., we have A2, B1, C3 as invariants in the quotation content. This is just another way of saying that we need to permute the person vector components [1, 2, 3] by the same operator r, which was the group index for the quotative MARGIN, in order to give us the starting array (corresponding to I, the identity array for the quotation content). This starting array would thus be

$$\begin{bmatrix} A & B & C \\ 2 & 1 & 3 \\ \rho & \alpha & \chi \end{bmatrix}$$

QUOTATION CONTENT

is then derived by regarding this array as the starting array and then permuting the case vector with the operations of the group, viz. Table V.

TABLE V

	A	B	C	Corresponding valid case-cast-person combination			One possible surface structure realization of this		
	2	1	3						
I	ρ	α	χ	αB1	ρA2	χC3	SB1	OA2	XC3
r	α	ρ	χ	αA2	ρB1	χC3	SA2	OB1	XC3
s	χ	α	ρ	αB1	ρC3	χA2	SB1	OC3	XA2
rs	α	χ	ρ	αA2	ρC3	χB1	SA2	OC3	XB1
sr	χ	ρ	α	αC3	ρB1	χA2	SC3	OB1	XA2
rsr	ρ	χ	α	αC3	ρA2	χB1	SC3	OA2	XB1

Corresponding data is found in section 5 under group index r quotative margin.

4.2.3 *Quotative Margin Group Index s*

When s ≡ (1′) (2′ 3′) is group index for the quotative margin,

QUOTATIVE MARGIN

is represented by the array

$$\begin{bmatrix} A & B & C \\ 1 & 2 & 3 \\ \alpha & \chi & \rho \end{bmatrix}$$

which determines αA1, χB2, ρC3 for the quotative margin and A1, B3, C2 as invariants for quotation content. For reasons given under r (4.2.2), we get to the starting array for the quotation content by permuting the components of the person vector by the quotative MARGIN group index operation s to get

$$\begin{bmatrix} A & B & C \\ 1 & 3 & 2 \\ \alpha & \chi & \rho \end{bmatrix}$$

as starting array for

QUOTATION CONTENT

whose full specification in terms of pronominal reference is now as in Table VI.

TABLE VI

	A	B	C	Corresponding valid case-cast-person combination			One possible surface structure realization of this		
	1	3	2						
I	α	χ	ρ	αA1	ρC2	χB3	SA1	OC2	XB3
r	ρ	χ	α	αC2	ρA1	χB3	SC2	OA1	XB3
s	α	ρ	χ	αA1	ρB3	χC2	SA1	OB3	XC2
rs	χ	ρ	α	αC2	ρB3	χA1	SC2	OB3	XA1
sr	ρ	α	χ	αB3	ρA1	χC2	SB3	OA1	XC2
rsr	χ	α	ρ	αB3	ρC2	χA1	SB3	OC2	XA1

Corresponding data will be found in section 5 under group index s, quotative margin.

4.2.4 *Quotative Margin Group Index rs*

When rs ≡ (1′ 3′ 2′) is group index for the quotative margin,

QUOTATIVE MARGIN

is represented by the array

$$\begin{bmatrix} A & B & C \\ 1 & 2 & 3 \\ \chi & \alpha & \rho \end{bmatrix}$$

which determines $\alpha B2$, $\chi A1$, $\rho C3$ for the quotative margin, and A3, B1, C2 as invariants for the quotation content. For reasons given in (4.2.2) we get to the starting array for the quotation content by permuting the components of the person vector by the quotative MARGIN group index operation rs to get

$$\begin{bmatrix} A & B & C \\ 3 & 1 & 2 \\ \chi & \alpha & \rho \end{bmatrix}$$

as starting array for

QUOTATION CONTENT

whose full specification in terms of pronominal reference is now as in Table VII.

TABLE VII

	A	B	C	Corresponding valid case-cast-person combination			One possible surface structure realization of this		
	3	1	2						
I	χ	α	ρ	αB1	ρC2	χA3	SB1	OC2	XA3
r	χ	ρ	α	αC2	ρB1	χA3	SC2	OB1	XA3
s	ρ	α	χ	αB1	ρA3	χC2	SB1	OA3	XC2
rs	ρ	χ	α	αC2	ρA3	χB1	SC2	OA3	XB1
sr	α	ρ	χ	αA3	ρB1	χC2	SA3	OB1	XC2
rsr	α	χ	ρ	αA3	$\digamma$C2	χB1	SA3	OC2	XB1

Corresponding data is found in section 5 under group index rs quotative margin.

4.2.5 *Quotative Margin Group Index sr*

When sr $\equiv$ (1′ 2′ 3′) is group index for the quotative margin,

QUOTATIVE MARGIN

is represented by the array

$$\begin{bmatrix} A & B & C \\ 1 & 2 & 3 \\ \rho & \chi & \alpha \end{bmatrix}$$

which determines αC3, ρA1, χB2 for the quotative margin and A2, B3, C1 as invariants for the quotation content. For reasons given in (4.2.2) we get to the starting array for the quotation content by permuting the components of the person vector by the quotative MARGIN index operation sr, to get

$$\begin{bmatrix} A & B & C \\ 2 & 3 & 1 \\ \rho & \chi & \alpha \end{bmatrix}$$

as starting array for

QUOTATION CONTENT

whose full specification in terms of pronominal reference is now as in Table VIII.

TABLE VIII

	A	B	C	Corresponding valid case-cast-person combination			One possible surface structure realization of this		
	2	3	1						
I	ρ	χ	α	αC1	ρA2	χB3	SC1	OA2	XB3
r	α	χ	ρ	αA2	ρC1	χB3	SA2	OC1	XB3
s	χ	ρ	α	αC1	ρB3	χA2	SC1	OB3	XA2
rs	α	ρ	χ	αA2	ρB3	χC1	SA2	OB3	XC1
sr	χ	α	ρ	αB3	ρC1	χA2	SB3	OC1	XA2
rsr	ρ	α	χ	αB3	ρA2	χC1	SB3	OA2	XC1

Corresponding data is found in section 5 under group index sr quotative margin.

4.2.6 *Quotative Margin Group Index rsr*

When rsr ≡ (1′ 3′) (2′) is group index for the quotative margin,

QUOTATIVE MARGIN

is represented by the array

$$\begin{bmatrix} A & B & C \\ 1 & 2 & 3 \\ \chi & \rho & \alpha \end{bmatrix}$$

which determines αC3, ρB2, χA1 for the quotative margin, and A3, B2, C1 as invariants for the quotation content. For reasons given in (4.2.2) we get to the starting array for the quotation content by permuting the components of the person vector by the quotative MARGIN index operation rsr to get

$$\begin{bmatrix} A & B & C \\ 3 & 2 & 1 \\ \chi & \rho & \alpha \end{bmatrix}$$

as starting array for

QUOTATION CONTENT

whose full specification in terms of pronominal reference is now as in Table IX.

TABLE IX

	A	B	C	Corresponding valid case-cast-person combination			One possible surface structure realization of this		
	3	2	1						
I	χ	ρ	α	αC1	ρB2	χA3	SC1	OB2	XA3
r	χ	α	ρ	αB2	ρC1	χA3	SB2	OC1	XA3
s	ρ	χ	α	αC1	ρA3	χB2	SC1	OA3	XB2
rs	ρ	α	χ	αB2	ρA3	χC1	SB2	OA3	XC1
sr	α	χ	ρ	αA3	ρC1	χB2	SA3	OC1	XB2
rsr	α	ρ	χ	αA3	ρB2	χC1	SA3	OB2	XC1

Corresponding data is found in section 5 under group index rsr quotative margin.

5. COMPLETE DATA CHARTS FOR A SINGLE QUOTATIVE MARGIN

We pass now from theory to actual data. Thus the following are charts of representative data in English for the case of a single quotative margin, showing how the results obtained by the permutation operations in section 4 are 'realized' in actual data in English. Under each pronoun we give the function-cast-person triple, thus determining the pronominal reference. The reader is invited to check these pronominal references against those predicted by the theory in section 4.

Quotative Margin (Group Index I)	Quotation Content (Group Index shown in right-hand column)	
I (Abe) *said to you* (Bill) SA1 OB2	*'I saw you yesterday'* SA1 OB2	(I)
	'You saw me yesterday' SB2 OA1	(r)
	'I saw him yesterday' SA1 OC̲3	(s)
	'You saw him yesterday' SB2 OC̲3	(rs)
	'He saw me yesterday' SC̲3 OA1	(sr)
	'He saw you yesterday' SC̲3 OB2	(rsr)

Invariants for the quotation content A1, B2, C3. The theory corresponding to this is worked out in section 4.2.1. The reader is invited to check the pronominal references there.

Quotative Margin (Group Index r)	Quotation Content (Group Index shown in right-hand column)	
You (Bill) *said to me* (Abe) SB2 OA1	*'I saw you yesterday'* SB1 OA2	(I)
	'You saw me yesterday' SA2 OB1	(r)
	'I saw him yesterday' SB1 OC̲3	(s)
	'You saw him yesterday' SA2 OC̲3	(rs)
	'He saw me yesterday' SC̲3 OB1	(sr)
	'He saw you yesterday' SC̲3 OA2	(rsr)

Invariants in the quotation content A2, B1, C3. The theory corresponding to this is found in section 4.2.2, where the reader is invited to check the pronominal reference.

Quotative Margin (Group Index s)		Quotation Content (Group Index shown in right-hand column)		
I (Abe) *said to him* (Charlie)		'*I saw you yesterday*'		
SA1	OC3	SA1	OC2	(I)
		'*You saw me yesterday*'		
		SC2	OA1	(r)
		'*I saw him yesterday*'		
		SA1	O<u>B</u>3	(s)
		'*You saw him yesterday*'		
		SC2	O<u>B</u>3	(rs)
		'*He saw me yesterday*'		
		S<u>B</u>3	OA1	(sr)
		'*He saw you yesterday*'		
		S<u>B</u>3	OC2	(rsr)

Invariants in quotation content are A1, C2, B3. The theory corresponding to this is found in section 4.2.3, where the reader is invited to check the pronominal reference.

Quotative Martin (Group Index rs)		Quotation Content (Group Index shown in right-hand column)		
You (Bill) *said to him* (Charlie)		'*I saw you yesterday*'		
SB2	OC3	SB1	OC2	(I)
		'*You saw me yesterday*'		
		SC2	OB1	(r)
		'*I saw him yesterday*'		
		SB1	OA3	(s)
		'*You saw him yesterday*'		
		SC2	OA3	(rs)
		'*He saw me yesterday*'		
		SA3	OB1	(sr)
		'*He saw you yesterday*'		
		SA3	OC2	(rsr)

Invariants for quotation content B1, C2, A3. The theory corresponding to this is found in section 4.2.4.

Quotative Margin (Group Index sr)		Quotation Content (Group Index shown in right-hand column)		
He (Charlie) *said to me* (Abe)		'*I saw you yesterday*'		
SC3	OA1	SC1	OA2	(I)
		'*You saw me yesterday*'		
		SA2	OC1	(r)
		'*I saw him yesterday*'		
		SC1	OB3	(s)
		'*You saw him yesterday*'		
		SA2	OB3	(rs)
		'*He saw me yesterday*'		
		S$\underline{B}$3	OC1	(sr)
		'*He saw you yesterday*'		
		S$\underline{B}$3	OA2	(rsr)

Invariants for quotation content are A2, C1, B3. The theory corresponding to this is found in section 4.2.5.

Quotative Margin (Group Index rsr)		Quotation Content (Group Index shown in right-hand column)		
He (Charlie) *said to you* (Bill)		'*I saw you yesterday*'		
SC3	OB2	SC1	OB2	(I)
		'*You saw me yesterday*'		
		SB2	OC1	(r)
		'*I saw him yesterday*'		
		SC1	O$\underline{A}$3	(s)
		'*You saw him yesterday*'		
		SB2	O$\underline{A}$3	(rs)
		'*He saw me yesterday*'		
		S$\underline{A}$3	OC1	(sr)
		'*He saw you yesterday*'		
		S$\underline{A}$3	OB2	(rsr)

Invariants in quotation content are C1, B2, A3. The theory corresponding to this is found in section 4.2.6.

6. SAMPLE DATA CHARTS FOR DOUBLE EMBEDDING OF QUOTATIVE MARGIN

In this section we merely present some sample combinations of double quotative margin so as to indicate the trend. Then we move towards proving a general theorem. There is no point in enumerating all 36 possible cases, this would be sheer dog-work.

EXAMPLE 1

First Quotative Margin (Group Index rs)	Second Quotative Margin (Group Index r)	Quotation Content (Group Index shown in right-hand column)	
You (B) *said to him* (C) SB2 OC3	*"You said to me* SC2 OB1	*'I hit you'"* SC1 OB2	(I)
		'You hit me'" SB2 OC1	(r)
Product of Group Indices (in order) $=$rs.r$=$rsr		*'I hit him'"* SC1 O$\underline{A}$3	(s)
and this resultant group index gives us the proper pronominal references in the quotation content which can be checked in section 4.2.6, i.e., where the case for a single quotative margin of group index rsr is calculated.		*'You hit him'"* SB2 O$\underline{A}$3	(rs)
		'He hit me'" S$\underline{A}$3 OC1	(sr)
		'He hit you'" S$\underline{A}$3 OB2	(rsr)

EXAMPLE 2

First Quotative Margin (Group Index r)	Second Quotative Margin (Group Index rs)	Quotation Content (Group Index given in right-hand column)	
You (B) *said to me* (A) SB2 OA1	*"You said to him* SA2 OC3	*'I hit you'"* SA1 OC2	(I)
		'You hit me'" SC2 OA1	(r)
Product of Group Indices (in order) $=$rrs$=$r^{2}s$=$s		*'I hit him'"* SA1 O$\underline{B}$3	(s)
and resultant s gives us the proper pronominal references in the quotation content which can be checked in section 4.2.3.		*'You hit him'"* SC2 O$\underline{B}$3	(rs)
		'He hit me'" S$\underline{B}$3 OA1	(sr)
		'He hit you'" S$\underline{B}$3 OC2	(rsr)

EXAMPLE 3

First Quotative Margin (Group Index s)		Second Quotative Margin (Group Index r)		Quotation Content (Group Index given in right-hand column)	
I (A) *said to him* (C)		*"You said to me*		*'I hit you'"*	
SA1	OC3	SB2	OA1	SC1 OA2	(I)
				'You hit me'"	
				SA2 O$\underline{C}$1	(r)
Product of Group Indices (in order)				*'I hit him'"*	
=s.r=sr				SC1 O$\underline{B}$3	(s)
and this resultant group index does give the proper referents in the quotation content (cf. section 4.2.5).				*'You hit him'"*	
				SA2 O$\underline{B}$3	(rs)
				'He hit me'"	
				S$\underline{B}$3 OC1	(sr)
				'He hit you'"	
				S$\underline{B}$3 OA2	(rsr)

EXAMPLE 4

First Quotative Margin (Group Index r)		Second Quotative Margin (Group Index s)		Quotation Content (Group Index given in right-hand column)	
You (B) *said to me* (A)		*"I said to him*		*'I hit you'"*	
SB2	OA1	SB1	OC3	SB1 OC2	(I)
				'You hit me'"	
				SC2 OB1	(r)
Product of Group Indices (in order)				*'I hit him'"*	
=r.s=rs				SB1 O$\underline{A}$3	(s)
and this resultant group index does give the proper referents in the quotation content (cf. section 4.2.4).				*'You hit him'"*	
				SC2 O$\underline{A}$3	(rs)
				'He hit me'"	
				S$\underline{A}$3 OB1	(sr)
				'He hit you'"	
				S$\underline{A}$3 OC2	(rsr)

EXAMPLE 5

First Quotative Margin (Group Index r)		Second Quotative Margin (Group Index r)		Quotation Content (Group Index given in right-hand column)	
You (B) *said to me* (A)		*"You said to me*		*'I hit you'"*	
SB2	OA1	SA2	OB1	SA1 OB2	(I)
				'You hit me'"	
				SB2 OA1	(r)
Product of Group Indices in order =r.r; from the multiplication table				*'I hit him'"*	
				SA1 OC3	(s)
$r^2 = I$					
and in fact we find that the pronominal references in this quotation content check with those found for I (cf. section 4.2.1).				*'You hit him'"*	
				SB2 OC3	(rs)
				'He hit me'"	
				SC2 OA1	(sr)
				'He hit you'"	
				SC3 OB2	(rsr)

EXAMPLE 6

First Quotative Margin (Group Index s)		Second Quotative Margin (Group Index s)		Quotation Content (Group Index given in right-hand column)	
I (A) *said to him* (C)		*"I said to him*		*'I saw you'"*	
SA1	OC3	SA1	OB3	SA1 OB2	(I)
				'You saw me'"	
				SB2 OA1	(r)
Product of Group Indices in order =s.s; from the multiplication table				*'I saw him'"*	
				SA1 OC3	(s)
$s^2 = I$					
and in fact we find that the pronominal references in the quotation content check with those found for I (cf. section 4.2.1).				*'You saw him'"*	
				SB2 OC3	(rs)
				'He saw me'"	
				SC3 OA1	(sr)
				'He saw me'"	
				SC3 OB2	(rsr)

EXAMPLE 7

A speaking to B

First Quotative Margin (Group Index rs)		Second Quotative Margin (Group Index rs)		Quotation Content (Group Index given in right-hand column)		
You (B) *said to him* (C)		*"You* (C) *said to him* (A)		*'I hit you'"*		
SB2	OC3	SC2	OA1	SC1 OA2		(I)
				'You hit me'"		
				SA2 OC1		(r)
Product (in order) of Group Indices:				*'I hit him'"*		
$\qquad$ (rs)^2=sr				SC1 OB3		(s)
and pronominal references will be found under sr (cf. section 4.2.5) and these do check with last column.				*'You hit him'"*		
				SA2 OB3		(rs)
				'He hit me'"		
				SB3 OC1		(sr)
				'He hit you'"		
				SB3 OA2		(rsr)

EXAMPLE 8

A speaking to B

First Quotative Margin (Group Index sr)		Second Quotative Margin (Group Index sr)		Quotation Content (Group Index given in right-hand column)		
He (C) *said to me* (A)		*"He* (B) *said to me* (C)		*'I hit you'"*		
SC3	OA1	SB3	OC1	SB1 OC2		(I)
				'You hit me'"		
				SC2 OB1		(r)
Product (in order) of Group Indices				*'I hit him'"*		
$\qquad$ (sr)^2=rs				SB1 OA3		(s)
and pronominal references will be found under rs of section 4.2.4 and these do check with the last column.				*'You hit him'"*		
				SC2 OA3		(rs)
				'He hit me'"		
				SA3 OB1		(sr)
				'He hit you'"		
				SA3 OC2		(rsr)

7. TRIPLE EMBEDDING

We give one example only of triple embedding before passing on to the general theorem.

A speaking to B, says

First Quotative Margin (Group Index rs)	Second Quotative Margin (Group Index rs)	Third Quotative Margin (Group Index rs)	Quotation Content (Group Index given in right-hand column)	

You (B)
   said to him (C)
	You (C)
	   said to him (A)
		You (A)
		   said to him (B)
			I hit you
			SA1 OB2
				(I)

			You hit me SB2 OA1	(r)
Product of Group Indices $=$ rs.rs.rs $=$ (rs)^3 $=$ I			*I hit him* SA1 OC3	(s)
			You hit him SB2 OC3	(rs)
			He hit me SC3 OA1	(sr)
			He hit you SC3 OB2	(rsr)

8. GENERAL N-EMBEDDING COMBINATION THEOREM

8.1 *The Theorem*

We are required to prove that:

(i) The assignment of function-cast-person to the quotation content is uniquely determined by the 'effective group index' of the quotative margin.

(ii) The 'effective group index' of a recursively embedded quotative margin[15] equals the group product of the individual group indices of the separate individual quotative margins, the order of the group factors from left to right being the same order as the order of their corresponding margins also from left to right.

(This general theorem has been exemplified in particular cases in the preceding two sections).

8.2 *The Proof*

We may assume with no loss of generality that *A speaks to B* (with C therefore in the background).[16] Then in the first (or left-most) margin, CAST is determined with respect to PERSON by the following array

---

[15] i.e. the effective group index of a string of quotative margins, each one being embedded in the one preceding it.

[16] Suppose it were not the case that A spoke to B, i.e., suppose the speaking was done between another pair of the cast. Then a simple permutation of the cast would cover this.

$$\begin{bmatrix} A & B & C \\ 1 & 2 & 3 \end{bmatrix}$$

because in the initial state as we have defined it, A is talking and therefore 1 (first person), B is talked-to and therefore 2 (second person), C is background and therefore 3 (third person).

There is still open to A, the speaker, a choice of function. For typographical convenience we shall use the symbols [S, O, X], but the reader is reminded that the treatment in the proof of this theorem would be completely unchanged if these symbols were interpreted as case (deep-structure) labels.

Suppose that A, the speaker, decides to use his first quotative margin corresponding to the permutation ω_1 of the unpermuted function set [S, O, X]. Here, of course, ω_1 can be any one of the operations of the symmetric group P_3 as we have defined it.

Thus the function-cast-person triples in margin 1 are given explicitly by the array

$$\omega_1 \text{ (Margin 1)} \Leftrightarrow \begin{bmatrix} \omega_1 \, [S, & O, & X] \\ A & B & C \\ 1 & 2 & 3 \end{bmatrix}$$

where the permutation ω_1 [S, O, X] will re-arrange that vector with its components in some other order with respect to the cast and person vectors.

Now to see how quotative margin 2 is affected by quotative margin 1 with regard to pronominal reference, we note that:

S in margin 1 always becomes 1st person in margin 2,

O in margin 1 always becomes 2nd person in margin 2,

X in margin 1 always becomes 3rd person in margin 2.

That is to say: in the starting array (or identity array) for margin 2, the SAME permutation ω_1, of the components of the function vector [S, O, X] made in margin 1, must now be made on the components of the person vector [1, 2, 3] in order to get the proper person assignment with respect to the cast for margin 2, i.e.,

$$I \text{ (Margin 2)} \Leftrightarrow \begin{bmatrix} \omega_1 \, [S, & O, & X] \\ A & B & C \\ \omega_1 \, [1, & 2, & 3] \end{bmatrix}$$

is the starting array for margin 2.

Once again, just as for margin 1, the speaker (A) still has open to him, a choice of function; let us represent this by the permutation ω_2 on the [S, O, X] set, already permuted according to the permutation of ω_1 of margin 1. Then the function-cast-person triple of margin 2 is given by[17]

[17]   It may be of help to the reader to observe here that for purposes of pronominal reference at any rate, the order of the columns in any array representing a margin is quite immaterial, so long as we preserve the integrity of alignment of the column vectors. Hence, application of permutations, as we have done, is a perfectly legitimate procedure.

$$\omega_2 \text{ (Margin 2)} \Leftrightarrow \begin{bmatrix} (\omega_1 \ \omega_2) \ [\text{S}, \ \text{O}, \ \text{X}] \\ \text{A} \quad \text{B} \quad \text{C} \\ \omega_1 \ [1, \ 2, \ 3] \end{bmatrix}$$

where the composite operator $(\omega_1 \ \omega_2)$ means that we operate on our vector first with ω_1 and then on the result of this first operation with ω_2; we enclose the composite operator with round brackets to denote that we regard it as essentially a single operator to be interpreted in this way. In fact, by the closure property of the symmetric group $(\omega_1 \ \omega_2)$ will always be a single operator of P_3.

Now, again for margin 3, we must make S, O, X in ω_2 (Margin 2) correspond respectively to 1, 2, 3 in I (Margin 3); therefore the starting array for margin 3 will be

$$\text{I (Margin 3)} \Leftrightarrow \begin{bmatrix} (\omega_1 \ \omega_2) \ [\text{S}, \ \text{O}, \ \text{X}] \\ \text{A} \quad \text{B} \quad \text{C} \\ (\omega_1 \ \omega_2) \ [1, \ 2, \ 3] \end{bmatrix}$$

and this is exactly the same form for I (Margin 2) but with one extra factor, namely ω_2, added to the group product in the correct order as specified by the theorem. Thus an induction is clearly suggested.

8.2.1 *The Induction*

ASSUME the following two correspondences hold for the case of n margins

$$\begin{cases} \text{I (Margin n)} \Leftrightarrow \\ \\ \omega_n \text{ (Margin n)} \Leftrightarrow \end{cases} \begin{bmatrix} (\omega_1 \ ... \ \omega_{n-1}) & [\text{S}, \ \text{O}, \ \text{X}] \\ & \text{A} \quad \text{B} \quad \text{C} \\ (\omega_1 \ ... \ \omega_{n-1}) & [1, \ 2, \ 3] \\ (\omega \ ... \ \omega_{n-1} \ \omega_n) & [\text{S}, \ \text{O}, \ \text{X}] \\ & \text{A} \quad \text{B} \quad \text{C} \\ (\omega_1 \ ... \ \omega_{n-1}) & [1, \ 2, \ 3] \end{bmatrix}$$

We need to prove that formulae of the same shape hold also for $(+1)$ margins.

From the assumed formula for ω_n (Margin n), we can get to the starting formula for Margin $(n+1)$ by making the same permutation $[1, 2, 3]$ in I (Margin $(n+1)$), as was the permutation of $[\text{S}, \text{O}, \text{X}]$ in ω_n (Margin n). This ensures that Subject in margin n goes to 1st person in margin $(n+1)$, etc. Thus

$$\text{I (Margin } (n+1)) \Leftrightarrow \begin{bmatrix} (\omega_1 \ ... \ \omega_{n-1} \ \omega_n) \ [\text{S}, \ \text{O}, \ \text{X}] \\ \text{A} \quad \text{B} \quad \text{C} \\ (\omega_1 \ ... \ \omega_{n-1} \ \omega_n) \ [1, \ 2, \ 3] \end{bmatrix}$$

Then, since speaker A is allowed an arbitrary permutation ω_{n+1} of function for margin $(n+1)$, we get

$$
_{n+1}(\text{Margin } (n+1)) \Leftrightarrow
\begin{bmatrix}
(\omega_1 \ \dots \ \omega_{n-1} \ \omega_n \ \omega_{n+1}) & [S, \ O, \ X] \\
& A \ \ B \ \ C \\
(\omega_1 \ \dots \ \omega_{n-1} \ \omega_n) & [1, \ 2, \ 3]
\end{bmatrix} \dots
$$

and these last two formulae for margin $(n+1)$ are of exactly the same shape as the corresponding formulae for margin n. Hence, if the formulae are true for any n, they will be true for $n+1$; but since the formulae are clearly true for $n = 1, 2$, they are therefore true for any integer value of n. QED.

APPENDIX I

Proof of relationships between the generating elements

The following relationships among the generating elements r, s were stated in section 2.8. We here supply the proof.

GIVEN r, s, such that I, r, s, rs, sr, rsr form a group with $r^2 = s^2 = (sr)^3 = I$. (Alternatively, start with $(rs)^3 = I$.)

R.T.P.
    (i) $rsr = srs$
    (ii) $(rsr)^2 = (srs)^2 = I$
    (iii) $srsr = rs$
    (iv) $rsrs = sr$
    (v) $rsrsr = s$
    (vi) $srsrs = r$
    (vii) $(rs)^3 = (sr)^3 = I$
    (viii) $r = r^{-1}$, etc.

PROOFS

of (i): We have given

    $(sr)^3 = I$ (defining relations)
    $srsrsr = I$

Post-multiply successively with r, s, r and remembering that $r^2 = I = s^2$, we have at once

    $srs = rsr$ QED

of (ii): From $(sr)^3 = srsrsr = I$ (given in defining relations)
we can bracket because of the law of associativity.

    $(srs)(rsr) = I$

From (i) $srs = rsr$

    $(srs)(srs) = I$
    $(srs)^2 = I$

Therefore

$$(rsr)^2 = I \qquad \text{QED}$$

of (iii): From $(sr)^3 = srsrsr = I$ (given)
Post-multiply successively by r, then by s; we get since $r^2 = s^2 = I$

$$srsr = rs \qquad \text{QED}$$

of (iv): From $(sr)^3 = srsrsr = I$
Pre-multiply by s, then post-multiply by r; we get since $r^2 = s^2 = I$

$$rsrs = sr \qquad \text{QED}$$

of (v) and (vi): From $(sr)^3 = I$

$$srsrsr = I$$

Pre-multiply by s; we get

$$rsrsr = s \text{ which is (v)}$$

Post-multiply original equation by r; we get

$$srsrs = r \text{ which is (vi)}$$

of (vii): From $srsrsr = I$ (given)
Pre-multiply by s, then post-multiply by s; we get

$$rsrsrs = s^2 = I$$
$$(rs)^3 = I = (sr)^3 \qquad \text{(which is vii)}$$

of (viii): clear.

PART TWO

RELIGIOUS

STRANGE DIMENSIONS OF TRUTH*

A sentence must never be interpreted out of context, as any scholar knows. It is pointless, furthermore, to suggest that separate sentences are true OUT of a context of linguistic and nonlinguistic experience. Recently, however, some theologians have claimed that no separate sentence can be wholly true EVEN IN context.

I refer specifically to William Hordern's *The Case for a New Reformation Theology* (Westminster Press, 1959). Hordern takes two approaches to make his point. The first starts from affirmations concerning the social function of language. The second deals with the presence of areas of meaning — of ambiguity — represented by the words of a language.

INFORMATION, UNDERSTANDING, AND TRUTH

As for the first, Hordern adopts the point of view that a "proposition is a tool; it has a task to perform, and to perform its task it must be spoken and it must be received" (58). Language, as a tool, must therefore — he implies — do its job of affecting someone EXACTLY. Inerrant propositions must "come into the understanding of the hearer, meaning precisely what the speaker meant by them" (59). This linkage from speaker to hearer must be so tight that "to express infallibly what the speaker wants to say, we must also say that it is impossible to hear it otherwise than the speaker intended it to be heard" (59). He would conclude that "An objective revelation is not inerrant unless it is inerrantly received", since the "subjective receiver of revelation is an indispensable link in the chain", and, following Kierkegaard, Hordern maintains that "there is NO TRUTH UNLESS THERE IS TRUTH TO ME" (p. 59, emphasis added). Thus "If there is to be inerrant revelation of propositions, the hearer would have to be as inerrant as the speaker" (59).

If we ask for the reason lying behind the adoption of this view of language we find in his book that it developed as a challenge to what he considers the "basic premise" of "fundamentalism or conservatism" — "that what God reveals is information" (57). He maintains with "modern theologians" that "what God reveals is not propositions nor information — what God reveals is God" (61-62; see also 55-

57, 68). Hordern rejects the fundamentalist view that information has been revealed to us by God since — he tells us — if he accepts information as being revealed this implies "with stunning logic" (57) that the Bible and the interpreting church must both be considered infallible — which he considers impossible. He then replaces this informational concept of revelation with that of revelation as being composed of the knowledge of God directly.

We have no objection to treating the contract of man with God in Christ as being part of — or one kind of — revelation. We object rather to the elimination of information from the total amount or kinds of revelation available to us.

Furthermore, we do not deny that language has social relevance and purpose, or that language is designed to communicate with and affect other people. What we deny is that language has ONLY the one function of linkage from one person to another. We claim that it includes also the purposes of man talking with himself; of formulating ideas for himself; of STORING ideas in sayings, legends, or libraries; the presentation of information or truth in such a way that it is AVAILABLE for others who THEN OR LATER are or will be PREPARED TO RECEIVE IT. It is the pair of concepts of availability on the one hand and preparedness for reception on the other hand which seem to me to have been overlooked (or perhaps rejected?) by Hordern.

These omissions may lead to ultimate skepticism if pushed to their logical conclusion. Let us assume, for example, that a teacher of very great scientific competence gives a lecture today to an audience of young graduate students. A tape recording is made of the lecture. Members of the class are asked to comment on or to repeat the day's lecture. Let us suppose that none of them understood the lecture. From the point of view of Hordern this would not be mere failure to understand truth — it would be evidence that the lecture was NOT INERRANT, specifically, and by implication would also be evidence that the lecture is NOT WHOLLY TRUE.

Three years later, when these same students have had further training, they listen to the old tape again. They now understand it. The material, which formerly was not truth by Hordern's treatment, would now become truth because it would have done what propositions are meant to do.

In order to avoid this conclusion, I would claim, on the contrary, that the initial lecture was in fact TRUE, and was in principle AVAILABLE. It needed, however, PREPARED RECEIVERS for its adequate reception.

Availability would imply that in order for material revealed to be at least IN PRINCIPLE understandable to adequate receivers, it could not be phrased in a heavenly language which was permanently opaque to all human beings. It might, on the other hand, be interpreted as being available only to persons with the proper experience. One component of such experience is available to people, on a natural level, if they can read easily.

Preparedness may involve a delay while further data is being made available through succeeding events. Understanding — but not the presence versus the absence of truth — would then be retroactive.

UNDERSTANDING is not in the same DIMENSION with truth. Jesus had some things to tell to his disciples which they were not prepared to receive fully at the moment, and which they would understand only in retrospect, but which I consider to have been fully true even before the disciples were able to understand these teachings. He stated that the Son of Man was to be killed, and was to rise the third day. The disciples did not understand this (Mark 9:31-32; Luke 9:44-45; 18:31-34), even though we now do. The written Scriptures were also at times understood in retrospect — as concerning the triumphal entry (John 12:16), or prophecies of Christ's coming (Luke 24:45). Similarly, lack of belief does not invalidate the truth of an utterance — as when Christ warned Peter about denial before the cock crew (John 13:38), or when the Jews did not 'understand' because they did not 'hear' (John 8:43). Nor does teaching in parables, partly hidden (cf. John 16:25), make an item false.

Christ, furthermore, claimed that truth came through human language. Even though "they understood not", He insisted that "he that sent me is true" and "I speak ... those things which I have heard of him" (John 8:26-28). And "they have kept thy word. ... For I have given unto them the words which thou gavest me; and they have received them, and have known surely that I came out from thee. ... I have given them thy word. ... Sanctify them through thy truth; thy WORD IS TRUTH" (John 17:6, 8, 14, 17).

LANGUAGE, AMBIGUITY, AND TRUTH

Hordern's second objection to considering revelation as containing true information lies in the fact that sentences can be ambiguous.

Specifically, he suggests that the sentence "God is love" (I John 4:8) is such that "we cannot consider it infallible" since "To many a hearer it will convey the wrong impression, because the word 'love' today has many connotations that cannot be applied to God" (64); to get the desired specific meaning of love from this context many other acts of God in the background history of the situation must be pointed out. Similarly, in reference to the sentence "Thou art the Christ" (Matt. 16:16-23), he states that "Far from being an infallible statement, even to the man who spoke it, the statement had an ambiguous meaning" (69), since Peter was rebuked for his further statements that seemed to have grown out of the immediate situation. Thus, for Hordern, ambiguity in a statement implies error in the statement itself.

If this were to be granted, it would follow inevitably that no statement is ever true. EVERY word has several different meanings — or, in technical terms, it covers an area of meaning — even though the differences be small. Each context in which the word occurs forces a slightly different meaning to the word — even if it be by an infinitesimal amount — in a way that the nonprofessional observer would not suspect. With a bit of thought, however, he can see that the exact physical activity implied by the word *drive* differs sharply in the phrases *to drive a car, to drive a horse, to drive a nail,* and *to drive a point home.* The ability of various contexts to force such changes of meaning is vital to the function of language itself. Without it, no learning could take place, no translation could ever be made, and communication would cease.

Since scientific statements, as well as statements of the man in the street, are all subject to analysis of the words contained in them as having a breadth of meaning, it would clearly follow that Hordern has in fact rejected the possibility of any wholly-true science. The turn of the wheel is curiously complete. Having, along with the liberals, rejected fundamentalism because it "seemed to require intellectual hari-kari" (cf. 108) in its relationships to science, etc. (cf. also 53, 60, 86, 92, 113), Hordern has in fact adopted a position which, in my view, in turn breeds intellectual hari-kari through denying full truth value to ANY of the statements or summaries or propositions of science.

DIMENSION OF TRUTH VERSUS ERROR

We now ask: How can we avoid Hordern's conclusion that ambiguity implies error? We can do so if we view statements as containing DIMENSIONS — as we hinted in the first section of this article.

The first of these dimensions of statement has TRUTH at one pole and ERROR at the other. We have in mind the ordinary meaning of the words true and false: Truth in a statement is based upon information which can be relied upon. Error and falsehood are reports of observation, information, or judgment which cannot be relied upon.

In this view a true statement about weather reflects the measurable facts of humidity, temperature, and so on. A person who operates on the basis of such a report will find himself acting adequately. As Edward J. Carnell says: "The true is the quality of that judgment or proposition which, when followed out into the total witness of facts in our experience, does not disappoint our expectation" (*An Introduction to Christian Apologetics* [1956] 45).

THE DIMENSION OF MAGNIFICATION

A second dimension of statements differs sharply from the first: WE DO NOT WISH TO APPLY DIRECTLY TO THIS CHARACTERISTIC OF STATEMENTS EITHER THE TERM TRUTH OR THE TERM ERROR. The contrast referred to is rather a difference which may be called HIGH MAGNIFICATION versus LOW MAGNIFICATION, using the optical term metaphorically. If we look at a fly under a low-powered magnifying glass we may be able to see the whole fly with considerable detail involved. If we wish to see much more detail about the structure of the fly, we must use a higher-powered micro-scope. The price we pay for this fine detail, however, is very great — the fly as a whole cannot be seen all at once. The PATTERN of the fly as a whole has disappeared from view. As others have said, one cannot find a face with a microscope. Sim-ilarly, as regards language, if one writes for a beginner an extremely intricate text-book on the laws of physics, including elaborate details, illustrations, reservations, implications, and the like, the beginner cannot adequately get information from the book.

Neither the detailed treatment nor one showing the overall pattern should be called true as such, and neither should be called false as such. Truth and error may both be found at EACH POLE of this kind of contrast. A detailed statement may be true or it may be false. Degree of detail in a statement is not of itself either true or false.

Language is adequate to accomplish the aim of communicating information at any level of magnification. One must not, however, demand that SIMULTANEOUSLY both exhaustive detail and general pattern must always be presented. It is only God who is able to grasp simultaneously ultimate pattern and infinite detail.

The Bible, in general, chooses to have a low amplification in order to have a high concentration of meaningful pattern present.

No scientific statement, on the other hand, can ever reach an ultimate degree of magnification. If one wishes to claim that a true statement must have the highest magnification, then no scientific statement can ever be true — there is always more detail possible. To equate truth with magnification is to abandon scientific discourse.

THE DIMENSION OF RELEVANCE

Degrees of RELEVANCE lead to a third dimension of statement.

Contextual resolution of ambiguity can be viewed in this light. Contexts cause changes in the meanings of words, as we indicated above, but they also force the hearer's SELECTION of those specific meanings which are relevant to the intention of the writer. In the phrase *to drive a nail*, one cannot rationally assume that the writer means 'to control the direction of movement of a nail by moving it with reins'. The context provided by a sentence, therefore, can — and often does — eliminate the irrelevant ambiguity inherent in an isolated word. Context provided by a para-graph — or a whole book — can also eliminate ambiguities inherent in isolated sentences. The sentence *God is love*, interpreted in the context of the Bible, is nar-rowed in the possible range of its meanings. Language, by context, is ADEQUATE to portray truth by using words each of which by itself would be ambiguous.

The technique by which language carries out its business of selecting specific, relevant, components out of multiple-available components has reference to the way in which words in context influence one another. The process is extremely powerful. Without it, no language could ultimately function, even though the process is not yet too well understood. (Compare Robert E. Longacre, "Items in Context: Their Bearing on Translation Theory", *Language*, 34 [1958], 482-491.)

Sharpness of focus on some one relevant part of the meaning of a word (or sentence) CAN ALWAYS BE INCREASED if one chooses. Sharpness is often achieved at the cost of more words, by a longer explanation. Yet, relevance is not magnification. Technical formulas, such as those of symbolic logic, have a kind of precision achieved by brevity, not amplification, since irrelevant words are pruned away. An artistically sharp-cut verbal sketch of a situation may make clear more effectively those parts of a person's character relevant to the author's interest than can a rambling ten-year diary.

We must keep truth tied to the power of language to reveal relevant pattern rather than tying truth to an unattainable infinity of irrelevant detail. One might assume that a story COULD be told with all details made explicit. This is impossible. The hare could then never catch the tortoise. Billions of molecular details would have to be specified, the story would stop, communication would cease, and truth could not exist in any way known to us now. Problems of round numbers, summaries of sermons, the use of *son* in the sense of 'descendant', and so on, take place in a perspective of the nature of language as adequate for truly communicating relevant information — relevant on different levels of magnification.

Can any statement then be true? According to Hordern, as the logic of his position would seem to me to lead him, the answer must be "No". According to my view of the nature of language, the answer must be "Yes".

I end, not with proof, but with a statement of one component of my personal faith: Fruitful discourse in science or theology requires us to believe that WITHIN THE CONTEXTS of normal discourse THERE ARE SOME TRUE STATEMENTS. Man MUST, sometimes, ACT as if he believed it — or die.

... WHAT'S ON MY MIND*

A PREVIEW

I am a scholar. The greatest proportion of my time is devoted to scholarship.
    I am a Christian. I am devoted to Christ, risen from the dead, my Lord.
    Is it strange to hybridize these two roles of mine? Let me give my first commercial:

The Word of God needs to be translated for the little tribes all around the world. I BELIEVE THAT IT IS ESPECIALLY APPROPRIATE THAT SCHOLARS BE INVOLVED IN BIBLE TRANSLATION.

If you are interested in studying HOW to analyze a language that has no alphabet or dictionary, write to the Summer Institute of Linguistics, Inc., Box 1960, Santa Ana, California 92702. If you want information regarding results, write the Wycliffe Bible Translators, Inc., Box 1960, Santa Ana, California 92702.
    Few of us remember that a large proportion of the pages of the Bible were written by the equivalent of Ph.D.'s. Daniel was on the level of a Ph.D., not a fuzzy-cheeked boy. He was under competitive examinations at the top of his culture in Israel, and enrolled in a graduate area study program ("skillful in all wisdom, and cunning in knowledge, and understanding science — whom they might teach the learning and the tongue of the Chaldeans", Daniel 1:4). When he presented his competitive doctoral dissertation, the king was honorary chairman of his committee.
    Moses was more than a Ph.D. Not only did he know all the wisdom of Egyptian engineering, but also all its hieroglyphics; he was a powerful orator (Acts 7:22). God broke his proud spirit and led him back to be identified with his people and to give us a large part of the Bible.
    But the scholars who wrote the Bible were also involved in social action.
    There is a rigid demand in the Word of God for a social order; and God in the Old Testament made rejection of social justice one of the bases for the rejection of the people of God.
    Our ancestors looked at the individual; we must now also look at society. Christ made the generalization that the poor would be with us always (Matthew 26:11). We may have the mistaken idea that we can get rid of poverty by medicine or other means, as is being attempted in India. But this allows more people to live — and the poor remain.

* *Stir, Change, Create* (Grand Rapids, Mich., Wm. B. Eerdmans, 1967), 9-15. Reprinted by permission.

There is a priority that an ethic of fairness and rugged individualism has to be careful of, lest it try to send rain only on the just. God sent His rain on the unjust as well. The sun rises on all, and the rain falls on all. If we allow our goodness to be applied only to someone who is good, then we refuse to apply goodness to someone who is bad. We reply with harsh words to someone who gives us harsh words, and eventually there is an automatic demand for evil to reply with evil. My actions at that point are not determined by my character but by the character of evil, and only good social action stimulates a good action from me. In the face of evil, then, can I be good? "Be ye therefore perfect, even as your Father in heaven is perfect" — whose social action gives rain upon the just and the unjust. Do not let evil control us, but let us control evil with good.

But where does a new social order come from, one producing social good? The answer is that in the plan of God a new social order sometimes has been initiated not by society as a whole, but by an individual within that society. Abraham was called out of Ur of the Chaldees, from a corrupt social order, and God promised that from him all society would be blessed. Abraham as an individual was the father of many nations, and as an heir to his faith, I am his child — socially.

And is there, then, a mother? The Bible says there is. In the book of Galatians we read about the Jerusalem which "is from above", which is the "mother of us all". Our own children are brought up in the womb of a culture, in the matrix of society. (Although Calvin would have called the Church, rather than a culture, our mother — see Book IV, Ch. 1, of his *Institutes*.) Whether I like it or not, my children in school are affected by the cultural climate. We have to keep our schools clean if we want a good chance of keeping our children clean.

The individual in culture is man, in the image of God, a citizen of heaven. What is it that man shares with God? Not fingernails, not hair, not eyebrows. Of course, the capacity for love and for joy — but these abstracts are very hard to study through science. There is one special thing, accessible to science, that we share with God. In the beginning was the WORD. In the beginning was ONE WHO COULD TALK — not a dynamo, not brute power, not some vague pantheistic all in all, but One who could talk to Himself in the Trinity, Father to Son, and Son to the Father. This ability to communicate, to think, to reason, to plan, is ours by the creative capacity of God. Not only can we mimic it, but we ourselves become creative.

Language is in the creative image of God.

This is an intended metaphor — not accidental — at the heart of the Bible. It is at the heart of the universe, and at the heart of personality. Without language you could not say, "I ought", or "I will". Nor could you say, "You must". Personality, in part, comes from language. Language expresses character. Jesus said, "I am the light of the world". He also said, "I am the truth". He, in person, is the truth, and He said of the Father, "Thy Word is truth", and "I have given them Thy Word".

Truth comes from the person first, and Christ is at the heart of all. I am not a

Platonist who looks for ultimate reality in ideas floating around in the abstract. I am a Christian who believes that Christ is the embodiment of truth, and that His words are therefore truth. Propositional revelation is true because it comes from a person who is true.

Another commercial:

Christ prayed to the Father, "I have given them Thy Word. ... So send I THEM — to give the Word." ... SO I AM A BIBLE TRANSLATOR.

If language is reflecting deeply the image of God, do not expect it to be simple, now or ever — nor for any theory to exhaust it. God could have made any animal, or any kind of a man He chose to make. But man as we know him, and as God wanted him to be, could not have been shaped like an elephant, have burrowed like a worm, been constrained by the mental limits of a bird or the communication restrictions of a moth. So it is with the incarnation of the message of God in the nature of Jesus Christ. Do not expect it to be simple. Language is complicated, because language has its source in PERSON.

Language identifies person. When God named Himself "I Am", He used language to identify the self-consciousness that can talk, since "in the beginning was the Word". Language identifies us. "Surely thou art also one of them — thy speech betrayeth thee." When the Ephraimites came to the ford of the Jordan they said "sibboleth" instead of saying "shibboleth" because they could not form the right groove in the blade of their tongue. Delete: 42,000 Ephraimites.

Next commercial:

They needed a practical course in phonetics!

Language is an identificational factor. In John 10:4 we read that the sheep hear His voice, and they follow Him. No other voice will they follow. The dead in the grave will hear the voice of the Son of God, and they will rise.

Life is deeper than language, and life is deeper than the intellect that works through language. Faith does not begin where logic leaves off. One of the most serious errors in our student world is the notion that logic precedes faith. But faith always, inevitably, and without exception must precede logic, intellect, judgment, and reason (and then it must go beyond them). Why? Logicians and mathematicians sometimes discuss the basis for our formal intellectual processes. A logician cannot begin until he adopts without proof (but by faith) some prelogical notions; he then prepares a set of axioms either with faith in their truth or arbitrarily, for an abstract meaningless system. Faith does not begin where logic leaves off: faith precedes logic. The intellect operates only within the matrix of faith, and faith goes on beyond the limits of its insights. And "he that cometh to God must believe that HE IS" (Hebrews 11:6). He who wants to be rational must first believe.

No wonder therefore that Christ said (Matthew 18:3): "Except you humble yourself as a little child, you cannot enter the kingdom of God." Why did He pray (Luke

10:21): "Father, I thank you, Lord of heaven and earth, that you have hidden these things from the wise and prudent, and have revealed them unto babes. Even so, Father, for it seemed GOOD. ..." Why was it good? It is good, because a child feels simultaneously with all things coming to him at once. The logical phase of adult intellect is limited to dealing with things in a rational, articulate, formal sense, one thing at a time. Words come out of our mouths one after another. The logician and the intellectual are limited by the nature of language and the academic rational process, one thing after another.

But life cannot operate by first building a head, and then a heart, and then a toe. The embryo has to grow them, mixed all up at once, and then differentiate them. A child learning a language reacts in a similar fashion. He does not memorize first the verbs, then the nouns, then the syntax. He learns all at once, in a matrix, or a network. It is simultaneous integration.

It is interesting to pretend that there are two computers inside us. The first is life's integrating computer which is not articulate. It cannot talk. It has groanings which cannot be uttered, because they cannot get into words. Why not? Because the elements are all together at once, coming from every direction in experience and mental storage. I hear what you are saying, I feel my emotions, and my glands circulate — all of this at once. Whatever I do with all of this afterward comes out of my mouth, through my 'rational computer', one word at a time.

God's computers are not our computers. His ways are not our ways. God can do it all at once and be rational, too. But I cannot be rational except by being articulate. This is far less competent than the child. All of us as linguists know this. All of us hurt when, after 25 years of age, we try to learn a language that requires the use of our first computers, which are stuck in a groove — and the child of six passes us by. Why? Because the life computer is an integrating computer, and the scholarly computer is a linear computer. Only as we become as children is it possible for us to have the mind of Christ and accept by faith the complexity of life, all at once, without understanding where it comes from, where it goes. Only then can we live as children with a new citizenship in heaven. Only then can we find God.

Language concentrates life's memories, truths and joys. It expresses them, and guides them, and concentrates them.

Language is a verbal telescope. We can see the galaxies in the pupil of the eye — but that pupil is only an eighth of an inch or so across. If I want to see a great distance, the image from inches of a telescope must be concentrated on the tiny surface of the pupil of my eye. A drama in two and a half hours can stir us to understand and experience something of life that we cannot see by just living, for life is too long. It is not concentrated enough. It is like the galaxy two billion light years away.

Words are like that telescope — they concentrate truth and joys. Words can concentrate revelation, and the Bible is a book of revelation. Some of the problems in the book of Genesis are nothing more than this, in my opinion. God, in order to get us to hear, had to concentrate words, as if in a verbal telescope. Although the stars look through a telescope as though one could reach out and touch them, it may take a little longer to get there in a space ship than one would think.

Language also directs and guides. The tongue is a rudder. With words we give thanks to God. If we cease to give thanks, we cease to believe. From Romans 1:21 we are led to understand that the intellectual who refused to bend his tongue to say "thank you" first, lost an essential axiom. Thinking himself wise, he became a fool. He lost the axiom which says that the fear of the Lord is the beginning of wisdom.

It is not enough to live a Christian life: there must also be WORDS used. Life is not enough of a witness. Social relevance, personal integrity, personal joy, and belief must be expressed in words.

And a final commercial:

These words of Christian witness need to be in THE VERNACULAR.

A Welshman once said to me, when I asked him about his mother tongue, "A man who loses his own language loses his SOUL." (He was a principal of a Baptist seminary, and I assume he was speaking in metaphorical terms!)

Some years ago I was talking with one of the greatest linguists that Denmark has produced. I said, "Why does not your country drop Danish and just use English — since you are teaching it nine years in your schools?" He drew himself up to his full tall height and said, "It is a good thing you asked a FRIEND that question!"

Then I said to him, "Look, I am not trying to be crude. I have given twenty-five years of my life to minority language groups, and some people say it is ridiculous. I have got to know why I am right. Why AM I right? Why haven't I wasted twenty-five years? You are a sophisticated, educated man and a member of a small language group. Tell me why."

He was speechless for a few moments (his initial reaction was in his integrating computer — and it took a while to bring it up to the conscious computer). Finally he said, in perfect English, "Well, you know, Pike, you lose your language and you have lost your moral substance. You have learned this at your mother's knee through stories in your own language, and it's — YOU."

THE LORD'S VOICE — AND OURS*

A linguistic element: "He that entereth in by the door is the Shepherd of the sheep. To him the porter openeth; and the sheep hear his voice; and he calleth his own sheep by name and leadeth them out. And when he putteth forth his own sheep, he goeth before them, and the sheep follow him: for they know his voice. And the stranger will they not follow, but will flee from him; for they know not the voice of strangers" (John 10:2-5).

Language is an extraordinary device. It indexes culture. It represents the personality structure. It identifies the individual. It is this identificational function which is so clearly and strikingly shown to us here. We recognize a person by his voice. We follow because we hear his voice, and hearing his voice, we trust him because we know him.

Personality expresses what a man is, and his words allow this to come out so that it is recognizable by others. The Lord has the voice of a shepherd; he has the touch that is recognizable by sheep — stupid, wandering, jittery lambs. But they follow the voice, and in the long run, every sheep will get to the fold. Not one will be lost, and not one will end up out of the way. They will end up in the fold, as they follow the voice.

In Revelation 3:19-20, the pattern is picked up again: "As many as I love, I rebuke (with my voice) and chasten." "Behold, I stand at the door, and knock; if any man hear my voice, and open the door, I will come in to him, and will sup with him, and he with me."

In linguistics we have to deal both with the words and the general character of the voice. While in Africa trying to see what the voice had to do with communication, I well remember working with an informant and one of my colleagues. If this informant were angry, he had breathy, rapid, powerful pronunciation — with lowered pitch, especially at the end of sentences. And along with this he would show his excitement by fast gestures and by rolling his wide-open eyes. If, however, he were talking to the Chief, and he wanted to show him respect, he would speak slowly, and quietly, with a slow nod of the head, and both hands rotated out flat. The voice identifies the man; the voice identifies the attitudes of the man — joy, sorrow, anger,

* *Stir, Change, Create* (Grand Rapids, Mich., Wm. B. Eerdmans, 1967), 104-106. Reprinted by permission.

fear, love (provided it is accompanied with the communicative gestures which go along with it).

Paul speaking at one time before a hostile audience said, "Men, brethren, and fathers, hear ye my defense which I make now unto you. And when they heard that he spake in the Hebrew tongue to them, they kept the more silence" (Acts 22:1-2). The language in which a man was born has power to reach deep into the soul. One informant said to the translator, "I don't mind if that one scolds me in English, but you scold me in MY OWN LANGUAGE."

A centurion was shaken by language (Acts 21:37-39). He had rescued Paul from a mob which would have torn him limb from limb, and as Paul was to be led into the castle for protection by the soldiers, he said unto the chief captain, "May I speak unto you, please?" who said, "Can you speak Greek? Aren't you one of the Egyptians we had trouble with last week? How do you speak Greek?" Paul said, "I am a Roman citizen, speaking Greek." And then he spoke in Hebrew, and he shook the audience, too. (Cf. Acts 21:37-38).

I seem to recall that C. S. Lewis somewhere (I have not located the spot) told of a man saying to his wife, "Is breakfast ready yet?" — with a snarling tone of voice — and she threw the skillet at him. I've often wondered what would happen if they called him into court, with the judge, saying to him, "Tell me what happened?" Suppose he answered, "Well, I was just coming down for breakfast and I asked, 'Is breakfast ready yet?', and she threw the skillet at me." But he lied. He said, "Is breakfast ready yet" PLUS a snarling tone superimposed. It was the PLUS that got the skillet!

Voice identifies the attitude. Voice identifies the message. Voice identifies the man, his culture, his language, and his soul.

It is not too surprising then that the Lord Jesus warns us about the use of our voice and our words. "A good man out of the good treasure of the heart brings forth good things: and an evil man out of the evil treasure brings forth evil things. But I say unto you, That every idle word that men shall speak, they shall give account thereof in the day of judgement" (Matthew 12:35, 36). Our words open up the veil and let our brothers know what we are; as we speak we calibrate ourselves. Unless a man is a powerfully competent hypocrite, his character will shine through his words fast.

But why the warning about idle words? Why cannot I be judged by what I say when I am on guard? Is it fair? Yes, it is fair. I fail by this test because, you see, when the GUARD IS DOWN, when the gate opens wide — for easy escape of heart's corruption, cursing, anger, sarcasm, or just plain lack of courtesy — BY OUR OFF-GUARD WORDS OUR CHARACTER IS MOST ESPECIALLY REVEALED.

SAN MIGUEL: L'ENVOI — 1967*

More than a decade passes once more. My wife and I were headed out to the Mixtec village after a long absence, for a final good-bye. We would tell our friends that they were on their own. Neither we — nor our colleagues who had followed us up for many years — could be expected back again.

The house, symbol of our guarantee to return, was being formally presented to the town, in a ceremony in which the governor of the state was to be represented. Linguistic and translation commitments had been met. We might never return.

This time I quote an account of the visit as I gave it to my Institute colleagues in Mexico City.

This trip out to San Miguel was different. I had to ask myself, "What will it be like now that we are leaving — all of us, the team?" I had left it before, but the team had not. I do not know of a spot on earth where there had been greater density of testimony, of faithful hour-by-hour and month-by-month telling of the Gospel to scores of Indians for three decades. I had watched my colleagues witness to school children passing by on their way to school, or coming in at recess. Others came to the house at all hours. Now we were leaving.

On the way to the village we went to visit the governor of the State of Oaxaca to prepare for the ceremony of presenting our home to the village of San Miguel for community use. I was impressed with the governor. He was tremendously interested in language, and in people. He was kindly and gentle, and perceptive. He was able to catch onto a mere suggestion — anything that you said about language in general or about other relationships. So that when I said of course the house itself wasn't particularly valuable he said, no, it was not the intrinsic value but the symbol which was important.

This time it was different travelling to San Miguel from Oaxaca. It took 25 flying minutes through the courtesy of the Missionary Aviation Fellowship, as over against four days on foot when I first went out. At the airstrip there was a band and a lot of people waiting for us. The schoolteachers had a program all lined up for presenting the house to the people. I spoke first, presenting the house. Then one of the old-time Mixtec teachers stood up and spoke in Mixtec and in Spanish. He

* *Stir, Change, Create* (Grand Rapids, Mich., Wm. B. Eerdmans, 1967), 157-160. Reprinted by permission.

commented especially that Pike had shown himself to be one with the town. He had carried rock on his back and had helped build a school and the town hall.

But the people of San Miguel interested me most. I found that in terms of Christian experience I could say firmly that I do not know a group of people anywhere in the world — either among my colleagues or in my church in the States — who are more firmly rooted in Christ, or more deeply committed to the Word of God. As far as I am concerned they are my equals, and in some respects they are my superiors. Intellectually, Angel is my equal. In terms of knowledge of the Scriptures, Max is my superior. Again and again as we commented on the Bible he would suggest Scripture references, and would tell me where they were to be found, chapter and verse. I would have had to use a concordance. There are two or three who know the Bible like that. One night Max came to ask me about two things in the New Testament which he could not understand. They were among the most obscure passages in Revelation. I asked if there were any more, and he said, no, that was all. As we talked, I would suggest related passages of Scripture, to be helpful. A couple of times he jumped ahead of me. When I had shown him the approach I was following, in each case he was quicker at finding the passages than I myself.

Among the Mixtec believers I also found counsellors in terms of certain areas of spiritual sensitivity. The day before we were to leave, Cipriano came to talk to me about another believer who had dropped having fellowship with the group of believers. He said to me, "I wonder if you have done right about this brother. Have you spoken to him about it?" I told him that this time I had decided to try a gentler approach, so I had not. Then Cipriano said, "You know, Pike, I wonder if you shouldn't speak to him — not a great deal, but 'just a little bit'. You know, the Scriptures say that we are supposed to. If we try and it doesn't work, that's all right, but I think we ought to try again — 'a little bit'. If we don't try, that's sin, too."

I was deeply moved. Here was a Mixtec believer leading me into the will of God. So the next day I did try. As we talked, he insisted that there was no cleavage, that his failure to attend meetings was because of his town duties, and so on. I told him that the other believers did not think this.

Then I made a suggestion to him, and later to the others. Instead of trying to build up just one total church meeting as a whole, why not supplement this 'particle' view of the church with a network of 'field' view. Suppose that whenever an individual goes to another believer's house they should include in their visit a time of Bible study and prayer? This might bring into fellowship those who do not meet with the larger group.

My basic hypothesis was that this would develop two levels of church relationship. One of them is the formal church; the other is the network of individuals — flexible for any time or place.

As I was with the Mixtecs for this last visit, I thought much about the Scripture concerning the ninety and nine sheep, and the one that was in the mountain alone.

Recently I had received a copy of an article attacking those of us involved in translating the Scriptures for such fragments. We are WASTING TOO MUCH MAN-POWER on so few, it said. While I was among the Mixtecs saying farewell, I asked myself once more, in a 30-year retrospect: Was it worth translating the New Testament for this group? My answer was an unequivocal 'Yes'. We went back to find not merely a halfway group of believers. We found strong and vigorous Christians who were our equals. They were not different from us. They were not just 'informants' or 'helpers' or 'natives', but our equals and our superiors. They were worth the translation of the New Testament. If I am worth it, they are worth it.

The Holy Spirit brought another portion of Scripture to mind, "Where your treasure is, there will your heart be also." And I began to reflect upon my professional linguistic research and writing in relation to the investment of years among the Mixtec Indians. Just before leaving Ann Arbor for the house presentation ceremony in Mexico, I had received copies of the second edition of my major work, *Language in Relation to a Unified Theory of the Structure of Human Behavior*. As a part of the ceremony, I presented a copy to the official government representative. Just before I left Michigan we had also had a little ceremony. In our Water Polo Club at the University, a person who publishes a book is allowed to buy coffee for the crowd, so I begged for the honor. The chairman picked up the rather heavy volume and said, "Hmm, about three and a half pounds." Another spoke up, "Premature?" I had to reply, "Hardly — I've been working on it 17 years."

"Where is my treasure?" I asked myself. "Is it in these books?" No, I knew that my treasure was in Cipriano and Bernardo, and other Mixtec brothers who now know the Bible better than I do. It is in Cipriano who told me that I would be a sinner if I did not speak to my erring brother again, win or lose. It is Ricardo around whom the solid core of Mixtec believers has grown. It is in my first informant Bernardo, now waiting in heaven for us, and in his widow. This, I told the Lord, is my treasure. It won't get obsolete, and it won't rust.

This is my treasure, and there is also my heart. Nor is it waste.

PART THREE

POETIC

'FLYÍNG THROUGH 'FOG//*

I can't see where we're góing .../

    (The Pílot knows/)

Clóuds block my view,/ with móuntains near ...//

    (The Pílot stéers/)

The aírport,/ I cannot téll.//

    (The Pílot knows it wéll//)

A glímpse belów—/ will it hélp as séems?/

    (The pílot rides the béam/)

* *Stir, Change, Create* (Grand Rapids, Mich., Wm. B. Eerdmans, 1967), 70. Reprinted by permission. (Horizontal lines indicate intonation, slash lines are pauses.)

THY SPÉECH BETRÁYETH THEE//*

Relaxed, soft

slow   *Hǒw*:can I téll who you ǎre?/ [a‹·]

Every *ídle wǒrd*

márks your tráck

with prívate scént.

Speed up   Èvery vǒwel, èvery tǒne, èvery 'R̈' [a‹·]

gives a tráce of your órigin

and your bént from afǎr.// [əfə‹·]

Faster, with staccato   Clues to crónies and your wǒrks

stress groups   are wràpped úp in áccent chírps

(= early decrescendo)

Líttle Bȉrd!/ [bə·d]

Dǒn't you trý to flǔ·—/

Júst denȳ

and skwáwk and crý//

Slow down signalled   (ánd bé prepáred to dȉě·

by first word

Little Bȉrd). [bə·d]

Fast staccato   Chǎracter will oǔt/

just as sóftly

and as lǒudly

as yóu shóuǔ/

Relaxed   ǒr póuˇ./

---

* *Mark My Words* (Grand Rapids, Wm. B. Eerdmans, 1971), 107. Reprinted by permission. Additional phonetic markings and instructions by Pike, to duplicate reading by him Feb. 18, 1970.

PIKE — A BIOGRAPHICAL SKETCH

Kenneth L. Pike is tall and lanky with graying hair, glasses and deep lines in his face. Perhaps 'intense' is the adjective his students use most frequently when describing him. When illustrating a point, his motions are so vigorous that the chalk resounds and frequently breaks against the blackboard.

Blackboards have been resounding all over the world: in the University of Michigan where he became Associate Professor of Linguistics in 1948 and where he has been Professor of Linguistics since 1954; in Arkansas until 1942, then at the University of Oklahoma in Norman where he was co-director of the local Summer Institute of Linguistics courses from 1938 through 1950, and director from 1951 through 1970; in Seattle, Washington, Grand Forks, N.D., Boston, Mass., England, Australia, and Germany, where as President of the Summer Institute of Linguistics, Inc. (a sister corporation of the Wycliffe Bible Translators), he has visited and lectured at branches of the Institute.

Since 1935 more than 10,000 students have been enrolled in one of those seven institutes. The vast majority of them have needed linguistics as a tool for translating the Bible into one of the little-known languages and therefore, Pike likes a theory that can be applicable to a practical problem. His theories usually are.

His first breakthrough was a method in the analysis of tone languages — not published until 1948. Second, he developed a theory of the structure of phonetics (1943). Third he analyzed the intonation of American English (1942, 1945). His book *Phonemics* (1947) grew out of the need for a textbook for linguistic students. These four books are still being sold throughout the world, and parts have been translated into Japanese, French, and Spanish.

Pike also developed the tagmemic theory of linguistics (see his *Language ... Behavior* Part I, 1954; Part II, 1955; Part III, 1960; 2nd ed. 1967), and at present he is working on semantics as well as on the application of mathematical concepts to language analysis. Because of his close tie-in with people studying and analyzing languages, he wants his theory to be empirically workable; he wants a generalization which can be applied to a practical situation.

He enjoys watching the application and development of any theory and as he directs students doing their research for a doctoral dissertation, he makes himself readily available for consultation — although the interview may take place at some airport as he waits for his plane to be called.

He is at an airport frequently since he is at the University of Michigan only two out of every three years. The third year is spent at a workshop (in Mexico, Peru, Ecuador, Bolivia, Philippines, Nigeria, Ghana, New Guinea, Nepal, or some other remote area) consulting with his colleagues of the Summer Institute of Linguistics, and helping them in their research in pre-literate languages. Sometimes at a single workshop, he consults with people working on two dozen different languages. When he was in Nepal, one of his brothers commented, "He says he decided not to climb Mt. Everest. He didn't give his reason for not doing so, but I suppose it was because there was nobody up there to teach linguistics to."

Pike's influence in linguistics is world-wide, not just in relation to his far-flung colleagues, but he has given papers in academic circles in many capitals of the world, and in 1972 one entire section of the XIth International Congress of Linguists to be held in Bologna, Italy, will be devoted to tagmemics, the linguistic theory of his own invention.

Easier for the uninitiated to follow are the 'monolingual demonstrations' that he performs while both linguists and nonlinguists listen and watch breathlessly. Pike meets, for the first time on the platform, a person whose language he does not know. In fact he has not even been told what the language is, nor in what part of the world it is spoken. Hesitatingly, the Unknown begins to talk, and Pike writes his words in a sprawling phonetic script on one of a half dozen blackboards. Then using gestures and objects instead of English, or talking in an Indian language (Mixtec) of Mexico instead of a mutually understood language, Pike elicits names of things and a few adjectives perhaps. Soon, selecting one word from this blackboard and another word from that, he starts eliciting in the unknown language itself. Part of the fun is to see Unknown's surprise and delight when he hears his own language coming forth from the lips of the man with the vigorous chalk. Before the forty minutes are up, he has paradigms, pronouns, clauses, and maybe even sentences with several clauses.

He says he learned how to get into a language without an interpreter when, in 1935, he was living in a village in Mexico where none of the Mixtec-speaking people there knew English, and he himself knew no Spanish.

But the struggle with Mixtec was not a forty minute stint. He stayed with it until he, together with his colleague Donald Stark, had finished translating (in 1947) the New Testament into that dialect of Mixtec. It was published in 1951 and of all his publications, that is the one which is, to him, the most satisfying. The Mixtecs who became his friends, who helped him find the right words and combinations of words for the Book, and then read it, believed it, and put it into practice, are still very much on his heart.

Pike was born 60 years ago (June 9, 1912) in Woodstock, Conn. and perhaps his mother should have been able to predict that he would be a linguistic expert.

As a child and young teen-ager he loved making weird noises — any kind of non-speech or non-English sound. Sometimes he would arrive at one which was very pleasing to him, and he would repeat it until his mother called out, "Kenneth! That's enough!"

His father was a medical doctor (Univ. of Mich. 1898), and he and his bride went as missionaries to an Indian tribe in Alaska but within two years poor health forced them home. To him the next best place was some place where he was really 'needed'. That is why Pike and his seven brothers and sisters grew up in a small country town.

In that big family, everybody had to do his share of work and even the smaller children were responsible for certain chores — bringing in wood for the several stoves, walking a quarter of a mile to pick up the day's milk, etc. Pike hated and still hates 'routine', so he grew up thinking of himself as 'lazy'. Even now he spurs himself on with such Scripture verses as, "The sluggard will not plow by reason of the cold; therefore shall he beg in harvest, and have nothing" (Pro. 20:4).

While at Gordon College, Boston, Pike became concerned for the millions in China who did not know of Christ's love for them. He memorized the number of millions in each province and he applied to a mission to be one to go and give them the good news. The mission turned him down because he was too nervous. They said he could not take China. Looking back, Pike says they were right — he is still nervous; and it is better that he went elsewhere.

The first place was Mexico, in 1935. He had majored in New Testament Greek, so the change to translation of the Bible for minority groups seemed right when W. Cameron Townsend asked him to join him for that purpose. Within a year Townsend was asking him to write a book on phonetics for missionaries. Pike figured that was nonsense — he did not like to write and he did not know enough — but he did order a number of linguistic books and start reading. In the summer of 1937, at Townsend's urging, he studied at the Linguistic Society of America, sessions then held at the University of Michigan. Somehow Townsend had seen good potential in skinny, jittery Pike, and he encouraged him to undertake tasks he never would have attempted on his own.

At Michigan it was Professor Charles Fries who was his shade tree, helping him to get a scholarship, encouraging him to continue his studies (he got his Ph.D. in 1942), and giving him advice in general.

His classes and especially informal talks with Professor Edward Sapir stimulated him to develop a technique for analyzing the tone of the Mixtec language. Then he used that same technique in helping members of the Summer Institute of Linguistics to analyze other tone languages.

One of the forces which throughout the years has driven Pike in his linguistic work is the responsibility he felt for his colleagues who were analyzing languages in preparation for Bible translation. Always one of them was waiting for help on a problem he did not know the answer to.

In 1938 he found someone to share this burden. He and Evelyn Griset (Townsend's niece) were married and a few weeks after their honeymoon, out in the Mixtec village, they read a page or two of Bloomfield's *Language* every day and discussed it at the dinner table. In later years when they went to Peru, Ecuador, or some other country, for a workshop, she too served as a consultant. When they finally got back to Connecticut for a visit with Pike's family, his father watched Evelyn for a while and then commented, "She's Kenneth, but with a feminine personality." Their three children, two girls and a boy, loved travelling because, shut up in a car or on a train, they had their parents all to themselves for a while. Pike was a great storyteller and could keep a yarn going for the entire length of the trip. One of the family favorites was about a giant who would leap over the clouds and work himself out of one near-catastrophe after another.

Once the family had arrived at their destination, a variety of duties took Pike's time. It was not just linguistics that he was teaching, but attitudes. He wanted his students to ask concerning a new theory, "Is it useful?" and "What would happen if I looked at my data through these new glasses?" To help them remember, he made up a few proverbs, "Good technology gives rapid success, but breadth of exposure to theoretical conflict gives independence and flexibility in times of stress."

But it is not easy to master another theory — or another language. Tensions may get pretty high. Pike sometimes expresses his own feelings, and encourages his students, with his poetry. His comment on II Corinthians 12:9 went like this:

Tension[1]
String — taut stretched —
Snap not! Nor grieve
When frightful bow draws
Forth the haunting fear.
Please, Lord, play on.

Every week when he is in Ann Arbor, Pike teaches a college-age Bible class there. When in the summer time he is in Norman, Okl., twice a week he spends twenty minutes vividly presenting portions of the Bible to the students. But he does not forget linguistics even during those short sessions. For example, one day he said, "Language was built by God to do a job ... Have you never wondered at the metaphor in the first verse of the Gospel of John? 'In the beginning was the Word' ... Language reflects the image of God, so could you expect it to be anything other than beautiful, elegantly patterned, glorious, and difficult? ... So thank God for language and ask Him to help you this summer to learn something of the answer to the question, 'What is language that You made it?' "

1971   EUNICE V. PIKE

---

[1] From: *Stir, Change, Create* (Grand Rapids, Mich., Wm. B. Eerdmans, 1967), 63. Used by permission.

MAJOR ACADEMIC ACHIEVEMENTS AND AWARDS

ThB, Gordon College, 1933
PhD, University of Michigan, 1942
Phi Alpha Chi; Phi Kappa Phi
Lloyd Postdoctoral Fellow, University of Michigan, 1945-1946
Permanent Council Member, International Phonetic Association
President, Linguistic Society of America, 1961
Distinguished Faculty Achievement Award, University of Michigan, 1966
Doctor of the Humanities (honorary), Huntington College, Huntington, Indiana, 1967
Visiting Professor, Linguistic Society of Europe, Kiel, Germany, summer, 1968
Fellow, Center for Advanced Study in the Behavioral Sciences, Palo Alto, California, 1968-1969

BIBLIOGRAPHY

LINGUISTIC

Books and Monographs

1942   *Pronunciation*, Vol. I of *An Intensive Course In English for Latin American Students* (Ann Arbor, English Language Institute of the University of Michigan).

1943   *Phonetics: A Critical Analysis of Phonetic Theory and a Technic for the Practical Description of Sounds* (= *University of Michigan Publications in Language and Literature* 21) (Ann Arbor, University of Michigan Press).

1945   *The Intonation of American English* (= *University of Michigan Publications in Linguistics* 1) (Ann Arbor, University of Michigan Press).

1947   *Phonemics: A Technique for Reducing Languages to Writing* (= *University of Michigan Publications in Linguistics* 3) (Ann Arbor, University of Michigan Press).

1948   *Tone Languages: A Technique for Determining the Number and Type of Pitch Contrasts in a Language, with Studies in Tonemic Substitution and Fusion* (= *University of Michigan Publications in Linguistics* 4) (Ann Arbor, University of Michigan Press).

1951   *Axioms and Procedures for Reconstruction in Comparative Linguistics: An Experimental Syllabus* (Santa Ana, Calif., Summer Institute of Linguistics). (Revised, 1957).

1954, 1955, 1960   *Language in Relation to a Unified Theory of the Structure of Human Behavior*, Part I, Chs. 1 through 7; Part II, Chs. 8 through 10; Part III, Chs. 11 through 17; Preliminary Edition (Glendale [now Santa Ana], Calif., Summer Institute of Linguistics).

1966   *Tagmemic and Matrix Linguistics Applied to Selected African Languages* (= Final Report, Contract OE 5-14-065) (Washington, D.C., U.S. Office of Education). (Reprinted in *Summer Institute of Linguistics Publications in Linguistics and Related Fields* — Appendix omitted — 1971.)

1967   *Language in Relation to a Unified Theory of the Structure of Human Behavior*, 2nd revised ed. (The Hague, Mouton.)

1970a   (editor, with Austin Hale) *Tone Systems of Tibeto-Burman Languages of Nepal*, Part I: *Studies on Tone and Phonological Segments*; Part II: *Lexical Lists and Comparative Studies* Part III: *Texts, I*; Part IV: *Texts, II* (= *Occasional Papers of the Wolfenden Society on Tibeto-Burman Linguistics*) (Urbana, University of Illinois).

1970b   (with Richard E. Young and Alton L. Becker) *Rhetoric: Discovery and Change* (New York, Harcourt, Brace and World).

Articles and Pamphlets

1937a   "Likenesses, Differences and Variation of Phonemes in Mexican Indian Languages and How to Find Them", *Investigaciones Lingüísticas* 4:1-2, 134-139.

1937b   "Una Leyenda Mixteca", *Investigaciones Lingüísticas* 4:3-4, 262-270.

1938a   "Practical Suggestions Toward a Common Orthography for Indian Languages of Mexico",
         Investigaciones Lingüísticas 5:1-2, 86-97.
1938b   *Phonemic Work Sheet* (Santa Ana, Calif., Summer Institute of Linguistics).
1943   "Taxemes and Immediate Constituents", *Language* 19, 65-82.
1944   "Analysis of a Mixteco Text", *International Journal of American Linguistics* 10, 113-138.
1945a   "Mock Spanish of a Mixteco Indian", *International Journal of American Linguistics* 11,
         219-224.
1945b   (with Aileen Traver and Virginia French) "Step-by-Step Procedure for Marking Limited
         Intonation with its Related Features of Pause, Stress, and Rhythm", *Teaching and Learning
         English as a Foreign Language*, by Charles C. Fries (Ann Arbor, Mich., English Language
         Institute, University of Michigan).
1945c   "Tone Puns in Mixteco", *International Journal of American Linguistics* 11, 129-139.
1946a   "The Flea: Melody Types and Perturbations in a Mixtec Song", *Tlalocan* 2, 128-133.
1946b   "Another Mixteco Tone Pun", *International Journal of American Linguistics* 12, 22-24.
1946c   "Phonemic Pitch in Maya", *International Journal of American Linguistics* 12, 82-88.
1946d   *Cuendu Nanga* [Funny Stories] (with Angel Merecias and other Mixtecs) (Mexico, D.F.:
         Instituto Lingüístico de Verano).
1947a   "A Text Involving Inadequate Spanish of Mixteco Indians", *International Journal of American
         Linguistics* 13, 251-257.
1947b   "On the Phonemic Status of English Diphthongs", *Language* 23, 151-159.
1947c   "Grammatical Prerequisites to Phonemic Analysis", *Word* 3, 155-172.
1947d   (with Eunice Pike) "Immediate Constituents of Mazatec Syllables", *International Journal of
         American Linguistics* 13, 78-91.
1948a   "Problems in the Teaching of Practical Phonemics", *Language Learning* 1, 3-8.
1948b   (with Donald Sinclair) "The Tonemes of Mezquital Otomi", *International Journal of American
         Linguistics* 14, 91-98.
1948-1949   "Cuento Mixteco de un Conejo, un Coyote, y la Luna", *Revista Mexicana de Estudios
         Antropológicos* 10, 133-134.
1949a   (with Charles C. Fries) "Coexistent Phonemic Systems", *Language* 25, 25-50.
1949b   "A Problem in Morphology-Syntax Division", *Acta Linguistica* 5, 125-138.
1951a   *Bibliography of the Summer Institute of Linguistics* (Glendale, Calif., Summer Institute of
         Linguistics).
1951b   "The Problems of Unwritten Languages in Education", Report in the UNESCO meeting
         of Experts in the Use of Vernacular Languages (Paris, UNESCO).
1952a   "More on Grammatical Prerequisites", *Word* 8, 106-121.
1952b   "Operational Phonemics in Reference to Linguistic Relativity", *Journal of the Acoustical
         Society of America* 24, 618-625.
1953a   "Intonational Analysis of a Rumanian Sentence", *Cahiers Sextil Puscariu* 2 (University of
         Washington, Seattle, Dept. of Romance Languages and Literatures), 59-60.
1953b   "A Note on Allomorph Classes and Tonal Technique", *International Journal of American
         Linguistics* 19, 101-105.
1955a   "Meaning and Hypostasis", *Monograph* 8 (Georgetown University, Institute of Languages
         and Linguistics), 134-141.
1955b   (with Eunice V. Pike) *Live Issues in Descriptive Linguistics* (Santa Ana, Calif., Summer
         Institute of Linguistics). (2nd ed. 1960).
1956a   "As Correntes da Linguistica Norteamericana", *Revista Brasileira de Filologia* 2, 207-216.
1956b   (with Willard Kindberg) "A Problem in Multiple Stresses", *Word* 12, 415-428.
1956c   "Towards a Theory of the Structure of Human Behavior", *Estudios Antropológicos Publicados
         en Homenaje al Doctor Manuel Gamio* (Mexico, D.F.), 659-671.
1957a   "Grammemic Theory in Reference to Restricted Problems of Morpheme Classes", *Interna-
         tional Journal of American Linguistics* 23, 119-128.
1957b   "Grammemic Theory", *General Linguistics* 2, 35-41.
1957c   (with David Beasley) "Notes on Huambisa Phonemics", *Lingua Posnaniensis* 6, 1-8.
1957d   "Abdominal Pulse Types in Some Peruvian Languages", *Language* 33, 30-35.
1957e   "Language and Life: A Training Device for Translation and Practice", *Bibliotheca Sacra* 114,
         347-362. (Other sections listed under Religious bibliography.)

1958a   (with Esther Matteson) "Non-Phonemic Transition Vocoids in Piro (Arawak)", *Miscellanea Phonetica* 3, 22-30.
1958b   "Interpenetration of Phonology, Morphology, and Syntax", *Proceedings of the Eighth International Congress of Linguists* (Oslo, University Press), 363-374.
1958c   "On Tagmemes, *née* Gramemes", *International Journal of American Linguistics* 24, 273-278.
1958d   (with Rachel Saint) "Notas sobre Fonémica Huarani (Auca)", *Estudios Acerca de las Lenguas Huaraní (Auca), Shimigae y Zápara: Publicaciones Científicas de Ministerio de Educación del Ecuador*, 4-17.
1959a   (with Ralph P. Barrett and Burt Bascom) "Instrumental Collaboration on a Tepehuan (Uto-Aztecan) Pitch Problem", *Phonetica* 3, 1-22.
1959b   "Language as Particle, Wave, and Field", *The Texas Quarterly* 2:2, 37-54.
1960a   "Linguistic Research as Pedagogical Support", *Papers of the National Conference on the Teaching of African Languages and Area Studies*, ed. by John G. Broder (Georgetown University), 32-39.
1960b   "Towards a Theory of Change and Bilingualism", *Studies in Linguistics* 15, 1-7.
1960c   "Nucleation", *The Modern Language Journal* 44, 291-295. (Reprinted: 1961, *ILT News* [Journal of the Institute of Language Teaching, Waseda University, Tokyo] 6, 1-5; 1963, *Philippine Journal for Language Teaching* 1, 1-7, 20; 1965, Harold B. Allen (ed.), *Teaching English as a Second Language* [New York, McGraw-Hill], 67-74.)
1961a   "Stimulating and Resisting Change", *Practical Anthropology* 8, 267-274.
1961b   "Compound Affixes in Ocaina", *Language* 37, 570-581.
1961c   (with Milton Warkentin) "Huave: A Study in Syntactic Tone with Low Lexical Functional Load", *A William Cameron Townsend en el Vigesimoquinto Aniversario del Instituto Lingüístico de Verano* (Mexico, D.F., Instituto Lingüístico de Verano), 627-642.
1962a   (with Rachel Saint) "Auca Phonemics", *Studies in Ecuadorian Indian Languages* I (Norman, Oklahoma, Summer Institute of Linguistics and the University of Oklahoma), 2-30.
1962b   "Practical Phonetics of Rhythm Waves", *Phonetica* 8, 9-30.
1962c   "Dimensions of Grammatical Constructions", *Language* 38, 221-244.
1963a   (with Graham Scott) "Pitch Accent and Non-Accented Phrases in Fore (New Guinea), *Zeitschrift für Phonetik, Sprachwissenschaft und Kommunikationsforschung* 16, 179-189.
1963b   "Choices in Course Design", *The Teaching of Linguistics in Anthropology* (= *Memoir* 94) (American Anthropological Association), 315-332.
1963c   "Theoretical Implications of Matrix Permutation in Fore (New Guinea)", *Anthropological Linguistics* 5:8, 1-23.
1963d   "A Syntactic Paradigm", *Language* 39, 216-230.
1963e   "The Hierarchical and Social Matrix of Suprasegmentals", *Prac Filologicznych* 18, 95-104.
1964a   "A Linguistic Contribution to Composition: A Hypothesis", *Journal of the Conference on College Composition and Communication* 15, 82-88.
1964b   (with Mildred Larson) "Hyperphonemes and Non-Systematic Features of Aguaruna Phonemics", *Studies in Languages and Linguistics in Honor of Charles C. Fries*, ed. by A.H. Marckwardt (Ann Arbor, The English Language Institute of the University of Michigan), 55-67.
1964c   (with Barbara Erickson) "Conflated Field Structures in Potawatomi and in Arabic", *International Journal of American Linguistics* 30, 201-212.
1964d   "Beyond the Sentence", *Journal of the Conference on College Composition and Communication* 15, 129-135.
1964e   "Discourse Analysis and Tagmeme Matrices", *Oceanic Linguistics* 3, 5-25.
1964f   (with Alton L. Becker) "Progressive Neutralization in Dimensions of Navaho Stem Matrices", *International Journal of American Linguistics* 30, 144-154.
1964g   "Stress Trains in Auca", *In Honour of Daniel Jones*, ed. by D. Abercrombie, D.B. Fry, P.A.C. MacCarthy, N.C. Scott, and J.L.M.Trim (London, Longmans, Green), 425-431.
1964h   "Name Fusions as High-Level Particles in Matrix Theory", *Linguistics* 6, 83-91.
1964i   "On Systems of Grammatical Structure", *Proceedings of the Ninth International Congress of Linguists*, ed. by H.G. Lunt (The Hague, Mouton), 145-154.
1965a   "Language — Where Science and Poetry Meet", *College English* 26, 283-292.

1965b   "Non-Linear Order and Anti-Redundancy in German Morphological Matrices", *Zeitschrift für Mundartforschung* 32, 193-221.

1966a   "A Guide to Publications Related to Tagmemic Theory", *Current Trends in Linguistics* 3, ed. by T.A. Sebeok, 365-394.

1966b   "On the Grammar of Intonation", *Proceedings of the Fifth International Congress of Phonetic Sciences*, ed. by E. Zwirner and W. Bethge (Basel, S. Karger), 105-119.

1967a   "Suprasegmentals in Reference to Phonemes of Item ,of Process, and of Relation", *To Honor Roman Jakobson* (The Hague, Mouton), 1545-1554.

1967b   "Tongue-Root Position in Practical Phonetics", *Phonetica* 17, 129-140.

1967c   "Grammar as Wave", *Monograph* 20 (Georgetown University, Institute of Languages and Linguistics), 1-14.

1968a   "How to Make an Index", *Publications of the Modern Language Association of America* 83, 991-993.

1968b   "Matrix Permutation as a Heuristic Device in the Analysis of the Bimoba Verb", *Lingua* 21, 321-345.

1968c   "Indirect Versus Direct Discourse in Bariba", *Proceedings of the Conference on Language and Language Behavior*, ed. by M. Zale (New York, Appleton-Century-Crofts), 165-173.

1969a   "Language as Behavior and Etic and Emic Standpoints for the Description of Behavior", *Social Psychology: Readings and Perspective*, ed. by E.F. Borgatta (Chicago, Rand, McNally), 114-131. (Reprinted from *Language in Relation to a Unified Theory of the Structure of Human Behavior*.)

1969b   (with Ivan Lowe) "Pronominal Reference in English Conversation and Discourse: A Group Theoretical Treatment", *Folia Linguistica* 3, 68-106.

1970a   "The Role of Nuclei of Feet in the Analysis of Tone in Tibeto-Burman Languages of Nepal", *Prosodic Feature Analysis*, ed. by Leon, Faure and Rigault (= *Studia Phonetica* 3), 153-161.

1970b   *Toward the Description of the Languages of the World: On Phonemic, Word, and Clause Formats of Comparable Descriptions*, Study prepared for the Burg Wartenstein Symposium #49 (New York, Wenner-Gren Foundation for Anthropological Research).

1970c   (with Maria Hari and Doreen Taylor) "Tamang Tone and Higher Levels", *Tone Systems of Tibeto-Burman Languages of Nepal* I, ed. by Pike and Hale (see above), 82-124.

1971a   "More Revolution: Tagmemics", Ch. 7 of *Reading about Language*, ed. by C. Laird and R.M. Gorrell (New York, Harcourt, Brace, Jovanovich), 234-247.

1971b   "Implications of the Patterning of an Oral Reading of a Set of Poems", *Poetics* 1, 38-45.

1971c   "Crucial Questions in the Development of Tagmemics — the Sixties and the Seventies", *Monograph* 24 (Georgetown University, Institute of Languages and Linguistics), 79-98.

RELIGIOUS

Books

1946   (with Donald Stark, Evelyn Pike, and Angel Merecias) *Cuendú ndaã* [True Tales] (Mexico, D.F., Instituto Lingüístico de Verano).

1947a   *Yãhá kúu kartá jã ní chaa pálú ápoxli nuũ náyʌ v ñúũ filipó: La Epístola del Apóstol San Pablo a los Filipenses* (a diglot, with Angel Merecias) (Mexico, D.F., Sociedad Biblica Americana).

1947b   (with Donald Stark and Angel Merecias) *Tũhun vãha ni chaa makú: El Santo Evangelio según San Marcos* (diglot) (Mexico, D.F., Sociedad Biblica Americana).

1950   (with Donald Stark) *Yãhá cácuu carta jã ní chaa San Juan apóstol: Las Epístolas de San Juan Apostol* (Mexico, D.F., Instituto Lingüístico de Verano).

1951   (with Donald Stark and Angel Merecias) *Testemento Jaa Maa Jitoho-yo Jesucristo: El Nuevo Testamento de Nuestro Señor Jesucristo* (diglot, Mixteco-Spanish). (Cuernavaca, Mexico, Tipografía Indígena).

1957   (with Donald Stark) *Tuhun vaha ni chaa San Juan: El Santo Evangelio según San Juan* (Cuernavaca, Mexico, Tipografía Indígena).

330   BIBLIOGRAPHY

1960   (with Donald Stark) *Ja ni casaha chaa apostol: Los Hechos de los Apóstoles* (Cuernavaca,
        Mexico, Tipografía Indígena).
1962   *With Heart and Mind: A Personal Synthesis of Scholarship and Devotion* (Grand Rapids,
        Mich., Wm. B. Eerdmans).
1967   *Stir, Change, Create: Poems and Essays* (Grand Rapids, Mich., Wm. B. Eerdmans).
1971   *Mark My Words* (Grand Rapids, Mich., Wm. B. Eerdmans). (Also poetic.)

Articles and Pamphlets

1947   *God's Guidance and Your Life's Work*. (Chicago, Ill., Inter-Varsity Christian Fellowship).
        (Reprinted, 1955, by Wycliffe Bible Translators, Santa Ana, California.)
1948   "Living on Manna", *The Sunday School Times* (May 1), 3-4.
1951   "We'll Tell Them, But in What Language?", *His* 12:2, 8-11, 14.
1957a   "Gold, Frankincense, and Myrrh", *The King's Business* 48:12, 16-17.
1957b   "Why I Believe in God", *His* 18:2, 3-7, 32-33.
1957c   "Prescription for Intellectuals", *Eternity* 8:8, 11, 44-45.
1957, 1958 "Language and Life: A Stereoscopic Window on the World", *Bibliotheca Sacra* 114,
        141-156, 255-262, 115, 36-43.
1958a   "Serving our Colleagues", *His* 18:5, 5-7.
1958b   "The Sin of Independence", *His* 18:8, 5-7.
1958c   "The Individual", *Eternity* 9:9, 18-19.
1959a   "Marriage", mimeograph.
1959b   *Our Own Tongue Wherein We Were Born: The Work of the Summer Institute of Linguistics
        and the Wycliffe Bible Translators* (= *The Bible Translator* 10:2). (Reprinted, 1960, The
        Summer Institute of Linguistics, Santa Ana, California.)
1959c   "Intellectual Idolatry", *His* 19:5, 5-6.
1959d   "Walking", *The King's Business* 50:4, 10-11.
1959e   "Finishing the Sentence — A Linguistic Parable", *His* 19:6, 39-40.
1959f   "Why the Angels are Curious", *The King's Business* 50:9, 12-13.
1959g   "Cause-and-Effect in the Christian Life", *His* 20:11, 33-34.
1960a   "Building Sympathy", *Practical Anthropology* 7, 250-522.
1960b   "Players", *His* 20:9, 41-42.
1960c   "When Failure is Success", *The Alliance Witness* 95:21, 5.
1960d   "Why is There a Moral Code", *The King's Business* 51:10, 10-11.
1961a   "Stimulating and Resisting Change", *Practical Anthropology* 8, 267-274.
1961b   "Strange Dimensions of Truth", *Christianity Today* 5:690-692.
1961c   "Current Strategy in Missions", *His* 22:1, 9, 13-14.
1962   "Left-Handed", *His* 22:9, 36-47.
1964   "Man or Robot", *Eternity* 15:2, 9-11.
1965   "Christianity and Science", *The Church Herald* 22:4, 4-6.
1966a   "Tempted to Quit", *The Church Herald* 23:6, 14-15. (Reprinted in *The Christian Athlete*
        [Feb. 1968], 11.)
1966b   "The Disillusioned Scholar", *The Church Herald* 23:30, 15, 30.
1966c   "God in History", *The Church Herald* 23:2, 4-5, 22.
1967a   "The Courage to Face Tension", *The Church Herald* 24:21, 11.
1967b   "Abraham My Father", *The Alliance Witness* 102:25, 9, 19.
1968a   "Intergenerational Cleavage", *Translation* (January-February), 4-5.
1968b   "Review of *You! Jonah!* (by J.T. Carlisle)", *Christianity Today* 13:2, 22-23.
1968c   "Mental Tension", *The King's Business* 58:2, 30-31.
1968d   "Termites and Eternity", *His* 28:7, 4-5.
1969   "Guest Editorial: On Finding God's Role for You", *Missionary Messenger* (organ of the
        Eastern Mennonite Board of Missions and Charities), 45:8, 24-23.

POETIC

(Books: *Stir, Change, Create* and *Mark My Words*, listed under Religious)

1958   "Flaming Candle", *His* 18:7, 30.
1966   "Crushed", *Translation* (Spring), 12.
1968a   "Pre-literate Tribe", *Translation* (January-February), 2.
1968b   "Not by Bread Alone", *The Church Herald* (May), 11.
1968c   "In War — or Fuss", *Overflow* 2:1, 16.
1968d   "The Day Before Christmas", *Overflow* 2:1, 8.
1969   "Fear" (2 poems), *His* 29:9, 13.
1970   "Five Poems", *Essays in Honor of Claude M. Wise* (A.J. Bronstein, C.L. Shaver, and G. Stevens) (Hannibal, Mo., The Standard Printing Co.), 67-72.

INDEX

mario makes a move

Jill McElmurry

schwartz & wade books · new york

To my amazing family

Mario liked to invent amazing moves.

Twirly Ballet Arms

Tail, Don't Fail

Bowling Ball

Crazy Wave

Upside-Down Around

Rocket to Mars

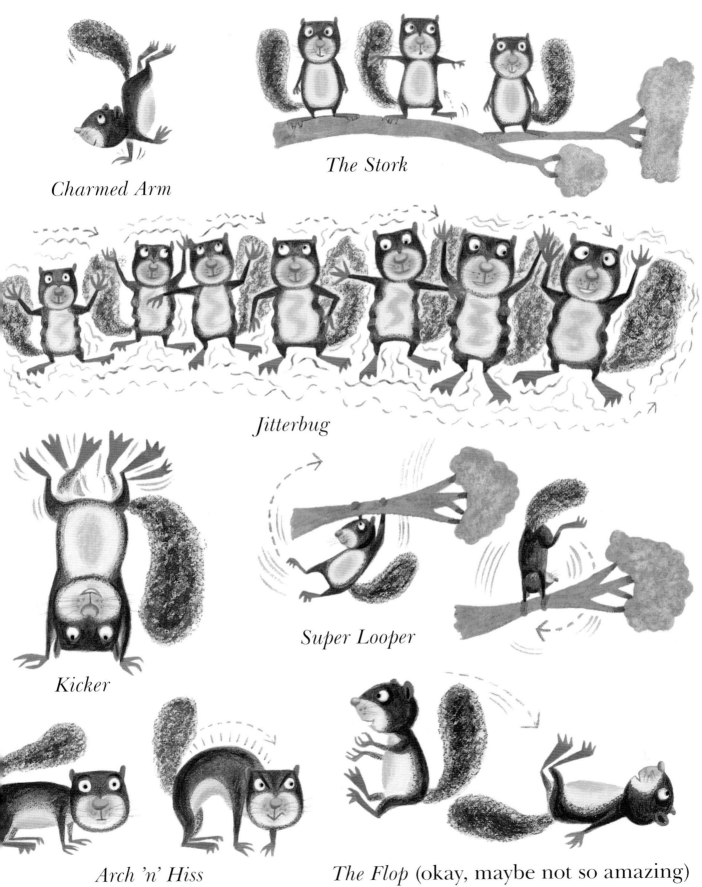

Charmed Arm

The Stork

Jitterbug

Kicker

Super Looper

Arch 'n' Hiss

The Flop (okay, maybe not so amazing)

"Look! Look!" said Mario.

"Amazing!" said Mario's dad.

"Artistic!" said Mario's mom.

"Astonishing!" said his grandpa.

"Alarming!" said his auntie.

"Aaaaa!" said his cousins, who didn't know words.

"Look! Look!" Mario said to Isabelle.

"That's nice," said Isabelle.

"NICE?" said Mario. "I think you mean amazing. Or astonishing, maybe."

"Hmmm," said Isabelle.

"It's called the Amazing Amazer," said Mario.

"Oh," said Isabelle.

"Aren't you amazed?" said Mario.

"I guess," said Isabelle.

"You don't know an amazing move when you see one," said Mario. "I'd like to see *you* try it."

"No problem," said Isabelle.

How to Do Isabelle's Amazing Move

"I don't think we can be friends anymore," said Mario.

"Why not?" said Isabelle, straightening her glasses.

"Because you stole my move," he said.

"I did not steal your move," she said.

"Did so!" said Mario.

"That wasn't your move," said Isabelle. "That was *my* move."

"You can't have a move!" said Mario.

"Why not?" said Isabelle. "Anyone can have a move.

"See?"

"Oh, dear," said Mario.

"What are you doing?" said Isabelle the next day.

"Finding sticks," said Mario.

"Why?"

"It's my new hobby," said Mario.

"What about your amazing move?"

"Anyone can have an amazing move," said Mario. "*I* have amazing sticks."

"Hmmm," said Isabelle.

"Aren't you amazed?" said Mario.

"They're just sticks."

"You don't know an amazing stick when you see one," said Mario.

"Your move is more amazing than that stick," said Isabelle.

"My move was dumb. I got rid of it," said Mario.

"Too bad. I wanted you to teach it to me."

"Really?" said Mario.

"Really," said Isabelle.

"But you said it was NICE," said Mario.

"I meant to say it was elegant."

"Elegant?" said Mario.

"And graceful."
"Graceful?!" said Mario.
He dropped his stick.

"You know," said Mario,
"I want you to teach me
your move, too!"

So Isabelle taught Mario her move . . .
and Mario taught Isabelle the
Amazing Amazer . . .

And then they mashed the two moves together and invented the Even More Amazingly Amazing Amazer.

And everyone was amazed.

IF YOU ARE A SQUIRREL

1. Your brain is the size of a walnut.   ←walnut

2. You Probably Live in a tree.

3. You like to eat acorns, nuts, seeds, and roots, and sometimes you'll even eat insects, caterpillars, or BABY BIRDS!

4. You have a bushy tail.

5. You have FOUR FRONT teeth that never STOP Growing.

6. You have THUMBS on your feet.   BRANCH
   THUMB

7. Also, you sweat through your feet.

8. You are one of hundreds of species in a number of families, including Tree squirrels, ground squirrels, and FLYING squirrels

9. Your first ancestor Lived about 35 million Years AGO!

10. You can run as fast as 20 miles per HOUR.

11. You bury your Food, although sometimes you forget where.

12. You ARE considered cute by some and pesky by others.

13. YOU MAKE amazing moves.

↑   ↑   ↑↑   ↑   ↑

Library of Congress Cataloging-in-Publication Data
McElmurry, Jill.
Mario makes a move / Jill McElmurry.—1st ed.
p. cm.
Summary: Mario and Isabelle, two squirrels, teach each other their amazing dance moves. Includes facts about squirrels.
ISBN 978-0-375-86854-2 (trade) — ISBN 978-0-375-96854-9 (glb)
[1. Squirrels—Fiction. 2. Dance—Fiction.] I. Title.
PZ7.M4784485Mar 2012
[E]—dc23
2011011014

The text of this book is set in Baskerville.
The illustrations were rendered in gouache on watercolor paper.
Book design by Becky Terhune and Rachael Cole
MANUFACTURED IN MALAYSIA
10 9 8 7 6 5 4 3 2 1
First Edition